UNIVERSITIES AND THE SUSTAINABLE DEVELOPMENT FUTURE

Since the mid-1970s, a series of international declarations that link environment and sustainable development to all aspects of higher learning have been endorsed and signed by universities around the world. Although university involvement in sustainable-development research and outreach has increased substantially, systematic learning from higher-education engagements has been limited.

Universities and the Sustainable Development Future offers institutions of higher learning around the world practical guidelines that can be applied contextually to produce credible evidence regarding the outcome and impact of their teaching, research, and transnational-partnering activities. Drawing on innovative applications of lessons from experience with international-development cooperation, this book demonstrates the utility of a flexible framework that will inspire substantial improvements in the ways universities evaluate and improve their sustainable-development undertakings aimed at promoting *Agenda 2030*.

This book promotes an inclusive evaluation framework that will allow universities to illuminate sustainable-development outcomes, and it provides a cutting-edge resource for students, scholars, and policy makers with an interest in sustainable development, climate change, and evaluation challenges.

Dr. Peter H. Koehn is Professor of Political Science, a University of Montana Distinguished Scholar, a Fulbright New Century Scholar, and a recipient of the Association of Public and Land Grant Universities 2011 Michael P. Malone award for international leadership. He is the founding director of the University of Montana's Office of International Programs and its academic programs in International Development Studies and Global Public Health. He has taught and conducted research in Ethiopia, Nigeria, Eritrea, China, and Finland.

Dr. Juha I. Uitto is Director of the Independent Evaluation Office of the Global Environment Facility (GEF). He has held various evaluation positions with the GEF and the United Nations Development Programme, during which he has conducted and managed a large number of programmatic and thematic evaluations of international cooperation at the global, regional, and country level. Dr. Uitto has published widely on topics related to environment and natural resources management, sustainable development, environmental hazards, and evaluation.

"Universities have a choice: to contribute unthinkingly to critical trends that are leading to social, economic and ecological disruption and volatility, or to knowingly participate in forging a future where risk is minimised and systemic wellbeing for all is pursued as the guiding value. By underlining the urgency, meaning, and practicability of the task, this thorough and comprehensive book can make a major contribution to bringing sustainability to the centre of higher education's attention and effort – where it surely must belong."

– Professor Stephen Sterling, Centre for Sustainable Futures,
University of Plymouth, UK

"This book expands the conceptual design and utilization of the evaluations of education for sustainable development (ESD) and transnational sustainable development (TSD). Important concepts include capacity, stakeholder inclusion, systemic change, outcomes, and impacts. If utilized by educators, evaluators, researchers and practitioners, the information in this book will enhance evaluation, ESD, TSD, our species, and the planet."

– Dr. Debra Rowe, Sustainable Energies & Social
Sciences, Oakland Community College

"As the 2030 Agenda for Sustainable Development takes its first steps, this timely book asks a critical question: how can we know what kind of impact universities are making on fostering sustainable development around the world? By taking a big picture view of our environmental context, Koehn and Uitto put forward a framework that universities and their stakeholders will find enormously valuable for making evidence-based decisions about how best they can achieve impact."

– Anne-Claire Hervy, Associate Vice President for International Development
and Programs, Association of Public and Land Grant Universities (APLU)

"This book is a valuable contribution to the small but growing literature on the environment and evaluation. It is uniquely accessible to the non-technical reader and should be read widely."

– Saraswathi Menon, Former Chair, United Nations Evaluation Group

"Today there is growing international recognition of the importance of education for sustainable development in light of the Sustainable Development Goals (SDGs) adopted by the global community. This timely and pragmatic publication provides us with insights into how universities already make and can make significant future contributions to sustainable development. The book will be of enormous value to academics and senior administration in higher education institutions around the world."

– Matthias Barth, Professor of Education for Sustainability,
Leuphana University of Lueneburg

"Universities and the Sustainable Development Future is truly breaking new ground in the fields of sustainable development, higher education, and evaluation for three reasons. It constitutes the first systematic study on the topic. Second, it provides tools for assessing the contribution of universities to sustainable development. Third, it forces to think about the overall nature and role of universities in connection with the big issues of the years ahead. Considering how essential universities are for the training of the professionals and citizens of tomorrow, and considering how sustainable development is key for the future of the planet, the issues tackled in this book are of outmost urgency."

— *Jean-Marc Coicaud, Rutgers School of Law, Rutgers University*

"Universities must play a key role in ensuring that our society becomes sustainable economically, socially, environmentally, culturally and politically. It is my earnest hope that sustainable development occupies the centerpiece of all university programs of teaching, research, and outreach, and especially for student activities, be they classroom study, extra-curriculum activities, or internships, to develop our young people dedicated and committed to sustainability. Therefore, this book by Peter Koehn and Juha Uitto is so important. I would even venture to suggest that the title should be Universities for Sustainable Development."

— *Ryokichi Hirono Professor Emeritus, Seikei University*

UNIVERSITIES AND THE SUSTAINABLE DEVELOPMENT FUTURE

Evaluating Higher-Education Contributions to the 2030 Agenda

Peter H. Koehn and Juha I. Uitto

Routledge
Taylor & Francis Group
LONDON AND NEW YORK

earthscan
from Routledge

First published 2017
by Routledge
2 Park Square, Milton Park, Abingdon, Oxon OX14 4RN

and by Routledge
711 Third Avenue, New York, NY 10017

Routledge is an imprint of the Taylor & Francis Group, an informa business

British Library Cataloguing-in-Publication Data
A catalogue record for this book is available from the British Library

Library of Congress Cataloging-in-Publication Data
A catalog record for this title has been requested

ISBN: 978-1-138-21252-7 (hbk)
ISBN: 978-1-138-21253-4 (pbk)
ISBN: 978-1-315-44996-8 (ebk)

Typeset in Bembo
by Apex CoVantage, LLC

To a sustainable-development future informed by evidence of outcomes and impacts and shaped by universities committed to informing rural and urban, remote and connected persons in all regions of the world

CONTENTS

BOXES

ACRONYMS AND ABBREVIATIONS

AAAA	Addis Ababa Action Agenda
AACC	American Association of Community Colleges
AASHE	Association for the Advancement of Sustainability in Higher Education
AERC	African Economic Research Consortium
Agenda 2030	Sustainable Development Agenda adopted at the United Nations 2015 Summit
AICPA	American Institute of Certified Public Accountants
AISHE	Assessment Instrument for Sustainability in Higher Education
AIU	Albukhary International University, Malaysia
AUA	Alternative University Appraisal
BIQ	benchmark indicator question
CCMCP	Climate Change Mitigation Capacity Program
CFC	chlorofluorocarbon
CGEA	Council for Higher Education Accreditation
COHRED	Council on Health Research for Development
CSR	corporate social responsibility
CSU	Colorado State University
Danida	Danish International Development Agency[1]
DANS	Disciplinary Association Network for Sustainability
DESD	United Nations Decade of Education for Sustainable Development
DfID	UK Department for International Development
EHEA	European Higher Education Area
ENQA	European Network of Quality Assessment Agencies
ESD	Education for Sustainable Development
EU	European Union
FAO	Food and Agriculture Organization

GAP	Global Action Programme (for DESD)
GEF	Global Environment Facility
GIS	Geographical Information Systems
glocal	global/local linked
GRI	Global Reporting Initiative
GTZ	German Technical Cooperation (now GIZ)
GUPES	Global Universities Partnership on Environment and Sustainability
HEA	Higher Education Academy
HEASC	Higher Education Associations Sustainability Consortium
HEI	higher-education institution
HESI	Higher Education Sustainability Initiative
IAU	International Association of Universities
ICT	information and communication technology
IDRC	International Development Research Centre, Canada
IPCC	Intergovernmental Panel on Climate Change
IUC	institutional university cooperation program
LiFE	Learning in Future Environments index
M&E	Monitoring and Evaluation
MDG	Millennium Development Goals
MDP	Master's in Development Practice
MEPI	Medical Education Partnership Initiative
MESA	Mainstreaming Environment and Sustainability in African Universities
NAAL	National Academy for Academic Leadership
NCHE	National Council for Higher Education, Uganda
NGO	non-governmental organization
NVAO	Accreditation Organization of the Netherlands (Nederlands – Vlaamse accreditatieorganisatie)
PAT	Partnership Assessment Toolkit
PEARL	Partnership for Enhancing Agriculture in Rwanda through Linkages
PPBL	problem- and project-based learning
ProSPER.Net	Promotion of Sustainability in Postgraduate Education and Research Network
PSLSA	participatory sustainable-livelihoods-systems appraisal
QCA	qualitative comparative analysis
RAE	Royal Academy of Engineering
RCE	Regional Centre of Expertise on Education for Sustainable Development
RCT	randomized controlled trial
REDD	Reducing Emissions from Deforestation and Forest Degradation
RMIT	Royal Melbourne Institute of Technology University
RPCs	research-program consortia

SAQ	self-awareness question
SD	sustainable development
SDC	Swiss Agency for Development and Cooperation
SDGs	Sustainable Development Goals
Sida	Swedish International Development Cooperation Agency
SJTIHE	Shanghai Jiao Tong Institute of Higher Education
SSCSAEDI	Smart Strategic Coalition for Sustainable Agricultural and Economic Development in Indonesia
STAMP	Bellagio Sustainability Assessment and Measurement Principles
STARS	Sustainability Tracking and Rating System
TBL	triple bottom line
TC	transnational competence
THE-QS	Times Higher Education-Quacquarelli Symonds
THEP	transnational higher-education partnership
TOR	terms of reference
TSD	transnational sustainable development
UBC	University of British Columbia
UDS	University for Development Studies, Ghana
ULSF	University Leaders for a Sustainable Future
UNDP	United Nations Development Programme
UNEG	United Nations Evaluation Group
UNEP	United Nations Environment Programme
UNESCO	United Nations Educational, Social and Cultural Organization
UNMUL	Universitas Mulawarman, Rare, Indonesia
USAID	United States Agency for International Development
USHEPiA	University Science, Humanities and Engineering Partnerships in Africa
USM	Universiti Sains Malaysia
VLIR-UOS	Flemish Interuniversity Council (Belgium)
WHO	World Health Organization
WWDR	United Nations World Water Development Report

Note

1 Strictly speaking, no longer. It's now: "Danida is the term used for Denmark's development cooperation, which is an area of activity under the Ministry of Foreign Affairs of Denmark."

FOREWORD

Robert B. Gibson

In the beginning we were storytellers. That was how we got along in the world. Through most of the human record, we remained storytellers. Then, slowly and only recently, we shifted to measuring and evaluating.

The book you have now opened is both a product of and a response to that new strategy for getting along. Most obviously, this book is about measuring and evaluating. But it is also a book about reversing our slide into ever-deeper unsustainability, and unsustainability is a side effect of measuring and evaluation. Or at least it is a side effect of the ways by which measuring and evaluation have served the agenda of scientific and economic advancement.

It does not follow that measuring and evaluation are inappropriate tools for the pursuit of sustainability. However, application to sustainability does entail a significant change in their objectives and perhaps also in their character.

In service to conventional modern progress, measuring and evaluating have favored parts over wholes, tangible evidence over inherent character, and confidence in reason over traditional reticence. They have facilitated fragmentation, manipulation, and hubris. As a consequence they have contributed to great perils as well as astounding accomplishments.

The notion of sustainability retains much of the modern package. But in contrast to the dominant modern practice, it respects interconnections, embraces complexity, and favors humility. By focusing on sustainability, Peter Koehn and Juha Uitto, along with other pioneers in this field, are taking the calculating tools into unfamiliar territory. They are preparing the ground for a new story about measuring and evaluating.

As it turns out, they are also contributing to a new story about sustainability. While sustainability is frequently presented as an invention of the late twentieth century, its roots are deep.

Long before the rise of measuring and evaluating, sustainability was a central human concern. We find it at the heart of all the old stories.

Old sustainability

Most of what we may claim to know about the old sustainability has been inferred from scattered archaeological and anthropological evidence and from what remains of the old stories. But the essentials are clear enough.

For 90-some percent of the human experience, all of us were hunters, gatherers, and foragers. We moved from place to place with the seasons and the resources, gradually learning more about how to survive and thrive. Stories passed our slowly accumulated understandings from the elders of one generation to the children of the next. They told us what to eat, where to go, how we came to be, how to get along with each other, and how we fit in with everything else.

Learning expanded over centuries and millennia, and the stories evolved, as stories do. Some stories incorporated impressively detailed ecological, nutritional, and medical knowledge. Others involved sophisticated means of building cooperation and managing conflict. But the learning was for continuing successfully, not for seeking more control of nature to gain more wealth for the individual or community. We were nomads. Material wealth was a burden to lug from place to place – the less, the better.

Moreover, little was simple or certain. More or less unreliable spirits inhabited everything, and everything was connected. The stories that survived to be retold emphasized what had worked before, the consequences of failed innovation, and the dangers of over-confidence. The old stories were sustainability strategies for a world in which change was risky.

Measurement and evaluation

Measuring and evaluating arose in cultures that began to embrace change – cultures that needed better tools for controlling, adjusting, and manipulating. Measuring and evaluating helped us become more powerful, more confident, and more dangerous. Such changes were not embraced quickly or easily, however. That took millennia.

Farming made a difference. Sedentary life permitted accumulation. Agriculture involved more alteration and control of the environment. Sometimes, it demanded major public works – terracing, irrigation, storage facilities, roads – and, consequently, administrators, rulers, cities, armies, and the proliferating rest. These brought new requirements for measuring and evaluating in units of extent and value – harvests, taxes, booty, commodities, the trajectories of cannon balls. And so we adopted cubits and ducats, measured the behavior of falling objects, converted to Arabic numerals, and accepted double-entry bookkeeping.

Threats to the established order were suspect, and resistance was common. Eventually, however, the calculating tools rose to define modern science, economics, and technology. Then they proceeded to swallow all else. Life began to be organized around wages and prices, revolutions per minute, GDP, bandwidth, and gigabytes.

Stories

Stories remained, of course. Increasingly, however, they have featured the world of measuring and evaluating. The predominant stories today, the ones with most audience and influence, are in algorithms and spreadsheets, accounts, rankings, and projections. Even stories in the old forms now arise in the world of measurement and evaluation, adopt their media, and reinforce their supremacy. The calculating tail now wags the storied dog.

Or maybe measuring and evaluating have become the big dog and it wags the tale.

None of this would be a significant worry if the results of the new approach were consistently cheerful. But they are not. Measuring and evaluating have supported modern science, economics, technology, and industry. They have helped us become powerful beyond our past imaginings but also dangerous beyond our demonstrated capacities for correction.

Our celebrated powers today lie in manipulation and material enrichment – in using nature as a resource for increasingly ambitious reorganization into goods and services for human satisfactions.

Our failings are in imprudence, insufficiency, and maldistribution. We are demanding already too much and every year still more of the biosphere's carrying capacity for humans than can be maintained over time. Meanwhile, billions of people suffer serious material deficiency. And most of the gains from our still-expanding takings and leavings are going to those who need them least.

These are the three pillars of unsustainability. Each of them interacts with the others. Together they imperil present wellbeing and steal from future generations. While none of our failings are necessary or incorrigible, all of them are in one way or another supported and perpetuated by the prevailing structures of measurement and evaluation, motivation and management. Our failings are maintained by the dominant narratives – the main stories that we now tell – and by the insufficiency of stories about other possibilities.

Measurement and evaluation in the service of sustainability

Collectively, we are now enormously better informed, and many of us are much better off than we have ever been. Nonetheless, we all face highly uncertain prospects.

To improve these prospects, we will probably need to draw from the old learning as well as the new capabilities – to combine the fitting-in wisdom of the old sustainability with the change-making capabilities of measuring and evaluation.

In the following pages, Peter Koehn and Juha Uitto do just that. They have assembled components for a new story about measuring and evaluating for sustainability.

Heroic ambitions are in play here. As we have seen, measuring and evaluating are not natural allies of sustainability. Adopting progress toward sustainability as a serious objective demands more attention to uncertainties, interactions, and lasting consequences than has been common in the world of reporting on progress. A new story with measurement and evaluation serving lasting wellbeing will not come easy.

Given the challenges, it is especially suitable that the authors have assigned the task of developing this story to universities, which are themselves oddly promising combinations of tradition and innovation, fragmentation and solidarity.

We can imagine many different stories about the results. We can safely predict, however, that if, centuries from now, forensic researchers dig back into residual university records from the early twenty-first century, they won't be seeking the now-revered data on undergraduate entrance grades, graduate-student completion ratios, or endowment and research funding received per annum. Much more likely, they will be investigating the responses to inter-generational crime.

Perhaps they will be hoping to uncover how we managed to confront climate change and the other great threats to biospheric support systems and human persistence before it was entirely too late. Maybe they will be looking for what finally moved us to act, what experiments in learning and practice were eventually helpful, why we succeeded in some things, and why we failed (so unnecessarily, it will seem in retrospect) in others.

Whatever the specifics may be, the result of any success will put us back to storytelling. And the new stories will not be about how we gained dominion. They will be back to the old theme – what we have learned about getting along with the world and each other.

Robert B. Gibson
Professor, School of Environment,
Resources and Sustainability,
University of Waterloo, Canada

FOREWORD

Rob D. van den Berg

Some of the most urgent issues of our times have been put on the global agenda by science. Sometimes through unexpected innovation; sometimes through consequences that became clear later. The hole in the ozone layer is a good example. Science was at the birth of the problem. In the late 1920s, an American chemist, Thomas Midgley Jr., focused on solving a problem in air conditioning and refrigeration systems, which used a variety of compounds which were either toxic, flammable or explosive. Rather than to see his house explode or his family poisoned, Dr. Midgley aimed for a new compound that had none of these qualities. He developed the first chlorofluorocarbon (CFC) compound – more followed, and they quickly replaced the old compounds. Another success story for science supporting technological innovation and development? Not quite.

Just as a scientist was responsible for creating CFCs in the first place, science also was responsible for discovering potential negative effects of the new compounds. In 1972 the United States became concerned about increasing air pollution from aircraft. The US Academy of Sciences was asked to prepare a report, which it duly delivered in 1976. This contained the surprising finding that credible scientific evidence existed that CFCs escaping into the atmosphere would lead to depletion of the ozone layer. This layer is of crucial importance, protecting Earth from harmful ultraviolet radiation. In 1985 scientists reported for the first time on the famous ozone layer hole over the Antarctic region, and the issue became political, leading to one of the finest moments in the history of international collaboration: a nearly global abandonment of the production and consumption of CFCs, and, in 2010, the first reports that the ozone layer is recovering from the onslaught of CFCs.

More examples can be given. The Industrial Revolution was made possible through countless innovations inspired by science and technology, which led to an unsustainable economy focused on non-renewable energy. The Club of Rome was one of the first in 1972 to ask attention for the "limits to growth" related to unsustainable use of resources. Although the Club advertised itself as consisting of "world citizens", it was based on scientific insights. In 1987 its baton was taken over by UN World Commission on Environment and Development, better known as the Brundtland Commission, with the first definition of sustainable development, focusing on meeting the needs of present as well as future generations. In 1988 the Intergovernmental Panel on Climate Change (IPCC) followed, putting the issue of climate change on the global agenda. Science is a motor for development, but also looks forward and warns if the road taken leads to disaster.

Science has also uncovered the reasons behind many failures in international development. When agricultural extension remained very ineffective in Africa in the Eighties of the previous century, it took research to identify why this was the case. As a synthesis report of 1995 of the Food and Agriculture Organization of the United Nations[1] clearly demonstrated, women were not targeted in agricultural extension as they tended to not own the land, were marginalized in decision making processes, tended to be poor, and small-holders producing subsistence crops. Agricultural extension in the Eighties was focused on export crops, technological innovation and the men who owned the land. . . . Studies like the FAO synthesis report were crucial in shifting attention to gender and small holder issues.

While scientists have played a major role in these developments, both in causing problems and helping to solve them, the role of universities has been relatively out of the limelight. As centers for learning and research, they have contributed immensely to our insights into current and future problems. They undoubtedly have a direct contribution through research programs focused on the major issues of our times, whether this be poverty, equity, gender, diseases, agricultural development, conflict, governance and a multitude of others. They have perhaps an even more important indirect contribution through the countless scientists who work in the public and private sectors, in civil society organizations and in the philanthropic institutions. All these scientists have been trained in universities. They bring the theories and insights incorporated in their education to their new environment. One could make a case that the Sustainable Development Goals (SDGs) mean the return of a scientific approach to development, rather than a technocratic one. The Millennium Development Goals (MDGs), the predecessors of the SDGs, were focused on what politicians could hope to deliver. While science can support such efforts through solving relatively narrow problems, these efforts on their own do not build societies that are socially, economically and environmentally sustainable. The SDGs can be perceived as a science inspired return to complexity and interconnectedness.

The SDGs have been criticized by scientists as well, and some of this criticism is focused on the perceived lack of realism in these goals. Two conflicting strands of scientific work emerge in the debate about sustainability and sustainable development. One strand aims for reductionism to identify powerful solutions to problems. Another strand focuses on a better understanding of underlying causes of problems in our societies, our economies and the environment, and how to solve these. While it may be argued that both strands are inherently scientific and need to co-exist, universities may not always have sufficient overview to get the best out of both of them and combine them where needed.

If universities could contribute to a better understanding of sustainability and sustainable development, on where reductionism and technocratic solutions play a role and where integration and multi-disciplinary approaches are necessary, this would be great. If universities would have a better understanding of the role they play in societies, their role could potentially become more beneficial. This book explores the contribution that evaluation can play in this process of self-reflection.

Evaluation in universities can make substantial progress. While evaluation is playing a role in many universities, the authors look for inspiration at the experiences of international development evaluation to develop a comprehensive evaluation framework, focusing on processes, outcomes and impacts. This comprehensive framework is a strong effort to introduce and further develop good evaluation practices for the specific requirements of universities tackling sustainability. It focuses not only on the processes of education and research in universities, but also on how universities interact with society. Last, but not least important, it develops a perspective on the evaluation capacity needed to implement the comprehensive framework. This book should be recommended reading not only for evaluators in universities, but also for their governing boards and leadership, as well as the management of faculties and departments. While many universities seem to be increasingly in the grip of managers that apply the tools of business administration to ensure that the "bottom-line" is met, evaluation can potentially play an important role to help and support a focus in universities on how research and education can be made more relevant to the major problems of our times.

Rob D. van den Berg
President, International Development Evaluation Association
Visiting Professor, King's College London
Visiting Fellow, Centre for Development Impact,
Institute of Development Studies (IDS), University of Sussex

Note

1 FAO (1995). A synthesis report of the Africa region – Women, agriculture and rural development. Rome, FAO, accessed on 30 November 2016 at http://www.fao.org/docrep/x0250e/x0250e.htm#TopOfPage

INTRODUCTION

Today, a plethora of university activities are devoted to "sustainable development." *Sustainable development*, how are you situated among the multitude of contemporary university undertakings? *Sustainable development*, how do we know when our university has hastened your arrival? These framing questions both guide our inquiry and illuminate pathways to meaningful sustainability evaluations by higher-education institutions.

Twenty-first-century universities engage in diverse actions under the rubric of sustainable development. *Universities and the Sustainable Development Future: Evaluating Higher-Education Contributions to the 2030 Agenda* is concerned with internal sustainable-development activity in curricular, teaching, research,[1] and (to a lesser extent) estate-management initiatives and with external-outreach engagements. In particular, we aim to address the paucity of published work that treats the academic side of university sustainable-development evaluation. In this connection, the transnational higher-education partnership (THEP) – an increasingly popular vehicle for collaborative North-South, South-South, and triangular (North-South-South) research and sustainable-development undertakings (Koehn, 2012; Koehn and Obamba, 2014) – merits special attention. With the university as the center of analysis, we include, within the scope of the study, partnerships with other higher-education institutions, governments, and non-governmental organizations (NGOs) – including private businesses and community associations.[2]

Our principal interest in this book is with the "how can we know what happens" and "so what" questions. As the 2015 International Year of Evaluation drew to a close,[3] world leaders attending the United Nations September 2015 Summit adopted the 2030 Agenda for Sustainable Development with its attendant universal Sustainable Development Goals (SDGs). It is timely, therefore, to step back and assess whether the university is making, and can make, a sustainable-development difference (Gibson, 2005, p. 162). Stakeholders – including donors, the public, international organizations, accrediting agencies, and participants in transnational-sustainable-development (TSD) ventures – need to know if universities are advancing sustainable development or, at least, are on the right track. This inquiry also is important for universities themselves, as they invest substantial resources, faculty time, and prestige in sustainable-development endeavors.

Evaluation of academic institutions and programs is not a new concept. In some cases, evaluation – especially external independent evaluation – is seen as a threat, particularly when it is linked to funding by governments or donors. Our aim is to promote credible independent evaluation and not to use the tool as a punitive mechanism. The framework for analysis presented in Part III is built on a critical review of current university approaches to evaluation, lessons from international-development experience, an extensive body of literature on the subject, and personal insights. The novel framework is intended to help universities ascertain whether their sustainable-development actions are contributing to desired outcomes and to enhance learning about how such actions can be improved.

While many universities have pursued estate-management greening initiatives (sustainable campus physical operations such as food service, waste disposal, mobility, and buildings), the more challenging areas of curricula, research, and outreach generally have lagged behind (see, for instance, Jones, Selby, and Sterling, 2010, p. 5; Cotton and Winter, 2010, p. 40; Sterling and Maxey, 2013, p. 6; Wals and Blewitt, 2010, p. 59; Ralph and Stubbs, 2014, p. 76; Wright, 2002, pp. 111–116; Sileshi, 2016, p. 190). In the new millennium, however, a number of universities around the world have introduced undergraduate and post-graduate academic programs in sustainability and sustainable development (see, for instance, Ryan and Cotton, 2013, p. 152; Desha and Hargroves, 2014, p. 193).[4] In 2004, for instance, Arizona State University "founded the full degree-granting School of Sustainability, which has steadily grown to over six hundred undergraduate majors and nearly one hundred graduate students" (Cortese, 2012, p. 28).

Although university involvement in TSD research, teaching, and outreach has increased substantially, systematic learning from these involvements has been "weak" (Jones, Bailey, and Lyytikäinen, 2007, p. 24). Further, the extent to which higher-education initiatives have influenced development outcomes, particularly in the Global South, is widely contested. Contestations raise issues of focus, measurement, methods, asymmetry, and bias. Given the limitations encountered in available evaluations of higher-education undertakings, a major concern of *Universities and the Sustainable Development Future* involves identifying ways that evaluation processes can be improved, expanded, and made more powerful.

Reliable evaluations only are valuable to the extent that sustainable development is important. Here, we consider sustainable development as a concept and intention. Chapter 2 elaborates on the ways universities can contribute to a future ennobled by sustainable development.

Sustainable development and higher education's mission and position

The origins of sustainable development lie in the World Commission on Environment and Development chaired by the former Norwegian prime minister Gro Harlem Brundtland. In the report submitted to the United Nations in 1987, the commission defined "sustainable development" as "development that meets the needs of the present without compromising the ability of future generations to meet their own needs."[5] In the ensuing decades, the terms "sustainable development" and "sustainability" often have been used interchangeably (Derrick, 2013, p. 48). However, Hayden Washington (2015, pp. 363–366, 371–372) maintains that "sustainability" is a broader and harmonious concept in comparison with "sustainable development,"[6] a term that he argues *requires* unsustainable economic growth. In an alternative conceptualization that we find useful, Susan Baker (2016, pp. 9, 24, 45) articulates the term "sustainable development" as a social-change-directed blend of the "potential of an ecosystem to subsist over time" (sustainability) joined with viable (inter-generational) economic pathways (development). Baker's definition encompasses and interweaves the iconic three interacting pillars of sustainable development: economic, ecological, and social.[7] We further envision pathways to wellbeing in non-material senses as challenging and replacing economic-growth pathways in a transnational-sustainable-development future that honors Earth's biosphere capacity and environmental limits (also see Waas, et al., 2015, pp. 90, 93).

Clearly, the environment/poverty nexus is at the core of the sustainable-development challenge (see, for instance, Ospina, 2000, p. 33; PEI, 2009; Sachs, 2015, p. 11; Baker, 2016, p. 24). Sustainable development envisions improvements in current living conditions for those who are disadvantaged,[8] advancing intra-/inter-generational and inter-species equity and justice (Waas, et al., 2015, p. 89), and preserving the ability of future generations in all world regions to meet their needs and realize their aspirations through common but differentiated responsibility.[9] Sustainable development requires "maintaining the capacity of ecological systems to support social and economic systems" (Berkes, Colding, and Folke, 2003, p. 2; also Gibson, 2005, p. 95) and vice versa. The wellbeing of human beings and non-humans, now and in the future, is at stake in sustainable-development interfaces.[10]

Sustainable development is a dynamic, ongoing process rather than an end point: "a way of managing possible feasible scenarios for the future . . ." (Ospina, 2000, p. 33). Therefore, "it is better to speak about promoting, not achieving, sustainable development" (Baker, 2016, p. 9) and to embrace a precautionary approach in the face of inevitable risks and uncertainties (Waas, et al., 2015, p. 89). Both incremental and systemic changes can contribute to the realization of evolving sustainable-development objectives (Shriberg, 2004, p. 73). Low-carbon and no-carbon pathways feature prominently in promising sustainable-development visions (e.g., Koehn, 2016, p. 63).

While "ill-defined, politically contentious, manipulable, and at times contradictory" (Roberts and Parks, 2007, pp. 223–224),[11] sustainable development has emerged as a popular, adaptable, and encompassing (McFarlane and Ogazon, 2011, pp. 84–85; Stockmann, 2012, p. 5) guiding principle for innovative academic programming and transnational collaboration. The vagueness of the construct also has resulted in establishment of a widely diverse set of academic programs devoted to development studies and has introduced special evaluation challenges.

Underlying the 2005–2014 United Nations Decade of Education for Sustainable Development's inspirational objective of promoting "education as a basis for a more sustainable human society" (Bourn and Morgan, 2010, pp. 272–273)[12] is recognition that education, environmental protection, and sustainable development are connected in multiple and interdependent ways. Indeed, the fundamental transformation of conceptualization and action that sustainable development requires of individuals, institutions, and societies ensures that higher learning will remain at the core of the TSD pursuit (Barth and Rieckmann, 2016, p. 100).

Although observers fault them for having graduated actors who establish and perpetuate unsustainable patterns and practices,[13] the world's universities are particularly well-positioned to identify and model[14] the change pathways[15] required to address challenges of transitioning to sustainable development. In Simon Marginson's (2007, p. xii) words, "universities are both part of the problem, and part of the solution." They are innovative and forward-looking institutions, better positioned to adopt a longer time perspective on sustainability's extended "natural time horizon for results" (Sachs, 2015, p. 493) than are business and political actors preponderantly subject to short-term pressures (Derrick, 2013, p. 47). Most are at least semi-independent agents, suffused with passion, vision, moral responsibility to advance a sustainable future (Cortese, 2003, p. 17; Cotton and Winter, 2010, p. 40; Ralph and Stubbs, 2014, p. 74); they display commitment to transferring knowledge generated to society (Barth and Rieckmann, 2016, p. 100), to public service, to accommodating society's changing needs (Razak, et al., 2013, p. 141),[16] and to reflecting on practice (Stewart, Keusch, and Kleinmann, 2011, p. 309). They possess sufficient infrastructure, interdisciplinary and transdisciplinary capacity, and the potential to bridge science and policy as well as to address interconnected global, national, and local sustainable-development needs (Katehi, 2012, pp. 120, 122; Ralph and Stubbs, 2014, p. 74). They graduate future generations of leaders and informed citizens who will determine TSD outcomes and impacts (Chambers, 2013, p. 310). Increasingly, Northern and Southern institutions of higher learning are transnationally partnered (see Koehn and Obamba, 2014). In short, the potential impact of universities on sustainable development is "vastly greater than any other single sector of society" (Disterheft, et al., 2013, p. 2). And, fortuitously, "the higher education sector is uniquely placed to influence the ways in which sustainability is assessed and measured" (Derrick, 2013, p. 47).

The sustainable-development intention

Since the introduction of the term by the World Commission on Environment and Development (WCED, 1987), sustainable development has taken on dimensions of a mantra among its proponents in and out of academe. For decades, the United Nations Development Programme (UNDP) has been in the forefront of advocates for sustainable human development. As early as 1990, UNDP's Human Development Report elaborated on the concept of sustainable development, emphasizing the linkages between human development, use of natural resources, and the protection of the environment (HDR, 1990). The agency recognized poverty as one of the biggest threats to the environment, as poor countries and poor people use environmental resources unsustainably for their short-term needs.

As the Millennium Development Goals (MDGs) drew to a close, the post-2015 agenda and its evaluation implications began to take shape. Focusing attention to interlinkages among poverty, human wellbeing, and the environment, *Agenda 2030* and the SDGs are intended to stimulate action for people, planet, and prosperity. The process culminating in the adoption of the agenda was a major show of political will across continents. Unlike in the case of the previous MDGs, the *2030 Agenda for Sustainable Development* is not only focused on the developing countries but globally applicable. Furthermore, evaluation has been built into the SDGs.[17]

At the UN Sustainable Development Summit in September 2015, five of the eight MDGs blended into seventeen more demanding SDGs for 2015–2030 that are connected to 169 specific action targets (Sengupta, 2015; Haas, 2015, pp. 78–81).[18] New financing to the tune of US$3 trillion remained to be found (Sengupta, 2015),[19] and, although insiders acknowledge that outcomes and impacts "must be measured" (e.g., Sachs, 2015, p. 493), representatives of the countries that adopted *Agenda 2030* postponed deciding how to measure whether SDG targets are being met (Sengupta, 2015). Although the SDGs are universal, the fact that they are intended to reflect national realities, capacities, and levels of development – and to respect national policies and priorities – suggests a central role for country-led evaluation and data (Uitto, 2016).

In December 2015, 195 nations attending the United Nations Climate Summit in Paris reached a milestone agreement that, in the words of the French negotiator Laurent Tabiana, forms a "universally accepted basis for negotiations" on moving toward a sustainable low-carbon future.[20] Earlier in the year, the Third United Nations Conference on Disaster Risk Reduction, held in the Japanese city of Sendai, set forth a new agenda that highlights the importance of climate change and variability in its final document (Uitto and Shaw, 2016).

Bilateral and multilateral donors have promoted the application of sustainable-development concepts on the ground in developing countries and provided evidence of the crucial linkages between poverty and environment (see, for instance, Hansen, 2007; PEI, 2009). Universities have been eager to introduce sustainable-development programs and to join in related project initiatives. Interested parties have established a multiplicity of continental and international networks devoted to advancing higher education's involvement in TSD (see Michelsen, 2016, pp. 46–47; Desha and Hargroves, 2014, pp. 28–29, 52, 173–177).

Although differences remain in emphases among those focusing on economic growth, environment, climate change, and disaster risk reduction, a near global consensus has arisen around the intention to bring about sustainable development.[21] Upfront, we want to establish that sustainable development is a forward-looking vision we also endorse. In addition, we fully expect that future international and domestic agendas will be driven more than ever by TSD intentions.

Although universities should be and, for the most part, want to be an integral part of tomorrow's sustainable-development overtures, they have not been centrally involved in setting the international agenda (Moja, 2008, p. 164; Tarabini, 2010, p. 209; Koehn and Obamba, 2014, p. 7). For instance, tertiary-level institutions[22] lacked official-sector representation at the 2002 World Summit on Sustainable Development in South Africa (Moja, 2008, p. 164). It is particularly striking that "higher education is not mentioned as an instrument for achieving even one of the eight Millennium Development Goals . . . [even though] attainment of every single one of them will be much easier if a country has a strong and productive higher education system" (Bloom, 2003, p. 142; also King, 2009, p. 34; Yusuf, Saint, and Nabeshima, 2009, pp. xxii–xxiii). Similarly, the *2030 Agenda for Sustainable Development*[23] does not assign any role for post-secondary education to advance sustainable development, apart from ensuring equal access to tertiary education for all.

Oversight has not dampened higher-education's enthusiasm for participation in sustainable-development efforts, however. Since the mid-1970s, a series of international declarations that link sustainability to all aspects of higher learning have been endorsed and signed by universities around the world.[24] By 2013, more than four hundred universities[25] in fifty-plus countries had committed to the sustainability-literacy in teaching, research, and outreach objectives embodied in the 1990 *Talloires Declaration* (Derrick, 2013, p. 60).[26] In 1993, delegates to the 1,200-member International Association of Universities (IAU) Round Table adopted the *Kyoto Declaration on Sustainable Development*, which pledged to develop institutional capacity to teach, conduct research, and engage in action according to "sustainable development principles" (Jones, Selby, and Sterling, 2010, p. 3; also Wright, 2002, p. 108). Among other provisions, the *Swansea Declaration* of 1993 "appealed for universities of richer countries to aid in the evolution of university environmental sustainability programs in less wealthy nations worldwide" (Wright, 2002, p. 108). The 1997 *Thessaloniki Declaration* argues for a holistic approach to environmental education that links global sustainability with "poverty, population, food security, democracy, human rights, peace and health and a respect for traditional cultural and ecological knowledge" (Wright, 2004, p. 12; also Wright, 2002, p. 109). The role of higher education in sustainable development is highlighted in the 2009 *Abuja Declaration on Sustainable Development in Africa* (Lozano, et al., 2013, p. 12). The 2012 *Higher Education for Sustainability Initiative for Rio+20*, signed by universities in more than forty countries, treats sustainability opportunities as "special responsibilities."[27]

All relevant international declarations refer to the need to include sustainable development across the curriculum and to develop interdisciplinary and trans-disciplinary research[28] as well as public outreach, to promote sustainability in university operations, and to encourage post-secondary institutions to cooperate proactively with each other and with other stakeholder organizations (Wright, 2004, pp. 8–10, 13–17; Lozano, et al., 2013, pp. 12–18). A small number demonstrate interest in evaluating sustainability initiatives (Derrick, 2013, p. 50; Lozano, et al., 2013, pp. 16–17). University leadership is to be manifest through teaching and enhancing student capabilities, by encouraging relevant research, by disseminating knowledge through public engagement, by adopting sustainable practices, and by building sustainable societies (Sawahel, 2012).

Nevertheless, the vast majority of universities in the world remain unengaged with sustainable development (Lozano, et al., 2013, p. 11), and endorsing one or more declarations can amount to little more than a university public-relations move, or "greenwashing" (Wright, 2002, pp. 110–111). In most cases, evidence of core higher-education institutional and societal impact attributable to signing a major declaration has not been forthcoming (Wright, 2002, p. 118; Ramos and Pires, 2013, p. 93).[29] For instance, a study conducted at the Royal Melbourne Institute of Technology (RMIT) University, "a leader in signing declarations and developing policy," found "a disappointing lack of action" and little influence on mainstream practices twelve years following the institution's initial engagement with the sustainability agenda (see Bekessy, Samson, and Clarkson, 2007, pp. 301–312). In Sweden, although "education on all levels is by law obliged to make sustainable development part of the curriculum," most universities offer at best a few courses in the field (Isaksson and Johnson, 2013, pp. 3692, 3696).[30]

Pathway to deeper policy involvement

Universities around the world, as ever-recharging repositories of critically needed knowledge and expertise, have vitally important and long-lasting contributions to make to the sustainable-development future. Through "demonstrating best practice in their operations, research and teaching" and by "educating future communities and leaders . . . universities have both multiple and multiplier effects on the sustainability of today's and future society" (Ralph and Stubbs, 2014, pp. 71–72). The special role of universities in the critical arenas of human wellbeing, climate, energy, biodiversity, water and oceans, forests, and fisheries is elaborated in Chapter 2. To succeed, higher-education institutions will need to strengthen existing partnerships and to be more proactive in international policy circles. In addition, they will need evaluative evidence to ensure that sustainable development occupies the front burner of contemporary political and economic decision making (Hardi, 2007, p. 24) and "to guide future direction" (Thomas and Tominaga, 2013, p. 58).

We measure what we care about (Hardi, 2007, p. 24). However, not everything can be measured, and actions leading to transformative changes are the ones that least lend themselves to quantification (Natsios, 2010). In *Universities and the Sustainable Development Future*, we make a case for moving beyond accounting for activities and outputs and on to evaluating the outcomes and impact of university-TSD endeavors. We will resist relying on a narrow set of measures and, instead, advocate for applying multiple approaches and methods – both quantitative and qualitative.

It is important for numerous reasons that we know whether higher-education initiatives are making a difference in contributing toward sustainable development. At the policy-setting table, the hand of universities will be enhanced to the extent that they are able to demonstrate that their actions contribute valuable and valued results. Demands for credible evidence (see Newcomer, El Baradei, and Garcia, 2013, p. 63; Collins, 2014, pp. 195–196) will only increase. This is where evaluation (and this book) comes in. Weakness in demonstrating effect and importance through convincing evaluation studies leads decision makers to weigh higher education's sustainable-development initiatives less seriously. Evaluations also are important within the broader context of education for sustainable development because "there is much skepticism in North and South about the larger development project given the paucity of evidence for its success in its first 50 years of existence" (McGrath and King, 2004, p. 179; also Porter and Goldman, 2013, pp. 10–11; Hales and Prescott-Allen, 2002, p. 31).

Purposively and effectively designed and implemented academic-project and institutional-program evaluations strengthen the case for university leadership in the TSD venture. At the same time, respected evaluations reinforce higher education's societal relevance, further embed sustainability in the university's identity (Roorda, 2013, p. 113), enhance approaches designed to prepare graduates for future sustainable-development challenges, advance co-learning with stakeholders (Hailemichael, 2013, p. 43; Chouinard and Cousins, 2013, p. 69; Hailemichael, 2013, p. 43), and inform collaborations with partners on sustainable-development-research and outreach initiatives (Koehn and Obamba, 2014, Chapter 8). In short, whatever universities fund and initiate to advance sustainable development internally and externally should be demonstrably compelling.

Defining evaluation

To begin, universities will be well-served by shared understanding of evaluation purposes and practice. While evaluation has been defined in many ways, most definitions involve the concept of making a "judgment of the value or worth of the subject of the evaluation" (Morra Imas and Rist, 2009, p. 8). Evaluation is carried out for multiple purposes, including generating new insights, action-pathway identification, policy and program improvement, shared and continuous institutional and public learning (Gibson, 2005, p. 155), and accountability for results achieved and resources used (also Meyer, 2012, p. 40; Deprez, 2012, p. 237; Waas, et al., 2015, p. 95). Therefore, evaluation can be formative, summative, and/or prospective (Morra Imas and Rist, 2009).

Monitoring (and its performance-management "cousin") involve the frequent and ongoing tracking of changes in inputs, activities, outputs, and preliminary outcomes in order to inform program implementation and improvement (Zint, 2011, p. 332; Poister, Aristigueta, and Hall, 2015, pp. 5, 27). Formative evaluation is conducted while the project or program is still being implemented. Monitoring resembles formative evaluation "except that the former does not imply that value judgments will be made, whereas the latter does" (Zint, 2011, p. 332). Process evaluations aim to determine the extent to which participants implemented planned activities as intended. Formative evaluation overlaps with process evaluation because of the common focus on operations (Morra Imas and Rist, 2009, p. 9). Summative evaluations typically draw on monitoring and process insights and occur following or near the end of interventions to determine the extent to which project, program, or policy features (as opposed to external factors) contributed to changes in outcomes and impacts (Zint, 2011, pp. 332–337).

Evaluation involves a rigorous, systematic, and evidence-based process of collecting, analyzing, and interpreting information to answer specific questions. Common steps in the evaluation process involve the identification of questions, relevant criteria, and target audiences; developing a research design that will guide the collection and analysis of collected data; disseminating results; and promoting the use of findings (Zint, 2011, p. 332). Useful evaluations provide assessments of what works and why and in what context; highlight intended and unintended results; and provide strategic, future-oriented lessons to guide decision makers and inform stakeholders. Although evaluation clearly has an accountability dimension for results achieved and resources used, it is most valuable when used by stakeholders for program improvement (or termination) and learning lessons for the future (see Patton, 2008; Waas, et al., 2015, p. 95; Zint, 2011, p. 332; Desha and Hargroves, 2014, p. 92). According to Porter and Goldman (2013, p. 16):

> Evaluation helps you understand change, both anticipated and unanticipated, and plan for what happens next. It does this by establishing why the level of performance is being achieved, what difference is being made, what has been learned, and what to do next in the implementation of a policy or programme. . . . Evaluation can helpfully distinguish between implementation failure – not doing things well – and theory failure – doing things well but not getting the desired result. Evaluation . . . seeks to support the development of utilization-focused answers to stakeholders' questions.

In a time of conflicting internal and external expectations and increasing governance complexity, evaluation assumes an especially prominent role (Simon and Knie, 2013, p. 405). To prepare the way for a tailored discussion of higher-education-TSD evaluations, we first consider the narrow consensus on key dimensions of comprehensive evaluations. Next, we identify the limitations of prevailing approaches. Then, in the interest of advancing sustainable-development-evaluation methods and approaches, we identify, in generic and adaptable terms, the defining characteristics of comprehensive and symmetrical evaluations. Part III of the book sets forth an evaluation framework for application to university sustainable-development activities.

Consensus dimensions

In the search for a framework that will illuminate sustainable-development activity at higher-academic institutions, we can start with an agreement that comprehensive evaluations need to cover inputs, processes, outputs, outcomes, and impacts (see Deardorff and van Gaalen, 2012, pp. 168–170). An *output* is a "tangible product (including services) of an intervention that is directly attributable to the initiative" (UNDP, 2011). Outputs relate to the extent (amount, volume) of completion of the goals that actors set for themselves (Hardi, 2007, p. 26; Poister, Aristigueta, and Hall, 2015, p. 58) rather than the conduct (*process*) of activities. Outputs are the type of results over which program and project managers can exert the most influence. However, the generation of outputs provides "no guarantee that outcomes will result" (Poister, Aristigueta, and Hall, 2015, p. 58). An *outcome* is the "actual or intended changes in development *conditions* that an intervention seeks to support" (UNDP, 2011, emphasis added). Sustainable-development conditions include policies, institutional capacities, and human capabilities. In the higher-education context, evidence of teaching-, research-, outreach-, and partnership-capacity development constitute prime condition-advancing outcomes of sustainable-development initiatives. Process-oriented-outcome criteria include motivations, intents, connectors, relationships, disincentives, rewards, and actions (Shriberg, 2004, p. 73; Deprez, 2012, p. 240).

In sustainable-development evaluations, *impact* involves high-level improvements in human wellbeing and the state of the environment. In his theoretical work on the evaluation of donor-supported development projects, Harvey Smith (2000, p. 209) points out that "some projects may achieve their objectives but not have any great impact on the community, while others may not achieve their objectives but nevertheless have a beneficial impact – possibly even greater than was foreseen by the original design" (also see Strele, 2012, pp. 173–174). The micro-macro paradox, where many projects are achieving their objectives but overall trends in global environmental impacts are declining, is recognized in the sustainable-development-evaluation field (see van den Berg, 2011; Uitto, 2014). Smith's insight calls attention to the importance of focusing on *how* higher-education's TSD research and outreach projects work in a given context.

In sustainable-development evaluations, the ultimate question is whether the intervention being evaluated actually has contributed to changing trends in social, economic, and environmental conditions. Who (and what) is directly and indirectly better off and worse off (Thabrew, Wiek, and Ries, 2009, p. 71)? Under what circumstances, and why? It is difficult to determine attribution for higher education's ultimate impacts.[31] Impacts typically are clouded when evaluated early on, and specific contributions are more difficult to distinguish from other influences as one comes closer in time to observable ultimate impacts. Impact pathways are complex, time lags are often lengthy, and there are multiple intervening factors and actors that can facilitate or hinder impact. Interventions can be categorized as complex when they are "inherently dynamic and emergent, rather than following a path that has been tightly defined in advance to achieve tightly specified objectives" (Rodgers, 2011, p. 35). We can identify at least five main sources of evaluation complexity (Raimondo, et al., 2016, pp. xxxvi–xxxvii): the nature of the program; the context within which the program is embedded; the interactions among the multiple stakeholders and agencies involved (Kruse, 2005, pp. 121–122); the nature of change and causality processes; and the nature of the evaluation process itself. Theory-based approaches offer one promising way of evaluating the results of complex sustainable-development initiatives (Vaessen and Todd, 2008, p. 232; Todd and Craig, 2014; Zint, 2011, p. 336).

The limited consensus on higher-education-partnership evaluation also holds that the most helpful assessments are relevant and of practical utility, are ongoing, and trigger remedial actions. The evaluation process itself should be transparent, broadly inclusive of project or program participants and stakeholders, and produce explanations that are understandable to a wide audience (Hardi, 2007, pp. 25, 28). It should explore gaps and complementary strengths (Klitgaard, 2004, p. 51). Curricular, research, and community-engagement initiatives should be subjected to transdisciplinary, integrated, and synergistic assessments rather than evaluated separately (Yarime, et al., 2012, p. 104; Cortese, 2003, pp. 17–18, 20–21; Ralph and Stubbs, 2014, p. 74). Evaluations should be inclusive of the temporal, spatial, and multiple-domain dimensions of sustainable development (Hardi, 2007, p. 23; Derrick, 2013; Stevens, 2012, p. 57; Bakkes, 2012, pp. 246, 248). In addition, evaluations should encompass individual (private) and social (collective) benefits and costs. In this connection, Schuller and Desjardins (2007, p. 45) provide an informative list of potential private and public non-monetary benefits of (higher) education that draws upon the work of Walter McMahon. Finally, credibility and an adequate level of independence must be assured.

Common weaknesses

Evidence suggests that prevailing evaluations of university sustainable-development initiatives tend to be unsystematic.[32] They focus on inputs, activities, and outputs rather than outcomes and impacts (Chapman and Moore, 2010, pp. 555, 557, 562; also Srivastava and Oh, 2010), overlook timeframe analysis (Derrick, 2013, pp. 48–49; Franz and Kirkpatrick, 2012, p. 71; Baker, 2016, p. 49), are not transparent, and are not widely available (Hoppers, 2001, p. 463). Many are in-house; few are external and independent. Monitoring, which "does not help you understand why something is happening," takes precedence over generating "in-depth evaluative evidence that provides guidance for improving interventions" (Porter and Goldman, 2013, pp. 15–16). Even the well-designed and well-implemented development-evaluation efforts possess important limitations (see Koehn and Uitto, 2014).

Asymmetry introduces a host of detrimental influences. Many evaluations of university sustainable-development efforts are asymmetrical in at least two respects. First, they are predominantly Northern designed and Northern directed. Second, they are preoccupied with Northern-donor interests. Asymmetrical evaluations arise from exclusive donor determinations of project indicators and baselines against which achievements are measured (Crossley, et al., 2005, p. 37). Northern funders also are prone to promote "ever-widening standardization" of evaluation metrics internationally (Taylor, 2008, p. 99; Neave, 2012, pp. 5–7). Pressure to borrow standardized, externally determined, indicators narrows opportunities to conduct contextually based evaluations that allow for different place-based operational definitions of sustainable development (Hardi, 2007, p. 28). In addition, the application of results-based approaches that place priority on upward compliance with donor interests works to the "detriment of more developmental uses of M&E evidence" (Porter and Goldman, 2013, p. 10; also Deprez, 2012, pp. 236–237).

The asymmetrical nature of Northern-designed development evaluations is further revealed by the disproportionate attention paid to monitoring performance and assessing results on only the Southern side of transnational partnerships (van den Berg and Feinstein, 2009, p. 35). Benefits that accrue to Northern institutions and societies often fall outside the purview of TSD evaluations (see Syed, et al., 2012).

Researchers, practitioners, and consultants are engaged in a search for relevant evaluation metrics in the fields of education and development (Walker, et al., 2009, p. 571; Africa-U.S. Higher Education Initiative, n.d., p. 3). However, consensus on specific metrics has yet to take shape within either field. Academic sustainable-development evaluation is further complicated by challenges of working within three discrete realms of activity (research, development practice, and learning) and three levels of analysis (individual, organizational, and societal). Critical analysis of the ways in which the possibilities and constraints imposed by donors affect higher-education outcomes and impacts also needs to be embedded in the evaluation process (see Samoff and Carrol, 2006). Eyben (2013, pp. 7–24) provides an insightful critical treatment of the results and evidence artifacts of the development-evaluation methods popular with Northern donors, including logical frameworks, payment by results, randomized-control trials, and cost-effectiveness analysis.

We now understand that it is not sufficient to evaluate individual projects in terms of their stated objectives. Although thousands of projects are mostly successful, global environmental problems keep mounting (see, for instance, van den Berg, 2011). The micro-macro paradox arises because successful projects are overwhelmed by other societal forces that work against their goals, such as environmentally harmful subsidies to continued fossil-fuel use, unsustainable agricultural techniques, and destructive armed conflicts. Therefore, it is essential that evaluation incorporates a holistic, foresight-expanding (Slaughter, 1995, p. xvii) picture that assesses whether the interventions that universities undertake are making a difference for the global environment and the lives of people that depend on it (see Uitto, 2014).

Universities and the Sustainable Development Future aims to pave the way for advances in the evaluation of university efforts intended to promote sustainable development. This is a challenging undertaking with the promise of considerable reward. To be clear, our goal is not to provide a universal blueprint. Rather, we intend to present and demonstrate the utility of a flexible and adaptable framework that will inspire substantial contextually based improvements in the ways universities evaluate their sustainable-development undertakings.

The rest of the book

Part I is devoted to articulating the contemporary roles of Northern and Southern higher-education institutions in the planet's sustainable-development future. Chapter 1 presents a framework for analyzing university engagement in sustainable development that addresses both transformative pathways and facilitating conditions. In addition, Chapter 1 explores the diverse ways that the contemporary university is and can be involved in sustainable-development activity through curricular innovations, research undertakings, estate management, outreach, transnational partnering, and stakeholder engagement. Building needed higher-education capacity to address challenges of sustainable development is included in this discussion. The special role of universities in the critical arenas of human wellbeing, freshwater scarcity, species extinction, deforestation and fisheries depletion, climatic change, and health provides the principal subject of discussion in Chapter 2. As repositories of skills and knowledge and change-tilted organizations, universities are uniquely positioned to contribute in each of these arenas.

Part II critically explores the landscape of university assessment and evaluation. Chapter 3 treats current higher-education assessment and evaluation practices in the North and South. Accreditation practices feature in this discussion. With a focus on sustainable-development activity, Chapter 4 addresses the limitations of existing assessment approaches and identifies opportunities for improvement. This chapter critically reviews prevailing university approaches to sustainable-development evaluation, introduces lessons from international-development-evaluative experience, and briefly explores pathways to change.

Part III is concerned with how institutions of higher learning in the North and South can support transitions to sustainable development through meaningful evaluation approaches and enhanced capacity. Chapter 5 identifies outcome and impact pathways, introduces theories of change that are generic to universities, and provides a process for selecting appropriate evaluation methods. Chapters 6 through 9 critically review prevailing university sustainable-development curricula, research, outreach, and transnational-partnering assessment approaches from process, outcome, and impact perspectives. The alternative framework cumulatively developed in these chapters for carrying out sustainable-development evaluations that help determine if university activities are making a difference applies inclusive, participatory, and innovative analytic strands. In Chapter 9, the proposed framework is utilized to assess several full-term higher-education-evaluation case studies with a view toward discovering what has worked and has not worked, identifying specific limitations, and suggesting improved future symmetrical-evaluation pathways. Chapter 10 is devoted to enhancing evaluation capacity at universities in North and South. Each Part III chapter offers specific guidance aimed at enhancing university outcome and impact evaluations.

Two concluding chapters constitute Part IV of the book. The penultimate chapter offers practical guidelines for applying the framework elaborated in Part III. We suggest here a core set of illustrative evaluation guidelines that can serve as a practical foundation with widespread utility for institutions of higher learning.

Embracing contextually driven outcome and impact evaluation provides universities with valuable insights that can be used in support of further TSD academic activities. In Chapter 12, we show how the comprehensive, but adaptable, framework and the practical guidelines suggested for outcome and impact inquiries in Part III of *Universities and the Sustainable Development Future* can help universities prepare for and address emerging and forthcoming challenges of sustainable development. The concluding chapter also identifies potential drivers who can successfully advance the book's recommended approaches for conducting university sustainable-development evaluations.

Notes

1 For one helpful enumeration of the focal issues and "approaches commensurate with sustainability principles" involved in sustainable-development research, see White (2013, p. 168).

2 According to former UNEP executive director Achim Steiner, partnerships across economic, social, and environmental sectors that support the integration of sustainable-development principles in national policies and programs can distinguish progress with the 2030 Agenda from the uneven and unfinished goals and targets of MDG7 (interview reported in Scherkenbach, 2013, pp. 36–37).

3 Although the United Nations Decade of Education for Sustainable Development (DESD) concluded at the end of 2014, UNESCO announced at the final DESD conference (in Nagoya, Japan, 2014) that, as a "concrete contribution to the post-2015 agenda," education for sustainable development would continue as a Global Action Programme (GAP) (see Michelsen, 2016, p. 53). DESD goals, which applied to informal education as well as to colleges and universities, include serving as the principal transformative agent of sustainable development and increasing future-thinking capacity. DESD evaluation reports indicate that specific national contexts shaped the application of education-for-sustainable-development goals (see Blewitt, 2015, p. 303), that sustainable development and education agendas are converging, that an increasing number of post-secondary institutions around the world are integrating sustainability approaches into their research and teaching endeavors, and that "there is now an increased recognition at the international policy level that education is essential to the advancement of sustainable development" (UNESCO, 2014, p. 9).

4 By February 2016, the Association for Advancing Sustainability in Higher Education (AASHE) listed 103 (overwhelmingly US-based and Canada-based) sustainability-focused doctoral programs (the vast majority in engineering), 476 masters programs, and 431 baccalaureate programs. However, the terms "sustainability" and "sustainable development" did not appear as a program indicator in most of these discipline-based programs (www.aashe.org/ [accessed 21 February 2016]).

5 United Nations (1987), Chapter 2, paragraph 1.
6 See also the broad definition of "sustainability" set forth by Arnim Wiek, et al. (2016, p. 241).
7 The second Bellagio Sustainability Assessment and Measurement Principle for sustainability assessment specifically refers to interactions, synergies, and tradeoffs among these three systems (Bakkes, 2012, pp. 244–245; see also Gibson, 2005, pp. 52, 55–62).
8 The gap-closing dimension of sustainable development draws attention to the moral as well as practical nature of the concept (Cullingford, 2004, pp. 245, 250).
9 On the Brundtland Commission's oft-cited and now iconic formulation of sustainable development in its *Our Common Future* report, see Fredericks (2014, pp. 21–24) and Baker (2016, pp. 25, 32–33, 45, 47–48, 50–51).
10 This conceptualization is consistent with the first principle of the Bellagio Sustainability Assessment and Measurement Principles (Bakkes, 2012, p. 244). On the key principles of sustainable development set forth in the Brundtland Report, see Box 2.6 in Baker (2016, p. 45).
11 The oxymoronic nature of the construct "sustainable development" stems from "a conflict between a desire to sustain something in the long term, but also to develop and make use of it" (Derrick, 2013, p. 48; Washington, 2015).
12 On the origins and development of the education for sustainable development concept, see Disterheft, et al. (2013, p. 9).
13 For instance, Anthony Cortese (2003, p. 16) maintains that "it is the people coming out of the world's best colleges and universities that are leading us down the current unhealthy, inequitable, and unsustainable path" (also see Wals and Blewitt, 2010, p. 70).
14 Cayuela, et al. (2013, p. 235) refer to this role as "becoming a test-bed for sustainability, and in that way contributing directly to the significant transitions required to reach a sustainable future."
15 The transition processes of sustainable development are "multi-scale, multi-domain, [and] multi-temporal." Sustainability processes are inherently dynamic. Consequently, a newly attained equilibrium can "become the pre-development phase of a new transition" (Hardi, 2007, p. 21).
16 As Kearsley Stewart, Gerald Keusch, and Arthur Kleinmann (2011, p. 309) put it, "no other institution can claim a serious engagement in all three domains of teaching, research, and service as strongly as universities."
17 Annually, at the High Level Political Forum, nations will report on "what they have done on the SDGs" (Nabarro, 2016, p. 15).
18 Newly added items were sustainable energy, resource security, and food security (Haas, 2015, p. 81).
    For details, see the UN's Sustainable Development Knowledge Platform (https://sustainabledevelopment.un.org/post2015/transformingourworld).
19 The July 2015 Addis Ababa Action Agenda (AAAA) adopted at the Third International Conference on Financing for Development launched a new global framework for financing sustainable development and began the process of securing resource commitments, particularly through development banks (Batra, Uitto, and Cando-Noordhuizen, 2016, p. 17).
20 See www.cop21.gouv.fr/en/a-major-step-forward-with-the-new-version-of-the-draft-agreement/ (accessed 7 December 2015). Thanks to widespread and rapid national adoptions, the Paris Agreement entered into force on 4 November 2016.
21 We acknowledge that the notion of sustainable development articulated here and advocated by the international regime is not shared and is even violently opposed in certain fundamentalist quarters.
22 Tertiary-level institutions encompass all post-secondary forms of education, including private and public universities and colleges, technical institutes, teaching colleges, and "other programs that lead to the award of [post-secondary] academic diplomas or degrees" (Yusuf, Saint, and Nabeshima, 2009, p. xxxi).

23 United Nations Resolution adopted by the General Assembly on 25 September 2015. "Transforming Our World: the 2030 Agenda for Sustainable Development." A/RES/70/1.

24 For a comprehensive list spanning 1972 through 2012, see Tilbury (2013, pp. 74–81) and Disterheft, et al. (2013, p. 14). On the early contribution of *Agenda 21*, see Sterling and Thomas (2006, pp. 350–351); Wright (2002, p. 108). *Agenda 21* consistently emphasizes the importance of adequate data and assessment (Fredericks, 2014, pp. 31–33).

    In 2005, the Government of the United Kingdom specifically highlighted the need to prepare professional graduates with "sustainability literacy" (Sterling and Thomas, 2006, p. 351).

25 For instance, the University of British Columbia (UBC) (see Moore, 2005, p. 327; Cayuela, et al., 2013).

26 On the role of the US-based University Leaders for a Sustainable Future (ULSF) in initiating the *Talloires Declaration*, which emphasized curricula, teaching, and learning, see Jones, Selby, and Sterling (2010, p. 3). The ULSF association also serves as secretariat for *Talloires Declaration* signatories (Togo, 2015, p. 35). The *University Charter for Sustainable Development* (*Copernicus Charter*) promulgated by the Conference of European Rectors in 1994 and signed by some 350 European university chief executives from thirty-seven countries by 2010, embodies the same emphasis as the *Talloires Declaration* while emphasizing the need for networking (Jones, Selby, and Sterling, 2010, p. 3; Wright, 2002, p. 109). The *Bonn Declaration*, adopted at the 2009 UNESCO World Conference on Sustainable Development, also affirmed the curricula, teaching, research, and community-engagement impetus (Jones, Selby, and Sterling, 2010, p. 3).

27 For details regarding the *Rio+20 People's Sustainability Treaty for Higher Education*, see Tilbury (2013, pp. 73–74). The *Rio+20* treaty on higher education requires that signatories specify how their universities will enhance education for sustainable development (Holm, et al., 2015, p. 165). Kenneth King and Robert Palmer (2013, p. 26) expected the SDGs to incorporate the *Rio+20* goal of enhancing the capacity of tertiary education to prepare graduates to promote sustainable development through teaching and curricular advancements.

28 On the connection of transdisciplinary research to sustainable development, see Hadorn, et al. (2006).

29 Further, some universities (e.g., the University of South Carolina) have undertaken major curricula and outreach initiatives without signing any declarations (Wright, 2002, p. 110).

30 The five Nordic countries (Sweden, Norway, Finland, Denmark, Iceland) either promote education-for-sustainable-development (ESD) initiatives or incorporate ESD in national-sustainability strategies (Holm, et al. 2015, p. 165). China has integrated sustainable development in national education-reform initiatives, and Japan has embedded education for sustainable development in national curriculum guidelines (Michelsen, 2016, p. 53).

31 Some evaluators treat the impact-attribution issue by comparing intervention results with counterfactual values (conditions sans intervention) or by comparing before-after situations.

32 In common with prevailing evaluation constraints under international environmental agreements (see Esty and Ivanova, 2002, p. 186), higher-education-TSD evaluations tend to lack coordination and consistency. Consequently, comparability across institutions is rarely accomplished.

Works cited

Africa-U.S. Higher Education Initiative. n.d. *Developing a Knowledge Center for the Africa-U.S. Higher Education Initiative: A Concept Paper.* Washington, DC: Association of Public and Land Grant Universities.

Baker, Susan. 2016. *Sustainable Development*, 2nd edition. London: Routledge.

Bakkes, Jan. 2012. "Bellagio Sustainability Assessment and Measurement Principles (BellagioSTAMP): Significance and Examples from International Environmental Outlooks." In *Sustainable Development, Evaluation and Policy-Making: Theory, Practise and Quality Assurance*, edited by Anneke von Raggamby and Frieder Rubik. Cheltenham, UK: Edward Elgar. Pp. 241–260.

Barth, Matthias; and Rieckmann, Marco. 2016. "State of the Art in Research on Higher Education for Sustainable Development." In *Routledge Handbook of Higher Education for Sustainable Development*, edited by Matthias Barth, Gerd Michelsen, Marco Rieckmann, and Ian Thomas. London: Routledge. Pp. 100–133.

Batra, Geeta; Uitto, Juha I.; and Cando-Noordhuizen, Lee. 2016. "From MDGs to SDGs: Evaluating Global Environmental Benefits." *Evaluation Matters* 1:16–23. African Development Bank, Independent Development Evaluation.

Bekessy, S. A.; Samson, K.; and Clarkson, R. E. 2007. "The Failure of Non-Binding Declarations to Achieve University Sustainability: A Need for Accountability." *International Journal of Sustainability in Higher Education* 8 (3):301–316.

Berg, Rob D. van den. 2011. "Evaluation in the Context of Global Public Goods." *Evaluation* 17 (4):405–415.

Berg, Rob D. van den; and Feinstein, Osvaldo. 2009. "Evaluating Climate Change and Development." In *Evaluating Climate Change and Development*, edited by Rob D. van den Berg and Osvaldo Feinstein. New Brunswick, NJ: Transaction Publishers. Pp. 1–40.

Berkes, Fikret; Colding, Johan; and Folke, Carl. 2003. "Introduction." In *Navigating Social-Ecological Systems: Building Resilience for Complexity and Change*, edited by Fikret Berkes, Johan Colding, and Carl Folke. Cambridge: Cambridge University Press. Pp. 1–25.

Blewitt, John. 2015. *Understanding Sustainable Development*, 2nd edition. London: Routledge.

Bloom, David E. 2003. "Mastering Globalization: From Ideas to Action on Higher Education Reform." In *Universities and Globalization: Private Linkages, Public Trust*, edited by Gilles Breton and Michel Lambert. Paris: UNESCO Publishing. Pp. 140–149.

Bourn, Douglas; and Morgan, Alun. 2010. "Development Education, Sustainable Development, Global Citizenship and Higher Education: Towards a Transformatory Approach to Learning." In *Global Inequalities and Higher Education: Whose Interests Are We Serving?*, edited by Elaine Unterhalter and Vincent Carpentier. Hampshire: Palgrave Macmillan. Pp. 268–286.

Cayuela, Alberto; Robinson, John B.; Campbell, Ann; Coops, Nicholas; and Munro, Alison. 2013. "Integration of Operational and Academic Efforts in Sustainability at the University of British Columbia." In *Sustainability Assessment Tools in Higher Education Institutions: Mapping Trends and Good Practices around the World*, edited by Sandra Caeiro, Walter L. Filho, Charbel Jabbour, and Ulisses M. Azeiteiro. Cham, Switzerland: Springer International Publishing. Pp. 223–236.

Chambers, Dianne P. 2013. "A Discipline-Based Model for Embedding Sustainability in University Curricula." In *Sustainability Assessment Tools in Higher Education Institutions: Mapping Trends and Good Practices around the World*, edited by Sandra Caeiro, Walter L. Filho, Charbel Jabbour, and Ulisses M. Azeiteiro. Cham, Switzerland: Springer International Publishing. Pp. 309–321.

Chapman, David W.; and Moore, Audrey S. 2010. "A Meta-Look at Meta-Studies of the Effectiveness of Development Assistance to Education." *International Review of Education* 56:547–565.

Chouinard, Jill A.; and Cousins, J. Bradley. 2013. "Participatory Evaluation for Development: Examining Research-Based Knowledge from within the African Context." *African Evaluation Journal* 1 (1):66–74.

Collins, Christopher S. 2014. "Can Funding for University Partnerships between Africa and the US Contribute to Social Development and Poverty Reduction?" *Higher Education* 68:943–958.

Cortese, Anthony D. 2003. "The Critical Role of Higher Education in Creating a Sustainable Future." *Planning for Higher Education* 2 (March–May):15–22.

Cortese, Anthony D. 2012. "Promises Made and Promises Lost: A Candid Assessment of Higher Education Leadership and the Sustainability Agenda." In *The Sustainable University: Green Goals and New Challenges for Higher Education Leaders*, edited by James Martin and James E. Samels. Baltimore: The Johns Hopkins University Press. Pp. 17–31.

Cotton, Debby; and Winter, Jennie. 2010. "'It's Not Just Bits of Paper and Light Bulbs': A Review of Sustainability Pedagogies and Their Potential for Use in Higher Education." In *Sustainability Education: Perspectives and Practice across Higher Education*, edited by Paula Jones, David Selby, and Stephen Sterling. London: Earthscan. Pp. 39–55.

Crossley, Michael; Herriot, Andrew; Waudo, Judith; Mwirotsi, Miriam; Holmes, Keith; and Juma, Magdallen. 2005. *Research and Evaluation for Educational Development: Learning from the PRISM Experience in Kenya*. Oxford, UK: Symposium Books.

Cullingford, Cedric. 2004. "Conclusion: The Future: Is Sustainability Sustainable?" In *The Sustainability Curriculum: Facing the Challenge in Higher Education*, edited by John Blewitt and Cedric Cullingford. London: Earthscan. Pp. 245–252.

Deardorff, Darla K.; and van Gaalen, Adinda. 2012. "Outcomes Assessment in the Internationalization of Higher Education." In *The Sage Handbook of International Higher Education*, edited by Darla K. Deardorff, Hans de Wit, John Heyl, and Tony Adams. Los Angeles, CA: Sage. Pp. 167–190.

Deprez, Steff. 2012. "Development of a Learning-Oriented Monitoring System for Sustainable Agriculture Chain Development in Eastern Indonesia." In *Governance by Evaluation for Sustainable Development: Institutional Capacities and Learning*, edited by Michal Sedlacko and Andre Martinuzzi. Cheltenham, UK: Edward Elgar. Pp. 233–252.

Derrick, Stephen. 2013. "Time and Sustainability Metrics in Higher Education." In *Sustainability Assessment Tools in Higher Education Institutions: Mapping Trends and Good Practices around the World*, edited by Sandra Caeiro, Walter L. Filho, Charbel Jabbour, and Ulisses M. Azeiteiro. Cham, Switzerland: Springer International Publishing. Pp. 47–63.

Desha, Cheryl; and Hargroves, Karlson C. 2014. *Higher Education and Sustainable Development: A Model for Curriculum Renewal*. London: Routledge.

Disterheft, Antje; Caeiro, Sandra; Azeiteiro, Ulisses M.; and Filho, Walter L. 2013. "Sustainability Science and Education for Sustainable Development in Universities: A Way for Transition." In *Sustainability Assessment Tools in Higher Education Institutions: Mapping Trends and Good Practices around the World*, edited by Sandra Caeiro, Walter L. Filho, Charbel Jabbour, and Ulisses M. Azeiteiro. Cham, Switzerland: Springer International Publishing. Pp. 3–27.

Esty, Daniel C.; and Ivanova, Maria H. 2002. "Revitalizing Global Environmental Governance: A Function-Driven Approach." In *Global Environmental Governance: Options & Opportunities*, edited by Daniel C. Esty and Maria H. Ivanova. New Haven, CT: Yale School of Forestry & Environmental Studies. Pp. 181–203.

Eyben, Rosalind. 2013. "Uncovering the Politics of 'Evidence' and 'Results': A Framing Paper for Development Practitioners." www.bigpushforward.net

Franz, Jennifer; and Kirkpatrick, Colin. 2012. "Integrating Sustainable Development into Impact Assessments: How Effective Is the European Commission?" In *Governance by Evaluation for Sustainable Development: Institutional Capacities and Learning*, edited by Michal Sedlacko and Andre Martinuzzi. Cheltenham, UK: Edward Elgar. Pp. 63–85.

Fredericks, Sarah. 2014. *Measuring and Evaluating Sustainability: Ethics in Sustainability Indexes.* London: Routledge.

Gibson, Robert B. 2005. *Sustainability Assessment: Criteria and Processes.* London: Earthscan.

Haas, Peter M. 2015. "Issue Linkage and the Prospects for SDGs' Contribution to Sustainability." In *Transitions to Sustainability*, edited by Francois Mancebo and Ignacy Sachs. New York: Springer. Pp. 77–82.

Hadorn, Gertrude H.; Bradley, David; Pohl, Christian; Rist, Stephan; and Weismann, Urs. 2006. "Implications of Transdisciplinarity for Sustainability Research." *Ecological Economics* 60:119–128.

Hailemichael Taye. 2013. "Evaluating the Impact of Agricultural Extension Programmes in Sub-Saharan Africa: Challenges and Prospects." *African Evaluation Journal* 1 (1):38–45.

Hales, David; and Prescott-Allen, Robert. 2002. "Flying Blind: Assessing Progress toward Sustainability." In *Global Environmental Governance: Options & Opportunities*, edited by Daniel C. Esty and Maria H. Ivanova. New Haven, CT: Yale School of Forestry & Environmental Studies. Pp. 31–52.

Hansen, Stein. 2007. *The Economic Case for Investing in Environment: A Review of Policies, Practice and Impacts of Relevance to Norwegian Partner Countries.* Oslo: NORAD.

Hardi, Peter. 2007. "The Long and Winding Road of Sustainable Development Evaluation." In *Impact Assessment and Sustainable Development: European Practice and Experience*, edited by Clive George and Colin Kirkpatrick. Cheltenham, UK: Edward Elgar. Pp. 15–30.

Holm, Tove; Sammalisto, Kaisu; Grindsted, Thomas S.; and Vuorisalo, Timo. 2015. "Process Framework for Identifying Sustainability Aspects in University Curricula and Integrating Education for Sustainable Development." *Journal of Cleaner Production* 106:164–174.

Hoppers, Wim. 2001. "About How to Reach the Truth in Development Co-Operation: ODA/DFID's Education Papers." *International Journal of Educational Development* 21:463–470.

Human Development Report (HDR). 1990. *Concept and Measurement of Human Development.* Published for the United Nations Development Programme (UNDP). Oxford: Oxford University Press.

Isaksson, Raine; and Johnson, Mikael. 2013. "A Preliminary Model for Assessing University Sustainability from the Student Perspective." *Sustainability* 5:3690–3701.

Jones, Nicola; Bailey, Mark; and Lyytikäinen, Minna. 2007. *Research Capacity Strengthening in Africa: Trends, Gaps and Opportunities.* London: Overseas Development Institute.

Jones, Paula; Selby, David; and Sterling, Stephen. 2010. "Introduction." In *Sustainability Education: Perspectives and Practice across Higher Education*, edited by Paula Jones, David Selby, and Stephen Sterling. London: Earthscan. Pp. 1–16.

Katehi, Linda P. B. 2012. "A University Culture of Sustainability: Principle, Practice and Economic Driver." In *Global Sustainability and the Responsibilities of Universities*, edited by Luc E. Weber and James J. Duderstadt. London: Economica. Pp. 117–127.

King, Kenneth. 2009. "Higher Education and International Cooperation: The Role of Academic Collaboration in the Developing World." In *Higher Education and International Capacity Building: Twenty-Five Years of Higher Education Links*, edited by David Stephens. Oxford, UK: Symposium Books. Pp. 33–49.

King, Kenneth; and Palmer, Robert. 2013. *Post-2015 Agendas: Northern Tsunami, Southern Ripple? The Case of Education and Skills.* Working paper #4. Geneva: Network for International Policies and Cooperation in Education and Training (NORRAG).

Klitgaard, Robert. 2004. "Evaluation of, for, and through Partnerships." In *Evaluation & Development: The Partnership Dimension*, edited by Andres Liebenthal, Osvaldo N.

Feinstein, and Gregory K. Ingram. New Brunswick, NJ: Transaction Publishers. Pp. 43–57.

Koehn, Peter H. 2012. "Transnational Higher Education and Sustainable Development: Current Initiatives and Future Prospects." *Policy Futures in Education* 10 (3):274–282.

Koehn, Peter H. 2016. *China Confronts Climate Change: A Bottom-Up Perspective.* New York: Routledge.

Koehn, Peter H.; and Obamba, Milton O. 2014. *The Transnationally Partnered University: Insights from Research and Sustainable Development Collaborations in Africa.* Gordonsville, VA: Palgrave Macmillan.

Koehn, Peter H.; and Uitto, Juha I. 2014. "Evaluating Sustainability Education: Lessons from International Development Experience." *Higher Education* 67 (5):621–635.

Kruse, Stein-Erik. 2005. "Meta-evaluations of NGO Experience: Results and Challenges." In *Evaluating Development Effectiveness*, edited by George K. Pitman, Osvaldo N. Feinstein, and Gregory K. Ingram. World Bank Series on Evaluation and Development, Volume 7. New Brunswick, N.J.: Transaction Publishers. Pp. 109–127.

Lozano, Rodrigo; Lukman, Rebeka; Lozano, Francisco J.; Huisingh, Donald; and Lambrechts, Wim. 2013. "Declarations for Sustainability in Higher Education: Becoming Better Leaders, through Addressing the University System." *Journal of Cleaner Production* 48:10–19.

Marginson, Simon. 2007. "Preface: The Open Horizon." In *Prospects for Higher Education: Globalization, Market Competition, Public Goods and the Future of the University*, edited by Simon Marginson. Rotterdam: Sense Publishers. Pp. xi–xv.

McFarlane, Donovan A.; and Ogazon, Agueda G. 2011. "The Challenges of Sustainability Education." *Journal of Multidisciplinary Research* 3, No. 3 (Fall):81–107.

McGrath, Simon; and King, Kenneth. 2004. "Knowledge-Based Aid: A Four Agency Comparative Study." *International Journal of Educational Development* 24:167–181.

Meyer, Wolfgang. 2012. "Should Evaluation Be Revisited for Sustainable Development?" In *Sustainable Development, Evaluation and Policy-Making: Theory, Practise and Quality Assurance*, edited by Anneke von Raggamby and Frieder Rubik. Cheltenham, UK: Edward Elgar. Pp. 37–54.

Michelsen, Gerd. 2016. "Policy, Politics and Polity in Higher Education for Sustainable Development." In *Routledge Handbook of Higher Education for Sustainable Development*, edited by Matthias Barth, Gerd Michelsen, Marco Rieckmann, and Ian Thomas. London: Routledge. Pp. 40–55.

Moja, Teboho. 2008. "Institutional Challenges and Implications for HEIs: Transformation, Mission and Vision for the 21st Century." In *Higher Education in the World 3: New Challenges and Emerging Roles for Human and Social Development.* GUNI Series on the Social Commitment of Universities 3. London: Palgrave Macmillan. Pp. 161–169.

Moore, Janet. 2005. "Seven Recommendations for Creating Sustainability Education at the University Level: A Guide for Change Agents." *International Journal of Sustainability in Higher Education* 6 (4):326–339.

Morra Imas, Linda G.; and Rist, Ray C. 2009. *The Road to Results: Designing and Conducting Effective Development Evaluations.* Washington, DC: The World Bank.

Nabarro, David. 2016. "SDGs: No One Will Be Left Behind." *Africa Renewal* 30, No. 1 (April):14–15.

Neave, Guy. 2012. *The Evaluative State, Institutional Autonomy and Re-Engineering Higher Education in Western Europe: The Prince and His Pleasure.* London: Palgrave Macmillan.

Newcomer, Kathryn; El Baradei, Laila; and Garcia, Sandra. 2013. "Expectations and Capacity of Performance Measurement in NGOs in the Development Context." *Public Administration and Development* 33:62–79.

Ospina, Gustavo L. 2000. "Education for Sustainable Development: A Local and International Challenge." *Prospects* 30 (1):31–40.

Patton, Michael Q. 2008. *Utilization-Focused Evaluation*, 4th edition. Los Angeles, CA: Sage.

Poister, Theodore H.; Aristigueta, Maria P.; and Hall, Jeremy L. 2015. *Managing and Measuring Performance in Public and Nonprofit Organizations: An Integrated Approach*, 2nd edition. San Francisco, CA: Jossey-Bass.

Porter, Stephen; and Goldman, Ian. 2013. "A Growing Demand for Monitoring and Evaluation in Africa." *African Evaluation Journal* 1 (1):10–18.

Poverty-Environment Initiative (PEI). 2009. *Making the Economic Case: A Primer on the Economic Arguments for Mainstreaming Poverty-Environment Linkages into National Development Planning*. Nairobi: UNDP-UNEP Poverty-Environment Initiative.

Raimondo, Estelle; Bamberger, Michael; and Vaessen, Jos. 2016. "Introduction." In *Dealing with Complexity in Development Evaluation: A Practical Approach*, edited by Michael Bamberger, Jos Vaessen, and Estelle Raimondo. Los Angeles, CA: Sage. Pp. xxxv–xliv.

Ralph, Meredith; and Stubbs, Wendy. 2014. "Integrating Environmental Sustainability into Universities." *Higher Education* 67:71–90.

Ramos, Tomas; and Pires, Sara M. 2013. "Sustainability Assessment: The Role of Indicators." In *Sustainability Assessment Tools in Higher Education Institutions: Mapping Trends and Good Practices around the World*, edited by Sandra Caeiro, Walter L. Filho, Charbel Jabbour, and Ulisses M. Azeiteiro. Cham, Switzerland: Springer International Publishing. Pp. 81–99.

Razak, Dzulkifli A.; Sanusi, Zainal A.; Jegatesen, Govindran; and Khelghat-Doost, Hamoon. 2013. "Alternative University Appraisal (AUA): Reconstructing Universities' Ranking and Rating toward a Sustainable Future." In *Sustainability Assessment Tools in Higher Education Institutions: Mapping Trends and Good Practices around the World*, edited by Sandra Caeiro, Walter L. Filho, Charbel Jabbour, and Ulisses M. Azeiteiro. Cham, Switzerland: Springer International Publishing. Pp. 139–154.

Roberts, J. Timmons; and Parks, Bradley C. 2007. *A Climate of Injustice: Global Inequality, North-South Politics, and Climate Policy*. Cambridge: MIT Press.

Rodgers, Patricia J. 2011. "Implications of Complicated and Complex Characteristics for Key Tasks in Evaluation." In *Evaluating the Complex: Attribution, Contribution, and Beyond*, edited by Kim Forss, Mita Marra, and Robert Schwartz. New Brunswick, NJ, and London: Transaction Publishers. Pp. 33–52.

Roorda, Niko. 2013. "A Strategy and a Toolkit to Realize System Integration of Sustainable Development (SISD)." In *Sustainability Assessment Tools in Higher Education Institutions: Mapping Trends and Good Practices around the World*, edited by Sandra Caeiro, Walter L. Filho, Charbel Jabbour, and Ulisses M. Azeiteiro. Cham, Switzerland: Springer International Publishing. Pp. 101–119.

Ryan, Alex; and Cotton, Debby. 2013. "Times of Change: Shifting Pedagogy and Curricula for Future Sustainability." In *The Sustainable University: Progress and Prospects*, edited by Stephen Sterling, Larch Maxey, and Heather Luna. London: Routledge. Pp. 151–161.

Sachs, Jeffrey D. 2015. *The Age of Sustainable Development*. New York: Columbia University Press.

Samoff, Joel; and Carrol, Bidemi. 2006. "Influence: Direct, Indirect and Negotiated: The World Bank and Higher Education in Africa." In *Knowledge, Power and Dissent: Critical Perspectives on Higher Education and Research in Knowledge Society*, edited by Guy Neave. Paris: UNESCO Publishing. Pp. 133–180.

Sawahel, Wagdy. 2012. "University Leaders Worldwide Sign Sustainability Declaration." *University World News* 223 (25 May).

Scherkenbach, Carmen. 2013. "Environmental Targets." *Human Dimensions* 3 (August): 35–37.

Schuller, Tom; and Desjardins, Richard. 2007. *Understanding the Social Outcomes of Learning*. Paris: Organization for Economic Co-Operation and Development (OECD).

Sengupta, Somini. 2015. "After Years of Negotiations, U.N. Sets Development Goals to Guide All Countries." *New York Times*, 26 September, p. A6.

Shriberg, Michael. 2004. "Assessing Sustainability: Criteria, Tools, and Implications." In *Higher Education and the Challenges of Sustainability: Problematics, Promise, and Practice*, edited by Peter B. Corcoran and Arjen E. J. Wals. Dordrecht: Kluwer. Pp. 73–86.

Sileshi Sisaye. 2016. *Ecology, Sustainable Development and Accounting*. New York: Routledge.

Simon, Dagmar; and Knie, Andreas. 2013. "Can Evaluation Contribute to the Organizational Development of Academic Institutions? An International Comparison." *Evaluation* 19 (4):402–418.

Slaughter, Richard A. 1995. *The Foresight Principle: Cultural Recovery in the 21st Century*. Westport, CT: Praeger.

Smith, Harvey. 2000. "Transforming Education through Donor-Funded Projects: How Do We Measure Success?" In *Globalisation, Educational Transformation and Societies in Transition*, edited by Teame Mebrahtu, Michael Crossley, and David Johnson. Oxford: Symposium Books. Pp. 207–218.

Srivastava, Prachi; and Oh, Su-Ann. 2010. "Private Foundations, Philanthropy, and Partnership in Education and Development: Mapping the Terrain." *International Journal of Educational Development* 30 (5):460–471.

Sterling, Stephen; and Maxey, Larch. 2013. "Introduction." In *The Sustainable University: Progress and Prospects*, edited by Stephen Sterling, Larch Maxey, and Heather Luna. London: Routledge. Pp. 1–14.

Sterling, Stephen; and Thomas, Ian. 2006. "Education for Sustainability: The Role of Capabilities in Guiding University Curriculum." *International Journal of Innovation and Sustainable Development* 1 (4):349–369.

Stevens, Candice. 2012. "A Basic Roadmap for Sustainability Assessments: The SIMPLE Methodology." In *Sustainable Development, Evaluation and Policy-Making: Theory, Practise and Quality Assurance*, edited by Anneke von Raggamby and Frieder Rubik. Cheltenham, UK: Edward Elgar. Pp. 57–72.

Stewart, Kearsley A.; Keusch, Gerald T.; and Kleinmann, Arthur. 2011. "Bridging the Local and the Global: Values and Moral Experiences in Global Health." In *Global Health and Global Health Ethics*, edited by Solomon Benatar and Gillian Brock. Cambridge: Cambridge University Press. Pp. 304–310.

Stockmann, Reinhard. 2012. "Understanding Sustainability Evaluation and Its Contributions to Policy: Making." In *Sustainable Development, Evaluation and Policy-Making: Theory, Practise and Quality Assurance*, edited by Anneke von Raggamby and Frieder Rubik. Cheltenham, UK: Edward Elgar. Pp. 3–20.

Strele, Martin. 2012. "Participatory Livelihoods System Appraisal: A Learning-Oriented Methodology for Impact Assessment." In *Governance by Evaluation for Sustainable Development: Institutional Capacities and Learning*, edited by Michal Sedlacko and Andre Martinuzzi. Cheltenham, UK: Edward Elgar. Pp. 173–190.

Syed, Shamsuzzoha B;. et al. 2012. "Developed-Developing Country Partnerships: Benefits to Developed Countries?" *Globalization and Health* 8 (17). DOI: 10.1186/1744–8603–8–17

Tarabini, Aina. 2010. "Education and Poverty in the Global Development Agenda: Emergence, Evolution and Consolidation." *International Journal of Education and Development* 30 (2):204–212.

Taylor, Peter. 2008. "Introduction." In *Higher Education in the World 3: New Challenges and Emerging Roles for Human and Social Development*. GUNI Series on the Social Commitment of Universities 3. London: Palgrave Macmillan. Pp. xxiv–xxvii.

Thabrew, Lanka; Wiek, Arnim; and Ries, Robert. 2009. "Environmental Decision Making in Multi-Stakeholder Contexts: Applicability of Life Cycle Thinking in Development Planning and Implementation." *Journal of Cleaner Production* 17:67–76.

Thomas, Vinod; and Tominaga, Jiro. 2013. "Development Evaluation in an Age of Turbulence." In *Evaluation and Turbulent Times: Reflections on a Discipline in Disarray*, edited by Jan-Eric Furubo, Ray C. Rist, and Sandra Speer. New Brunswick, NJ: Transaction Publishers. Pp. 57–70.

Tilbury, Daniella. 2013. "Another World Is Desirable: A Global Rebooting of Higher Education for Sustainable Development." In *The Sustainable University: Progress and Prospects*, edited by Stephen Sterling, Larch Maxey, and Heather Luna. London: Routledge. Pp. 71–85.

Todd, David; and Craig, Rob. 2014. "Assessing Progress towards Impacts in Environmental Programmes Using the Field Review of Outcomes to Impacts Methodology." In *Evaluating Environment in International Development*, edited by Juha I. Uitto. London: Routledge. Pp. 62–86.

Togo, Muchaiteyi. 2015. "Development, Use and Significance of the Unit-Based Sustainability Assessment Tool for Universities in Africa and Asia." In *Mainstreaming Environment and Sustainability in African Universities: Stories of Change*, edited by Heila Lotz-Sisitka, Gitile Naituli, Amanda Hlengwa, Mike Ward, Ayobami Salami, Akpezi Ogbuigwe, Mahesh Pradhan, Marie Neeser, and Sanne Lauriks. Grahamstown: Rhodes University Environmental Learning Research Centre. Pp. 34–64.

Uitto, Juha I. 2014. "Evaluating Environment and Development: Lessons from International Cooperation." *Evaluation* 20 (1):44–57.

Uitto, Juha I. 2016. "The Environment-Poverty Nexus in Evaluation: Implications for the Sustainable Development Goals." *Global Policy* 7 (3):441–447.

Uitto, Juha I.; and Shaw, Rajib. 2016. "Sustainable Development and Disaster Risk Reduction: Introduction." In *Sustainable Development and Risk Reduction*, edited by Juha I. Uitto and Rajib Shaw. Tokyo: Springer Japan. Pp. 1–12.

United Nations. 1987. *Report of the World Commission on Environment and Development: Our Common Future*. New York: United Nations.

United Nations Development Programme (UNDP). 2011. *Evaluation Policy*. New York: UNDP. www.undp.org/evaluation/policy.htm

United Nations Economic and Social Council (UNESCO). 2014. *Shaping the Future We Want: UN Decade of Education for Sustainable Development (2005–2014)*. Paris: UNESCO.

Vaessen, Jos; and Todd, David. 2008. "Methodological Challenges of Evaluating the Impact of the Global Environment Facility's Biodiversity Program." *Evaluation and Program Planning* 31:231–240.

Waas, Tom; Huge, Jean; Verbruggen, Aviel; and Block, Thomas. 2015. "Navigating towards Sustainability: Essential Aspects of Assessment and Indicators." In *Sustainability: Key Issues*, edited by Helen Kopnina and Eleanor Shoreman-Ouimet. London: Routledge. Pp. 88–108.

Walker, Melanie; McLean, Monica; Dison, Arona; and Peppin-Vaughn, Rosie. 2009. "South African Universities and Human Development: Towards a Theorisation and Operationalisation of Professional Capabilities for Poverty Reduction." *International Journal of Educational Development* 29:565–572.

Wals, Arjen E. J.; and Blewitt, John. 2010. "Third-Wave Sustainability in Higher Education: Some (Inter)national Trends and Developments." In *Sustainability Education:*

Perspectives and Practice across Higher Education, edited by Paula Jones, David Selby, and Stephen Sterling. London: Earthscan. Pp. 55–74.

Washington, Hayden. 2015. "Is 'Sustainability' the Same as 'Sustainable Development'?" In *Sustainability: Key Issues*, edited by Helen Kopnina and Eleanor Shoreman-Ouimet. London: Routledge. Pp. 359–376.

White, Rehema M. 2013. "Sustainablity Research." In *The Sustainable University: Progress and Prospects*, edited by Stephen Sterling, Larch Maxey, and Heather Luna. London: Routledge. Pp. 168–191.

Wiek, Arnim; Bernstein, Michael J.; Foley, Rider; Cohen, Matthew; Forrest, Nigel; Kuzdas, Christopher; Kay, Braden; and Keeler, Lauren W. 2016. "Operationalising Competencies in Higher Education for Sustainable Development." In *Routledge Handbook of Higher Education for Sustainable Development*, edited by Matthias Barth, Gerd Michelsen, Marco Rieckmann, and Ian Thomas. London: Routledge. Pp. 241–260.

World Commission on Environment and Development (WCED). 1987. *Our Common Future*. Oxford: Oxford University Press.

Wright, Tarah S. A. 2002. "Definitions and Frameworks for Environmental Sustainability in Higher Education." *Higher Education Policy* 12 (2):105–120.

Wright, Tarah S. A. 2004. "The Evolution of Sustainability Declarations in Higher Education." In *Higher Education and the Challenge of Sustainability: Problematics, Promise, and Practice*, edited by Peter B. Corcoran and Arjen E. J. Wals. Dordrecht: Kluwer Academic Publishers. Pp. 7–20.

Yarime, Masaru; Trencher, Gregory; Mino, Takashi; Scholz, Roland W.; Olson, Lennart; Ness, Barry; Frantzeskaki, Niki; and Rotmans, Jan. 2012. "Establishing Sustainability Science in Higher Education Institutions: Towards an Integration of Academic Development, Institutionalization, and Stakeholder Collaborations." *Sustainability Science* 7 (Supplement 1):101–113.

Yusuf, Shahid, Saint, William; and Nabeshima, Kaoru. 2009. *Accelerating Catch-Up: Tertiary Education for Growth in Sub-Saharan Africa*. Washington, DC: The World Bank.

Zint, Michaela. 2011. "Evaluating Education for Sustainable Development Programs." In *World Trends in Education for Sustainable Development*, edited by Walter L. Filho. Frankfurt: Peter Lang. Pp. 329–347.

PART I

The role of today's universities in advancing sustainable development

1

CONCEPTUAL FRAMEWORK FOR UNDERSTANDING UNIVERSITY ENGAGEMENT IN SUSTAINABLE DEVELOPMENT

In the introduction, we found that universities around the world are demonstrating growing interest in introducing sustainable-development programs and eagerness to join in related project initiatives. In most cases, actualizing the arising motivation among higher-education institutions in the North and South to participate in the sustainable-development endeavor requires broad-based institutional change. Part I of *Universities and the Sustainable Development Future* is devoted to exploring the ways that institutions of higher learning are attempting to advance sustainable development and the directions they are headed. Chapter 1 is concerned with pathways to change that incorporate sustainable development. The special role of universities in the critical arenas of human wellbeing, climate, energy, biodiversity, water and oceans, and health provides the principal subject of discussion in Chapter 2.

Today, the future of higher education in most fields is tied to institutional and faculty capacity to anticipate and prepare graduates for boundary-spanning challenges, for integrating glocally (Disterheft, et al., 2013, p. 8) and across time scales. University personnel assume responsibility for creativity, synergy, and initiative in the face of cascading change and uncertainty (Williams, 2002, p. 106); for effective participation on and leadership of multinational and multidisciplinary teams; and for coordination within vast research clusters and networks (Simon and Knie, 2013, p. 407). They must respond to shifting employers' demands for technical/technological expertise and practical sustainability competencies (Desha and Hargroves, 2014, p. xxi; Rowe and Hiser, 2016, p. 317), to demands for life-long learning, to humanity's interest in equitable and sustainable pathways, and to calls for effective participation in political processes and policy making that advance sustainable development. These and other forward-looking dimensions of higher learning are central to transnational-sustainable-development (TSD) research, outreach, and curricular evaluation.

Moving Southern and Northern universities to engage actively and urgently with sustainable development requires the identification of pathways to change and the presence of key facilitating conditions. For institutional transformations to occur, approaches to change must be holistic and penetrating. Given its cross-disciplinary scope and institution-wide applicability, the sustainable-development mission is consistent with these fundamental change prerequisites. Factors that either facilitate or hinder this mission at individual universities include material resources, human capabilities, and participant orientations and dispositions. The presence or absence of key facilitating conditions is contextually determined and varies from site to site.

Our framework for analyzing university engagement in sustainable development addresses both transformative pathways and facilitating conditions. We approach the underlying structure of change comprehensively in terms of the paramount functions of post-secondary institutions. Embedded in this analysis is consideration of commonly encountered barriers and drivers that condition the actualization of sustainable-development initiatives. The growing contribution of transnational linkages to insight flows and organizational change also receives attention in this chapter.

The four legs of university involvement in sustainable development

A holistic approach to analyzing university involvement in sustainable development works with the four legs of estate management, curriculum, research, and outreach. Teaching and research are recognized core functions among universities around the world. Although interest in sustainable development in terms of research and curricula transformation is increasing worldwide, action on both fronts either has lagged behind or has concentrated on the margins; narrowly focused traditional subject matters organized in disciplinary silos still prevail. This section of Chapter 1 explores contemporary trends in sustainable-development knowledge and expertise generation and transmission. Three arenas of particular consequence for sustainable development are considered in depth: curricula transformation, linking research with action, and systemic change. Estate management is covered briefly here because it is an amply treated topic that falls outside of the focus of this book.

Estate management

Estate management refers to the physical-operations side of university activity. Higher-education operations policies that directly and indirectly bear upon sustainability include energy usage, greenhouse-gas emissions, waste disposal, building, supply-chain management, landscaping, and transportation (Vaughter, et al., 2013, pp. 2259, 2261–2262).

Universities in a wide range of countries – including India, Japan, the United States, Spain, and Sweden – have succeeded in integrating sustainability in estate-management policies when champions bridged campus-operations units and academic departments and participants mobilized funding for innovations (Vaughter, et al., 2013, p. 2259). The University of Cape Town is the first university in Africa to commit to reporting its carbon footprint on a consistent basis (McGibbon and Van Belle, 2015, p. 82). In a top-down and uniform approach, the UK Higher Education Funding Council mandates that higher-education institutions "adopt target reductions in greenhouse gas emissions by 2020 and 2050 in line with government commitments for country wide reductions" (Derrick, 2013, p. 53). While "greening" campus operations is important, the focus of this book is on the deeper levels represented by the other three legs of sustainability-transformed institutions and individuals (see Dahl, 2014, p. 193).

Curriculum

Future progress toward sustainable development rests on success in preparing current and next-generation professionals in multiple fields – "not only sustainability professionals!" (Wiek, et al., 2016, p. 241; also Rowe and Hiser, 2016, p. 317) – with sustainability perspectives and relevant skills so that they can "actively shape sustainable development processes" (Vettori and Rammel, 2014, p. 51). University educators and some governments have introduced steps in this direction, although current initiatives fall short in vision, scope, and intensity. For instance, although the Government of Australia's 2009 National Action Plan for Education for Sustainability "aims to integrate education for sustainability into all university subject areas," sustainability learning, especially in terms of interpersonal skills and cultural understanding, remains to be addressed in most higher-education specialist and generalist programs in the country (Date-Huxtable, Ellem, and Roberts, 2013, p. 346). In Australia, consequently, the "results of large-scale evaluations of individual curriculum initiatives have been disappointing" (de la Harpe and Thomas, 2009, p. 76). More widely, a nascent development with considerable curriculum promise connects sustainability science, which aims to "bridge the gap between science and society and to link knowledge to action for sustainability" with the emerging transformative field of education for sustainable development (Disterheft, et al., 2013, p. 9; Barth and Michelsen, 2013, p. 107; Mochizuki and Yarime, 2016).

Sustainable-development learning connects disciplines, continents, and generations. The 2008 report of the International Commission on Education for Sustainable Development Practice identified a pressing worldwide need to educate a "new generation of development practitioners" who possess the core competencies needed to secure positions and to work fluidly at the intersection of multiple professional disciplines as well as across national borders (Shaw and Kim, 2008). Given that the glocal challenges of sustainable development do not honor boundaries, virtually all academic fields and institutions of higher learning are potential contributors. Interdisciplinary and transdisciplinary approaches[1] take on particular meaning (Disterheft, et al., 2013, p. 9) and are of special utility. Some areas of study – including poverty reduction and increasing the long-term well-being of the poor, natural-resource and biodiversity conservation, agricultural sciences, environmental management, development administration/management, and climate-change mitigation and adaptation – place sustainability at the core of their cross-boundary academic enterprise (Shaw and Kim, 2008, pp. iii, 11, 13; Koehn and Rosenau, 2010, chapter 9).

There is considerable overlap in the interwoven challenges that fields addressing sustainable development confront and the transnational skills their graduates require. The International Commission on Education for Sustainable Development Practice concluded that "in a fragile planet that requires management of countless complex and delicate natural and social systems, future generations will require all the cross-disciplinary expertise that they can muster" (Shaw and Kim, 2008, p. 55; also Mochizuki and Yarime, 2016, pp. 19, 21). Indeed, "the ability to bridge disciplines and transform specialized knowledge into integrated practice" has become "one of the defining competencies of universities in this millennium" (Anderson, 2008). Nevertheless, embedding sustainable development across the higher-education curriculum remains a challenging and largely unfulfilled enterprise (Ryan and Cotton, 2013, pp. 151–152).

Consequently, graduating professionals with the cross-disciplinary expertise needed to succeed in sustainable-development arenas requires additional attention by many institutions of higher learning. Building higher-education capacity to graduate competent TSD professionals is critically needed in low-income countries of the Global South as well as in the North. In Mamphela Ramphele's words (2003, p. 19), "it is the capability to create, access, and apply knowledge that determines how successfully a country can address the numerous development challenges it faces."

Clearly, then, "the challenges of sustainable development require a new and more systematic approach to teaching, learning and problem solving for development practitioners" (International Commission on Education for Sustainable Development Practice, cited in Shaw and Kim, 2008, p. iii). To date, in contrast, most curricula and teaching approaches to building human capabilities for sustainable development "have been limited in perspective and reach" (Parker, Ninomiya, and Cogan, 1999, p. 119; Desha and Hargroves, 2014, p. 176).[2] Curriculum reforms are far more likely to be cosmetic or bolt-on (education *about* sustainability in Stephen Sterling's categorization) rather than built-in (education *for* sustainability) or transformative (*sustainable education*) (Sterling and Thomas, 2006, p. 355; Sterling, 2004, pp. 59–60). Ad hoc learning in stand-alone courses limits the graduate's ability to address multidimensional sustainable-development challenges (Desha and Hargroves, 2014, p. 151; Sileshi, 2016, pp. 192–193).

Curriculum transformation in the interest of education for sustainability or sustainable-development education requires a comprehensive process strategy. The process begins by articulating a university-wide plan and identifying desired graduate attributes or competencies. In conjunction with faculty development, the curriculum-renewal process then maps learning pathways;[3] develops, revises, and implements courses; and monitors and evaluates learning outcomes (Desha and Hargroves, 2014, pp. 69, 71, 74, 79–80, 87, 89–92, 116, 131, 144).

An integrated curriculum for sustainable-development practitioners would draw upon multiple interconnected disciplines. Higher-education institutions around the world should seriously consider the range of rigorous multidisciplinary course work recommended in 2008 for the Master's in Development Practice (MDP) by the International Commission on Education for Sustainable Development Practice. The sustainable-development curriculum proposed for the ideal MDP includes courses in economic and policy analysis, tropical agriculture, global health, energy and the environment, managing multisectoral development projects, and science and technology, and it culminates in a transdisciplinary practical exercise (Shaw and Kim, 2008, pp. 33–35).[4] Hub programs focused on a distinct sustainable-development challenge could be established as regional centers of expertise (Shaw and Kim, 2008, p. 36).

Transnational-sustainable-development competence

Because *"globalization is de-territorializing the skills and competencies it rewards"* (Suarez-Orozco and Qin-Hilliard, 2004, p. 6, emphasis in original), the leaders of tertiary-education institutions throughout the world confront converging transnational skill-development and curricular-building expectations. For students who graduate from professional-education programs, demonstrated technical expertise offers one key to success in sustainable-development endeavors (also Arima, 2009, p. 3; Roorda, Corcoran, and Weakland, 2012, p. 334; Barth, et al., 2007, p. 417) provided that domain competence can be integrated on an interdisciplinary and transdisciplinary basis (Mochizuki and Fadeeva, 2010, p. 392). Transnational competence (TC) constitutes an equally indispensable dimension of preparation for deeply interconnected and increasingly interdependent twenty-first-century sustainable-development contexts. Given that graduates increasingly change occupations and encounter new professional-mobility challenges and that the challenges of sustainable development often manifest themselves transnationally, transnational competence is likely to assume ever greater value as a life-long learning asset. TC's transformative potential is strongest at educational institutions in the developing world that urgently seek to graduate professionals who are connected to workforce needs and qualified to shrink South-North divides.

The TC framework is one of several conceptually and empirically grounded skill-set conceptualizations that offer special value in approaching TSD challenges (see Koehn and Rosenau, 2010, chapter 9). There is considerable overlap, for instance, between TC and the sustainable-development-competency framework developed and operationalized by Arnim Wiek and colleagues (Wiek, Withycombe, and Redman, 2011; Wiek, et al., 2016). In *Universities and the Sustainable Development Future*, we specifically apply TC as transnational-sustainable-development competence and treat the skills encompassed as a critically important curriculum-outcome objective. This elaboration will come into play at several points in the course of the book, most notably in the Chapter 6 discussion of evaluating sustainable-development-learning outcomes.

Transnational competence involves holistic, practical applications of five sets of clearly differentiated, interlinked, and conceptually embedded human capabilities: analytic, emotional, creative/imaginative, communicative, and functional (see Koehn and Rosenau, 2010, pp. 8–9).[5] TC accompanies and enriches disciplinary expertise (Roorda, 2013, p. 106; Sullivan, 2005, pp. 254, 285) and is at least partially transferrable to multiple milieus (Blewitt, 2004, p. 33). The following paragraphs apply the five TC-framework dimensions to sustainable-development-curricula development.

Specialized knowledge about sustainable development rapidly becomes obsolete and, therefore, must be secured continuously. *Analytic* competence primarily involves developing the ability to search for, locate, select, assemble, organize, interpret, critically assess, and apply relevant generic and context-specific knowledge, data, and rules – in short, learning how to learn (Pusch, 2009, p. 71; Salmi, 2002, p. 28). The transnationally competent professional possesses the ability to analyze the key components and dynamics of complex systems across sectors and scales (Wiek, Withycombe, and Redman, 2011, p. 207), to scan disciplines for relevant input (Wiek, et al., 2011, p. 9, 2016, p. 243), and to discern how the intersection of local, national, and transnational natural and social processes constrain, contribute to, and shape the interdependent challenges of sustainable development. The TC curriculum includes rigorous analysis of distant and proximate social-ecological developments and linkages that cross disciplinary boundaries and challenge sustainable development (Koehn and Rosenau, 2010, p. 86). The TC analytic framework highlights the importance of recognizing and utilizing the linear and non-linear processes embedded in sustainable development (Roorda, Corcoran, and Weakland, 2012, p. 334) and applying systems concepts such as inertia, feedback loops, cause-effect chains, resilience, whole-of-life analysis, triggering events, tipping points, and cascading effects (Wiek, et al., 2016, pp. 243–244; Desha and Hargroves, 2014, p. 140).[6] The specific skills that require learning "change as research and innovation push out the frontiers of each subject and change the tools available for retrieving knowledge" (McMahon, 2009, pp. 259–260).

In contrast to the tendency for education for sustainable development to reflect an anthropocentric bias (Kopnina and Meijers, 2012, p. 192), the TC-directed curriculum emphasizes learning about sustainable development from diverse peoples and natural contexts.[7] By comparing similar phenomena across multiple national perspectives, underlying processes (rather than just events) associated with sustainable development, holistic (including subjective[8]) wellbeing, and inter-generational equity become apparent.

The wicked problems of sustainable development challenge higher educators to incorporate anticipatory-knowledge management in their courses. Anticipatory-knowledge management, exchange, and implementation techniques involve valuing different ways of understanding phenomena, enhanced methods of accessing and navigating today's wealth of information, extrapolating from recent trends, and developing in-depth understanding of how action occurs, policies are changed, and outcomes are influenced. Methods of anticipatory learning include scenario-building tools (Nilsson, 2012, pp. 56–57; Salter, Robinson, and Wiek, 2010, pp. 704–705, 712), sustainability visioning (Brundiers, Wiek, and Redman, 2010, p. 310), appreciative inquiry, systematically reorienting prior to changing (Adamson, Nixon, and Su, 2013, p. 3), environmental scanning, cross-impact matrices (Slaughter, 1995, p. 38), forecasting from simulation models, and Delphi techniques (Deprez, 2012, pp. 236–237; Wiek, et al., 2016, p. 245). "Sensemaking" (or continuously interpreting information in ways that illuminate connections among people, places, and events) helps discern emerging patterns, uncover key forces at play, anticipate trajectories, and identify promising leverage points and action opportunities (Deprez, 2012, pp. 236–237; also Wiek, Withycombe, and Redman, 2011, pp. 205, 207–209). Among persons working along the edge of intersecting boundaries, the envisioning process carries special meaning because "when visions vividly describe a desired future, they have the magnetic power to draw us toward them and galvanize action" (Cortes and Wilkinson, 2009, p. 18).

For students of sustainable-development practice, abilities to open up and adapt to unfamiliar and ambiguous cultural influences and transboundary experiences (Pusch, 2009, pp. 67, 69–70) and to welcome diverse transnational perspectives constitute especially valuable components of an *emotional-competence* skill set. The welcoming skill requires recognition that there are many values worth living by and withholding judgmental attributions based on perceived socio-economic, ethnic, religious, and/or political differences. Further, the emotionally competent transnational spanner derives satisfaction, meaning, and enrichment (Barth, et al., 2007, p. 424) from transboundary interactions. Abilities to assume a genuine interest in new patterns of language, family life, cuisine, customs, etc. and to maintain respect for a multiplicity of different (including non-mainstream) values, beliefs, traditions, experiences, challenges, and preferred communication styles provide additional TC-enhancing emotional skills.

Forging empathic bridges and connectedness with other people constitutes another vital dimension of transnational emotional competence (also see Roorda, 2013, p. 106; Pusch, 2009, p. 70; Arima, 2009, p. 5). Learning to grasp the perspectives of others quickly, while retaining some identity distance, is a key step toward developing empathic capability. In the context of sustainable-development work, empathy initially involves identifying and respecting differences in value orientations, needs, pains, resilience, and aspirations (Williams, 2002, pp. 110–111; Wiek, Withycombe, and Redman, 2011, p. 211). Mature emphatic competence involves the ability to perceive challenges of sustainable development from multiple vantage points, switching "back and forth between disciplinary perspectives, time perspectives (past-present-future), space perspectives (local-regional-global), cultural perspectives and . . . even between human and other or more-than-human perspectives" (Wals and Blewitt, 2010, p. 66).

Self-confidence, or a sense of personal transnational efficacy tempered with compassion and humility (see Rondinelli, 2009, p. 39), constitutes the culminating emotional skill. Transnational self-efficacy strengthens the sustainable-development professional's willingness to "take risks and seek out more demanding challenges" (Goleman, 1995, pp. 89–90). Emotional competency includes passion for constructive involvement in sustainable development (Roorda, Corcoran, and Weakland, 2012, p. 334) and the "caring" or stewardship dimension of ecological literacy (Blewitt, 2004, p. 29). Activating awareness of personal commitments and objectives can help students and practitioners maintain motivation in the face of complex transnational and transboundary challenges and in the wake of disappointments.

Creativity is particularly important in TSD practice because "sustainability requires the ability to cope with, adapt to, and shape change without losing options for future adaptability" (Folke, Colding, and Berkes, 2008, pp. 353–354). Four closely related skills promote transnational *creative/imaginative competence*. The first involves the catalytic ability to foresee and mobilize the synergistic relevance of diverse group perspectives in collective transboundary problem solving (Goleman, 1998, p. 27; Wiek, et al., 2011, p. 10). Diversity provides a "proven way to increase the randomness of concept combinations" (Johansson, 2004, p. 79). The successful mixing and merging of dissimilar backgrounds and viewpoints can produce collective accomplishments that exceed the sum total of the separate contributions (Moran, Harris, and Moran, 2007, p. 229).

Another creative/imaginative skill is the ability to articulate novel transnational syntheses of multisource knowledge and aspirations (Cortes and Wilkinson, 2009, pp. 18, 23). Creative professionals are able to inspire counterparts of diverse identities, disciplines, and locations in the design and nurturing of previously unimagined and contextually appropriate paths to sustainable development (e.g., see Wals and Blewitt, 2010, pp. 66, 70). In crafting transnationally acceptable sustainability visions, it also can be useful to utilize and adapt lessons from evaluation research.

A closely related creative capacity is the continuous cognitive flexibility to (co-) envision new categories and paradigms, unmet needs, viable alternative futures, processes, and roles that are mutually acceptable among collaborators who possess diverse identities (see Koehn and Rosenau, 2010, p. 13; Tilbury, 2004, p. 105; Pusch, 2009, p. 69; Wiek, Withycombe, and Redman, 2011, p. 209). Practitioners with the ability to tap into diverse indigenous and global socio-cultural and technical sources for inspiration – the fourth creative/imaginative skill – will be more likely to perceive synergistic potentials, to envision transnationally acceptable and imaginative rather than costly alternatives, and to identify innovative and shared syntheses. A critical part of the search for creative sustainable-development approaches will concentrate on "visions of smaller-scale, more environmentally sound and more democratic and nested resource management systems that are self-organizing, adaptive, and resilient" (Berkes, Colding, and Folke, 2003, p. 21).

Sustainable-development educators need to guide learners in the creative TC art of "possibility." Universities prepare learners to envision and advance preferred and motivating futures.[9] By engaging graduating practitioners in reflection about challenging alternatives and drawing attention to the power of human agency, "a sense of possibility enables us to look at what has been done, what can be done, and what can exist" (Finn and Jacobson, 2008, p. 47). The stirring poem "The Edge," written in 1997 by fifteen-year-old Indian student Lavanya Krishnan,[10] heightens our appreciation for the importance and urgency of preparing graduating professionals throughout the world with skills they will need to confront tomorrow's transnational sustainability challenges creatively:

> Strolling along the stream of Today,
> I came upon the Edge . . .
> The Edge of now,
> The start of tomorrow,
> The golden boat of possibility
> Beckoning to follow.

For individuals preparing to be boundary-spanning sustainable-development professionals, "the value of basic and effective oral, written, and presentational communication skills cannot be overestimated" (Williams, 2002, p. 115; also Shaw and Kim, 2008, p. 70). The first key *communicative skill* is facility in the spoken and written language used by one's counterparts. While personal linguistic fluency in another language can be an immense behavioral asset, achieving it is impractical in transnational situations involving multiple and revolving first languages.[11] Such interactions call for skill in interpretation and in using an interpreter.[12] Further, TC-prepared professionals around the world who seek to access information or support for sustainable-development activities need to be proficient using English in these communication circumstances. For instance, "English is often necessary for securing funds for development either through international organizations or private funding sources" (McKay, 2002, p. 17). Transnationally skillful actors also develop proficiency in nonverbal communicative behavior and in interpreting facial expressions, gestures, posturing, use of space, body movement, pace, and other cues.

Effective transnational communication further requires attentive listening and understanding (Williams, 2002, p. 115). Transnationally competent sustainable-development professionals employ all four dimensions of deep listening in their work with disadvantaged communities: "your ears, your eyes, your undivided attention, and your heart" (Sarkissian, 2009, p. 105). Additional TC-communicative abilities include engaging in meaningful dialogue, facilitating mutual self-disclosure, code switching, mindful reframing (Ting-Toomey, 2009, pp. 103–104), and resolving communication misunderstandings. One promising use of ICT (information and communication technology) in sustainable-development contexts involves linking skilled and committed diaspora members with homeland information and capacity-building needs, either directly with local governments or communities or in cooperation with international/indigenous NGOs. For instance, Somalinet, a large digital diaspora, functions, in part, as a platform for discussion regarding how to rebuild Somalia (Brinkerhoff, 2007, pp. 192–196, 200).

Sustainable-development professionals operating in today's interconnected world further require transnational *functional competence*. Functional adroitness enables the actor to integrate, connect, and apply policy and procedural insights, empathy, imagination, and communicative proficiency through transboundary collective actions in usable ways that resolve logistical challenges and "get things done" (Wiek, Withycombe, and Redman, 2011, p. 210; also Wiek, et al., 2016, p. 243).[13] Functionally capable sustainable-development professionals also are adept at nurturing instrumental transboundary relationships, teams, networks, alliances, and partnerships. Successful sustainability managers are distinguished by "their ability to engage with others and deploy effective relational and interpersonal competencies" (Williams, 2002, p. 110).

A set of transnational operational skills underlies effective social and technical problem solving and project/task performance in transboundary sustainable-development situations. The first core TC functional skill involves the ability to relate to stakeholders and to develop and maintain positive interpersonal relationships grounded in the mutual discovery of common aspirations and in trust building (Ojelay-Surtees, 2007). In TC-centered curricula, students and graduated professionals initially focus on enhancing their ability to establish and sustain friendly, trusting relationships across nationality and other defining lines. Gaining trust is the pivotal ingredient in successful transnational-relationship building and mutual learning. In this connection, the importance of spending time socially with one's professional counterpart and getting to know his/her family, interests, and aspirations (Williams, 2002, pp. 111, 115–117) often is underestimated. Eventually, "if it passes the tests of reliability, delivering on promises, not being underhanded and being honest, the relationship moves on to a possibly more enduring state of 'deep trust'" (Williams, 2002, p. 116).

Operational competence requires skill in overcoming technical and social problems, conflicts, and uncertainties along with action skills such as the ability to secure and sustain the participation of key stakeholders and to achieve collective goals when dealing with TSD challenges and tensions among globalization and localization pressures (Koehn and Rosenau, 2010, p. 16; Fadeeva, et al., 2014, p. 8; Roorda, 2013, p. 106; Roorda, Corcoran, and Weakland, 2012, p. 334; Wiek, Withycombe, and Redman, 2011, p. 205). Successful task accomplishment and sustainable-development problem solving (also Wiek, et al., 2016, p. 242) are key objectives of functional-competence education. One way that graduates demonstrate functional competence in concrete settings is by acting in ways that generate "a temporary outcome that is considered the most sustainable given what we know, value and strive for at that moment in time" (Wals, et al., 2016, p. 28).

Capacities to "leverage diversity" (Goleman, 1998, p. 27), mobilize communities and contextually available resources, coordinate and focus stakeholders, draw upon the skills of other specialists (Desha and Hargroves, 2014, p. 140), and account for "unintended consequences and cascading effects" (Wiek, et al., 2016,

p. 247) provide additional functional assets. Unique to sustainable-development professionals, managing for sustainability involves learning (1) how to maintain and enhance diversity, adaptability, and renewal capacity, (2) means of incorporating and retaining redundancy, and (3) ways to retain flexibility and spread risks (Berkes, Colding, and Folke, 2003, p. 15; Folke, Colding, and Berkes, 2008, pp. 354, 356, 361). Mastery of strategic planning, theories of change, adaptation and mitigation interventions, and power mapping can be particularly valuable in this functional-competence connection to sustainable development (Wiek, et al., 2016, pp. 247–248).

Functional TC further encompasses the capacity to forge compromises and collaborations through cross-boundary negotiation. TC educators prepare students for the interpersonal and interprofessional challenges involved in interdisciplinary and transdisciplinary teamwork (Roorda, 2013, p. 106; Gordon, 2009, pp. 63, 65; Barth, et al., 2007, pp. 420, 423; Stauffacher, et al., 2006, p. 255), gaining allies, establishing legitimacy, and building long-term partnerships with stakeholders inside and outside of academe (Wiek, et al., 2011, p. 8, 2016, p. 250) by emphasizing respectful and trusting social relationships, along with tact and skill in coordinating diverse political, economic, cultural, and ecological resources and applying participatory methodologies (Shaw and Kim, 2008, pp. 22, 68; Folke, Colding, and Berkes, 2008, p. 356).[14] Paul Williams (2002, p. 116) notes that "the acid test of a robust relationship is considered to be the ability to manage conflict and criticism – the potential to disagree and fallout, but a willingness to move on without harming the relationship."

Finally, in the interest of advancing social justice and ecological health, transnational functional competence requires rigor and vigor in ethics and advocacy. Foremost within the advocacy skill subset is the normative ability (see Wiek, Withycombe, and Redman, 2011, p. 209) to act in ways that advance changes in those domestic and international economic, social, institutional, and legal/policy conditions that produce the systematic disparities that constrain ecological sustenance and human wellbeing. Along with skill in issue bundling and policy framing (see Koehn, 2010), TC graduates learn to build, activate, and assess[15] professional and societal resources that mitigate socio-economic inequities, power differentials, exclusionary policies, and other institutionalized constraints on sustainable development. By expanding the capabilities of disadvantaged and vulnerable persons, functionally competent professionals contribute to poverty reduction and population wellbeing (Walker, et al., 2009, pp. 567–569, 571). To foster sustainable development, some universities in South America, Africa, and Asia explicitly strive to educate responsible "graduates who serve as agents of socioeconomic change" (Juma and Yee-Cheong, 2005, p. 96; also Walker, et al., 2009, pp. 555–556).

Curricula transformations

The transnational-sustainable-development-competence framework provides the basis for the introduction of meaningful course and curricular design. At most universities around the world, providing TC preparation for sustainable development requires curriculum transformation.[16] On one hand, sustainability would be infused throughout the curriculum of each disciplinary area (Sterling and Thomas, 2006, p. 363). At the same time, in Anthony Cortese's (2003, p. 18) words, "education would have the same 'lateral rigor' across, as the 'vertical rigor' within, the disciplines."

Curricula transformations require focus shifts to "processes rather than things, dynamics rather than static states, and wholes rather than parts" (Blewitt, 2015, pp. 307–308; also Sterling, 2009, p. 114). A solution-oriented sustainability-learning approach incorporates "systems-thinking competence, future-thinking or anticipatory competence, value-thinking or normative competence, strategic-thinking competence, interpersonal competence, and integrated problem-solving competence" (Wiek and Kay, 2015, p. 29; also Roorda, 2013, p. 106; Wiek, et al., 2016, p. 242).[17] A TSD curriculum focused along these lines is likely to gain traction among students, particularly in the South,[18] because of the clear connection among "skills for work and skills for life" (King and Palmer, 2013, p. 32; also Barth, et al., 2007, p. 417). Moreover, the envisioned curriculum transformation would catalyze parallel reconceptualizing and reconfiguring processes for teaching, research, and community engagement (Wals and Blewitt, 2010, p. 70).

Universities in some Southern countries already have initiated programs in sustainable development that incorporate many of the curriculum objectives articulated here and related learning activities. For instance, Costa Rica's EARTH University offers a comprehensive sustainable-development education that emphasizes "practical learning, entrepreneurial capabilities, ethics and values, teamwork, group problem-solving, communication skills, vertical and horizontal integration of the curriculum, and fostering of social sensitivity through the acquisition of community development skills" (Juma and Yee-Cheong, 2005, p. 97). After one year of study, masters and PhD students at TERI University in India participate in semester-long projects that address problems of poverty and environmental degradation (Neelakantan, 2009, p. A20). Ghana's University for Development Studies (UDS) emphasizes the cultivation by students of skills in addressing poverty, including participatory rural appraisal. UDS also arranges for all students to live for extended periods in rural communities, where they work on designing development projects in collaboration with local people and private entrepreneurs (Zaglul and Sherrard, 2005, pp. 39–40, 44, 47). In Uganda, Busitema University's Change Project has mainstreamed education-for-sustainable-development and incorporated community-outreach activities into its teacher-training programs (Andama and Suubi, 2015, pp. 127–129). The mission of Heliopolis University, established by the Sekem Development Foundation and the Sekem Group of companies in 2012, is to "empower our students to be the champions of sustainable development within the Egyptian community" (cited in Mader, 2014, p. 71). Since 2005, Mexico's Monteray Institute of Technology "has been implementing an integrated, interconnected and multidisciplinary approach for fostering sustainable development which includes a short course for sustainable development 'champions'" (Desha and Hargroves,

2014, p. 192). The vision of Albukhary International University (AIU), Malaysia, is to "graduate students from marginalized groups as agents of change" dedicated to poverty alleviation. Through its sustainable-livelihood approach, AIU "plans and implements [partnered] development projects based on the needs and strengths of the community from within" that aim to benefit both local community members and students (Gapor, et al., 2014, p. 262).[19]

Pedagogical imperatives

Generating valuable TSD competency requires critical, complementary, and inter-active pedagogical approaches that "flourish in the formal curriculum and through informal learning" (Ryan and Cotton, 2013, p. 164; Sterling and Thomas, 2006, p. 352; Sterling, 2013, p. 38). According to Katja Brundiers, Arnim Wiek, and Charles Redman (2010, p. 309), the "literature on sustainable development calls for pedagogical innovations that provide interactive, experiential, transformative, and real-world learning."[20] Interdisciplinary sharing and collaboration is a common ingredient that encompasses a variety of pedagogical and innovative approaches to sustainable-development learning (Cortese, 2003, p. 16; Cotton and Winter, 2010, p. 40; Mochizuki and Fadeeva, 2010, p. 393). Further, TSD-focused pedagogical approaches emphasize participatory learning (Sterling and Thomas, 2006, p. 353; Sterling, 2013, p. 38).[21] Classroom humor helps motivate students to develop "lateral thinking and creativity" regarding the complex issues that suffuse sustainable development and can reduce resistance to change (Mulder, et al., 2013, pp. 36–37).

Higher-education programs for sustainable-development educators and practitioners find utility in interactive skill-focused practical exercises that emphasize the value of individual- and group-learning processes (Barth and Michelsen, 2013, p. 114; Andama and Suubi, 2015, p. 129). Case studies involving bounded narratives of actual social-ecological complexities and development challenges and related policy issues that combine qualitative- and quantitative-data-analysis techniques can be incorporated into a wide range of courses (e.g., Ban, et al., 2015, pp. 37, 40). Peer role-play activities enable graduating practitioners to nurture empathy, motivation, solidarity with nature and people (Brundiers, Wiek, and Redman, 2010, p. 310), and other TC-emotional skills. For some future sustainable-development practitioners, particularly those who will work in village and urban-neighborhood settings, it will be useful to learn how to engage lay publics in performances (skits, storytelling, artwork, dance, song) that join indigenous visualization with imagining sustainable futures and innovative approaches to glocal challenges (Sarkissian, 2009, p. 105).

Other valuable sustainable-development pedagogies engage students in teams whose members possess diverse backgrounds and interests on class-based or action-research projects that address specific, usually micro-level, challenges to poverty reduction and sustainable development. Well-designed, theoretically informed, and reflective learning activities are explicitly and clearly connected to intended applied outcomes (Rowe and Johnston, 2013, pp. 46, 50). Rowe and Hiser (2016,

p. 327) suggest that students and community members collaborate in designing action-research projects that address "compelling issues in the defined community." Teamwork that identifies and addresses local and regional challenges of sustainable development helps to prepare graduates to collaborate on future transnational projects and to develop the optimistic and empowered mindset required of change agents (Rowe and Hiser, 2016, pp. 316, 320, 328; Cortese, 2003, p. 19).[22] Close to home, university-greening operations offer opportunities for integrated sustainable-development learning experiences (see Desha and Hargroves, 2014, pp. 175, 188). The University of British Columbia explicitly "cross-fertilizes" academic and operational activities and facilitates campus integration through a horizontal central management entity that cuts across vertical structures (Cayuela, et al., 2013, pp. 227–228, 235).[23]

One promising approach that involves learners in inquiry-based research for applied practice is problem- and project-based learning (PPBL). PPBL involves "student-centered, self-directed and collaborative learning that focuses on real-world issues" and can include engagement with stakeholders (Wiek, et al., 2014, pp. 432, 434; Ban, et al., 2015, p. 38; Mulder, 2013, pp. 39, 44). Drawing on problem- and project-based learning principles, instructors in the undergraduate course in Information Systems linked reflective practice with the campus-operations goal of reducing the University of Cape Town's carbon footprint (McGibbon and Van Belle, 2015, pp. 81, 85–86). PPBL experiences aim to enhance competencies that will be of value to TSD practitioners in such areas as problem analysis, transnational communication and negotiation, teamwork, partnership building, stakeholder collaboration, project design, planning and budgeting, and project management (Shaw and Kim, 2008, p. 27).

The acquisition of TC skills by sustainable-development professionals is advanced by practical experience through overseas study, mutual-service-learning, internship, research, and project-based fieldwork programs (Brundiers, Wiek, and Redman, 2010, pp. 311–312). Skill development (especially in the emotional, creative, and communicative domains) is enhanced by placing students of sustainable development in unfamiliar overseas-learning locations. Year-long overseas-immersion programs, including South-South exchanges, at partner universities in TSD-challenged locations are likely to be especially rewarding both professionally and personally. The ideal TC field-learning program would be hosted by a committed partner (often an NGO), involve hands-on professional training and individual work assignments guided by an experienced mentor, apply knowledge to action for sustainability (Brundiers, Wiek, and Redman, 2010, p. 312), treat failure as part of the learning process, engage cultural and disciplinary diversity (Barth and Michelsen, 2013, p. 114), and culminate in a comprehensive field-experience reflection (Shaw and Kim, 2008, p. 30).

Obstacles to TSD education and promising change processes

Faculty availability often constitutes the foremost barrier to implementing TSD-curriculum initiatives. Teaching multidimensional, emerging sustainability themes is challenging for faculty schooled in single-discipline perspectives and learning approaches (Ban, et al., 2015, p. 35; Andama and Suubi, 2015, p. 133). In addition, not all faculty are equipped to convey the fundamentals of transnational competence. Therefore, ongoing attention needs to be devoted to enhancing the TC of faculty members who are responsible for transmitting sustainable-development competencies to learners (Disterheft, et al., 2013, p. 16; Desha and Hargroves, 2014, p. 9).

At the grassroots level, PPBL approaches are limited by differing student and stakeholder schedules and intermittent participation and turnover among student participants (Wiek, et al., 2014, p. 443; Ban, et al., 2015, p. 38; Daneri, Trencher, and Petersen, 2015, p. 19; Andama and Suubi, 2015, p. 133). To mitigate problems that arise from scheduling and time constraints and inconsistent learning approaches, Katja Brundiers and colleagues (2014, pp. 222–223) recommend progressive integration across the curriculum of a required introductory course where students practice key aspects of PPBL, followed by a cumulative series of PPBL courses and internships. Availability of a "transacademic interface manager" can facilitate PPBL integration for students and faculty.

Institutional change

Institutional change often is a prerequisite for curricula change. Transforming curricula in the direction of sustainable education involves a long-term process characterized by pervasive institutional penetration and depth of thinking and learning (Thomas, 2016, pp. 58–59, 61). Dianne Chambers (2013) provides us with a promising process-based model for embedding sustainability in university curricula that is discipline grounded. Her approach involves five phases designed to impact institutional change. Chambers' process model is centered on the influential role that ground-level academics can play in determining the details of curricula changes, expected learning outcomes, and the pace of implementation (Thomas, 2016, pp. 61, 63).

The first stage ("discovery") commences with a dialogue about sustainability among curriculum leaders. This phase includes an audit of current course offerings, gap identification, and securing buy-in from leading faculties. Careful engagement with early adopters and other potential champions facilitates change over the long-term (Chambers, 2013, p. 317; also Andama and Suubi, 2015, p. 130; Desha and Hargroves, 2014, p. 94).

During the second phase ("discipline-based planning"), academics in each discipline would be briefed about the core components of sustainable development, and the contributions of early adopters would be "showcased to demonstrate what is possible" (Chambers, 2013, p. 317). The aim of this crucial stage is to ensure that faculty understand and accept the integrative reasoning behind the short-term (curriculum integration) and long-term ("positive impact on society and the environment through the actions of graduates") objectives of the change initiative. Along the way, disciplinary teams produce discussion papers that "identify how the major sustainability issues relevant to their discipline" relate to needed course offerings and "what graduates in their field should know to empower them in their professional lives" (Chambers, 2013, p. 318).[24] Hegarty and colleagues (2011) demonstrate that effectively designed stand-alone courses can foster "crucial, transferable" sustainable-development skills. They report favorably on the approach used at RMIT University that involved a compulsory first-year undergraduate course on "Sustainability: Society and Environment" for students studying in environmental, youth-work, legal-and-dispute-studies, psychology, and social-science programs. The course included "identifying the role/contribution of each discipline/field to action on 'wicked' sustainability problems, and the generic skills which enable that action" (Hegarty, et al., 2011, pp. 454, 456, 459, 465). Desha and Hargroves (2014, pp. 107–110) further suggest that a first-year "flagship" course (complemented by an "armada" of supporting courses and a capstone learning experience) can "kick-start" interest in and learning about sustainable development. However, these authors also point to several potent pitfalls of the flagship approach.

The challenges of transnational sustainable development cannot be completely addressed by any single field of study. Chambers' third change-process stage ("cross-discipline coordination") focuses on inter-departmental and cross-disciplinary collaboration. Cross-disciplinary and interdisciplinary teams of academics gain insight regarding the perspectives of other disciplines and discuss ways to promote holistic learning across the campus (Chambers, 2013, p. 319).

The fourth phase ("design and implementation") involves detailed individual and team work centered on "reconceptualizing and redesigning subjects" to fit new campus-wide curricula that approach sustainable development holistically. Top-level institutional support for faculty training often is needed at this stage (Chambers, 2013, p. 319).

Finally, and of special relevance to the focus of *Universities and the Sustainable Development Future*, successful curriculum-change processes require "progress reporting." At this stage, curricula developments and professional preparation are monitored and evaluated on a university-wide basis. Successes are recognized and "celebrated," and areas requiring further attention are identified. Newly arriving faculty are continuously integrated into the institution's sustainability-curriculum mission (Chambers, 2013, p. 320).

Research

Higher-education institutions function as society's primary repository of knowledge and expertise. In light of this responsibility, university faculty and researchers are committed to and engaged in generating knowledge that can be used for classroom and societal learning.

Waas, Verbruggen, and Wright (2010, pp. 629–630, 634, emphasis in original) define university research for sustainable development as "*all* [applied and fundamental; monodisciplinary and multidisciplinary] *research conducted within the institutional context of a university that contributes to sustainable development*." Along with other international declarations, the Kyoto Protocol (principle 4) "implores universities to undertake research and action in sustainable development" (Wright, 2002, p. 116).[25] Embracing this charge requires the sustained creation of dedicated "quality researchers" (Jones, Bailey, and Lyytikäinen, 2007, p. 19).

In contrast to the slow-moving process of curricula change, university-research priorities can be adjusted more flexibly and fluidly (Cayuela, et al., 2013, p. 233). Nevertheless, non-interactive research that excludes stakeholder engagement is problematic. Given the complexity presented by sustainability challenges, "analytical and normative input from diverse actors"[26] is essential, although the specific extent of engagement is left open to "negotiation among the equal partners (researchers-users) without prescribing it" (Talwar, Wiek, and Robinson, 2011, pp. 381–383).

Local and traditional knowledge also offer "a rich source of lessons for social-ecological adaptations" (Berkes, Colding, and Folke, 2003, p. 13). Integrating multiple sources of knowledge to draw out sustainable-development lessons nested in social and ecological diversity, disturbance, and resilience facilitates the discovery of adaptive innovations that increase flexibility and opportunities and avoid flips into undesirable stability domains (Berkes, Colding, and Folke, 2003, pp. 21–23; Fadeeva, et al., 2014, p. 6). Social and ecological resilience are vital components of sustainability because "loss of resilience leads to reduced capacity to deal with change." Likewise, species that appear to be redundant, and overlapping social practices and institutional functions, "may become of critical importance for regenerating and reorganizing the system after disturbance and disruption" (Folke, Colding, and Berkes, 2008, pp. 354–355, 361–363).

In *Universities and the Sustainable Development Future*, we often are concerned with transprofessional enhancements. Interdependent sustainability challenges cannot be treated in lonely silos that stretch precariously upward. The most daunting sustainable-development problems involve "wicked issues" that "bridge and permeate jurisdictional, organizational, functional, professional and generational boundaries" and often become "entangled in a web of other problems creating a kind of dense and complicated policy swamp" (Williams, 2002, p. 104). To be useful in advancing problem-oriented knowledge, therefore, sustainable-development research must "focus on linkages between the biological, chemical, economic, geological, physical, political and social systems, and . . . search for dynamic and cross-systemic explanations" (Waas, Verbruggen, and Wright, 2010, p. 630).

We can illustrate the multidisciplinary nature of sustainable-development-knowledge generation and dissemination by reference to the challenge of chronic hunger in sub-Saharan Africa.[27] Applications of agricultural science are useful for understanding biophysical influences on crop yields and for identifying technical approaches and access to inputs that could boost secure food production over the long-term. Geography and environmental science contribute to understanding local land and water conditions, GIS (Geographical Information Systems) mapping, and interactions with climate change. Engineering illuminates community-infrastructure requirements, gaps, and potential. Economic analysis works with household-income data, market opportunities and risks, capital needs, international-trade and monetary policies, and sustainable and equitable paths to breaking the grip of poverty. Anthropology reveals local priorities, indigenous and adapted innovations, and fertility trends. Public health engages community nutrition, infectious and chronic disease, and health issues that condition sustainable-development processes. Political science highlights local, national, and international governance constraints on sustainable development; explores political-economic conflict and migration; and identifies policy options. Public administration equips for financial management, facilitates understanding of local and national long-term institutional capacity (including project-management skills and NGO/population strengths), and addresses stakeholder participation in contextual-mapping, needs-assessment, planning, monitoring, maintenance, and (short- and long-run) evaluation processes.

The sustainable-development researcher is not expected to master the specialized knowledge and tools that distinguish each of these fields. However, s/he should possess a solid grasp of "the essential questions that must be answered in order to move forward," be able to think laterally and span critical knowledge boundaries (see Shaw and Kim, 2008, p. 22), be capable of articulating global visions in local terms (Fadeeva and Mochizuki, 2010, p. 253) and local visions in global terms, and be positioned to identify policy strengths and drawbacks. At present, "very few professionals are trained and prepared" in this way (Shaw and Kim, 2008, pp. 17–18).[28] Globally, many higher-education programs are particularly deficient in preparing graduates with the skills needed to work in research teams of specialists from many countries and fields (Shaw and Kim, 2008, p. iii).

Linking research with action

Growing higher-education interest in sustainable development dovetails with the ascendance of application-oriented research (Simon and Knie, 2013, p. 406; Talwar, Wiek, and Robinson, 2011, p. 379). Informed by critical thinking and inspired by purpose built on social justice and equity, action research aims to "bring about deep, lasting and meaningful change and improvements" at individual, collectivity, and community-wide levels (Wahr and de la Harpe, 2016, pp. 162, 164–166, 172–173, 175).

Sustainable-development-action research requires solid specialist preparation coupled with transdisciplinary participation on shifting teams of scientists and practitioners who engage wicked issues and collaborate on problem solving. Co-production of knowledge through stakeholder/user interactivity (Talwar, Wiek, and Robinson, 2011, pp. 379–380, 382; Wahr and de la Harpe, 2016, pp. 165, 167, 173; Mochizuki and Yarime, 2016, p. 20; Rowe and Hiser, 2016, p. 323)[29] and "contributing to theory while having local impact and global relevance" feature in impactful sustainability research (White, 2013, pp. 168, 173, 183; Wahr and de la Harpe, 2016, pp. 168, 175).

Collaborative-action research infuses within participating universities "the potential to overcome the many institutional barriers to education for sustainability" (Sibbel, Hegarty, and Holdsworth, 2013, p. 401). For instance, participatory-action research enhances the professional development of teaching staff and informs curriculum transformation (Sibbel, Hegarty, and Holdsworth, 2013, pp. 397, 401; White, 2013, p. 173; Andama and Suubi, 2015, p. 134; Wahr and de la Harpe, 2016, p. 175). Action research feeds smoothly into the development of valuable transdisciplinary case studies (see Stauffacher, et al., 2006, pp. 253, 256–257, 262, 269; Scholz, et al., 2006).

Joining scholarship, teaching, and active learning contributes in important ways to transformative education. Rehema White (2013, p. 177) notes that transformative sustainability learning involves "teaching-led research" along with "research-led teaching." Clemens Mader (2014, p. 76) heralds the higher-educational and societal transformative potential inherent in the co-creation of teaching and research initiatives in partnership with community groups and organizations. Community-based research is a close "cousin" of action research (Rowe and Hiser, 2016, p. 322). The United Nations' teacher-education programme for a sustainable future, the International Institute for Sustainable Communities, and the Urban Sustainability Directors' Network all provide helpful assistance for student/community-action-research projects (Rowe and Hiser, 2016, p. 320).

In addition, the synergistic transformative-learning process (head, hands, and heart) aims at changing frames of reference (Sipos, Battisti, and Grimm, 2008, pp. 71, 75). The imperative of transforming personal lifestyles as well as professional competencies appears as point 5 in the *People's Sustainability Treaty for Higher Education* (cited in Tilbury, 2013, pp. 73–74; Rowe and Johnston, 2013, p. 49).

TSD-outreach initiatives

With extensive connections to civil society and government agencies, universities are well-positioned to act as "brokers for sustainability within and beyond the communities to which they belong" (Cayuela, et al., 2013, p. 224). University sustainable-development-outreach initiatives involve both specific project objectives (instrumental approach) and stakeholder-capacity development (comprehensive approach). The instrumental approach, which focuses on performance of a predetermined set of specific sustainable-development activities, advocates the participation of external community members because "of their better knowledge of local conditions and constraints (environmental, social, and economic), and their better ability to enforce rules, monitor behavior, and verify actions" (Platteau, 2005, p. 277).[30] Community participation is viewed as "as an end in itself" in the comprehensive approach, which emphasizes developing the capacity to engage in sustainable development among local collectivities and requires sustained support for organizing efforts among community stakeholders (Platteau, 2005, pp. 278, 281, 291).

Stakeholders grounded in local experiential knowledge constitute a key sustainable-development-outreach partner. Sustainability-advancing stakeholders are "diverse in terms of their perceptions, beliefs, incentives and behavior" (Mochizuki and Yarime, 2016, p. 20).

In recent years, Northern aid agencies have placed increased emphasis on "knowledge as something to be produced [i.e., to be derived from local and contextual discoveries] rather than simply transferred." This shift has resulted in growing "recognition of and even support to indigenous knowledge and national knowledge systems in the South" (King and McGrath, 2004, pp. 135, 140; McGrath and King, 2004, p. 179). George Dei and Alireza Asgharzadeh (2006, p. 67) recognize that "at the heart of any global solution to poverty alleviation and economic growth lie the issues of local peoples, their indigenous knowledges, and their locally constructed solutions" (also see Siebert, 2012). Local and traditional wisdom also offer "a rich source of lessons for social-ecological adaptations" (Berkes, Colding, and Folke, 2003, p. 13; Tikly, 2005, p. 307). Although the longtime series of observations preserved in experiential knowledge systems are not sufficient by themselves to maintain sustainable development in today's globally interdependent world, it is crucial for adaptive learning that innovation-seekers avoid homogenizing, diluting, or diminishing the diversity of indigenous insights (Folke, Colding, and Berkes, 2003, pp. 371–372). Combining multiple sources of knowledge to draw out sustainable-development lessons nested in social and ecological diversity and disturbance facilitates the discovery of adaptive innovations that help build resilience (Berkes, Colding, and Folke, 2003, pp. 21–23). Adaptation "may concentrate on reducing the impacts of change, or it may take advantage of new opportunities created by change" (Folke, Colding, and Berkes, 2003, pp. 355, 375). Therefore, adaptation can be viewed as a promising university-outreach opening for societal transformation (Pelling, O'Brien, and Matyas, 2015).

Potent barriers and drivers

Sustainable-development curricula, research, and outreach barriers and drivers differ by individual inclination, institutional conditions (including available resources), local contextual grounding (Chambers, 2013, p. 320), and the presence or absence of stakeholder demand (Holm, et al., 2015, p. 170). In light of these influences, the potency of particular obstacles and opportunities varies from place to place, by type of activity, and over time.

Faculty members and researchers are inclined to champion sustainable development based on professional concerns, career considerations, and personal-value commitments. The strength of these motivators varies from individual to individual and is conditioned by institutional and societal facilitators and barriers. Potent drivers include intrinsic personal commitment to and action on behalf of sustainable-development objectives among educational leaders (Lotz-Sisitka, Agbedahin, and Hlengwa, 2015, p. 25; Holm, et al., 2015, pp. 169–170), external recognition and rewards, inclusive rather than strictly hierarchical leadership structures (Mader, 2014, p. 78; Sibbel, Hegarty, and Holdsworth, 2013, p. 393), and participation in ventures that promise to result in progress in the desired direction. In the field of accounting, for instance, "sustainability has broadened the issue of corporate social responsibility (CSR) to include environmental and ecological factors in triple bottom line (TBL) reporting for transparency and accountability of business performances to the various stakeholders. Sustainability accounting and reporting have now emerged as an important area of accounting education and scholarship" (Sileshi, 2016, pp. 8, 63, 68–70, 112).[31]

Powerful barriers to action include perceived irrelevancy of sustainable-development initiatives to one's disciplinary focus and career path, lack of institutional or unit support for innovative course and pedagogical initiatives (Wiek, 2016, p. 245), competing personal interests (Mader, 2014, p. 78), perceived lack of time or curriculum space, the departure of key champions (Desha and Hargroves, 2014, pp. 68, 87, 168), and the absence of shared responsibility for cross-institution action on behalf of sustainable development. Without buy-in, concrete support, and participation from top administrators (including deans) responsible for sustainable-development programming and for articulating the university-wide perspective (that is, presidents, vice chancellors, rectors, provosts, chief international officers, and research vice presidents), university curriculum, research, and outreach transitioning will not be forthcoming and sustained (Biddle, 2002, p. 120).

Sustainability-research and curriculum barriers include academic silos, lack of faculty understanding of sustainable development and contextual conditions, pedagogical rigidity, and competing priorities (Ralph and Stubbs, 2014, pp. 79, 85; Sibbel, Hegarty, and Holdsworth, 2013, p. 397; Cortese, 2003, p. 19; Cotton and Winter, 2010, p. 42; Tilbury, 2013, p. 81; Desha and Hargroves, 2014, p. 46).[32] Senior-management leadership, solid links with clear benefits for promotion, tenure, and merit evaluations, and demonstrated student interest[33] are common drivers in curriculum transformations (Cayuela, et al., 2013, p. 234; Ralph and Stubbs, 2014, pp. 80, 85; Wiek, 2016, p. 258). To succeed in introducing systemic change, bottom-up initiatives must be in concert with genuine and extensive support from the upper reaches of university administration (Sibbel, Hegarty, and Holdsworth, 2013, p. 397; de la Harpe and Thomas, 2009, pp. 78–79)[34] – including flexible workloads, support for professional development, seed funding and budgetary support, and recognition awards (Desha and Hargroves, 2014, pp. 94, 104). A university-wide strategic-policy direction coupled with financial incentives is particularly influential in the research domain (Ralph and Stubbs, 2014, pp. 80, 83, 85).

Institutional histories, resources, and recruitment outcomes ensure that drivers and barriers will play out differentially across institutions of higher learning. Although resource constraints are commonly encountered across-the-board, differences are likely to be particularly pronounced among universities in the North and South. For instance, most public and private universities in Africa, confronted with massification and other extreme pressures, can afford to devote few of their meager domestic resources to sustainable-development-research undertakings or community-engagement projects (Jowi, 2009, pp. 272–273; Samoff and Carrol, 2004, p. 136). In the North, universities face competing institutional agendas, increasing operational costs, and revenue and accountability constraints that confine their involvement in transnational (and even local) sustainable-development activity (Knight, 2008, p. 22; Johnstone and Marcucci, 2010, pp. 18–20; Daneri, Trencher, and Petersen, 2015, p. 19). Evaluation initiatives face similar challenges. Sustainability barriers and drivers are revisited in the conclusion to this book when we consider how participants can successfully implement the evaluation recommendations set forth in Part III.

Change advocacy

University communities tend to view new initiatives with suspicion (Biddle, 2002, p. 15) and to resist extensive revisions of established academic programs. However, for every major impediment, one can find pivotal and feasible barrier-busters. Inspiring opportunities abound for a "new shared worldview of North-South relations" that involves stronger and more effective policies and actions that address poverty and vulnerability and inspire research on promising TSD pathways. Transnationally experienced role models and mentors understand that "we would not pursue scientific and technological advances so fervently if we did not value human life and our common humanity so passionately" (Kao and Reenan, 2006, p. 15) and are able to transmit this core sustainable-development passion among colleagues and students. Ideally, engaging actionable perspectives on mitigation and adaptation "would include a large-scale, multinational and multidisciplinary effort, including engineers, climate scientists, economists, political scientists, sociologists, economic and environmental planners, and policy makers, and it would require the integral participation and guidance of scholars and policy makers [and community/group members] from the global South" (Roberts and Parks, 2007, pp. 213, 217–218, 231, 233, 235, 241). Online hubs enable cost-effective transnational sharing of research findings and case-study lessons (Ban, et al., 2015, p. 41).

Introducing systemic change

In the sustainable-development arena, we expect actors affiliated with universities to be in the forefront of change initiatives. At the core of sustainable development are the fields of agricultural sciences, public administration (government policies and interventions), engineering, and environmental studies (including natural-resource conservation and climatic stabilization). Each of these professional fields of study contributes valuable insights on challenges and pathways to improved and sustained quality of life. The ability of higher-education actors in these and other fields to bring about change rests in large part on the presence or absence of key drivers and barriers.

University faculty and students are responsible for preparing for the future. They are eager to advance knowledge and to discover new and improved ways of performing tasks. They interact at the edges of innovation. When their passions are activated, they are prone to advocate change.

At the university level, systemic or comprehensive change involves movement toward Stephen Sterling's "sustainable education" stage (Sterling, 2009, pp. 106, 113–115). The requisite paradigm shift would encompass curriculum transformation (teaching and learning-related research), changes in the physical facility and institutional culture, community/civic engagement in "its immediate environs, and the wider region . . . nationally and internationally," and wide and deep synergetic connections and collaborations (Sterling, 2013, pp. 41–42; also Cortese, 2003, p. 16; Ralph and Stubbs, 2014, p. 71). Most tertiary-education institutions have not yet embedded sustainability in all their operations to the whole-institution extent (Sterling and Thomas, 2006, pp. 349, 367; Ralph and Stubbs, 2014; Wals and Blewitt, 2010, p. 60; Vettori and Rammel, 2014, p. 50).[35] Prospects for systemic change are enhanced when sustainability principles are framed in ways that resonate with the multiple constituencies that comprise today's institutions of higher learning (Sylvestre and Wright, 2016, p. 310).

Catalyzing transnational-sustainable-development involvement among universities in the North and South

Transnational higher-education partnerships (THEPs) assume a special role in light of the potent barriers to sustainable-development involvement that constrain universities around the world and the ample opportunities for exciting and potentially decisive collaborations that exist. Many Southern universities are severely constrained by material- and human-resource deficits (e.g., Andama and Suubi, 2015, p. 133). While many Northern universities find themselves fiscally challenged when seeking to engage in transnational-research and sustainable-development activity, policy makers in high-income countries simultaneously are searching for approaches that will involve adjustments in prevailing unsustainable domestic systems of production, distribution, and consumption (also see Fadeeva, et al., 2014, pp. 8–9). Transnational-insight flows realized through symmetrical higher-education partnering offer a promising resource for enabling action-research collaboration on matters of mutual concern (Wooltorton, et al., 2015, pp. 429–430) and advancing sustainable-development inquiry, learning, and innovation (Mochizuki and Yarime, 2016, p. 21).

Transnational insight flows

The contemporary global governance stage is crowded and diverse. Sheer numbers limit the capacity of all participants, including those with expertise in sustainable-development and those backed by armed force, to steer the course of events. The value of transnational-, transnetwork-insight sharing is heightened as the influence of singular and domestic actors is restricted by the interdependent nature of sustainable-development challenges, unfolding centralizing and decentralizing pressures on information movement, forces advancing globalization, and fragmenting and integrating dynamics. In brief, sustainable development depends on the sharing of perspectives, insights, and contributions across countries and institutions. Multisited (especially South-North) insights and impacts and the rising need for transnational collaboration infuse future-unveiling perspectives and pathways to sustainable development.[36]

Curricular collaborations

Transnational partnering among institutions of higher learning opens manifold opportunities for sustainable-development curricular innovations that are beyond the capacity of any single university to provide. The most promising THEP options include student-educational exchanges, guided experiential and problem-based learning, collaborative-action research with classroom applications (Sipos, Battisti, and Grimm, 2008, p. 76), and faculty exchanges. Length of assignment at the partner institution is a crucial consideration when assessing student and faculty outcomes. King (2009, p. 38) finds the short-term visits that prevail today far less rewarding in terms of local insights and contributions than the much longer commitments made in the 1960s by Northern academics working at African universities on regular contracts with "a small amount of supplementation on their return home."[37] King argues, and we concur, that "the *minimum time* to allow a visitor to become somewhat more local is a term or a semester, but, better still, an academic year" (emphasis added).

At the same time, domestic-curricula outcomes remain important given that few university students are able to take advantage of education-abroad opportunities (Peterson, 2015). Often, one finds the deepest concentration on sustainable development in curricula strands, including interdisciplinary minors, concentrations, and certificates. Integrating sustainability across the curriculum merits serious attention among Southern and Northern universities. These efforts can be inspired and guided by THEPs.

Insights from indigenous knowledge

Increasingly, Northern researchers find that symmetrical partnering with Southern colleagues is a condition for undertaking useful sustainable-development-research projects in the South. Insights from indigenous knowledges contribute expanded and dynamic understandings of social and natural systems that are vital for sustainable development (Dei and Asgharzadeh, 2006, pp. 53–54, 56, 58, 64, 67; also Okolie, 2003, pp. 249–250). Contributions based on indigenous knowledge and Southern scholarship play a critical role in evidence-based policy making aimed at advancing widely shared goals such as reducing poverty and hunger, alleviating suffering, and protecting life-support systems (Crewe and Young, 2002, p. vii). Strengthening research and project-participation opportunities at the grassroots enhances the contributions of indigenous insights.

Facilitating grassroots contributions

Sustainability educators need to be extraordinarily nimble as they search for transnational insights into wicked and emerging issues. They also will need to bear in mind that cross-border challenges often grow out of local circumstances and that community innovations can lend themselves to wider applications. By enabling grassroots initiatives to flourish, devolution offers the prospect of mobilizing active and committed community residents who are aware of the needs to conserve natural resources and to maintain valuable infrastructure (Koehn, 1995, p. 78).

Devolution can be expanded and strengthened through strategic support. Some bilateral and multilateral donors actively support grassroots-research-capacity building in the South. The principal funders of individual-researcher-capability initiatives are bilateral agencies, including the Danish International Development Agency (Danida), the Canadian International Development Research Centre (IDRC), and the Swiss Agency for Development and Cooperation (SDC) (Jones, Bailey, and Lyytikäinen, 2007, pp. 14–15, 20). In Africa, bilaterals often provide research funding, support for research and dissemination infrastructure, training materials, and other forms of local university-capacity building. Multilateral donors have concentrated on supporting sector-specific research networks, such as the African Economic Research Consortium (AERC) and the University Science, Humanities and Engineering Partnerships in Africa (USHEPiA) program (Jones, Bailey, and Lyytikäinen, 2007, pp. 15, 17). The United Nations Environmental Programme (UNEP)'s Mainstreaming Environment and Sustainability in African Universities (MESA) Partnership focuses on capacity building, including an international training program on education for sustainability and a ten-year action and training plan directly aimed at "building capacity for responding to environmental issues, risks and associated sustainable development challenges" (Pradhan, Waswala-Olewe, and Ayombi, 2015, pp. 9–10).

In another grassroots-TSD initiative, existing Regional Centres of Expertise on Education for Sustainable Development (RCE) support transdisciplinary research and community-engagement activities focused on "the social, cultural, economic and environmental sustainability projects most relevant to the local region, [that] are informed by the traditional knowledge and experience of regional practitioners" (Mader, 2014, pp. 67–68). Simultaneously, RCE-networking capabilities enable direct linkages to the ways that similar challenges are being addressed by locally relevant approaches in other parts of the world (Mader, 2014, p. 68).

Brain circulation

For university educators in the Global South, the transnational flow of information, knowledge, and expertise offers opportunities to leapfrog into a brighter horizon. Moving forward, Calestous Juma argues, requires jettisoning the "old-fashioned metaphor of the 'brain drain.'" According to Juma (2005, pp. 18–19), Southern institutions of higher learning should focus on "figuring out how to tap the expertise of those who migrate and upgrade their skills while in the diaspora, not engage in futile efforts to stall international migration." In other words, facilitating the transnational migration or "brain circulation" of transnationally competent academics and professionals offers low-income countries one insight-promising path along the road to sustainable development (also see Altbach, 2004, pp. 14–15).

Building university capacity to engage effectively in sustainable development

The sustainable-development-promoting curricula, research, and outreach shifts highlighted in this chapter are dependent upon "profound transformation" of institutions of higher learning (Fadeeva, et al., 2004, p. 20; also Sterling and Maxey, 2013, p. 7). Shaping, and reshaping, professional programs that are positioned to graduate transnational-sustainable-development practitioners is a systemic transformative task that requires gaps analysis, curricular reform, pedagogical modifications, research and outreach reorientations, and institutional commitment. Educators themselves must first develop competence to advance education for sustainable development in their respective fields (see Blewit, 2015, p. 310; Desha and Hargroves, 2014, p. 71).

At universities that opt to place institution-wide priority on sustainable development, combined curricula and co-curricula (including interdisciplinary minors and certificates), research endeavors, and outreach initiatives will address a broad range of wicked, interrelated, intergenerational, and emerging issues and ethical dilemmas in holistic fashion (Sterling, 2013, p. 28; Sterling and Thomas, 2006, p. 353; Rowland, 2012, p. x; Cayuela, et al., 2013, p. 228; Remington-Doucette, et al., 2013, p. 422). Such forward-looking institutions of higher education will mobilize professional fields of study to help advance "creative societies" (Fadeeva, et al., 2004, p. 9). They will be distinguished as transdisciplinary "centres of transformation and critical enquiry" (Sterling, 2013, p. 28).

While comprehensive transnational-sustainable-development academic programs remain to be organized and delivered, many of the curriculum and pedagogical pieces are in place at universities around the world. Existing components remain to be connected, adapted transprofessionally, aligned with faculty-teaching skills and research interests and student-career aspirations, and integrated into unique and enriched TSD-program initiatives. Parallel capacity-building efforts that are widely supported and linked to program innovations also are needed to bring about the institutional transformation of universities in the North and South. Transformation for sustainable development competes with internationalization and other pressing challenges facing contemporary higher education. The requisite changes are so extensive and penetrating that institution-wide commitments to sustainable development will only be embedded in university DNA (Sylvestre and Wright, 2016, p. 310) when a broad base of internal and external stakeholders commit to focusing on "what most counts for the sustainable future of our world" (Fadeeva, et al., 2014, p. 20; also Desha and Hargroves, 2014, p. 70).

Developing a framework for evaluating curricular, research, outreach, and partnering transformations will enable universities in the North and South to determine how the processes and institutional changes they instigate are progressing, to identify the factors that are facilitating and hampering progress, and to ascertain what intended and unintended outcomes and impacts have resulted. Part III of *Universities and the Sustainable Development Future* is devoted to framework development. Before reaching that mountaintop, however, it is helpful to explore the principal challenges of sustainable development that contemporary universities are grappling with.

Notes

1 In contrast to multidisciplinarity (collaboration among experts from different disciplines), interdisciplinarity and transdisciplinarity involve the "dissolution of disciplinary boundaries" and the explicit "sharing of methods, perspectives, and ways of knowing" (Remington-Doucette, et al., 2013, pp. 406–407). These authors understand transdisciplinarity to include the integration and co-production of "academic knowledge with the practical or traditional knowledge of actors and stakeholders from outside academia."

2 One notable exception is the 2008 report and recommendations of the International Commission on Education for Sustainable Development Practice supported by the John D. and Catherine T. MacArthur Foundation and based at Columbia University's Earth Institute.

3 Mapping learning pathways includes assigning competencies to one or more courses and creating an integrated learning-outcome statement for each course (Desha and Hargroves, 2014, p. 141).

4 Critics note that the MDP model "pays insufficient attention to 'social action' competence" (Fadeeva and Mochizuki, 2010, p. 252). See "functional competence" in the TC model presented below.

5 In contrast to the TC transnational-sustainable-development framework, more commonly encountered "laundry lists" lack unifying themes that guide the identification of core competencies (Wiek, Withycombe, and Redman, 2011, pp. 204–205).

For evidence regarding the utility of TC skills in real-world problem solving, see Koehn (2006).

6 Useful learning in this connection includes qualitative system analysis, modeling, and causal-chain and root-cause analyses (Wiek, et al., 2016, p. 244).

7 Also see point 4 of the *People's Sustainability Treaty for Higher Education*, cited in Tilbury (2013, p. 73).

8 Subjective wellbeing, encompassing "how people experience and evaluate their life as a whole," is an essential component of a "multi-dimensional" conceptualization of human wellbeing (OECD, 2013, pp. 10, 181).

9 John Blewitt (2015, p. 306) adds that, when conducted inclusively, the visioning process acts "as a bridge to incorporate intercultural and indigenous perspectives and knowledge."

10 Cited in Ramanathan and Link (1999, pp. 235–236).

11 Respondents in the RAND study ranked foreign-language fluency nineteenth out of nineteen skills that define a successful professional career in an international organization, and the authors of this study caution that "serious negotiations will always require professional translators" (Bikson, et al., 2003, pp. 25, 27).

12 Sustainable-development practitioners also can use communication networks to e-mail documents to telecommuters who possess specific foreign-language proficiency for overnight translation (Bikson, et al., 2003, p. 49).

13 In this sense, functional capability employs the eight competencies embedded in the concept *gestaltungskompetenz* (see, for instance, Dyer, 2007, p. 402; Wals and Blewitt, 2010, pp. 61–62).

Although functional competence requires activating all five TC competencies, "there is no single way but multiple ways to do so" (Wiek, Withycombe, and Redman, 2011, p. 212). Moreover, when individuals lack all five TC skills, they can still use functional group-mobilizing capability to "find and build teams capable of applying the suite of competencies necessary for sustainability problem-solving" (Wiek, et al., 2016, p. 258).

14 Useful learning in this connection includes project- and conflict-management approaches, stakeholder-workshop-facilitation methods, and group-consensus-building techniques (Wiek, et al., 2016, p. 250).

15 Useful learning in this connection includes sustainability-assessment methods, risk analysis, and impact-assessment techniques (Wiek, et al., 2016, p. 247).

16 A related way to view sustainable-development-curriculum transformation is through the triple lens of the knowledge, skills, and values capability requirements advanced by Parker, Wade, and Atkinson (2004). Knowledge and understanding covers diversity; social justice and equity; interdependence; natural, human, and social capital; and the new limits of dynamic human-nature interactions (Ramos and Pires, 2013, p. 93; Disterheft, et al., 2013, p. 8). Required skills include cooperation (Fredericks, 2014, p. 34) and conflict resolution, critical thinking, natural-resource maintenance and restoration, poverty reduction, and the ability to challenge injustice effectively. Key values and attitudes are concern for the environment; commitment to sustainable development, justice, and equity; respect for diversity; and confidence that people can make a difference. The requisite knowledge, skills, and values draw heavily on non-economic social-science and humanities learning, areas that tend to be relatively neglected at many universities (Jones, Bailey, and Lyytikäinen, 2007, p. 25).

17 As we have seen in the discussion above, these five competencies, plus a sixth (meta-competence) introduced in Wiek, et al. (2016, p. 243), are encompassed in the more comprehensive transnational-competence framework.

18 As early as 2006, UNESCO urged sub-Saharan African countries to mainstream education for sustainable development (see Aklilu Dalelo, 2015, p. 186).

19 On the Universiti Sains Malaysia (USM)'s commitment to promoting sustainable development with "particular attention to the disempowered *bottom billion*," see Razak, et al. (2013, p. 148, emphasis in original). Although integrating sustainability into all its activities receives full support and resource allocations from USM's leaders, an assessment undertaken by Koshy, et al. (2013, pp. 238–239, 246) found few cases where staffers "infused sustainability issue/s into the curriculum, research and out of campus community activities they are involved in."

20 These principles guide the progressive program offered by the School of Sustainability at Arizona State University (Brundiers, Wiek, and Redman, 2010, pp. 310, 314–316, 320). Other US leaders in providing community-linked experiential learning opportunities are Oberlin College's Oberlin Project (Daneri, Trencher, and Petersen, 2015), the Sustainability Institute at Portland State University's ecodistrict collaboration with the City and County of Portland (Rowe and Hiser, 2016, p. 320), and George Mason University's integrated undergraduate research and sustainability program's capstone action-research project (Rowe and Hiser, 2016, p. 321).

21 For instance, using the household-environmental-assessment tool, EcoCal encourages students to calculate, evaluate, and address their ecological footprint (Blewitt, 2004, p. 34).

22 See the discussion of Ithaca College students' exemplary engagement with local EcoVillage projects found in Desha and Hargroves (2014, p. 178).

23 In contrast, education for sustainability in campus operations has been ad hoc and short-lived at the Royal Melbourne Institute of Technology (RMIT) (Bekessy, Samson, and Clarkson, 2007, p. 308).

24 Mochizuki and Fadeeva (2010, pp. 399–400) stress the importance of close consultation with stakeholders outside the university environs when identifying needed sustainable-development competencies for local contexts.

25 Interestingly, the Paris Agreement is basically silent on this, apart from technology research and climate-change research.

26 Fruitful sources of diversity for synthesizing sustainable-development research include users, transinstitutional partnerships, academic insiders and outsiders, and multiple cross-sector participants (Rickinson and Reid, 2016, p. 155).

27 This discussion is adapted from Shaw and Kim (2008, pp. 11, 20–25, 61–64, 66–68); see also Koehn and Rosenau (2010, Chapter 9).

28 A major UNDP evaluation on the poverty-environment nexus found that disciplinary limitations (especially among the economists in the organization) hampered understanding of sustainable development and cooperation.

29 Talwar, Wiek, and Robinson (2011, p. 389) identify five differences in the organizational and product expectations of users and researchers that can constrain the interactivity process.

30 For instance, the Megaphon Uni program at the University of Graz, Austria, identifies "regionally relevant social challenges that can be taken up in the educational and research programmes of the university" through mutual learning with all affected stakeholders (Mader, 2014, pp. 71–74; also Zimmermann, et al., 2014, p. 141); also read about the reach-out and reach-in exchanges that RCE Kitakyushu, Japan, and its ten local universities engage in with community stakeholders (Mader, 2014, pp. 71–72).

31 On corporate-carbon accounting, see Sileshi (2016, pp. 158–162). The Global Reporting Initiative (GRI) provides common standards and guidelines for reporting corporate sustainability performance to internal and external stakeholders (ibid, pp. 103–109). The comprehensive CSR reports prepared by Finnish companies according to GRI guidelines cover "environmental issues, employee welfare and ethical behavior, as well as corporate involvement in community-based projects, natural disaster help, support for education and donations to charities and youth groups, among others" (ibid, p. 171). Transparency in corporate sustainability reports "includes all transactions that the business has conducted, and the accounting principles that are used to measure, record and report them" (ibid., p. 164).

32 Ways to overcome such barriers are presented in Chapter 12.

33 To facilitate student involvement, the Higher Education Academy (HEA) provides practical support for student partnerships in designing curricula (Rowe and Hiser, 2016, p. 320).

34 For additional step-by-step process recommendations for introducing systemic change, see de la Harpe and Thomas (2009, p. 78).

35 Sterling (2013, p. 41) finds that the UK's Plymouth University has "much to commend it" in these respects (see also Jones, Selby, and Sterling, 2010, p. 7). The College of the Atlantic in Maine weaves sustainable-energy projects into its operations and curriculum (see Cardwell, 2015). Northern Arizona University revamped 120 courses in most disciplines so that sustainability constituted the context and/or content of learning and inserted sustainability as a key thrust of its liberal-studies requirement for all majors (Cortese, 2003, p. 20). The University of Florida and Leuphana University Luneborg are exceptional in their holistic reorientation of curricula, research, pedagogy, and governance (Vettori and Rammel, 2014, p. 50). Along with an action orientation and humanism, sustainability constitutes a "core pillar" at Leuphana University Luneborg. Employing a "whole-of-institution" approach, Leuphana University "combines research, education and institutional activities and, as such, seeks to transform itself as well as the region it serves" (Mader, 2014, p. 74). See Mader (2014, p. 74) for a detailed description of Leuphana University Luneborg's sustainability-embedded curriculum and its regionally relevant and community-partnered student-research program.

36 The evaluation of THEPs devoted to sustainable development provides the subject for Chapter 9.

37 Including the lead author of this book.

Works cited

Adamson, Bob; Nixon, Jon; and Su, Feng. 2013. "Preface." In *The Reorientation of Higher Education: Challenging the East-West Dichotomy*, edited by Bob Adamson, Jon Nixon, and Feng Su. Hong Kong: Comparative Education Research Centre, The University of Hong Kong. Pp. 1–10.

Aklilu Dalelo. 2015. "Sustainability Issues in the Geography Curriculum for an Undergraduate Programme: The Case of Addis Ababa University, Ethiopia." In *Mainstreaming Environment and Sustainability in African Universities: Stories of Change*, edited by Heila Lotz-Sisitka, Gitile Naituli, Amanda Hlengwa, Mike Ward, Ayobami Salami, Akpezi Ogbuigwe, Mahesh Pradhan, Marie Neeser, and Sanne Lauriks. Grahamstown: Rhodes University Environmental Learning Research Centre. Pp. 185–199.

Altbach, Philip G. 2004. "Globalisation and the University: Myths and Realities in an Unequal World." *Tertiary Education and Management* 10:3–25.

Andama, Edward; and Suubi, Ujeyo M. S. 2015. "Mainstreaming Education for Sustainable Development in Teacher Education at Busitema University, Uganda." In *Mainstreaming Environment and Sustainability in African Universities: Stories of Change*, edited by Heila Lotz-Sisitka, Gitile Naituli, Amanda Hlengwa, Mike Ward, Ayobami Salami, Akpezi Ogbuigwe, Mahesh Pradhan, Marie Neeser, and Sanne Lauriks. Grahamstown: Rhodes University Environmental Learning Research Centre. Pp. 127–134.

Anderson, Kathy L. 2008. "Bridging Disciplines to Bridge Global Divides: Interdisciplinary Approaches to the Millennium's Most Challenging Dilemmas." Paper presented at the World Universities Forum, Davos, Switzerland, 31 January.

Arima, Akito. 2009. "A Plea for More Education for Sustainable Development." *Sustainability Science* 4:3–5.

Ban, Natalie C.; Boyd, Emily; Cox, Michael; Meek, Chanda L.; Schoon, Michael; and Villamayor-Tomas, Sergio. 2015. "Linking Classroom Learning and Research to Advance Ideas about Social-Ecological Resilience." *Ecology and Society* 20 (3):35–42.

Barth, Matthias; Godemann, Jasmin; Rieckmann, Marco; and Stoltenberg, Ute. 2007. "Developing Key Competencies for Sustainable Development in Higher Education." *International Journal of Sustainability in Higher Education* 8 (6):416–430.

Barth, Matthias; and Michelsen, Gerd. 2013. "Learning for Change: An Educational Contribution to Sustainability Science." *Sustainability Science* 8:103–119.

Bekessy, S. A.; Samson, K.; and Clarkson, R. E. 2007. "The Failure of Non-Binding Declarations to Achieve University Sustainability: A Need for Accountability." *International Journal of Sustainability in Higher Education* 8 (3):301–316.

Berkes, Fikret; Colding, Johan; and Folke, Carl. 2003. "Introduction." In *Navigating Social-Ecological Systems: Building Resilience for Complexity and Change*, edited by Fikret Berkes, Johan Colding, and Carl Folke. Cambridge: Cambridge University Press. Pp. 1–25.

Biddle, Sheila. 2002. *Internationalization: Rhetoric or Reality?* New York: American Council of Learned Societies.

Bikson, Tora K.; Treverton, Gregory F.; Moini, Joy; and Lindstrom, Gustav. 2003. *New Challenges for International Leadership: Lessons from Organizations with Global Missions.* Santa Monica: RAND.

Blewitt, John. 2004. "Sustainability and Lifelong Learning." In *The Sustainability Curriculum: Facing the Challenge in Higher Education*, edited by John Blewitt and Cedric Cullingford. London: Earthscan. Pp. 24–42.

Blewitt, John. 2015. *Understanding Sustainable Development*, 2nd edition. London: Routledge.

Brinkerhoff, Jennifer M. 2007. "Contributions of Digital Diasporas to Governance Reconstruction in Fragile States: Potential and Promise." In *Governance in Post-Conflict*

Societies: Rebuilding Fragile States, edited by Derick W. Brickerhoff. London: Routledge. Pp. 185–203.

Brundiers, Katja; Savage, Emma; Mannell, Steven; Lang, Daniel J.; and Wiek, Arnim. 2014. "Educating Sustainability Change Agents by Design: Appraisals of the Transformative Role of Higher Education." In *Sustainable Development and Quality Assurance in Higher Education: Transformation of Learning and Society*, edited by Zinaida Fadeeva, Laima Galkute, Clemens Mader, and Geoff Scott. New York: Palgrave Macmillan. Pp. 196–229.

Brundiers, Katja; Wiek, Arnim; and Redman, Charles L. 2010. "Real-World Learning Opportunities in Sustainability: From Classroom into the Real World." *International Journal of Sustainability in Higher Education* 11 (4):308–324.

Cardwell, Diane. 2015. "Tackling Climate Change, One Class at a Time." *New York Times*, 1 July, pp. B1–B2.

Cayuela, Alberto; Robinson, John B.; Campbell, Ann; Coops, Nicholas; and Munro, Alison. 2013. "Integration of Operational and Academic Efforts in Sustainability at the University of British Columbia." In *Sustainability Assessment Tools in Higher Education Institutions: Mapping Trends and Good Practices around the World*, edited by Sandra Caeiro, Walter L. Filho, Charbel Jabbour, and Ulisses M. Azeiteiro. Cham, Switzerland: Springer International Publishing. Pp. 223–236.

Chambers, Dianne P. 2013. "A Discipline-Based Model for Embedding Sustainability in University Curricula." In *Sustainability Assessment Tools in Higher Education Institutions: Mapping Trends and Good Practices around the World*, edited by Sandra Caeiro, Walter L. Filho, Charbel Jabbour, and Ulisses M. Azeiteiro. Cham, Switzerland: Springer International Publishing. Pp. 309–321.

Cortes, Carlos E.; and Wilkinson, Louise C. 2009. "Developing and Implementing a Multicultural Vision." In *Contemporary Leadership and Intercultural Competence: Exploring the Cross-Cultural Dynamics within Organizations*, edited by Michael A. Moodian. Los Angeles, CA: Sage. Pp. 17–31.

Cortese, Anthony D. 2003. "The Critical Role of Higher Education in Creating a Sustainable Future." *Planning for Higher Education* 2 (March–May):15–22.

Cotton, Debby; and Winter, Jennie. 2010. "'It's Not Just Bits of Paper and Light Bulbs': A Review of Sustainability Pedagogies and Their Potential for Use in Higher Education." In *Sustainability Education: Perspectives and Practice across Higher Education*, edited by Paula Jones, David Selby, and Stephen Sterling. London: Earthscan. Pp. 39–55.

Crewe, Emma; and Young, John. 2002. *Bridging Research and Policy: Context, Evidence and Links*. Working paper #173. London: Overseas Development Institute.

Dahl, Arthur L. 2014. "Sustainability and Values Assessment in Higher Education." In *Sustainable Development and Quality Assurance in Higher Education: Transformation of Learning and Society*, edited by Zinaida Fadeeva, Laima Galkute, Clemens Mader, and Geoff Scott. New York: Palgrave Macmillan. Pp. 185–195.

Daneri, Daniel R.; Trencher, Gregory; and Petersen, John. 2015. "Students as Change Agents in a Town-Wide Sustainability Transformation: The Oberlin Project at Oberlin College." *Current Opinion in Environmental Sustainability* 16:14–21.

Date-Huxtable, Elizabeth; Ellem, Gary; and Roberts, Tim. 2013. "The Low-Carbon Curriculum at the University of Newcastle, Australia." In *Sustainability Assessment Tools in Higher Education Institutions: Mapping Trends and Good Practices around the World*, edited by Sandra Caeiro, Walter L. Filho, Charbel Jabbour, and Ulisses M. Azeiteiro. Cham, Switzerland: Springer International Publishing. Pp. 345–357.

Dei, George J. S.; and Asgharzadeh, Alireza. 2006. "Indigenous Knowledges and Globalization: An African Perspective." In *African Education and Globalization: Critical*

Perspectives, edited by Ali A. Abdi, Korbla P. Puplampu, and George J. S. Dei. Lanham, MD: Lexington Books. Pp. 53–78.

Deprez, Steff. 2012. "Development of a Learning-Oriented Monitoring System for Sustainable Agriculture Chain Development in Eastern Indonesia." In *Governance by Evaluation for Sustainable Development: Institutional Capacities and Learning*, edited by Michal Sedlacko and Andre Martinuzzi. Cheltenham, UK: Edward Elgar. Pp. 233–252.

Derrick, Stephen. 2013. "Time and Sustainability Metrics in Higher Education." In *Sustainability Assessment Tools in Higher Education Institutions: Mapping Trends and Good Practices around the World*, edited by Sandra Caeiro, Walter L. Filho, Charbel Jabbour, and Ulisses M. Azeiteiro. Cham, Switzerland: Springer International Publishing. Pp. 47–63.

Desha, Cheryl; and Hargroves, Karlson C. 2014. *Higher Education and Sustainable Development: A Model for Curriculum Renewal*. London: Routledge.

Disterheft, Antje; Caeiro, Sandra; Azeiteiro, Ulisses M.; and Filho, Walter L. 2013. "Sustainability Science and Education for Sustainable Development in Universities: A Way for Transition." In *Sustainability Assessment Tools in Higher Education Institutions: Mapping Trends and Good Practices around the World*, edited by Sandra Caeiro, Walter L. Filho, Charbel Jabbour, and Ulisses M. Azeiteiro. Cham, Switzerland: Springer International Publishing. Pp. 3–27.

Dyer, Alan. 2007. "Inspiration, Enchantment and a Sense of Wonder . . . Can a New Paradigm in Education Bring Nature and Culture Together again?" *International Journal of Heritage Studies* 13, Nos. 4–5 (July–September):393–404.

Fadeeva, Zinaida; Galkute, Laima; Mader, Clemens; and Scott, Geoff. 2014. "Assessment for Transformation: Higher Education Thrives in Refining Quality Systems." In *Sustainable Development and Quality Assurance in Higher Education: Transformation of Learning and Society*, edited by Zinaida Fadeeva, Laima Galkute, Clemens Mader, and Geoff Scott. New York: Palgrave Macmillan. Pp. 1–22.

Fadeeva, Zinaida; and Mochizuki, Yoko. 2010. "Higher Education for Today and Tomorrow: University Appraisal for Diversity, Innovation and Change towards Sustainable Development." *Sustainability Science* 5:249–256.

Finn, Janet L.; and Jacobson, Maxine. 2008. *Just Practice: A Social Justice Approach to Social Work*, 2nd edition. Peosta, IA: Eddie Bowers Publishing.

Folke, Carl; Colding, Johan; and Berkes, Fikret. 2008. "Synthesis: Building Resilience and Adaptive Capacity in Socio-Ecological Systems." In *Navigating Social-Ecological Systems: Building Resilience for Complexity and Change*, edited by Fikret Berkes, Johan Colding, and Carl Folke. Cambridge: Cambridge University Press. Pp. 352–387.

Fredericks, Sarah. 2014. *Measuring and Evaluating Sustainability: Ethics in Sustainability Indexes*. London: Routledge.

Gapor, Salfarina A.; Aziz, Abd M. A.; Razak, Dzulkifli A.; and Sanusi, Zainal A. 2014. "Implementing Education for Sustainable Development in Higher Education: Case Study of Albukhary International University, Malaysia." In *Sustainable Development and Quality Assurance in Higher Education: Transformation of Learning and Society*, edited by Zinaida Fadeeva, Laima Galkute, Clemens Mader, and Geoff Scott. New York: Palgrave Macmillan. Pp. 255–281.

Goleman, Daniel. 1995. *Emotional Intelligence*. New York: Bantam Books.

Goleman, Daniel. 1998. *Working with Emotional Intelligence*. New York: Bantam Books.

Gordon, Frances. 2009. "Interprofessional Capability as an Aim of Student Learning." In *Interprofessional Education: Making It Happen*, edited by Patricia Bluteau and Ann Jackson. New York: Palgrave Macmillan. Pp. 59–79.

Harpe, Barbara de la; and Thomas, Ian. 2009. "Curriculum Change in Universities: Conditions That Facilitate Education for Sustainable Development." *Journal of Education for Sustainable Development* 3 (1):75–85.

Hegarty, Kathryn; Thomas, Ian; Kriewaldt, Cathryn; Holdsworth, Sarah; and Bekessy, Sarah. 2011. "Insights into the Value of a 'Stand-Alone' Course for Sustainability Education." *Environmental Education Research* 17 (4):451–469.

Holm, Tove; Sammalisto, Kaisu; Grindsted, Thomas S.; and Vuorisalo, Timo. 2015. "Process Framework for Identifying Sustainability Aspects in University Curricula and Integrating Education for Sustainable Development." *Journal of Cleaner Production* 106:164–174.

Johansson, Frans. 2004. *The Medici Effect*. Cambridge: Harvard Business School Press.

Johnstone, D. Bruce; and Marcucci, Pamela N. 2010. *Financing Higher Education Worldwide: Who Pays? Who Should Pay?* Baltimore: Johns Hopkins University Press.

Jones, Nicola; Bailey, Mark; and Lyytikäinen, Minna. 2007. *Research Capacity Strengthening in Africa: Trends, Gaps and Opportunities*. London: Overseas Development Institute.

Jones, Paula; Selby, David; and Sterling, Stephen. 2010. "Introduction." In *Sustainability Education: Perspectives and Practice across Higher Education*, edited by Paula Jones, David Selby, and Stephen Sterling. London: Earthscan. Pp. 1–16.

Jowi, James O. 2009. "Internationalization of Higher Education in Africa: Developments, Emerging Trends, Issues and Policy Implications." *Higher Education Policy* 22 (3):263–281.

Juma, Calestous. 2005. "Reinventing Growth." In *Going for Growth: Science, Technology and Innovation in Africa*, edited by Calestous Juma. London: Smith Institute. Pp. 10–21.

Juma, Calestous; and Yee-Cheong, Lee. 2005. *Innovation: Applying Knowledge in Development*. London: Earthscan.

Kao, Audiey; and Reenan, Jennifer. 2006. "*Wit* Is Not Enough." In *Professionalism in Medicine: Critical Perspectives*, edited by Delese Wear and Julie M. Aultman. New York: Springer. Pp. 211–232.

King, Kenneth. 2009. "Higher Education and International Cooperation: The Role of Academic Collaboration in the Developing World." In *Higher Education and International Capacity Building: Twenty-Five Years of Higher Education Links*, edited by David Stephens. Oxford, UK: Symposium Books. Pp. 33–49.

King, Kenneth; and McGrath, Simon. 2004. *Knowledge for Development? Comparing British, Japanese, Swedish, and World Bank Aid*. London: Zed Books.

King, Kenneth; and Palmer, Robert. 2013. *Post-2015 Agendas: Northern Tsunami, Southern Ripple? The Case of Education and Skills*. Working paper #4. Geneva: Network for International Policies and Cooperation in Education and Training (NORRAG).

Knight, Jane. 2008. "The Internationalization of Higher Education: Complexities and Realities." In *Higher Education in Africa: The International Dimension*, edited by Damtew Teferra and Jane Knight. Chestnut Hill, MA: Enter for International Higher Education, Boston College. Pp. 1–43.

Koehn, Peter H. 1995. "Decentralization for Sustainable Development." In *Development Management in Africa: Toward Dynamism, Empowerment, and Entrepreneurship*, edited by Sadiq Rasheed and David Luke. Boulder: Westview Press. Pp. 71–81.

Koehn, Peter H. 2006. "Health-Care Outcomes in Ethnoculturally Discordant Medical Encounters: The Role of Physician Transnational Competence in Consultations with Asylum Seekers." *Journal of Immigrant and Minority Health* 8, No. 2 (April):137–147.

Koehn, Peter H. 2010. "Climate Policy and Action 'Underneath' Kyoto and Copenhagen: China and the USA." *Wiley Interdisciplinary Reviews (WIREs): Climate Change* 1 (March–April):405–417.

Koehn, Peter H.; and Rosenau, James N. 2010. *Transnational Competence: Empowering Professional Curricula for Horizon-Rising Challenges*. Boulder, CO: Paradigm Publishers.

Kopnina, Helen; and Meijers, Frans. 2012. "Education for Sustainable Development (ESD): Exploring Theoretical and Practical Challenges." *International Journal of Sustainability in Higher Education* 15 (2):188–207.

Koshy, Kanayathu C.; Nor, Norizan M.; Sibly, Suzyrman; Rahim, Asyirah A.; Jegatesen, Govindran; and Muhamad, Malik. 2013. "An Indicator-Based Approach to Sustainability Monitoring and Mainstreaming at Universiti Sains Malaysia." In *Sustainability Assessment Tools in Higher Education Institutions: Mapping Trends and Good Practices around the World*, edited by Sandra Caeiro, Walter L. Filho, Charbel Jabbour, and Ulisses M. Azeiteiro. Cham, Switzerland: Springer International Publishing. Pp. 237–258.

Lotz-Sisitka, Heila; Agbedahin, Adesuwa V.; and Hlengwa, Amanda. 2015. " 'Seeding Change': Developing a Change-Oriented Model for Professional Learning and ESD in Higher Education Institutions in Africa." In *Mainstreaming Environment and Sustainability in African Universities: Stories of Change*, edited by Heila Lotz-Sisitka, Gitile Naituli, Amanda Hlengwa, Mike Ward, Ayobami Salami, Akpezi Ogbuigwe, Mahesh Pradhan, Marie Neeser, and Sanne Lauriks. Grahamstown: Rhodes University Environmental Learning Research Centre. Pp. 16–33.

Mader, Clemens. 2014. "The Role of Assessment and Quality Management in Transformations towards Sustainable Development: The Nexus between Higher Education, Society and Policy." In *Sustainable Development and Quality Assurance in Higher Education: Transformation of Learning and Society*, edited by Zinaida Fadeeva, Laima Galkute, Clemens Mader, and Geoff Scott. New York: Palgrave Macmillan. Pp. 66–83.

McGibbon, Carolyn; and Van Belle, Jean-Paul. 2015. "Integrating Environmental Sustainability Issues into the Curriculum through Problem-Based and Project-Based Learning: A Case Study at the University of Cape Town." *Current Opinion in Environmental Sustainability* 16:81–88.

McGrath, Simon; and King, Kenneth. 2004. "Knowledge-Based Aid: A Four Agency Comparative Study." *International Journal of Educational Development* 24:167–181.

McKay, Sandra L. 2002. *Teaching English as an International Language: Rethinking Goals and Approaches*. Oxford: Oxford University Press.

McMahon, Walter W. 2009. *Higher Learning, Greater Good: The Private and Social Benefits of Higher Education*. Baltimore: Johns Hopkins University Press.

Mochizuki, Yoko; and Fadeeva, Zinaida. 2010. "Competences for Sustainable Development and Sustainability: Significance and Challenges for ESD." *International Journal of Sustainability in Higher Education* 11 (4):391–403.

Mochizuki, Yoko; and Yarime, Masaru. 2016. "Education for Sustainable Development and Sustainability Science: Re-Purposing Higher Education and Research." In *Routledge Handbook of Higher Education for Sustainable Development*, edited by Matthias Barth, Gerd Michelsen, Marco Rieckmann, and Ian Thomas. London: Routledge. Pp. 11–24.

Moran, Robert T.; Harris, Philip R.; and Moran, Sarah V. 2007. *Managing Cultural Differences: Global Leadership Strategies for the 21st Century*. Amsterdam: Elsevier.

Mulder, Karel F.; Ferrer-Balas, Didac; Segalas-Coral, Jordi; Kordas, Olga; Nikiforovich, Eugene; and Pereverza, Katerina. 2013. "Being Scared Is Not Enough! Motivators for Education for Sustainable Development." In *Sustainability Assessment Tools in Higher Education Institutions: Mapping Trends and Good Practices around the World*, edited by Sandra Caeiro, Walter L. Filho, Charbel Jabbour, and Ulisses M. Azeiteiro. Cham, Switzerland: Springer International Publishing. Pp. 29–45.

Neelakantan, Shailaja. 2009. "A Young University in India Focuses on Real-World Industry and Sustainability." *Chronicle of Higher Education*, 9 January, p. A20.

Nilsson, Måns. 2012. "Tools for Learning-Oriented Environmental Appraisal." In *Governance by Evaluation for Sustainable Development: Institutional Capacities and Learning*, edited by Michal Sedlacko and Andre Martinuzzi. Cheltenham, UK: Edward Elgar. Pp. 45–60.

Ojelay-Surtees, Bimla. 2007. *Building Trust in Diverse Teams: The Toolkit for Emergency Response*. Dorset, UK: Oxfam GB.

Okolie, Andrew C. 2003. "Producing Knowledge for Sustainable Development in Africa: Implications for Higher Education." *Higher Education* 46 (2):235–260.

Organization of Economic Cooperation and Development (OECD). 2013. *OECD Guidelines on Measuring Subjective Well-Being.* Paris: OECD Publishing.

Parker, Jenneth; Wade, Ros; and Atkinson, Hugh. 2004. "Citizenship and Community from Local to Global: Implications for Higher Education of a Global Citizenship Approach." In *The Sustainability Curriculum: Facing the Challenge in Higher Education,* edited by John Blewitt and Cedric Cullingford. London: Earthscan. Pp. 63–77.

Parker, Walter C.; Ninomiya, Akira; and Cogan, John. 1999. "Educating World Citizens: Toward Multinational Curriculum Development." *American Educational Research Journal* 36, No. 2 (Summer):117–145.

Pelling, Mark; O'Brien, Karen; and Matyas, David. 2015. "Adaptation and Transformation." *Climatic Change* 133:113–127.

Peterson, Patti M. [Presidential Advisor for Global Initiatives, American Council on Education] 2015. "A Flat Lens for a Round World?" Keynote address at the Defining a 21st Century Education for a Vibrant Democracy Conference, University of Montana, Missoula, 26 October.

Platteau, Jean-Philippe. 2005. "Institutional and Distributional Aspects of Sustainability in Community-Driven Development." In *Evaluating Development Effectiveness,* edited by George K. Pitman, Osvaldo N. Feinstein, and Gregory K. Ingram. World Bank Series on Evaluation and Development, Volume 7. New Brunswick, NJ: Transaction Publishers. Pp. 275–297.

Pradhan, Mahesh; Waswala-Olewe, Brian M.; and Ayombi, Mariam. 2015. "Introducing the UNEP Mainstreaming Environment and Sustainability in African Universities Partnership Programme." In *Mainstreaming Environment and Sustainability in African Universities: Stories of Change,* edited by Heila Lotz-Sisitka, Gitile Naituli, Amanda Hlengwa, Mike Ward, Ayobami Salami, Akpezi Ogbuigwe, Mahesh Pradhan, Marie Neeser, and Sanne Lauriks. Grahamstown: Rhodes University Environmental Learning Research Centre. Pp. 5–15.

Pusch, Margaret D. 2009. "The Interculturally Competent Global Leader." In *The Sage Handbook of Intercultural Competence,* edited by Darla K. Deardorff. Thousand Oaks, CA: Sage. Pp. 66–84.

Ralph, Meredith; and Stubbs, Wendy. 2014. "Integrating Environmental Sustainability into Universities." *Higher Education* 67:71–90.

Ramanathan, Chathapuram S.; and Link, Rosemary J. 1999. "Future Visions for Global Studies in Social Work." In *All Our Futures: Principles and Resources for Social Work Practice in a Global Era,* edited by Chathapuram S. Ramanathan and Rosemary J. Link. Albany: Brooks/Cole, Wadsworth. Pp. 219–236.

Ramos, Tomas; and Pires, Sara M. 2013. "Sustainability Assessment: The Role of Indicators." In *Sustainability Assessment Tools in Higher Education Institutions: Mapping Trends and Good Practices around the World,* edited by Sandra Caeiro, Walter L. Filho, Charbel Jabbour, and Ulisses M. Azeiteiro. Cham, Switzerland: Springer International Publishing. Pp. 81–99.

Ramphele, Mamphela. 2003. "The University as an Actor in Development: New Perspectives and Demands." In *African Higher Education: Implications for Development,* edited by Cheryl R. Doss, Robert E. Evanson, and Nancy L. Ruther. New Haven, CT: Yale Center for International and Area Studies. Pp. 1–21.

Razak, Dzulkifli A.; Sanusi, Zainal A.; Jegatesen, Govindran; and Khelghat-Doost, Hamoon. 2013. "Alternative University Appraisal (AUA): Reconstructing Universities' Ranking and Rating toward a Sustainable Future." In *Sustainability Assessment Tools in*

Higher Education Institutions: Mapping Trends and Good Practices around the World, edited by Sandra Caeiro, Walter L. Filho, Charbel Jabbour, and Ulisses M. Azeiteiro. Cham, Switzerland: Springer International Publishing. Pp. 139–154.

Remington-Doucette, Sonya M.; Connell, Kim Y. H.; Armstrong, Cosette M.; and Musgrove, Sheryl L. 2013. "Assessing Sustainability Education in a Transdisciplinary Undergraduate Course Focused on Real-World Problem Solving: A Case for Disciplinary Grounding." *International Journal of Sustainability in Higher Education* 14 (4):404–433.

Rickinson, Mark; and Reid, Alan. 2016. "Synthesis of Research in Higher Education for Sustainable Development." In *Routledge Handbook of Higher Education for Sustainable Development*, edited by Matthias Barth, Gerd Michelsen, Marco Rieckmann, and Ian Thomas. London: Routledge. Pp. 142–160.

Roberts, J. Timmons; and Parks, Bradley C. 2007. *A Climate of Injustice: Global Inequality, North-South Politics, and Climate Policy*. Cambridge: MIT Press.

Rondinelli, Dennis A. 2009. "Changing Concepts of Leadership in a Globalizing Society." In *Leadership for Development: What Globalization Demands of Leaders Fighting for Change*, edited by Dennis A. Rondinelli and John M. Heffron. Boulder, CO: Kumarian Press. Pp. 27–47.

Roorda, Niko. 2013. "A Strategy and a Toolkit to Realize System Integration of Sustainable Development (SISD)." In *Sustainability Assessment Tools in Higher Education Institutions: Mapping Trends and Good Practices around the World*, edited by Sandra Caeiro, Walter L. Filho, Charbel Jabbour, and Ulisses M. Azeiteiro. Cham, Switzerland: Springer International Publishing. Pp. 101–119.

Roorda, Niko; Corcoran, Peter B.; and Weakland, Joseph P. 2012. *Fundamentals of Sustainable Development*. London: Routledge.

Rowe, Debra; and Hiser, Krista. 2016. "Higher Education for Sustainable Development in the Community and through Partnerships." In *Routledge Handbook of Higher Education for Sustainable Development*, edited by Matthias Barth, Gerd Michelsen, Marco Rieckmann, and Ian Thomas. London: Routledge. Pp. 315–330.

Rowe, Debra; and Johnston, Lucas F. 2013. "Learning Outcomes: An International Comparison of Countries and Declarations." In *Higher Education for Sustainability: Cases, Challenges, and Opportunities from across the Curriculum*, edited by Lucas F. Johnston. New York: Routledge. Pp. 45–59.

Rowland, Paul. 2012. "Foreword." In *The Sustainable University: Green Goals and New Challenges for Higher Education Leaders*, edited by James Martin and James E. Samels. Baltimore: The Johns Hopkins University Press. Pp. ix–xi.

Ryan, Alex; and Cotton, Debby. 2013. "Times of Change: Shifting Pedagogy and Curricula for Future Sustainability." In *The Sustainable University: Progress and Prospects*, edited by Stephen Sterling, Larch Maxey, and Heather Luna. London: Routledge. Pp. 151–161.

Salmi, Jamil. 2002. "Higher Education at a Turning Point." In *Higher Education in the Developing World: Changing Contexts and Institutional Responses*, edited by David W. Chapman and Ann E. Austin. Westport, CT: Greenwood Press. Pp. 23–43.

Salter, Jonathan; Robinson, John; and Wiek, Arnim. 2010. "Participatory Methods of Integrated Assessment: A Review." *WIRES: Climate Change* 1:697–717.

Samoff, Joel; and Carrol, Bidemi. 2004. "The Promise of Partnership and Continuities of Dependence: External Support to Higher Education in Africa." *African Studies Review* 47 (1):67–199.

Sarkissian, Wendy. 2009. *Kitchen Table Sustainability: Practical Recipes for Community Engagement with Sustainability*. London: Earthscan.

Scholz, Roland W.; Lang, Daniel J.; Wiek, Arnim; Walter, Alexander I.; and Stauffacher, Michael. 2006. "Transdisciplinary Case Studies as a Means of Sustainability Learning:

Historical Framework and Theory." *International Journal of Sustainability in Higher Education* 7 (3):226–251.

Shaw, Amy; and Kim, Jae. 2008. *Report from the International Commission on Education for Sustainable Development Practice*. Brooklyn, NY: A. J. Bart.

Sibbel, Anne; Hegarty, Kathryn; and Holdsworth, Sarah. 2013. "Action Research in Communities of Practice to Develop Curricula for Sustainability in Higher Education." In *Sustainability Assessment Tools in Higher Education Institutions: Mapping Trends and Good Practices around the World*, edited by Sandra Caeiro, Walter L. Filho, Charbel Jabbour, and Ulisses M. Azeiteiro. Cham, Switzerland: Springer International Publishing. Pp. 387–404.

Siebert, Stephen. 2012. *The Nature and Culture of Rattan: Reflections on Vanishing Life in the Forests of Southeast Asia*. Honolulu: University of Hawaii Press.

Sileshi Sisaye. 2016. *Ecology, Sustainable Development and Accounting*. New York: Routledge.

Simon, Dagmar; and Knie, Andreas. 2013. "Can Evaluation Contribute to the Organizational Development of Academic Institutions? An International Comparison." *Evaluation* 19 (4):402–418.

Sipos, Yona; Battisti, Bryce; and Grimm, Kurt. 2008. "Achieving Transformative Sustainability Learning: Engaging Head, Hands, and Heart." *International Journal of Sustainability in Higher Education* 9 (1):68–86.

Stauffacher, Michael; Walter, Alexander I.; Lang, Daniel J.; Wiek, Arnim; and Scholz, Roland W. 2006. "Learning to Research Environmental Problems from a Functional Socio-Cultural Constructivism Perspective." *International Journal of Sustainability in Higher Education* 7 (3):252–275.

Sterling, Stephen. 2004. "Higher Education, Sustainability, and the Role of Systemic Learning." In *Higher Education and the Challenge of Sustainability: Problematics, Promise, and Practice*, edited by Peter B. Corcoran and Arjen E. J. Wals. Dordrecht: Kluwer Academic Publishers. Pp. 49–70.

Sterling, Stephen. 2009. "Sustainable Education." In *Science, Society, and Sustainability: Education and Empowerment for an Uncertain World*, edited by Donald Gray, Laura Colucci-Gray, and Elena Camino. New York: Routledge. Pp. 105–118.

Sterling, Stephen. 2013. "The Sustainable University: Challenge and Response." In *The Sustainable University: Progress and Prospects*, edited by Stephen Sterling, Larch Maxey, and Heather Luna. London: Routledge. Pp. 17–50.

Sterling, Stephen; and Maxey, Larch. 2013. "Introduction." In *The Sustainable University: Progress and Prospects*, edited by Stephen Sterling, Larch Maxey, and Heather Luna. London: Routledge. Pp. 1–14.

Sterling, Stephen; and Thomas, Ian. 2006. "Education for Sustainability: The Role of Capabilities in Guiding University Curriculum." *International Journal of Innovation and Sustainable Development* 1 (4):349–369.

Suarez-Orozco, Marcelo M.; and Qin-Hilliard, Desiree B. 2004. "Globalization: Culture and Education in the New Millennium." In *Globalization: Culture and Education in the New Millennium*, edited by Marcelo M. Suarez-Orozco and Desiree B. Qin-Hilliard. Berkeley, CA: University of California Press. Pp. 1–37.

Sullivan, William M. 2005. *Work & Integrity: The Crisis and Promise of Professionalism in America*, 2nd edition. San Francisco, CA: Jossey-Bass.

Sylvestre, Paul; and Wright, Tara. 2016. "Organisational Change and Organisational Learning for Promoting Higher Education for Sustainable Development." In *Routledge Handbook of Higher Education for Sustainable Development*, edited by Matthias Barth, Gerd Michelsen, Marco Rieckmann, and Ian Thomas. London: Routledge. Pp. 310–314.

Talwar, Sonia; Wiek, Arnim; and Robinson, John. 2011. "User Engagement in Sustainability Research." *Science and Public Policy* 38 (5):379–390.

Thomas, Ian. 2016. "Challenges for Implementation of Education for Sustainable Development in Higher Education Institutions." In *Routledge Handbook of Higher Education for Sustainable Development*, edited by Matthias Barth, Gerd Michelsen, Marco Rieckmann, and Ian Thomas. London: Routledge. Pp. 56–71.

Tikly, Leon. 2005. "The New Partnership for African Development: Implications for Skills Development." In *International Handbook on Globalisation, Education and Policy Research*, edited by Joseph Zajda. Dordrecht: Springer. Pp. 293–314.

Tilbury, Daniella. 2004. "Environmental Education for Sustainability: A Force for Change in Higher Education." In *Higher Education and the Challenge of Sustainability: Problematics, Promise, and Practice*, edited by Peter B. Corcoran and Arjen E. J. Wals. Dordrecht: Kluwer Academic Publishers. Pp. 97–112.

Tilbury, Daniella. 2013. "Another World Is Desirable: A Global Rebooting of Higher Education for Sustainable Development." In *The Sustainable University: Progress and Prospects*, edited by Stephen Sterling, Larch Maxey, and Heather Luna. London: Routledge. Pp. 71–85.

Ting-Toomey, Stella. 2009. "Intercultural Conflict Competence as a Facet of Intercultural Competence Development." In *The Sage Handbook of Intercultural Competence*, edited by Darla K. Deardorff. Thousand Oaks: Sage. Pp. 100–120.

Vaughter, Philip; Wright, Tarah; McKenzie, Marcia; and Lidstone, Lauri. 2013. "Greening the Ivory Tower: A Review of Educational Research on Sustainability in Post-Secondary Education." *Sustainability* 5:2252–2271.

Vettori, Oliver; and Rammel, Christian. 2014. "Linking Quality Assurance and ESD: Towards a Participative Quality Culture of Sustainable Development in Higher Education." In *Sustainable Development and Quality Assurance in Higher Education: Transformation of Learning and Society*, edited by Zinaida Fadeeva, Laima Galkute, Clemens Mader, and Geoff Scott. New York: Palgrave Macmillan. Pp. 49–65.

Waas, Tom; Huge, Jean; Verbruggen, Aviel; and Wright, T. 2010. "University Research for Sustainable Development: Definition and Characteristics Explored." *Journal of Cleaner Production* 18:629–636.

Wahr, Fiona; and Harpe, Barbara de la. 2016. "Changing from within: An Action Research Perspective for Bringing about Sustainability Curriculum Change in Higher Education." In *Routledge Handbook of Higher Education for Sustainable Development*, edited by Matthias Barth, Gerd Michelsen, Marco Rieckmann, and Ian Thomas. London: Routledge. Pp. 161–180.

Walker, Melanie; McLean, Monica; Dison, Arona; and Peppin-Vaughn, Rosie. 2009. "South African Universities and Human Development: Towards a Theorisation and Operationalisation of Professional Capabilities for Poverty Reduction." *International Journal of Educational Development* 29:565–572.

Wals, Arjen E. J.; and Blewitt, John. 2010. "Third-Wave Sustainability in Higher Education: Some (Inter)national Trends and Developments." In *Sustainability Education: Perspectives and Practice across Higher Education*, edited by Paula Jones, David Selby, and Stephen Sterling. London: Earthscan. Pp. 55–74.

Wals, Arjen E. J.; Tassone, Valentina C.; Hampson, Gary P.; and Reams, Jonathan. 2016. "Learning for Walking the Change: Eco-social Innovation through Sustainability-Oriented Higher Education." In *Routledge Handbook of Higher Education for Sustainable Development*, edited by Matthias Barth, Gerd Michelsen, Marco Rieckmann, and Ian Thomas. London: Routledge. Pp. 25–39.

White, Rehema M. 2013. "Sustainability Research: A Novel Mode of Knowledge Generation to Explore Alternative Ways for People and Planet." In *The Sustainable University: Progress and Prospects*, edited by Stephen Sterling, Larch Maxey, and Heather Luna. London: Routledge. Pp. 168–191.

Wiek, Arnim; and Kay, Braden. 2015. "Learning While Transforming: Solution-Oriented Learning for Urban Sustainability in Phoenix, Arizona." *Current Opinion in Environmental Sustainability* 16:29–36.

Wiek, Arnim; Withycombe, Lauren; and Redman, Charles L. 2011. "Key Competencies in Sustainability: A Reference Framework for Academic Program Development." *Sustainability Science* 6:203–218.

Wiek, Arnim; Withycombe, Lauren; Redman, Charles L.; and Mills, Sarah B. 2011. "Moving Forward: On Competence in Sustainability Research and Problem Solving." *Environment Magazine* 53, No. 2 (March–April):3–12.

Wiek, Arnim; Xiong, Angela; Brundiers, Katja; and van der Leeuw, Sander. 2014. "Integrating Problem- and Project-Based Learning into Sustainability Programs: A Case Study on the School of Sustainability at Arizona State University." *International Journal of Sustainability in Higher Education* 15 (4):431–449.

Wiek, Arnim; Bernstein, Michael J.; Foley, Rider; Cohen, Matthew; Forrest, Nigel; Kuzdas, Christopher; Kay, Braden; and Keeler, Lauren W. 2016. "Operationalising Competencies in Higher Education for Sustainable Development." In *Routledge Handbook of Higher Education for Sustainable Development*, edited by Matthias Barth, Gerd Michelsen, Marco Rieckmann, and Ian Thomas. London: Routledge. Pp. 241–260.

Williams, Paul. 2002. "The Competent Boundary Spanner." *Public Administration* 80 (1):103–124.

Wooltorton, Sandra; Wilkinson, Anne; Horwitz, Pierre; Bahn, Sue; Redmond, Janice; and Dooley, Julian. 2015. "Sustainability and Action Research in Universities: Towards Knowledge for Organisational Transformation." *International Journal of Sustainability in Higher Education* 16 (4):424–439.

Wright, Tarah S. A. 2002. "Definitions and Frameworks for Environmental Sustainability in Higher Education." *Higher Education Policy* 12 (2):105–120.

Zaglul, Jose; and Sherrard, Daniel. 2005. "Higher Education in Economic Transformation." In *Going for Growth: Science, Technology and Innovation in Africa*, edited by Calestous Juma. London: Smith Institute. Pp. 34–47.

Zimmermann, Friedrich M.; Raggautz, Andreas; Maier, Kathrin; Drage, Thomas; Mader, Marlene; Diethart, Mario; and Meyer, Jonas. 2014. "Quality System Development at the University of Graz: Lessons Learned from the Case of RCE Graz-Styria." In *Sustainable Development and Quality Assurance in Higher Education: Transformation of Learning and Society*, edited by Zinaida Fadeeva, Laima Galkute, Clemens Mader, and Geoff Scott. New York: Palgrave Macmillan. Pp. 131–152.

2

CONTEMPORARY SUSTAINABILITY EXPECTATIONS AND CHALLENGES FOR HIGHER EDUCATION

Sustainable development rests on critical analysis, foresight, capacity, and action. As repositories of skills and knowledge and change-tilted organizations, universities are uniquely positioned to contribute in each of these arenas. Unsurprisingly, therefore, we count on universities to be in the vanguard of long-term, future-directed initiatives like transnational sustainable development (TSD) that address threats to human wellbeing and environmental health.

The universally applicable *2030 Agenda for Sustainable Development* adopted by an unprecedented gathering of heads of state and government in September 2015 calls for "bold and transformative steps which are urgently needed to shift the world onto a sustainable and resilient path."[1] Fully recognizing the interlinkages among and the integrated nature of the three pillars of sustainability – social, economic, and environmental – the 2030 Agenda further identifies seventeen Sustainable Development Goals (SDGs) and 169 targets intended to stimulate action on multiple fronts that are critical for both humanity and the planet as a whole (UN, 2015). In addition, a "revitalized Global Partnership for Sustainable Development" is seen as central to mobilizing the requisite means and realizing the ambitious 2030 Agenda. The 2030 Agenda, then, provides the pivotal forward-looking context for this chapter's treatment of opportunities for university contributions to TSD.

Higher-education institutions around the world are indispensable participants in contemporary global efforts to advance sustainable development. Education – including university-level learning, research, and public outreach – must play a key role if TSD is to be advanced. The eviscerating risks of inaction confront all professional fields (Desha and Hargroves, 2014, p. 3). This chapter highlights the urgent challenges and diverse role expectations surrounding the sustainability agenda that engage universities.

Goal selection

Sustainable development encompasses a wide range of activity, including a multiplicity of efforts aimed at enhancing human health and wellbeing and reducing economic disparities and multiple steps designed to forestall environmental degradation and promote ecological health. Since it is impossible for one individual or a single university to address all dimensions of sustainable development, researchers and educators at different institutions of higher education who possess diverse professional interests are selecting different and even unique goals to pursue. The selection process lacks coordination on a country-wide, no less international, basis.

Broadly speaking, we can identify differences in the sustainable-development goals selected at Northern and Southern higher-education institutions. Southern universities tend to be primarily concerned with addressing economic disparities, while Northern universities are more likely to be concerned with ecological issues. The process also differs, with Northern university selections often faculty-driven and Southern university selections influenced by external forces such as government plans and donor interests. In the United States, for instance, the impetus for moving in the sustainable-development direction is most likely to "emerge from efforts of faculty members or administrators working in isolation or in small-scale collaborations" (Biddle, 2002, p. 40; also Koehn, Bolognese, and Deardorff, 2011). In Europe, the European Commission and various EU grant initiatives are likely to be in the lead. In much of the Global South, transnational partnerships supported by foundation funding are likely to provide the impetus for transforming professional programs.

Contemporary sustainability challenges

Understanding the basic nature of sustainable-development processes and challenges is a prerequisite for conducting useful outcome and impact evaluations. The evaluations launched by higher-education institutions need to build on existing scientific knowledge regarding the behavior and interaction of social, economic, and natural systems as well as system boundaries, components, and their emergent properties (Garcia and Zazueta, 2015).

Universities are positioned to muddle through the critical struggles of our time or to make sustainability a central dimension of informed and future-directed curriculum, research, outreach, and transnational-partnering initiatives (Cullingford, 2004, p. 251). In the long-term interest of sustainable development, the most advantageous option involves identifying, exploring, and learning from "visions of alternative socio-ecological futures and development pathways" with the potential to catalyze transformational outcomes (Weaver, et al., 2007, p. 150).

As Jorgen Randers reminds us, unsustainable ways "cannot be continued indefinitely." The "sustainability revolution" that is needed should lead to a prevailing focus on human (and ecological) wellbeing rather than material consumption

(Randers, 2012, pp. 12–13). In this endeavor, universities must be preoccupied with core issues of sustainability science, including:

- interactions between nature and society
- long-term environment and development directions that include considerations of population and consumption
- factors determining ecosystem and livelihood resilience and vulnerability
- timely warning of tipping-point conditions[2]
- incentive systems that promote moves toward sustainable trajectories
- development of monitoring and evaluation approaches that provide useful guidance for sustainability transitions.[3]

Most fundamentally, "educators are futurists; they must anticipate tomorrow's needs and equip today's students with the necessary skills to meet those needs" (Cushner and Trifonovitch, 1992, p. 300; also Sterling, 2013, p. 28). Some of tomorrow's futures already are emerging; others are nested along more distant horizons. Discerning and addressing uncertain futures calls for integrated and holistic research and learning approaches (Fadeeva and Mochizuki, 2010, p. 254; point 3 of the *People's Sustainability Treaty for Higher Education*, cited in Tilbury, 2013, p. 73). Anthropogenic changes in Earth's biosphere are occurring at a "faster rate than previously experienced in human history" (Berkes, Colding, and Folke, 2003, p. 1). Social-ecological resilience is the key to maintaining current equilibria in the face of rapid and unpredictable changes that carry the potential for costly, catastrophic, and irreversible "flips" into new and less-fulfilling stability domains. Malcolm Gladwell (2000, p. 9) popularized "that one dramatic moment . . . when everything can change all at once" as "the Tipping Point." A resilient social-ecological system "is synonymous with ecological, economic, and social sustainability" (Berkes, Colding, and Folke, 2003, pp. 14–15). Conversely, sustainability is threatened when the resilience of TSD-oriented institutions and natural systems is undermined.

"Wicked" sustainability challenges involve considerable complexity, urgency, and damage potential (Wiek, Withycombe, and Redman, 2011, p. 203). In this chapter, we treat several wicked problems that confront and engage university actors concerned with sustainable development. The discussion is meant to be illustrative since the overriding concern of our book is with evaluation issues.[4]

Population wellbeing in the face of growing inequity

Using a Cultural Futures Delphi technique, a panel of 182 scholars and practitioners from nine countries reached consensus on a dominant trend for the first quarter of the twenty-first century that embodies the interdependence theme and places sustainable development front and center. The international panel agreed that the dominant undesirable, but highly probable, arising development is increasing inequality within and among countries coupled with greater resource scarcity

(Parker, Ninomiya, and Cogan, 1999, pp. 120–124, 137). Others have extended concerns over finite-resource consumption to considerations of intergenerational equity (see Baker, 2016, pp. 48–49).

Overall, there is a poverty-environment TSD nexus based on the fact that poor people tend to depend more directly on environmental services for their livelihoods, as they work in primary production (such as agriculture), use firewood for energy, and rely on natural water sources and wells. Degradation of any of these resources, therefore, affects them immediately. A more controversial position holds that poor people harm the environment as they overexploit natural resources for their immediate needs. Therefore, the argument continues, sustainable development in poor countries demands economic growth that reduces poverty (Dasgupta, et al., 2005; Lufumpa, 2005). Others challenge this view as blaming the victims for environmental degradation. Political-ecology explanations focus more on issues of power and scale, thus producing a more nuanced picture (Blaikie and Muldavin, 2004; Gray and Moseley, 2005).

Anthropogenic pressures on the global environment

Research conducted at organizations such as the Stockholm Resilience Center suggests that anthropogenic pressures on the global environment have already exceeded planetary boundaries in three key dimensions: biosphere integrity, biogeochemical flows, and freshwater use (Rockström, et al., 2009). According to this research, land-system change and climate change are classified in the zone of uncertainty and increasing risk. In this discussion, we opt to treat four cascading threats to sustainable development of concern to Northern and Southern higher-education personnel and students in the new millennium: freshwater scarcity, species distinction, deforestation and fisheries depletion, and climatic change.

Freshwater scarcity

Water is fundamental to life on Earth, and all aspects of social and economic development depend on water (see Desha and Hargroves, 2014, pp. 7, 18). However, according to the UN Fourth World Water Development Report, water is at the center of complex, interdependent relationships:

> All of the activities that drive development also shape important political and economic decisions that influence how water resources are allocated and managed, . . . which often . . . exert substantial impacts on the quantity and quality of the water available, and thus on other development sectors.
>
> (WWDR4, 2012, p. 18)

The Sixth Sustainable Development Goal focuses on ensuring availability and sustainable management of water.[5] However, adequate and clean water is an underlying condition for achieving most of the other SDGs as well.[6] For instance, it will not be possible to achieve the goals of ending hunger and achieving food security,[7] or ensuring sustainable and reliable energy for all, without water.[8]

Water affects all sectors of our existence, most notably our ability to produce food and energy. Yet the world is facing increasing water scarcity, which is not equally distributed amongst people and geographical regions. Virtually all groundwater systems in North Africa and the Middle East are being depleted, and water levels in other large aquifers, such as the Guaraní in South America and the California Central Valley aquifer system, are shrinking (Richey, et al., 2015). Physical water scarcity currently mostly affects countries in the dry zones of the Middle East and North Africa, as well as South Asia and large areas of northern and western China. At the same time, the Colorado River system, on which much of southwestern United States depends on for its water and hydropower, is already in a situation of physical water scarcity. By far the largest number of countries of any region experiencing (especially economic) water stress are in sub-Saharan Africa (WWDR4, 2012).

The World Water Assessment (WWDR4, 2012) estimates that around 1.2 billion people live in areas of physical water scarcity, and another 500 million people are approaching that situation. In addition, 1.6 billion people live in areas facing economic water shortages – i.e., where countries lack the necessary infrastructure to provide their populations with freshwater from rivers and aquifers. Taken together, these conditions affect more than 40 percent of the world's population, and the shortfall figures are on the rise. According to the United Nations, by 2025 there will be 1.8 billion people in countries and regions with absolute water scarcity and two-thirds of the world's population are likely to be living under water-stressed conditions.[9]

It is important to note that water scarcity is both a natural and a human problem. The natural scarcity, which may be further exacerbated by climate change, is compounded by pollution, lack of financing and technologies to make clean water available, and political issues of distribution within and among countries. It is also notable that the water-scarce countries and regions are those where population growth remains highest and where the largest numbers of young people enter the labor force without adequate opportunities for employment. This creates political instability – as is obvious to any observer of the situation in the Middle East – and is a contributing factor to the current migration crisis.

Species extinction

Sustainable development rests in important ways on the maintenance of cultural and biological diversity (see Sachs, 2015, pp. 447–480; Baker, 2016, pp. 33, 209–214; Desha and Hargroves, 2014, pp. 6, 18). We are currently facing an unprecedented crisis in species extinction at a level that has never occurred during the time humans have inhabited the planet. Earth, over its history, has experienced five mass species extinctions prior to the current sixth one. The last of the previous mass species extinctions was 66 million years ago, when an asteroid hit is believed to have wiped out dinosaurs (Kolbert, 2014). Unlike the earlier ones, the current mass extinction is driven by human activities. A recent analysis found that by far the strongest drivers of biodiversity loss are overexploitation and agriculture (Maxwell, et al., 2016). Overexploitation refers to harvesting of species (logging, hunting, fishing, collecting for pet trade) at rates higher than can be compensated for by reproduction or regrowth. The expansion and intensification of agriculture, including livestock farming and aquaculture, has been calculated as imperiling 62 percent of the species listed as threatened or near-threatened in a 2016 study (Maxwell, et al., 2016).

The multidimensional drivers of species extinction "all relate ultimately to the adoption of our growth-orientated, economic development model" (Baker, 2016, pp. 212–214). Biodiversity loss threatens a broad range of ecosystem services and frustrates sustainable-development efforts (Baker, 2016, p. 211). SDG 15[10] highlights broad measures that need to be taken to halt biodiversity loss, including conservation and sustainable management of ecosystems, reducing the degradation of natural habitats, ending poaching and trafficking in endangered species, and preventing the impact of invasive species. SDG 15 further recognizes the close links of biodiversity conservation to economic issues, calling for integration of ecosystem and biodiversity values into national and local planning, development processes, poverty-reduction strategies, and accounts.

Deforestation and fisheries depletion

Deforestation affects the global environment in multiple ways. Deforestation caused by conversion of lands for agriculture, forestry monoculture, settlements, and industry destroys and fragments habitats that consequently become uninhabitable to numerous species. Forest loss also is critical for climate change because forests act as major sinks of atmospheric carbon. The causes of deforestation are again in the human domain and connected to our consumption patterns. Nearly 80 percent of tropical deforestation is estimated to be caused by the production of just three commodities: soy, beef, and palm oil (GEF, 2014). Palm oil has become the most widely used edible oil and a widespread ingredient in many foods, cosmetics, and other products.[11] An FAO (Food and Agriculture Organization) report (2009) concluded that human population growth combined with economic growth and urbanization leading to higher demand for quality food products will require a 70 percent increase in agricultural productivity by 2050. This would involve an additional annual production of 200 million tons of meat, as wealthier consumers in places like China switch to more meat consumption. To arrest negative pressures on the world's forest reserves, SDG 15 explicitly promotes the "implementation of sustainable management of all types of forests, halt deforestation, restore degraded forests and substantially increase afforestation and reforestation globally."[12]

At the same time, three-quarters of the world fisheries are already fully exploited or overexploited, as commercial-fishing fleets harvest the oceans on a global scale. The worst affected by fisheries depletion often are the poorest and most vulnerable people (PEI, 2015). For instance, according to the World Bank, coastal fisheries that provide fish protein and employment to some 60 million people, half of them women, are severely stressed by overfishing.[13] SDG 14[14] recognizes the urgent need to protect fisheries through multiple means, including regulating fish harvesting and overfishing, as well as by preventing marine pollution and sustainably managing and protecting marine and coastal ecosystems. Protecting the world fisheries will be crucial for achieving many of the central goals of *Agenda 2030*, including ending poverty (Goal 1) and ending hunger (Goal 2).

Climatic change

Add climate change to the above challenges, and the picture becomes even more complex and disturbing. Climate change is linked with virtually all sectors and areas of human activity (see, for instance, Smith, et al., 2014; Denton, et al., 2014, pp. 1109, 1112) with potential seriously to impede sustainable development (Denton, et al., 2014). Further, "sustainable development intersects with many of the drivers of climate change, especially regarding energy production and consumption and the ability to mitigate emissions" (Denton, et al., 2014, pp. 1109; also p. 1111).

While historically the current rich countries have generated the most global greenhouse-gas emissions, the situation is changing as predominantly agricultural countries rapidly industrialize and their economies expand. Among other anthropogenic drivers, increasing energy consumption in the dynamic economies of China and India poses a serious threat to future population health and global sustainability (see Koehn, 2016). Thus, "a key to sustainable development is the ability of these developing nations to pursue growth that conserves energy and resources without repeating and exacerbating the errors already committed by the developed nations" (Arima, 2009, p. 4).

SDG 13[15] focuses on climate, emphasizing the need both to combat climate change and to strengthen resilience and adaptive capacity toward its impacts. The frequently used shorthand, global warming, is misleading, as climate change appears to lead to increased variability in weather and differential effects in different geographical areas. The Intergovernmental Panel on Climate Change (IPCC)[16] warns that warming in the high-mountain areas could lead to less snow and ice, which could then affect river flows and, subsequently, further reduce water availability. IPCC further predicts, with high confidence, that increased temperatures will reduce crop yields, including those of maize and wheat – two of the three main crops consumed in the world alongside rice – by shortening the crop cycle. In short, climate-change policy makers confront critically important risks. Addressing climatic change is not only a matter of technological solutions or dealing with greenhouse-gas emissions. Climate change calls for integrated solutions that encompass the social, economic, and political alongside the environmental and technical. Indeed, attaining many of the other SDGs – such as those related to energy,[17] economic growth,[18] industry,[19] and consumption and production[20] – is needed in order to achieve climatic stabilization.

Conclusion

From the above illustrations, it is evident that sustainable development is a transnational imperative that truly encompasses the social, economic, and environmental dimensions. Although we have treated contemporary and future challenges of TSD discretely for the purpose of analysis, cross-sector planning and project integration is essential if universities are to succeed in addressing barriers and promoting drivers of sustainable change.[21] Most sustainable-development contexts require the involvement and empowerment of multiple stakeholders drawn from local experts and community interests (Ospina, 2000, p. 39), governments at all levels, non-profit NGOs, and the for-profit sector (Thabrew, Wiek, and Ries, 2009, p. 68).[22] Consequently, "improving stakeholder participation, coordination, and commitment beyond narrow self-interest is required" (Thabrew, Wiek, and Ries, 2009, p. 67; also Baker, 2016, pp. 52–53).

Given the complexity and continued uncertainty that confronts sustainable development, there is a clear need for continued research – especially interdisciplinary research – to comprehend interlinkages and pathways toward TSD (see Denton, et al., 2014, p. 1124). Universities must play a central role in this endeavor by initiating and conducting relevant and timely transnational research projects and educating students in integrated approaches. Furthermore, it is important that the results of such research and education contribute to sustainable development on the ground through outreach activities that engage societal actors.

Universities can play a key role in advancing TSD through generating new knowledge and understanding, inculcating students in this knowledge, and applying it to real-world situations. By promoting learning, innovation, and adaptive planning (Denton, et al., 2014, pp. 1124–1125), credible evaluation features prominently in this endeavor.

Today's university researchers, teaching faculty, students, and staff are extensively engaged with each of the issues introduced in this chapter and with other sustainable-development challenges in terms of their learning, basic and applied scholarly inquiry, and outreach activities. Just as it is impossible to analyze sustainable-development outcomes and impacts in silos or to address arising challenges through single disciplines and strictly technical fixes, evaluation systems must be comprehensive and integrated. Part II of *Universities and the Sustainable Development Future* explores university-evaluation practice with a focus on TSD undertakings.

Notes

1 See https://sustainabledevelopment.un.org/post2015/transformingourworld (downloaded on 22 September 2016).
2 On tipping points, see Baker (2016, p. 212).
3 Adapted from Table 1 in Disterheft, et al. (2013, p. 8).
4 For a thorough and current companion discussion, consult Baker (2016).
5 Goal 6. Ensure availability and sustainable management of water and sanitation for all.

6 Goal 15. Protect, restore, and promote sustainable use of terrestrial ecosystems, sustainably manage forests, combat desertification, and halt and reverse land degradation and halt biodiversity loss.
7 Goal 2. End hunger, achieve food security and improved nutrition, and promote sustainable agriculture.
8 Goal 7. Ensure access to affordable, reliable, sustainable, and modern energy for all.
9 See www.un.org/waterforlifedecade/scarcity.shtml (accessed 25 September 2016).
10 Goal 15. See endnote 6.
11 See www.worldwildlife.org/industries/palm-oil (accessed 25 September 2016).
12 Goal 15. See endnote 6.
13 See www.worldbank.org/en/topic/environment/brief/oceans (accessed 22 September 2016).
14 Goal 14. Conserve and sustainably use the oceans, seas, and marine resources for sustainable development.
15 Goal 13. Take urgent action to combat climate change and its impacts.
16 See http://unfccc.int/resource/docs/2015/cop21/eng/l09.pdf
17 Goal 7. See endnote 8.
18 Goal 8. Promote sustained, inclusive, and sustainable economic growth, full and productive employment, and decent work for all.
19 Goal 9. Build resilient infrastructure, promote inclusive and sustainable industrialization, and foster innovation.
20 Goal 12. Ensure sustainable consumption and production patterns.
21 Furthermore, although Goal 5 specifically focuses on gender equality and women's empowerment, it seems obvious that all of the other sixteen goals have a gender dimension as well.
22 Thabrew, Wiek, and Ries (2009, pp. 68–69, Figure 1) commend UNEP's Initiative on Capacity Building for Integrated Assessment and Planning for Sustainable Development as an example of an approach that develops collaborative projects involving all cross-sectoral stakeholders in a focal context and provides a post-disaster redevelopment model of an integrated planning and facilitation scenario.

Works cited

Arima, Akito. 2009. "A Plea for More Education for Sustainable Development." *Sustainability Science* 4:3–5.

Baker, Susan. 2016. *Sustainable Development*, 2nd edition. London: Routledge.

Berkes, Fikret; Colding, Johan; and Folke, Carl. 2003. "Introduction." In *Navigating Social-Ecological Systems: Building Resilience for Complexity and Change*, edited by Fikret Berkes, Johan Colding, and Carl Folke. Cambridge: Cambridge University Press. Pp. 1–25.

Biddle, Sheila. 2002. *Internationalization: Rhetoric or Reality?* New York: American Council of Learned Societies.

Blaikie, Piers M.; and Muldavin, Joshua S. S. 2004. "Upstream, Downstream, China, India: The Politics of Environment in the Himalayan Region." *Annals of the Association of American Geographers* 94 (3):520–548.

Cullingford, Cedric. 2004. "Conclusion: The Future: Is Sustainability Sustainable?" In *The Sustainability Curriculum: Facing the Challenge in Higher Education*, edited by John Blewitt and Cedric Cullingford. London: Earthscan. Pp. 245–252.

Cushner, Kenneth; and Trifonovitch, Gregory. 1992. "Understanding Misunderstanding: Barriers to Dealing with Diversity." In *Multicultural Education: A Global Approach*, edited by Don Bragaw and W. Scott Thomson. New York: American Forum for Global Education. Pp. 300–306.

Dasgupta, Susmita; Deichmann, Uwe; Meisner, Craig; and Wheeler, David. 2005. "Where Is the Poverty-Environment Nexus? Evidence from Cambodia, Lao PDR, and Vietnam." *World Development* 33 (4):617–638.

Denton, Fatima; Wilbanks, Thomas J.; Abeysinghe, Achala C.; Burton, Ian; Gao, Qingzhu; Lemos, Maria C.; Masui, Toshihiko; O'Brien, Karen L.; and Warner, Koko. 2014. "Climate-Resilient Pathways: Adaptation, Mitigation, and Sustainable Development." In *Climate Change 2014: Impacts, Adaptation, and Vulnerability. Part A: Global and Sectoral Aspects: Contribution of Working Group II to the Fifth Assessment Report of the Intergovernmental Panel on Climate Change*, edited by Christopher B. Field and Vincente R. Barros. Cambridge: Cambridge University Press. Pp. 1101–1131.

Desha, Cheryl; and Hargroves, Karlson C. 2014. *Higher Education and Sustainable Development: A Model for Curriculum Renewal*. London: Routledge.

Disterheft, Antje; Caeiro, Sandra; Azeiteiro, Ulisses M.; and Filho, Walter L. 2013. "Sustainability Science and Education for Sustainable Development in Universities: A Way for Transition." In *Sustainability Assessment Tools in Higher Education Institutions: Mapping Trends and Good Practices around the World*, edited by Sandra Caeiro, Walter L. Filho, Charbel Jabbour, and Ulisses M. Azeiteiro. Cham, Switzerland: Springer International Publishing. Pp. 3–27.

Fadeeva, Zinaida; and Mochizuki, Yoko. 2010. "Higher Education for Today and Tomorrow: University Appraisal for Diversity, Innovation and Change towards Sustainable Development." *Sustainability Science* 5:249–256.

Food and Agriculture Organization (FAO). 2009. *How to Feed the World in 2050*. Rome: U.N. Food and Agriculture Organization.

Garcia, J. R.; and Zazueta, Aaron. 2015. "Going beyond Mixed Methods to Mixed Approaches: A Systems Perspective for Asking the Right Questions." *IDS Bulletin* 46 (1):30–43.

Gladwell, Malcolm. 2000. *The Tipping Point: How Little Things Can Make a Big Difference*. Boston: Little, Brown and Company.

Global Environmental Facility (GEF). 2014. *Taking Tropical Deforestation Out of Commodity Supply Chains*. Washington, DC: Global Environment Facility.

Gray, Leslie C.; and Moseley, William G. 2005. "A Geographical Perspective on Poverty-Environment Interactions." *The Geographical Journal* 171 (1):9–23.

Koehn, Peter H. 2016. *China Confronts Climate Change: A Bottom-Up Perspective*. New York: Routledge.

Koehn, Peter H.; Bolognese, Kerry D.; and Deardorff, Darla K. 2011. "Enhancing International Research and Development-Project Activity on University Campuses: Insights from U.S. Senior International Officers." *Journal of Studies in International Education* 15, No. 4 (September):332–350.

Kolbert, Elizabeth. 2014. *The Sixth Extinction: An Unnatural History*. New York: Henry Holt and Company.

Lufumpa, C. L. 2005. "The Poverty-Environment Nexus in Africa." *African Development Review* 17 (3):366–381.

Maxwell, Sean I.; Fuller, Richard A.; Brooks, Thomas M.; and Watson, James E. M. 2016. "The Ravages of Guns, Nets and Bulldozers." *Nature* Comment 11 August 536:143–145.

Ospina, Gustavo L. 2000. "Education for Sustainable Development: A Local and International Challenge." *Prospects* 30 (1):31–40.

Parker, Walter C.; Ninomiya, Akira; and Cogan, John. 1999. "Educating World Citizens: Toward Multinational Curriculum Development." *American Educational Research Journal* 36, No. 2 (Summer):117–145.

Poverty-Environment Initiative (PEI). 2015. *Mainstreaming Environment and Climate for Poverty Reduction and Sustainable Development: A Handbook to Strengthen Planning and Budgeting Processes.* New York and Nairobi: UNDP-UNEP Poverty-Environment Initiative.

Randers, Jorgen. 2012. *2052: A Global Forecast for the Next Forty Years.* White River Junction, VT: Chelsea Green Publishing.

Richey, Alexandra S.; Thomas, Brian F.; Lo, Min-Hui; Famiglietti, James S.; Swenson, Sean; and Rodell, Matthew. 2015. "Uncertainty in Global Groundwater Storage Estimates in a Total Groundwater Stress Framework." *Water Resources Research* 51 (7):5198–5216.

Rockström, Johan; Steffen, Will; Noone, Kevin; Person, Åsa; Chapin, F. Stuart, III; Lambin, Eric; Lenton, Timothy M.; Scheffer, Marten; Folke, Carl; Schelinhuber, Hans Joachim; Nykvist, Björn; De Wit, Cynthia A.; Hughes, Terry; Van der Leeuw, Sander; Rodhe, Henning; Sörlin, Sverker; Snyder, Peter K.; Costanza, Robert; Svedin, Uno; Falkenmark, Malin; Karlberg, Louise; Corell, Robert W.; Fabry, Victoria J.; Hansen, James; Walker, Brian; Liverman, Diana; Richardson, Katherine; Crutzen, Paul; and Foley, Jonathan. 2009. "Planetary Boundaries: Exploring the Safe Operating Space for Humanity." *Ecology and Society* 14 (2):Art. 32.

Sachs, Jeffrey D. 2015. *The Age of Sustainable Development.* New York: Columbia University Press.

Smith, Kirk R.; Woodward, Alistair; Campbell-Lendrum, Diarmid; Chadee, Dave D.; Honda, Yasushi; Liu, Qiyong; Olwoch, Jane M.; Revich, Boris; and Sauerborn, Rainer. 2014. "Human Health: Impacts, Adaptation, and Co-Benefits." In *Climate Change 2014: Impacts, Adaptation, and Vulnerability. Part A: Global and Sectoral Aspects: Contribution of Working Group II to the Fifth Assessment Report of the Intergovernmental Panel on Climate Change,* edited by Christopher B. Field and Vincente R. Barros. Cambridge: Cambridge University Press. Pp. 709–754.

Sterling, Stephen. 2013. "The Sustainable University: Challenge and Response." In *The Sustainable University: Progress and Prospects,* edited by Stephen Sterling, Larch Maxey, and Heather Luna. London: Routledge. Pp. 17–50.

Thabrew, Lanka; Wiek, Arnim; and Ries, Robert. 2009. "Environmental Decision Making in Multi-Stakeholder Contexts: Applicability of Life Cycle Thinking in Development Planning and Implementation." *Journal of Cleaner Production* 17:67–76.

Tilbury, Daniella. 2013. "Another World Is Desirable: A Global Rebooting of Higher Education for Sustainable Development." In *The Sustainable University: Progress and Prospects,* edited by Stephen Sterling, Larch Maxey, and Heather Luna. London: Routledge. Pp. 71–85.

United Nations. 2015. *Transforming Our World: The 2030 Agenda for Sustainable Development.* A/RES/70/1. New York: United Nations.

Weaver, Paul; Rotmans, Jan; Turnpenny, John; Haxeltine, Alex; and Jordan, Andrew. 2007. "Methods and Tools for Integrated Sustainability Assessment (MATISSE): A New European Project." In *Impact Assessment and Sustainable Development: European Practice and Experience,* edited by Clive George and Colin Kirkpatrick. Cheltenham, UK: Edward Elgar. Pp. 149–163.

Wiek, Arnim; Withycombe, Lauren; and Redman, Charles L. 2011. "Key Competencies in Sustainability: A Reference Framework for Academic Program Development." *Sustainability Science* 6:203–218.

World Water Assessment (WWDR4). 2012. *Managing Water under Uncertainty and Risk: The United Nations World Water Development Report 4.* Paris: UNESCO.

PART II

Universities and sustainable-development evaluations

3

A REVIEW OF HIGHER-EDUCATION SUSTAINABLE-DEVELOPMENT-EVALUATION PRACTICES

Evaluations of various kinds and quality are an increasing preoccupation of higher-education institutions around the world. This chapter traces university-evaluation practices beginning with a generic overview. Our principal interest in *Universities and the Sustainable Development Future* is with evaluations that specifically address sustainable-development activity at post-secondary institutions. In Chapter 3, therefore, we also introduce university sustainable-development evaluation in the North and South. The ensuing chapter critically reviews existing university approaches to sustainable-development evaluation, introduces lessons from international-development evaluative experience, and proposes pathways to improvement.

The diverse landscape of evaluations of university work

When university activities are subject to review, the contemporary landscape is characterized by considerable diversity, ranging from assessment to full-fledged evaluation. Elements of diversity involve differing national policies, variation in the types of activities subject to evaluation by different actors, and multiple methods and purposes of analysis. In this landscape review, we use evaluation as the umbrella concept that incorporates assessment and accreditation.[1]

Assessment, assessment, assessment

Assessment is a learning process devoted to uncovering the current state of affairs in order to detect the presence or absence of progress by institutions of higher education in attaining identified goals that can involve any and all activities undertaken at universities. According to the National Academy for Academic Leadership (NAAL, n.d., p. 1), "assessment provides faculty members, administrators, trustees, and others with evidence, numerical or otherwise, from which they can develop useful information about their students, institutions, programs, and courses and also about themselves." Inputs, processes, and outputs are the principal interconnected subjects of higher-education assessments (NAAL, n.d., p. 2). The dominant discourse surrounding assessment is connected to "measurement and certification" rather than to long-term, sustainable, and impactful learning (Boud, 2007, p. 17).

Among US universities, "practically everybody assesses somebody else" (Astin, 1993, p. 1). The contemporary preoccupation of universities with assessments is driven by a number of forces. Faculty and students are concerned about learners' progress.[2] Government and private funders seek accountability for their contributions (see, for instance, Astin, 1993, p. 217). Boards and trustees share responsibility for maintaining and advancing institutional standing. Parents and prospective students are interested in ascertaining the relative "value" of colleges and universities and in comparative performance data. Accrediting organizations are concerned with learning outcomes. Managers are charged with undertaking cost-benefit analyses. Administrators are eager to demonstrate success to external and internal constituents (see Nelson, 2014, p. 1). In the words of the National Academy for Academic Leadership (n.d., p. 1), "the ability to engage in high-quality assessment has become a sine qua non for the college-level educator." In less glowing terms, Christopher Nelson (2014, p. 1), President of St. John's College (Annapolis), calls attention to the "feeding frenzy surrounding the issue of assessment."

Quality assessment "focuses on both accountability and improvement, providing information and judgements (not rankings) through an agreed upon and consistent process and well-established criteria" (Fadeeva, et al., 2014, p. 2). Quality can be measured according to inputs, process, and/or outputs; the principal output considerations are student-learning attainments – that is, the quality of graduates (Schwarz and Westerheijden, 2007a, pp. 19, 27). The forty-seven countries participating in the European Higher Education Area (EHEA) work with standards and guidelines for internal and external quality assurance that are linked to individually selected priorities and management approaches in the areas of teaching, research, and community engagement (Fadeeva, et al., 2014, p. 16).[3] However, a focus on sustainability has not yet become a guiding principal of university quality-assessment reporting (Mader, 2014, p. 78).

Assessment critiques

Higher-education assessments often are the subject of vigorous critiques based on methodological weaknesses, claims of hyperfactualization, preoccupation with curricular standardization,[4] reports focused on trivial issues (Mader, 2014, p. 78), an emphasis on test preparation rather than critical thinking and creativity (Kopnina and Meijers, 2012, p. 192), and conviction among many faculty members that any rewards generated pale in comparison with the required investments of time and effort (Roorda and Martens, 2008, p. 52; Pontuso and Thornton, 2008).[5] The workload imposed by accreditors often is perceived as overwhelming

(Schwarz and Westerheijden, 2007b, p. x), and the emphasis has been on compliance rather than innovation (Desha and Hargroves, 2014, p. 14).

Christopher Nelson (2014, pp. 1–2) further maintains that "current assessment models habitually and almost obsessively understate the responsibility of the student for his or her own learning and . . . overstate the responsibility of the teacher" (also see Boud, 2007, p. 17).[6] He concludes (pp. 2–3) that universities would be better off "repurposing" the considerable resources they dedicate to assessment toward reducing the number of large lecture classes that retard "true learning" through personal development.

Disparities in geographical coverage also characterize the overall pattern of assessments. In their review of published literature on higher education and sustainable development, Matthias Barth and Marco Rieckmann (2016, p. 104) found that a majority of articles report on research involving Europe, with only a handful treating African contexts.

Accreditation

The accreditation process aims to recognize quality post-secondary programs and institutions based on externally agreed-upon standards. Through periodic investigations and reviews, an independent supra-institutional accrediting body attests to the qualifications and value of the people, programs, degrees, and operations of particular universities and presents suggestions (even mandates) for improvement. In most counties, the institutional-accreditation process involves site visits conducted by agency-selected teams composed of administrators and faculty members from other universities that assess self-evaluation studies and feed reports into the agency's final accreditation decision. Institutional-accreditation criteria generally surround issues of university resources, curricular integrity, research output, and quality-assurance processes (Schwarz and Westerheijden, 2007a, pp. 21–22, 26–27). In the end, universities awarded "accredited" status are distinguished from those that fail to satisfy the accrediting body's standards. Unlike evaluation, therefore, accreditation results in "a formal summary judgement that leads to formal approval regarding the respective institution, degree type and/or programme" (Schwarz and Westerheijden, 2007b, p. x; Schwarz and Westerheijden, 2007a, pp. 2–3) that can carry profound consequences and remain in effect for the following five to ten years (see, for instance, Schwarz and Westerheijden, 2007a, p. 25). In this regard, therefore, accreditation more closely resembles performance auditing than it does evaluation.[7]

In the United States, seven private, non-profit, regionally focused agencies approved by the US Department of Education are responsible for accrediting colleges and universities.[8] Among these supra-institutional bodies, the Northwest Commission on Colleges and Universities is unique in that the scope of its review explicitly addresses "adaptability and sustainability" (standard 5).[9] The Disciplinary Associations Network for Sustainability (DANS) serves as an additional lever of curricula transformation. DANS focuses on "infusing sustainability into curricula in all academic disciplines," "creating standards (including tenure, promotion, and accreditation criteria," and "informing policy makers" (Rowe and Johnston, 2013, p. 50).

The management of accreditation has shifted from direct government control to non-governmental accrediting organizations in most European countries (Schwarz and Westerheijden, 2007b, p. ix; Schwarz and Westerheijden, 2007a, pp. 21–22; Välimaa, 2007, pp. 110, 120). In the Global South, most accrediting bodies are government organizations, including ministries of education.[10] In a few instances, professional bodies participate in transnational-certification processes. For instance, the Council on Health Research for Development (COHRED)'s *Fairness Index* for transnational partnerships includes a certification mechanism with guidelines, indicators, a measurement process, and a reporting system aimed at encouraging best collaborative practices, aligning mutual interests among partners, enhancing capacity in the South, and reducing inequities in the interest of stimulating socio-economic development (Musolino, et al., 2015).

Professional-accreditation agencies cover units and programs in their specific field when their stamp of approval is voluntarily sought by a university (Schwarz and Westerheijden, 2007a, p. 9). In the United States, professional-accreditation agencies exist for the fields of medicine, law, nursing, engineering, business and accounting, social work, teacher education, and public administration (Schwarz and Westerheijden, 2007a, pp. 25–26). Criteria and standards for accreditation primarily are shaped by the profession (Schwarz and Westerheijden, 2007a, p. 26).[11] Increasingly, the learning objectives and assessment criteria established by professional schools and associations and the standards insisted on by accrediting bodies encompass international- and intercultural-competency considerations (Biddle, 2002, p. 51; Koehn and Rosenau, 2010, p. xix; Rubaii and Calarusse, 2012, p. 235). The parallel demands of university-wide and professional-accreditation bodies contribute to reports of excessive and expensive evaluation burdens and "evaluation fatigue" (Schwarz and Westerheijden, 2007a, pp. 16, 27).

Cheryl Desha and Charlie Hargroves (2014, pp. 14, 61) envision program-accrediting agencies as potent drivers of education for sustainable development and find evidence of changing attitudes regarding the role of proactive accreditation in the engineering profession.[12] For instance, the UK Royal Academy of Engineering (RAE) "promotes sustainable development through a published set of twelve 'Guiding Principles' for engineering for sustainable development . . . and the importance of accreditation as a driver for curriculum renewal [and embedded competency expectations] is also reflected in . . . Australia and the United States" (Desha and Hargroves, 2014, p. 15).[13] In the absence of government mandates, these authors foresee a growing leadership role for accreditation agencies in nudging higher-education institutions to adopt outcome-based approaches to education for sustainable development through more rigorous requirements (Desha and Hargroves, 2014, pp. 14, 61). For Desha and Hargroves, the challenges to sustainable development explored in Chapter 2 mandate the rapid graduation of prepared professionals who can engage competently with current practitioners and decision makers. The available window for attaining gradual and sustained reductions in unsustainable global trajectories (given standard curriculum-renewal timeframes, the considerable time lag between accreditation reporting and actual curriculum change, and normal entry time into key decision-making roles) means that this "will be largely a postgraduate and professional development challenge" (Desha and Hargroves, 2014, pp. 18, 23–24, 41, 61, 85).[14]

University sustainable-development evaluations

Of primary interest in this book is the conduct of higher education's sustainable-development evaluations. Beyond the higher-education context, international agencies and NGOs have launched new evaluation tools that address system-wide effects, including the Environmental Sustainability Index and the Living Planet Index (see Hales and Prescott-Allen, 2002, pp. 40, 42–43).[15] Among these evaluation methods, the Ecological Footprint is particularly useful when dealing with university operations (see, for instance, Simon and Haertle, 2014), and the Wellbeing Assessment has potential applicability that will be adapted in connection with comprehensive outreach evaluations (Chapter 8).

There is a voluminous literature dealing with education-for-sustainable-development evaluation. In their seminal work on the subject, Niko Roorda and Pim Martens (2008, pp. 41–42) identify internal and external motivations for evaluating education for sustainable development. Internal evaluations can enhance awareness of, interest in, and support for issues related to curricula, operations, research, and outreach. Externally, evaluation results can promote applied learning and provide accessibility and transparency for funders and other stakeholders (see Bakkes, 2012, p. 252; Stevens, 2012, p. 62).[16] Indeed, much like other higher-education evaluations, sustainable-development evaluations now engage key stakeholders in the process. Early and optimized engagement helps to ensure that evaluations meet stakeholder needs (Bakkes, 2012, pp. 254–256) and that identified improvements are "situated, feasible, relevant . . . , context-specific" (Fadeeva, et al., 2014, p. 6), and acceptable (Stevens, 2012, p. 63).

Sustainable-development evaluations pay special attention to *why and how* results are attained or fail to be realized and *why and how* transformations of curricula, research, and outreach initiatives occur or do not occur. Evaluations are viewed as a process aimed at improvements rather than control (Välimaa, 2007, p. 108).

Integration with quality-management initiatives

Roorda and Martens (2008, pp. 41–42) maintain that integrating education for sustainable development in university quality-management initiatives is needed to ensure mainstreaming of sustainable development in higher-education institutions.[17] Oliver Vettori and Christian Rammel (2014, pp. 51, 56; also Rammel, Velazquez, and Mader, 2016, p. 331) further envision that "sustainable development can be viewed as an operational quality goal, but also as an objective and key value for the development of the institutional quality culture itself."[18] Fadeeva and colleagues (2014, pp. 1, 20) propose linking quality-assurance systems that address fitness of purpose ("what most counts for the sustainable future of our world") and fitness for transformation with sustainable-development objectives in order to facilitate the kinds of institutional transformations that advocates envision.

A participative quality-culture approach can leverage cross-sectional curricula, research, operations, and community-engagement transformations. This innovative approach to evaluation of university sustainable-development activity is built on stakeholder responsibility for specific sustainability initiatives as a quality issue (Vettori and Rammel, 2014, pp. 58–60); utilizes quality-culture concepts and sustainability principles as evaluative tools for reflection on institutional values,[19] processes, and practices (Vettori and Rammel, 2014, pp. 58–59; Rammel, Velazquez, and Mader, 2016, pp. 333–334), and requires "a profoundly different attitude to assessment that focuses not only on superimposed targets but is also helpful for [continuous] improvement of higher education practices as a social [collective] learning to change process" (Fadeeva, et al., 2014, p. 20).

Instruments specifically designed for assessing university sustainability activity

In recent years, evaluation proponents have developed assessment instruments specifically designed for university sustainability activity. Some of these approaches are introduced here. Promising components are woven into Part III of the book.

North American universities[20] favor participation in the Association for the Advancement of Sustainability in Higher Education's (AASHE) STARS (Sustainability Tracking and Rating System) launched in 2009 in response to a call by the Higher Education Associations Sustainability Consortium (HEASC), a network of mainstream higher-education associations, for development of a standardized-assessment tool (Urbanski and Rowland, 2014, pp. 154, 156; Rowe and Hiser, 2016, p. 320).[21] STARS evaluations are based on self-reports[22] that cover operations, curricula, research, community engagement, innovation, and governance (Vaughter, et al., 2013, pp. 2261, 2263; Urbanski and Rowland, 2014, p. 155) and address the economic, social, ecological, and health dimensions of sustainable development (Urbanski and Rowland, 2014, p. 154).[23] University-operations outputs tend to be of particular interest in STARS reporting (Vaughter, et al., 2013, p. 2263). Participating institutions receive a rating of bronze, silver, gold, or platinum. In 2015, Colorado State University became the first and only campus to record the highest possible (platinum) STARS rating (Ciaravola, 2015).

The Alternative University Appraisal (AUA) scheme launched in 2009 by members of ProSPER.Net (Promotion of Sustainability in Postgraduate Education and Research Network) is preferred by higher-education institutions in the Asia-Pacific region.[24] AUA is a self-reflection or peer-consultation scheme with emphasis on transformation, institutional empowerment, and outreach (Rammel, Velazquez, and Mader, 2016, p. 339; Gapor, et al., 2014, p. 257). AUA focuses on rating universities through surveys, dialogue, and stakeholder consensus rather than on rankings (Gapor, et al., 2014, pp. 256–257, 259; Razak, et al., 2013, pp. 146, 151). Its ultimate goal is to create a "dynamic community" that would share best practices[25] and mainstream sustainable development in higher education (Razak, et al., 2013, pp. 139, 146–148). Education, research, outreach, and governance constitute the focal dimensions of AUA assessments (Gapor, et al., 2014, p. 257).[26]

The Assessment Instrument for Sustainability in Higher Education (AISHE) developed in the Netherlands is widely used across Europe[27] to evaluate the extent to which sustainability has been incorporated in curricula, research, community outreach, and governance (Vaughter, et al., 2013, p. 2263).[28] Nico Roorda and Pim Martens (2008, p. 42) note the emphasis on learning assessment found in AISHE. A later, expanded version (AISHE 2.0) "consists of five modules, each with six indicators" assessed by consensus among all participants (discipline professionals, faculty members, students, and administrators) on a five-point ordinal scale (Roorda, 2013, p. 113). Higher stages of attainment are reached as education for sustainable development becomes systematically integrated into the organizational fabric, actively involves partners and stakeholders, and is linked with society (see Roorda, 2013, p. 115; Boer, 2013, p. 127; Rammel, Velazquez, and Mader, 2016, p. 339). AISHE audits involve (1) self-evaluations arising from consensus deliberations among AISHE auditors and a representative team from the university and (2) review of relevant documents to confirm that the consensus reached is verified (Boer, 2013, pp. 127–128). In the case of AISHE, internationally recognized certification using an expanded five-star system corresponding to the development stage reached (Boer, 2013, p. 129) has been effective in motivating increased integration of sustainable development at participating universities (Roorda and Martens, 2008, p. 48).

Stakeholders for university sustainable-development evaluations

A diverse set of stakeholders possess interest in knowing whether higher-education initiatives are making a difference in contributing toward sustainable development. Participatory-evaluation processes that ensure inclusion of measures of interest and importance to stakeholders and their weighting preferences are appreciated in this connection (see Salter, Robinson, and Wiek, 2010; Grafakos, Zevgolis, and Oikonomou, 2012, p. 193; Desha and Hargroves, 2014, p. 160). Lanka Thabrew, Arnim Wiek, and Robert Ries (2009, p. 68) explain that "given the need for cross-sectoral integrated planning, multi-stakeholder participation is expanding and becoming more complex in collaborative joint projects. . . . Participatory decision making encourages stakeholders to identify joint projects, contributions by different stakeholders, outcomes, and strategies for implementation."

In addition to the complex cast of multiple stakeholders encountered by international-development practitioners, Northern and Southern higher-education undertakings engage their own set of parties with sustainable-development-evaluation interests. Among the internal and the external university-linked stakeholders are individuals and boards responsible for university governance, organizations that manage the sustainability-assessment schemes discussed above, and potential employers (Desha and Hargroves, 2014, pp. 146, 159). University students are both concerned stakeholders and shapers of internal and external perceptions.[29]

Institutions in the South and North that are signatories to the Commitment to Sustainable Practices of Higher Education Institutions at Rio+20 (see Simon and Haertle, 2014) and to the Higher Education Sustainable Initiative (HESI) – follow-up to the Rio+20 Conference – are committed to improving their sustainability performance. UNEP's Platform for Sustainability Performance in Education[30] provides guidance on the assessment process and a list of useful sustainability-assessment tools (Mader, 2014, p. 68). HESI participants record sustainability plans and submit voluntary commitments to the Rio+20 registry (Simon and Haertle, 2014). Their stakeholders – including various international agencies, UN member states, and international NGOs (Simon and Haertle, 2014) – possess special interest in sustainable-development evaluations.

The overall higher-education track record of translating high-level commitments to sustainable-development objectives set forth in signed declarations into institutional transformation and meaningful action has not been impressive (Bekessy, Samson, and Clarkson, 2007, p. 302). Accountability for follow-through must be strengthened. Rewards for implementation and penalties for inaction need to be forthcoming (Bekessy, Samson, and Clarkson, 2007, p. 314). Institutional and program accreditations offer a nascent means of bringing about the requisite changes. Comprehensive evaluations accompanied by local, national, and international scrutiny (Bekessy, Samson, and Clarkson, 2007, p. 315) provide a more promising pathway to university accountability.

Notes

1 In contrast, Schwarz and Westerheijden (2007a, p. 3) use quality assurance "as an umbrella term, denoting accreditation and evaluation systems together."
2 For thoughtful recommendations on developing assessment skills for student learning, see Boud and Falchikov (2007, pp. 187–194); on self-assessment that engages life-long learning, see Tan (2007).
3 The European Network of Quality Assessment Agencies (ENQA) is composed of professional quality-assurance experts (Schwarz and Westerheijden, 2007a, p. 6).
4 Delese Wear and Julie Aultman (2006, p. vii) critique the "fixation with assessment" and the "constant surveillance for evidence or lack of professionalism" that characterizes the "audit culture" of contemporary academic medicine. They warn that "the richness, complexity, and contradictions of professionalism in medicine are being flattened into categorical attitudes or behaviors that evaluators (whose professionalism is rarely assessed) can check."
5 According to one outspoken faculty member (Snider, 2015, p. 5), "many administrative tasks are simply not worth completing. Outcomes assessment is nothing more than white collar featherbedding. It has no intellectual value and should be discontinued."
6 For a critique of student-assessment practices and recommendations for improvement, see Astin (1993).

7 Schwarz and Westerheijden (2007b, p. x) point out, however, that "accreditation 'borrows' so many methods from its 'older brother' evaluation, that the two sometimes seem so similar."

8 For a current list of accredited US colleges and universities, consult www.ope.ed.gov/accreditation/Database of accredited post-secondary institutions and programs
The Council for Higher Education Accreditation (CHEA) functions as the umbrella body for US accreditation organizations (Schwarz and Westerheijden, 2007a, p. 26).

9 See www.nwccu.org; click on standards and policies (accessed 19 April 2016).

10 See the Council for Higher Education Accreditation (CHEA)'s *International Directory* of more than 450 accreditation organizations (www.cheainternational.org/intdb/international_directory.asp). Uganda's accreditation agency is the National Council for Higher Education (NCHE) (Andama and Suubi, 2015, p. 134).

11 William Sullivan (2005, p. 4) points out that "in exchange for the privilege of setting standards for admission and authorizing practice, professions are legally obligated to maintain standards, even to discipline their own ranks, for the public welfare."

12 In accounting education, the American Institute of Certified Public Accountants (AICPA) has helped develop sustainability-accounting and CSR guidelines (Sileshi, 2016, pp. 165, 194–195).

13 The Engineering Council of the United Kingdom also recommends that engineering education incorporate specific sustainable-development principles (Desha and Hargroves, 2014, p. 60).

14 Desha and Hargroves (2014, p. 24) estimate the time lag from entry in a post-graduate program to arrival in key sustainability decision-making positions at eight to twelve years "depending on the pace and effectiveness of curriculum renewal efforts."

15 On the other hand, many World Bank project evaluations in the education sector have been diminished by the selection of inappropriate indicators and inadequate attention to substantiation of impacts and outcomes (Chapman and Moore, 2010, pp. 560, 562). For instance, "only one in five World Bank project evaluations had learning outcomes as an explicit objective" (Chapman and Moore, 2010, p. 560). Indeed, Samoff and Carrol (2006, p. 147) maintain that learning is "a frustratingly elusive concept" for economists and finance experts that often is "dimly perceived [as an outcome measure] in World Bank projects."

16 Our framework for TSD evaluations (Part III) encompasses both internal and external evaluators.

17 See the quality-management system based on sustainability introduced at the University of Graz (Zimmermann, et al., 2014, pp. 137–140, 143, 148).

18 They add that many quality-assurance efforts lack the "clearly defined purpose" that sustainability can provide and currently are perceived as an "externally imposed burden" (Vettori and Rammel, 2014, pp. 51, 53).

19 Values and ethics are important components of sustainable-development education because "behavior driven by an internal ethical motivation will have a wider and more lasting impact than behavior imposed by laws or regulations" (Dahl, 2014, p. 193).

20 STARS 2.0, released in 2013, "is expected to improve applicability of STARS to higher education institutions outside of the US and Canada" (Urbanski and Rowland, 2014, p. 155).

21 According to Ciaravola (2015), STARS is used at "nearly 700 universities and colleges on six continents across the globe." Urbanski and Rowland (2014, pp. 155, 160–168) report that more than three hundred institutions sought STARS rating by 2014; of these, 51 percent had attained a silver rating. Sustainability literacy and greenhouse-gas emissions reductions were among the lowest-scoring subcategories.

22 Aisling Tierney, Hannah Tweddell, and Chris Willmore (2015, p. 512) maintain that self-assessments that rely on existing systems are "more likely to embed ESD than utilizing external instruments that are viewed as 'add on,' not part of the internal structure academics work with."

23 In a parallel US community-college development, the American Association of Community Colleges (AACC) "produced the Green Genome (2012) self assessment tool and the new Climate Resiliency Guide (2014). Both frameworks stress the importance of community-based learning and stakeholder engagement" (Rowe and Hiser, 2016, p. 320).
24 Hokkaido University serves as the AUA secretariat (Razak, et al., 2013, p. 147).
25 On identifying "best" or "promising" practices, see Poister, Aristigueta, and Hall (2015, pp. 400–401).
26 AUA assessment subthemes, drawn from the DESD, include gender equality, health promotion, environment, cultural diversity, rural development, human security, and sustainable consumption (Razak, et al., 2013, p. 149).
27 Some UK higher-education institutions use the LiFE (Learning in Future Environments) index (see www.thelifeindex.org.uk).
28 AISHE certifications result in attainment of one of four "star" levels (Roorda and Martens, 2008, pp. 47–48).
29 On the impact of student projects on stakeholder visions and strategies resulting from the project-based Oberlin Project, see Daneri, Trencher, and Petersen (2015, pp. 14, 17, 19).
30 See www.eauc.org.uk/theplatform/home

Works cited

Andama, Edward; and Suubi, Ujeyo M. S. 2015. "Mainstreaming Education for Sustainable Development in Teacher Education at Busitema University, Uganda." In *Mainstreaming Environment and Sustainability in African Universities: Stories of Change*, edited by Heila Lotz-Sisitka, Gitile Naituli, Amanda Hlengwa, Mike Ward, Ayobami Salami, Akpezi Ogbuigwe, Mahesh Pradhan, Marie Neeser, and Sanne Lauriks. Grahamstown: Rhodes University Environmental Learning Research Centre. Pp. 127–134.

Astin, Alexander W. 1993. *Assessment for Excellence: The Philosophy and Practice of Assessment and Evaluation in Higher Education*. American Council on Education Series on Higher Education. Phoenix, AZ: ORYX Press.

Bakkes, Jan. 2012. "Bellagio Sustainability Assessment and Measurement Principles (BellagioSTAMP): Significance and Examples from International Environmental Outlooks." In *Sustainable Development, Evaluation and Policy-Making: Theory, Practise and Quality Assurance*, edited by Anneke von Raggamby and Frieder Rubik. Cheltenham, UK: Edward Elgar. Pp. 241–260.

Barth, Matthias; and Rieckmann, Marco. 2016. "State of the Art in Research on Higher Education for Sustainable Development." In *Routledge Handbook of Higher Education for Sustainable Development*, edited by Matthias Barth, Gerd Michelsen, Marco Rieckmann, and Ian Thomas. London: Routledge. Pp. 100–133.

Bekessy, S. A.; Samson, K.; and Clarkson, R. E. 2007. "The Failure of Non-Binding Declarations to Achieve University Sustainability: A Need for Accountability." *International Journal of Sustainability in Higher Education* 8 (3):301–316.

Biddle, Sheila. 2002. *Internationalization: Rhetoric or Reality?* New York: American Council of Learned Societies.

Boer, Pieternel. 2013. "Assessing Sustainability and Social Responsibility in Higher Education Assessment Frameworks Explained." In *Sustainability Assessment Tools in Higher Education Institutions: Mapping Trends and Good Practices around the World*, edited by Sandra Caeiro, Walter L. Filho, Charbel Jabbour, and Ulisses M. Azeiteiro. Cham, Switzerland: Springer International Publishing. Pp. 121–137.

Boud, David. 2007. "Reframing Assessment as If Learning Were Important." In *Rethinking Assessment in Higher Education: Learning for the Longer Term*, edited by David Boud and Nancy Falchikov. London: Routledge. Pp. 14–25.

Boud, David; and Falchikov, Nancy. 2007. "Developing Assessment for Informing Judgement." In *Rethinking Assessment in Higher Education: Learning for the Longer Term*, edited by David Boud and Nancy Falchikov. London: Routledge. Pp. 181–197.

Chapman, David W.; and Moore, Audrey S. 2010. "A Meta-Look at Meta-Studies of the Effectiveness of Development Assistance to Education." *International Review of Education* 56:547–565.

Ciaravola, Dell Rae. 2015. "CSU Earns First-Ever STARS Platinum Rating for Sustainability." source@colostate.edu 23 March.

Dahl, Arthur L. 2014. "Sustainability and Values Assessment in Higher Education." In *Sustainable Development and Quality Assurance in Higher Education: Transformation of Learning and Society*, edited by Zinaida Fadeeva, Laima Galkute, Clemens Mader, and Geoff Scott. New York: Palgrave Macmillan. Pp. 185–195.

Daneri, Daniel R.; Trencher, Gregory; and Petersen, John. 2015. "Students as Change Agents in a Town-Wide Sustainability Transformation: The Oberlin Project at Oberlin College." *Current Opinion in Environmental Sustainability* 16:14–21.

Desha, Cheryl; and Hargroves, Karlson C. 2014. *Higher Education and Sustainable Development: A Model for Curriculum Renewal*. London: Routledge.

Fadeeva, Zinaida; Galkute, Laima; Mader, Clemens; and Scott, Geoff. 2014. "Assessment for Transformation: Higher Education Thrives in Refining Quality Systems." In *Sustainable Development and Quality Assurance in Higher Education: Transformation of Learning and Society*, edited by Zinaida Fadeeva, Laima Galkute, Clemens Mader, and Geoff Scott. New York: Palgrave Macmillan. Pp. 1–22.

Gapor, Salfarina A.; Aziz, Abd M. A.; Razak, Dzulkifli A.; and Sanusi, Zainal A. 2014. "Implementing Education for Sustainable Development in Higher Education: Case Study of Albukhary International University, Malaysia." In *Sustainable Development and Quality Assurance in Higher Education: Transformation of Learning and Society*, edited by Zinaida Fadeeva, Laima Galkute, Clemens Mader, and Geoff Scott. New York: Palgrave Macmillan. Pp. 255–281.

Grafakos, Stelios; Zevgolis, Dimitrios; and Oikonomou, Vlasis. 2012. "Towards a Process for Eliciting Criteria Weights and Enhancing Capacity of Stakeholders in *ex ante* Evaluation of Climate Policies." In *Governance by Evaluation for Sustainable Development: Institutional Capacities and Learning*, edited by Michal Sedlacko and Andre Martinuzzi. Cheltenham, UK: Edward Elgar. Pp. 191–211.

Hales, David; and Prescott-Allen, Robert. 2002. "Flying Blind: Assessing Progress toward Sustainability." In *Global Environmental Governance: Options & Opportunities*, edited by Daniel C. Esty and Maria H. Ivanova. New Haven, CT: Yale School of Forestry & Environmental Studies. Pp. 31–52.

Koehn, Peter H.; and Rosenau, James N. 2010. *Transnational Competence: Empowering Professional Curricula for Horizon-Rising Challenges*. Boulder, CO: Paradigm Publishers.

Kopnina, Helen; and Meijers, Frans. 2012. "Education for Sustainable Development (ESD): Exploring Theoretical and Practical Challenges." *International Journal of Sustainability in Higher Education* 15 (2):188–207.

Mader, Clemens. 2014. "The Role of Assessment and Quality Management in Transformations towards Sustainable Development: The Nexus between Higher Education, Society and Policy." In *Sustainable Development and Quality Assurance in Higher Education: Transformation of Learning and Society*, edited by Zinaida Fadeeva, Laima Galkute, Clemens Mader, and Geoff Scott. New York: Palgrave Macmillan. Pp. 66–83.

Musolino, Najia; Lazdins, Janis; Toohey, Jacintha; and Ijsselmuiden, Carel. 2005. "COHRED Fairness Index for International Collaborative Partnerships." *Lancet* 385 (9975):1293–1294.

National Academy for Academic Leadership (NAAL). n.d. "Assessment and Evaluation in Higher Education: Some Concepts and Principles." www.thenationalacademy.org/readings/assessandeval.html accessed 21 April 2016.

Nelson, Christopher B. 2014. "Essay Criticizes State of Assessment Movement in Higher Education." *Inside Higher Education*, November. https://www.insidehighered.com accessed 21 April 2016.

Poister, Theodore H.; Aristigueta, Maria P.; and Hall, Jeremy L. 2015. *Managing and Measuring Performance in Public and Nonprofit Organizations: An Integrated Approach*, 2nd edition. San Francisco, CA: Jossey-Bass.

Pontuso, James F.; and Thornton, Saranna R. 2008. "Is Outcomes Assessment Hurting Higher Education?" *Thought & Action* 24 (Fall):61–69.

Rammel, Christian; Velazquez, Luis; and Mader, Clemens. 2016. "Sustainability Assessment in Higher Education Institutions: What and How?" In *Routledge Handbook of Higher Education for Sustainable Development*, edited by Matthias Barth, Gerd Michelsen, Marco Rieckmann, and Ian Thomas. London: Routledge. Pp. 331–346.

Razak, Dzulkifli A.; Sanusi, Zainal A.; Jegatesen, Govindran; and Khelghat-Doost, Hamoon. 2013. "Alternative University Appraisal (AUA): Reconstructing Universities' Ranking and Rating toward a Sustainable Future." In *Sustainability Assessment Tools in Higher Education Institutions: Mapping Trends and Good Practices around the World*, edited by Sandra Caeiro, Walter L. Filho, Charbel Jabbour, and Ulisses M. Azeiteiro. Cham, Switzerland: Springer International Publishing. Pp. 139–154.

Roorda, Niko. 2013. "A Strategy and a Toolkit to Realize System Integration of Sustainable Development (SISD)." In *Sustainability Assessment Tools in Higher Education Institutions: Mapping Trends and Good Practices Around the World*, edited by Sandra Caeiro, Walter L. Filho, Charbel Jabbour, and Ulisses M. Azeiteiro. Cham, Switzerland: Springer International Publishing. Pp. 101–119.

Roorda, Niko; and Martens, Pim. 2008. "Assessment and Certification of Higher Education for Sustainable Development." *Sustainability* 1 (1):41–53.

Rowe, Debra; and Hiser, Krista. 2016. "Higher Education for Sustainable Development in the Community and through Partnerships." In *Routledge Handbook of Higher Education for Sustainable Development*, edited by Matthias Barth, Gerd Michelsen, Marco Rieckmann, and Ian Thomas. London: Routledge. Pp. 315–330.

Rowe, Debra; and Johnston, Lucas F. 2013. "Learning Outcomes: An International Comparison of Countries and Declarations." In *Higher Education for Sustainability: Cases, Challenges, and Opportunities from across the Curriculum*, edited by Lucas F. Johnston. New York: Routledge. Pp. 45–59.

Rubaii, Nadia; and Calarusse, Crystal. 2012. "Cultural Competency as a Standard for Accreditation." In *Cultural Competency for Public Administrators*, edited by Kristen A. Norman-Major and Susan T. Gooden. Armonk, NY: M.E. Sharpe. Pp. 219–244.

Salter, Jonathan; Robinson, John; and Wiek, Arnim. 2010. "Participatory Methods of Integrated Assessment: A Review." *WIRES: Climate Change* 1:697–717.

Samoff, Joel; and Carrol, Bidemi. 2006. "Influence: Direct, Indirect and Negotiated: The World Bank and Higher Education in Africa." In *Knowledge, Power and Dissent: Critical Perspectives on Higher Education and Research in Knowledge Society*, edited by Guy Neave. Paris: UNESCO Publishing. Pp. 133–180.

Schwarz, Stefanie; and Westerheijden, Don F. 2007a. "Accreditation in the Framework of Evaluation Activities: A Comparative Study in the European Higher Education Area." In *Accreditation and Evaluation in the European Higher Education Area*, edited by Stefanie Schwarz and Don F. Westerheijden. Dordrecht, Netherlands: Springer. Pp. 1–41.

Schwarz, Stefanie; and Westerheijden, Don F. 2007b. "Preface." In *Accreditation and Evaluation in the European Higher Education Area*, edited by Stefanie Schwarz and Don F. Westerheijden. Dordrecht, Netherlands: Springer. Pp. ix–xii.

Sileshi Sisaye. 2016. *Ecology, Sustainable Development and Accounting*. New York: Routledge.

Simon, Kathleen; and Haertle, Jonas. 2014. "Rio+20 Higher Education Sustainability Initiative (HESI) Commitments: A Review of Progress, October 2014." HESI. http://sustainabledevelopment.un.org/index.php?menu=1073

Snider, John. 2015. "An Absolute Embarrassment: Administrative Bloat in Montana Higher Education." *Montana Professor* 25 (2):2–5.

Stevens, Candice. 2012. "A Basic Roadmap for Sustainability Assessments: The SIMPLE Methodology." In *Sustainable Development, Evaluation and Policy-Making: Theory, Practise and Quality Assurance*, edited by Anneke von Raggamby and Frieder Rubik. Cheltenham, UK: Edward Elgar. Pp. 57–72.

Sullivan, William M. 2005. *Work & Integrity: The Crisis and Promise of Professionalism in America*, 2nd edition. San Francisco, CA: Jossey-Bass.

Tan, Kelvin. 2007. "Conceptions of Self-Assessment: What Is Needed for Long-Term Learning?" In *Rethinking Assessment in Higher Education: Learning for the Longer Term*, edited by David Boud and Nancy Falchikov. London: Routledge. Pp. 114–127.

Thabrew, Lanka; Wiek, Arnim; and Ries, Robert. 2009. "Environmental Decision Making in Multi-Stakeholder Contexts: Applicability of Life Cycle Thinking in Development Planning and Implementation." *Journal of Cleaner Production* 17:67–76.

Tierney, Aisling; Tweddell, Hannah; and Willmore, Chris. 2015. "Measuring Education for Sustainable Development: Experiences from the University of Bristol." *International Journal of Sustainability in Higher Education* 16 (1):505–522.

Urbanski, Monika; and Rowland, Paul. 2014. "STARS as a Multi-Purpose Tool for Advancing Campus Sustainability in US." In *Sustainable Development and Quality Assurance in Higher Education: Transformation of Learning and Society*, edited by Zinaida Fadeeva, Laima Galkute, Clemens Mader, and Geoff Scott. New York: Palgrave Macmillan. Pp. 153–182.

Välimaa, Jussi. 2007. "Three Rounds of Evaluation and the Idea of Accreditation in Finnish Higher Education." In *Accreditation and Evaluation in the European Higher Education Area*, edited by Stefanie Schwarz and Don F. Westerheijden. Dordrecht, Netherlands: Springer. Pp. 101–125.

Vaughter, Philip; Wright, Tarah; McKenzie, Marcia; and Lidstone, Lauri. 2013. "Greening the Ivory Tower: A Review of Educational Research on Sustainability in Post-Secondary Education." *Sustainability* 5:2252–2271.

Vettori, Oliver; and Rammel, Christian. 2014. "Linking Quality Assurance and ESD: Towards a Participative Quality Culture of Sustainable Development in Higher Education." In *Sustainable Development and Quality Assurance in Higher Education: Transformation of Learning and Society*, edited by Zinaida Fadeeva, Laima Galkute, Clemens Mader, and Geoff Scott. New York: Palgrave Macmillan. Pp. 49–65.

Wear, Delese; and Aultman, Julie M. 2006. "Introduction." In *Professionalism in Medicine: Critical Perspectives*, edited by Delese Wear and Julie M. Aultman. New York: Springer. Pp. vii–xi.

Zimmermann, Friedrich M.; Raggautz, Andreas; Maier, Kathrin; Drage, Thomas; Mader, Marlene; Diethart, Mario; and Meyer, Jonas. 2014. "Quality System Development at the University of Graz: Lessons Learned from the Case of RCE Graz-Styria." In *Sustainable Development and Quality Assurance in Higher Education: Transformation of Learning and Society*, edited by Zinaida Fadeeva, Laima Galkute, Clemens Mader, and Geoff Scott. New York: Palgrave Macmillan. Pp. 131–152.

4

THE STATE OF HIGHER-EDUCATION SUSTAINABLE-DEVELOPMENT EVALUATION

Limitations and opportunities

Chapters 1 and 2 of *Universities and the Sustainable Development Future* presented a compelling case for the urgency of higher-education involvement in and evaluation of sustainable-development activity. The emerging curriculum, research, and community-engagement piece of this vitally important evaluation venture requires additional attention. This chapter critically reviews the state of current university and international-development sustainable-development-evaluation approaches and briefly explores pathways for change. Part III elaborates a novel framework for university evaluation of sustainable-development involvement that moves beyond existing approaches and encompasses the multiple sustainable-development initiatives encountered at contemporary institutions of higher learning in the South and North.

Limitations of existing higher-education evaluative approaches

Current sustainable-development evaluations are limited in the first instance by lack of sufficient effort. Most institutions of higher learning around the world either are not yet fully engaged in curriculum, research, and outreach initiatives or have not shown interest in systematically evaluating their undertakings (see Zint, 2011, p. 330). In their study of progress among the 272 commitments made by universities around the world in the Rio+20 Higher Education Sustainability Initiative (HESI), for instance, Kathleen Simon and Jonas Haertle (2014) found that only some schools published comprehensive strategic plans and only a few of these "listed concrete objectives, targets, key progress indicators, timelines, responsible persons/departments and/or other metrics to monitor the progress of their strategies."

Other limitations constrain the landscape for universities committed to evaluation. The following sections of this chapter consider some of these issues.

Absence of consensus and external accountability

A wide variety of voluntary university-assessment approaches exist and are in use.[1] There is scant uniformity in application. Among Rio+20 HESI institutions, for instance, only a "small few" report using STARS (Simon and Haertle, 2014).

In addition, agreement on validating or accrediting organizations for sustainable-development activities is lacking. Some sustainability assessments are meaningful in a reputational sense. Typically, however, education for sustainable development has been neither integrated with quality assurance nor widely linked to accreditation or any institutional penalties. The most notable exception is NVAO's (the Dutch and Flemish national organization for the accreditation of higher education) decision to incorporate sustainable development, as assessed by AISHE, as a formal part of the accreditation of universities in the Netherlands (Roorda and Martens, 2008, pp. 47–48).

In many respects, the absence of agreement on uniform-assessment tools and on standardized-learning outcomes (Brundiers, et al., 2014, p. 223) is not a matter for concern. In the realm of sustainable development, contextual diversity inevitably thwarts efforts to develop universally applicable evaluation approaches. In place of standardization, therefore, our framework for evaluating learning, research, outreach, and partnering outcomes and impacts seeks comprehensiveness and allows for selection according to unifying themes and contextual applicability. We are particularly interested in developing a framework with relevance and utility in underrepresented sustainability-evaluation regions – Africa, Asia, and South and Central America (Barth and Rieckmann, 2016, p. 111).

Lack of a comprehensive framework

University operations provide the overwhelming emphasis of prevailing sustainability-evaluation tools (Vaughter, et al., 2013, p. 2263). A study by Fischer, Jenssen, and Tappeser (2015, pp. 789, 791–792), for instance, found that only 34 percent of the indicators and criteria embodied in twelve popular sustainability-assessment tools dealt with education, research, and community outreach combined, whereas 67 percent of the total covered operations (particularly physical resources). In addition, assessment instruments like AISHE are mainly used in departments of education, engineering, and sciences; this departmental focus makes "cross-curricular comparison difficult, even within the same institution" (Vaughter, et al., 2013, p. 2263).

A critical component of a comprehensive framework for university sustainable-development evaluation involves student-learning outcomes. Specifically, competencies identified as useful need to be conceptually organized and operationalized. Fragmented reviews of the prevailing laundry lists of competencies are not helpful (Wiek, Withycombe, and Redman, 2011, pp. 204, 212). In their 2016 literature review, moreover, Arnim Wiek and colleagues (2016, p. 242; Wiek, Withycombe, and Redman, 2011, p. 212) encountered numerous published studies that "discuss different competencies concepts, but little on how to operationalize them for use in curricula and courses"[2] and in evaluation schemes. Indeed, only 5.8 percent of the 520 articles in key journals sampled by Barth and Rieckmann treated the assessment of learning outcomes.[3] In short, "little evidence-based research is focusing on what students actually learn and which competencies they develop" (Barth and Rieckmann, 2016, p. 107).

Outreach evaluations also can be weakened by limited scope. Chapter 3 reported on the growing consensus in support of participatory approaches to sustainable development that involve multiple stakeholders. Evaluations of stakeholder participation, however, tend to be restricted to those "directly related to the project while others who may be key stakeholders in a concurrent related project in a different sector are not included" (Thabrew, Wiek, and Ries, 2009, p. 68).

Methodological strengths and weaknesses

The time lag between university activities and sustainable-development outcomes and impacts presents serious methodological challenges (Oketch, McCowan, and Schendel, 2014, p. 7; Derrick, 2013, p. 53; Batra, Uitto, and Cando-Noordhuizen, 2016, p. 18).[4] Consequently, existing evaluations often fail to consider the longitudinal effects of education for sustainable development (Sterling, Warwick, and Wyness, 2016, p. 96).

Case studies constitute a popular evaluation methodology that can provide context-specific insights. However, existing examples tend to lack methodological rigor, to be predominantly descriptive (Barth and Rieckmann, 2016, p. 111), and to ignore linkage with additional methods (triangulation).

The development of generic assessment tools such as STARS and AISHE constitutes a form of benchmarking intended to offset the limitations of unique findings. Benchmarking encourages external cross-institutional comparisons that portray the range of performance within selected widely recognized parameters, highlight star performers and laggards, and enable peer universities to learn lessons from cutting-edge sustainability practices and strategies[5] (Poister, Aristigueta, and Hall, 2015, pp. 384–385, 400, 421; Esty and Ivanova, 2002, p. 195; Rammel, Velazquez, and Mader, 2016, p. 334). Benchmarking typically suffers from methodological problems, including absence of uniform data-collection procedures and lack of consistency in self-reported data (see, for instance, Urbanski and Rowland, 2014, p. 175).[6] Moreover, universities operate in environments that present challenges in contextual conditions of varying complexity and difficulty. Most importantly, benchmarked data "lend themselves primarily to measures of resources, outputs, and efficiency, but often not to measures of real outcomes" (Poister, Aristigueta, and Hall, 2015, pp. 390–392).

Strengths of the AISHE tool (see Chapter 3) are its process orientation,[7] its mix of qualitative and quantitative evidence (Razak, et al., 2013, p. 148), and the opportunities it provides to link with university quality-management initiatives. Shortcomings include its focus on single-study programs and its limited attention to research and community engagement (Lambrechts and Ceulemans, 2013, pp. 171–172). However, AISHE 2.0, developed in 2012, incorporates a more balanced focus on the four university roles relevant to sustainable development (Lambrechts and Ceulemans, 2013, p. 172).

A reported strength of AUA (Alternative University Appraisal) is its thorough scope (both macro and micro levels). However, AUA (and STARS) are resource-intensive and only "assess the existence of SD activities and not the impact of activities" (Gapor, et al., 2014, pp. 259–261). The output-focused nature of STARS assessments is apparent from member reports on curriculum, research, and student engagement (see Urbanski and Rowland, 2014, p. 176).

The logical-framework approach to evaluation is challenged when confronted by non-linear complexity. Complex programs are "fundamentally dynamic and emergent in response to needs and opportunities" (Rodgers, 2011, p. 36). There-fore, evaluating them requires approaches that take into account that the context is dynamic, and the evaluator's relationship to it also shifts, often in unpredict-able ways.[8] Garcia and Zazueta (2015, p. 30) argue that "any intervention involv-ing human institutions or environmental interaction is likely to be complex, and have non-linear chains of causality caused by tipping points, spatial and tempo-ral mismatches, and other surprises that do not follow the expected pathways to impact." There is a tendency for the logical-framework approach to undervalue the dynamic importance of human and systemic relationships and the roles of stakeholders and to oversimplify how sustainable development occurs.[9]

A theory-based-evaluation approach that appeals to us is realist inquiry (Paw-son, 2013). The realist approach places particular emphasis on the context in which interventions take place and the underlying assumptions about how interventions are expected to reach their goals (Miyaguchi and Uitto, 2015). The approach is particularly suited for evaluating complex programs with different causal mecha-nisms operating in various contexts (Stern, et al., 2012). Moreover, by treating logic models as temporary mental maps, evaluators can "remain alert for unex-pected or counter-intentional effects and . . . consider deviations from intended routes as an opportunity for learning and improvement" (Hummelbrunner, 2012, p. 265). Contribution analysis (Mayne, 2008) offers another useful tool in under-standing and confirming the theory of change of an intervention in a complex sit-uation. Supplementation with evaluation approaches that can deal with unknowns and complexity, such as outcome mapping, also can help offset the limitations of the logical-framework approach (Deprez, 2012, pp. 234–235, 240–241).

Outcome mapping is less problematic because it is primarily concerned with contribution (credible link to a meaningful effect) rather than attribution (causal link) and "models better what really happens in development: facilitating qualita-tive change in attitudes, beliefs and behaviors of relatively small groups of part-ners" (Powell, Molander, and Celebicic, 2012, p. 228; also Deprez, 2012, p. 248). Outcome mapping engages the contributions of multiple stakeholders at various levels and allows the evaluation process to spark continuously improved imple-mentation based on feedback and learning (Hailemichael, 2013, p. 44). Drawbacks are the withdrawal (migration) of respondents between baseline and final assessments and the different ways project implementers and boundary partners interpret progress markers (Powell, Molander, and Celebicic, 2012, p. 227).

Focus on rankings and recognition

Higher-education rankings that rely on bibliometrics and indicators of recognition like Nobel Prizes[10] awarded to faculty members and alumni and research funding (see Badat, 2010, pp. 122–124; Mohrman, 2010, p. 133; Szpaller, 2016) – including the Shanghai Jiao Tong Institute of Higher Education (SJTIHE)[11] and the Times Higher Education-Quacquarelli Symonds (THE-QS) listings[12] – disproportionately use readily available data on scholarly productivity "as a proxy for academic quality" (Hazelkorn, 2014, pp. 29–30). Such monodimensional rankings also assume prestige goals that are not relevant to institutions focused on sustainable development and developing locally relevant curricula (Taylor, 2008, p. 99) and encourage costly and imprudent races for world-class reputations (Hazelkorn, 2014, p. 43).

In any event, the construction of indices by which institutions are ranked is "arbitrary, inconsistent and based on convenience measures" (Harvey, 2008, p. 189; Mohrman, 2010, pp. 133–134). Since the indices are determined by the objectives of the ranking organizations, "there is no such thing as an objective ranking" (Hazelkorn, 2014, p. 29). Rankings such as the SJTIHE and THE-QS are "underpinned by questionable social science, arbitrarily privilege particular indicators and use shallow [quantitative] proxies as correlates of quality" (Badat, 2010, pp. 136, 125, 127, 131; also Harvey, 2008, p. 189; Hazelkorn, 2011, pp. 500–501). They also privilege "the physical, life, and medical sciences because these disciplines publish frequently with multiple authors" and, consequently, "often receive preferential treatment" (Hazelkorn, 2014, pp. 37, 502).

Of central relevance to sustainable-development evaluation, these global rankings "completely ignore the value of community engagement" (Badat, 2010, pp. 126, 131; also Jan Figel, cited in Fadeeva and Mochizuki, 2010, p. 252), each university's unique strengths and self-determined objectives (Thorp and Goldstein, 2010, p. A44), indicators of partnership symmetry and collaboration (Stromquist, 2013, p. 178; Hazelkorn, 2014, pp. 33–35; Salter, Robinson, and Wiek, 2010, p. 709), the impact of research on teaching (Hazelkorn, 2014, p. 31), and research relevance – particularly in terms of local- and regional-development needs, and the indispensable non-monetary assets that Southern partners contribute to collaborative-knowledge generation (Damtew, 2009, p. 165). By measuring impact in terms of citation counts, prevailing rankings are "unable to capture the way in which higher education and research makes an impact beyond the academy, for example on regional or civic engagement or on social, cultural, economic and environmental sustainability" (Hazelkorn, 2014, p. 31) and by encouraging innovation that brings about social change (Hazelkorn, 2014, p. 42).

Sustainability-ranking and rating systems, such as STARS, have become "part of the managerialism of higher education" (Derrick, 2013, p. 50). Participation can be viewed primarily in terms of immediate reputation and marketing opportunities rather than long-term impacts (Derrick, 2013, pp. 50, 52). In this connection, it is insightful to dissect the STARS "platinum" rating awarded in the first instance to Colorado State University (CSU) in 2015. CSU attained the highest ranking among all seven hundred STARS participants on the basis of its "broad spectrum of operations initiatives" plus curricular and research efforts. The output-focused nature of the STARS assessment is revealed by the criteria cited in CSU's news release heralding its first-ever platinum award: 962 credit courses that include sustainability, 532 non-credit continuing-education courses, more than 90 percent of all campus departments engaged in sustainability research (Ciaravola, 2015).

Input and output emphasis

It is not enough to evaluate that higher-education activities achieve their outputs (e.g., number of students and stakeholders reached). For instance, "medical schools are often rightfully criticized for measuring their success primarily in terms of academic outputs, such as papers written or grant funding secured, instead of explicit benefits to the health of the population they are intended to serve" (Olapade-Olaopa, et al., 2014, p. S20). Ensuring that higher-education undertakings actually are benefitting the natural environment and the people who depend on it is essential in ascertaining that universities are contributing to sustainable development.

In their review of research published on sustainability in post-secondary education in eight leading international journals, Philip Vaughter and colleagues (2013, pp. 2252, 2263–2264; also Holm, et al., 2015, p. 165; Disterheft, et al., 2013, p. 19) found that scholarly work is "concentrated on assessing measurable outputs for environmental externalities within institutional operations, with little examination of sustainability uptake and outcomes across broader institutional policies and practices." Roorda and Martens (2008, p. 42) agree that few assessment instruments "focus on the assessment of the research or the societal aspects of sustainable development in HEIs." In their review of the literature treating low-income and lower-middle-income countries, Moses Oketch, Tristan McCowan, and Rebecca Schendel (2014, pp. 5, 7) similarly found few development-impact studies in the higher-education research and service areas, although teaching and learning attracted attention. When they occur, moreover, outcome assessments are inconsistently linked to process assessments in ways that allow performance barriers to be detected and addressed (NAAL, n.d., p. 2).

It is important to note that indicators are not enough to provide a comprehensive picture of the results and impacts of sustainable-development interventions as, by definition, they are reductionist. Furthermore, using indicators for performance measurement – especially in research – can and has been found to provide a misleading picture due to annual fluctuations in research outcomes (Immonen and Cooksy, 2014). The risk is that use of indicators may favor activities producing short-term results rather than more meaningful long-term programs.[13] In addition, when impact analysis occurs, universities typically concentrate on environmental indicators and give short shrift to the social and economic aspects of sustainable development (Derrick, 2013, p. 5). Most importantly, relying on indicators does not explain causalities or why some interventions produce lasting results and under what circumstances.[14] A more balanced and theoretically informed treatment of short-term and long-term outcomes and impacts is needed.

Lessons from international-development evaluations

The world's experience with international-development evaluation is longer and deeper than it is with university evaluations of sustainable development.[15] This situation encourages us to draw upon lessons from the former (e.g., Miyaguchi and Uitto, 2015; Jones, Bailey, and Lyytikäinen, 2007) in advancing the latter. This section of this chapter begins with lessons to be avoided and concludes with lessons to be adopted and adapted. Both sets of insights will inform the higher-education-evaluation framework and recommendations set forth in Part III.

Lessons to avoid

The first lesson to avoid stems from misplaced focus. Given the evaluation focus on deliverables, for instance, we lack evidence that British Higher Education Links projects in rural development have attained successful impacts, behavioral changes, or institutional capacity-building outcomes (Pain, 2009, pp. 103, 110). A similar emphasis on project outputs coupled with failure to document, analyze, and explain outcomes and impacts has undermined the utility of most NGO evaluations (Kruse, 2005, pp. 111, 114–116).

Sweeping sectoral and program approaches are even more problematic than specific project evaluations of process and results are because, among other reasons, they are "not developed, implemented, and evaluated through a careful research process with the involvement of the people they are purportedly designed to impact" (Stoecker, 2005, p. 65). Single-sector evaluations also fail to account for the breadth of sustainable-development impacts (Weaver, et al., 2007, p. 150). Failure to interact extensively and intensively with intended beneficiaries and other stakeholders severely constrains evaluation results. One study based on donor-commissioned evaluation reports covering 240 NGO projects in the South found that evaluators never visited some projects and, therefore, relied solely upon written documentation and often conducted interviews with NGO staff but not with beneficiaries when they did visit (usually for two to four days) (Kruse, 2005, p. 111). Such short-term and shallow evaluation missions "are inadequate to evaluate and document processes of change and impact" (Kruse, 2005, p. 113).

A review of 410 evaluations of completed projects funded by the Global Environment Facility (GEF) revealed few failures, but only 15 percent of the interventions produced changes at the intended scale. Not reaching scale is associated with inattention to pathways to broader adoption and failure to address major systemic factors – that is, the full set of critical conditions hampering change. Evaluators need to be aware that the theory-of-change approach comes with blinders and that complex systems are resilient; there are limits to change prospects (Zazueta, 2014).

Another limitation often found in international-development evaluations is that they concern themselves with individual interventions in a complex landscape, which leads them to determine the outcomes of such interventions without paying attention to whether they truly make a difference (Uitto, 2014). A "micro-macro paradox" in which many interventions achieve their goals but overall the situation remains unchanged can be observed in sustainable development (Berg, 2011). Therefore, it is important that evaluations are designed in a way that recognizes the system within which an intervention takes place, its boundaries and components, and its emergent properties (Garcia and Zazueta, 2015).

Data overload also needs to be avoided (Deprez, 2012, p. 248). There are cases (e.g., GEF's experience in Brazil) of evaluation fatigue (Zazueta and Negi, 2014). Putting aside uncertainties that are peripheral to the principal evaluation conclusions conserves "valuable time for the audience as well as for the assessment team" (Bakkes, 2012, p. 253).

Lessons to adopt and adapt

Theory-based approaches to evaluation (Weiss, 1997) have proven to be useful and adaptable to many sustainable-development situations. The theory-of-change approach identifies key elements and chains of causality that lead directly or indirectly to attaining sustainable-development objectives (Zint, 2011, p. 336) and to increased benefits. The theory of change need not be completely accurate, but it "specifies a chain of causal assumptions that link inputs, processes, outputs and ultimate results, account for preconditioning factors and unforeseen events that . . . very often have determining effects on the ultimate outcomes and impacts" (Nilsson, 2012, p. 51). Did anticipated links among intervention drivers and outcomes and impacts remain valid and in effect during implementation (Hummelbrunner, 2012, pp. 254, 263)?[16] At the summative stage, look for evidence of indirect and direct impacts. How plausible is it that interventions contributed to observed sustainable-development outcomes and impacts (Hummelbrunner, 2012, pp. 254–255)? How likely is it that the impact would have occurred or would have occurred in a slower way without the intervention (Zazueta and Negi, 2014)? In addition, there are theory-based approaches that enable participants to evaluate in a prospective manner what would need to happen in the broader landscape for an intervention to contribute to a tangible impact after it has been completed and the immediate outcomes have been evaluated (Vaessen and Todd, 2008).

Time is an important consideration. Sustainable-development evaluations should capture long-term as well as short-term and intermediate impacts on environmental, economic, and social resources (Bakkes, 2012, p. 248; Derrick, 2013, pp. 52, 60). An explicit vision for end conditions provides an orientation point for backcasting studies (Bakkes, 2012, p. 244; Salter, Robinson, and Wiek, 2010, p. 705)[17] that take into account the decay time of impacts (Meyer, 2012, p. 49).

Outcome mapping is particularly useful as a parallel tool for evaluating long-term and medium-term outreach support to stakeholders. The focus is on the development of relationships, particularly with "boundary partners" (including "less powerful" and "potentially powerful" partners) associated with an outcome challenge. Evaluators look for quality changes in partners. What did they do? What worked and did not work (Powell, Molander, and Celebicic, 2012, pp. 216–218, 223, 225–226, 228; also Deprez, 2012, p. 241)? For whom? Findings are shared with and critically analyzed by boundary partners and other stakeholders (Deprez, 2012, p. 245).

Process analysis is rewarding. Consistent outcome mapping and continuous reflection/revision from the beginning of a project has been found to be valuable in support of East African impact-pathway evaluations. One key to success is the inclusion of boundary stakeholders as well as project partners in participatory evaluation. Enabling outcomes arise from iterative connections among capacity-building activities. Impact-pathway evaluators look for evidence of networking and social-institution leveraging (Jost, et al., 2014).

Outcomes-harvesting-evaluation approaches separate contributions from attribution. Diffuse impacts also need to be tracked because stakeholders and partners start introducing their own innovations even before interventions commence. The final mapping of harvested outcomes is not linear (Bretan, 2014). Pay attention to capturing unintended outcomes – for instance, partners sharing technology, stakeholders sharing lessons, stakeholder process reviews and transformations, intuitive improvisation, and stakeholder perspectives on effects (Bretan, 2014; Powell, Molander, and Celebicic, 2012, p. 230; Nilsson, 2012, p. 48). In "outcomes harvesting," it is rewarding to work backward to determine how change happened (process analysis). Ideally, in workshops, ask people: Who/what caused change? What was the role of the focal intervention? Was it decisive?

Barrier and driver analysis makes it easier to identify patterns and influences. The learned evaluative technique is mapping policy measures or other interventions against barriers/drivers in order that evaluators can explore whether actors have addressed one or more constraining and facilitating factors (Wörlen and van den Berg, 2014). Sustainable-development evaluations also need to account for the bottom-up process of aggregating impacts through far-reaching impact chains (Meyer, 2012, p. 47).[18]

GEF interventions that attained scale devoted attention to pathways to broader adoption from the design stage onward and adopted a comprehensive strategy that addressed how the intervention interacted with the rest of the system. Complexity theory is helpful because many actors and factors are in play in transformative change; there are long time lags in identifying sustainable-development impacts; and multiple confounding factors are at work (Zazueta, 2014; Zazueta and Negi, 2014). Look for different types of impacts: catalytic, enhanced quality, acceleration (Zazueta and Negi, 2014). Co-benefits and cross-cutting issues such as gender, resilience, and stakeholder engagement are now being mainstreamed in all GEF evaluations (Uitto, 2016, p. 111).

Multi-criteria analysis is useful in evaluation processes where complex outcomes and impacts cannot be quantified. Multi-criteria analysis calls for inclusion of different (subjective and objective) economic, ecological, and social measures that are relevant to the intervention under scrutiny in a stakeholder-involved process. According to Stelios Grafakos, Dimitrios Zevgolis, and Vlasis Oikonomou (2012, p. 193), "the main advantage of multi-criteria models is that they make possible the inclusion and consideration of a large amount of data, relationships and objectives which are often present in a specific sustainable development policy context." The narrow focus of sectoral analysis also calls for the adoption of extended-impact assessments or integrated assessments that address the multiple, wider, and cross-sectoral impacts of sustainable-development interventions (Weaver, et al., 2007, pp. 149–150). Integrated-assessment tools need to allow for tradeoffs among multiple generations and among socio-economic-technological and environmental impacts (Weaver, et al., 2007, p. 152).

Evaluators need to engage stakeholders early on in reaching agreement on evaluation methodologies (Zazueta and Negi, 2014). From experience with international-development evaluations, we learn that complex sustainable-development evaluations require multiple methods of data collection and analysis (Garcia and Zazueta, 2015). Evaluating relationships and collaborations requires qualitative methods. Interdisciplinary evaluation teams are essential. Impact evaluations require repeated measurement over time, continuous learning, and multiple adaptations and improvements (Bakkes, 2012, p. 256).

Pathway to improved higher-education sustainability evaluation

The limitations of prevailing evaluation approaches and higher-education rankings underscore the need to develop comprehensive-evaluation systems that incorporate process and convincingly explore the outcomes and impacts of sustainable-development-related teaching, research, and community outreach. We need to understand and appreciate the full impact of higher-education TSD initiatives. Many of the lessons learned from international-development experience with evaluations can be incorporated into a framework for evaluating university sustainable-development activity.

The pathway to improved sustainability evaluation is challenging. It involves measuring "what counts rather than what is easy" (Hazelkorn, 2014, p. 43). Outcomes and impacts will feature prominently in the novel pathway framework we elaborate in Part III.

Notes

1 See Chapter 3.
2 In an exceptional case, the authors of this article endeavor to operationalize their five-fold competency framework (Wiek, et al., 2016, pp. 243–252). In an earlier publication,

however, Arnim Wiek stops short of evaluating "the acquisition of these competencies" (Wiek, Withycombe, and Redman, 2011, p. 204).

3 More than half of the sampled articles treated curriculum development and teaching approaches combined (Barth and Rieckmann, 2016, p. 107).

4 Steve Bass and Alastair Bradstock (2013, p. 170) have unpacked some of the challenges that make evaluating sustainable development particularly difficult, including data inadequacies, multiple spatial and temporal levels, institutional resistance to evaluating sustainable development, difficulties in identifying and measuring spillover effects, and lack of formal sustainable-development-evaluation frameworks.

5 Potentially, benchmarking opens avenues for "collaborative competition" (Urbanski and Rowland, 2014, p. 164).

6 STARS operates with an elaborate data-correction process that includes random reviews, periodic audits, and anonymous "submission accuracy enquiries" (Urbanski and Rowland, 2014, p. 158).

7 AISHE assessments involve a five- to six-hour representative-group-consensus meeting led by the assessor (Roorda and Martens, 2008, p. 45).

8 In addition, the process of studying process invariably changes it.

9 For a detailed critical discussion of the logic model that is applied to the internationalization of higher-education institutions, see Deardorff and van Gaalen (2012, pp. 168–170).

10 The Nobel Prizes themselves have failed to keep up with the expanding reach of vital scientific contributions, leaving researchers in sustainability-focused fields such as climatology and ecology with virtually "no shot at the prestige, power and wealth that the Nobels bestow" (Popkin, 2016).

11 Across the entire African continent, only a couple of South African higher-education institutions (HEIs) have been included in the SJTIHE ranking of the world's top-five-hundred universities (Sörlin and Vessuri 2007, p. 20).

12 For a list of active global rankings in 2014, see Hazelkorn (2014, p. 29).

13 From environmental-education initiatives, we learn that evaluating outcomes is difficult when insufficient attention is devoted to describing and analyzing the implementation of program interventions. Additional cautions are raised about reliance on self-reports to the exclusion of direct measures of behavioral outcomes (Zint, 2011, p. 338).

14 Joe Ravetz (2007, p. 86) raises this rhetorical question: "Are the current efforts on counting indicators akin to those of medieval theologians, evaluating how many angels might dance on a pinhead?"

15 For instance, the BellagioSTAMP principles incorporated in the discussion that follows are "based on twenty years of experience in policy-oriented assessments in environment, natural resources and sustainable development" (Bakkes, 2012, p. 242).

16 Richard Hummelbrunner (2012, pp. 262–263) suggests that quickly elaborated impact diagrams offer a useful tool for clarifying "impact-creating processes" and understanding of "expected effects and the ways to achieve them."

17 In contrast to forecasting, backcasting "sets the target for a certain date and then analyzes the problem from the target to the present (backward in time)" (Sachs, 2015, p. 493).

18 By complementing traditional top-down evaluation approaches, bottom-up perspectives offer opportunities for "double-loop learning processes" (Nilsson, 2012, pp. 48, 50).

Works cited

Badat, Saleem. 2010. "Global Rankings of Universities: A Perverse and Present Burden." In *Global Inequalities and Higher Education: Whose Interests Are We Serving?*, edited by Elaine Unterhalter and Vincent Carpentier. Hampshire: Palgrave Macmillan. Pp. 117–141.

Bakkes, Jan. 2012. "Bellagio Sustainability Assessment and Measurement Principles (BellagioSTAMP): Significance and Examples from International Environmental Outlooks." In *Sustainable Development, Evaluation and Policy-Making: Theory, Practise and Quality*

Assurance, edited by Anneke von Raggamby and Frieder Rubik. Cheltenham, UK: Edward Elgar. Pp. 241–260.

Barth, Matthias; and Rieckmann, Marco. 2016. "State of the Art in Research on Higher Education for Sustainable Development." In *Routledge Handbook of Higher Education for Sustainable Development*, edited by Matthias Barth, Gerd Michelsen, Marco Rieckmann, and Ian Thomas. London: Routledge. Pp. 100–133.

Bass, Steve; and Bradstock, Alastair. 2013. "Evaluating Sustainable Development." In *Emerging Practices in International Development Evaluation*, edited by Stewart I. Donaldson, Tarek Azzam, and Ross F. Conner. Charlotte, NC: Information Age Publishing. Pp. 165–189.

Batra, Geeta; Uitto, Juha I.; and Cando-Noordhuizen, Lee. 2016. "Fron MDGs to SDGs: Evaluating Global Environmental Benefits." *Evaluation Matters* 1:16–23.

Berg, Rob D. van den. 2011. "Evaluation in the Context of Global Public Goods." *Evaluation* 17 (4):405–415.

Bretan, Maria E. A. N. 2014. "Evaluating Institutional Change and Long-Term Climate Change Adaption and Resilience Measures towards a National Drought Preparedness Policy in Brazil." Paper presented at the 2nd International Conference on Evaluating Climate Change and Development, GEF Independent Evaluation Office, Washington, DC, 4–6 November.

Brundiers, Katja; Savage, Emma; Mannell, Steven; Lang, Daniel J.; and Wiek, Arnim. 2014. "Educating Sustainability Change Agents by Design: Appraisals of the Transformative Role of Higher Education." In *Sustainable Development and Quality Assurance in Higher Education: Transformation of Learning and Society*, edited by Zinaida Fadeeva, Laima Galkute, Clemens Mader, and Geoff Scott. New York: Palgrave Macmillan. Pp. 196–229.

Ciaravola, Dell Rae. 2015. "CSU Earns First-Ever STARS Platinum Rating for Sustainability." source@colostate.edu 23 March.

Damtew Teferra. 2009. "Higher Education in Africa: The Dynamics of International Partnerships and Interventions." In *International Organizations and Higher Education Policy: Thinking Globally, Acting Locally?* edited by Roberta M. Bassett and Alma Maldonado-Maldonado. London: Routledge. Pp. 155–173.

Deardorff, Darla K.; and van Gaalen, Adinda. 2012. "Outcomes Assessment in the Internationalization of Higher Education." In *The Sage Handbook of International Higher Education*, edited by Darla K. Deardorff, Hans de Wit, John Heyl, and Tony Adams. Los Angeles, CA: Sage. Pp. 167–190.

Deprez, Steff. 2012. "Development of a Learning-Oriented Monitoring System for Sustainable Agriculture Chain Development in Eastern Indonesia." In *Governance by Evaluation for Sustainable Development: Institutional Capacities and Learning*, edited by Michal Sedlacko and Andre Martinuzzi. Cheltenham, UK: Edward Elgar. Pp. 233–252.

Derrick, Stephen. 2013. "Time and Sustainability Metrics in Higher Education." In *Sustainability Assessment Tools in Higher Education Institutions: Mapping Trends and Good Practices around the World*, edited by Sandra Caeiro, Walter L. Filho, Charbel Jabbour, and Ulisses M. Azeiteiro. Cham, Switzerland: Springer International Publishing. Pp. 47–63.

Disterheft, Antje; Caeiro, Sandra; Azeiteiro, Ulisses M.; and Filho, Walter L. 2013. "Sustainability Science and Education for Sustainable Development in Universities: A Way for Transition." In *Sustainability Assessment Tools in Higher Education Institutions: Mapping Trends and Good Practices around the World*, edited by Sandra Caeiro, Walter L. Filho, Charbel Jabbour, and Ulisses M. Azeiteiro. Cham, Switzerland: Springer International Publishing. Pp. 3–27.

Esty, Daniel C.; and Ivanova, Maria H. 2002. "Revitalizing Global Environmental Governance: A Function-Driven Approach." In *Global Environmental Governance: Options &*

Opportunities, edited by Daniel C. Esty and Maria H. Ivanova. New Haven, CT: Yale School of Forestry & Environmental Studies. Pp. 181–203.

Fadeeva, Zinaida; and Mochizuki, Yoko. 2010. "Higher Education for Today and Tomorrow: University Appraisal for Diversity, Innovation and Change towards Sustainable Development." *Sustainability Science* 5:249–256.

Fischer, Daniel; Jenssen, Silke; and Tappeser, Valentin. 2015. "Getting an Empirical Hold of the Sustainable University: A Comparative Analysis of Evaluation Frameworks across 12 Contemporary Sustainability Assessment Tools." *Assessment & Evaluation in Higher Education* 40 (6):785–800.

Gapor, Salfarina A.; Aziz, Abd M. A.; Razak, Dzulkifli A.; and Sanusi, Zainal A. 2014. "Implementing Education for Sustainable Development in Higher Education: Case Study of Albukhary International University, Malaysia." In *Sustainable Development and Quality Assurance in Higher Education: Transformation of Learning and Society*, edited by Zinaida Fadeeva, Laima Galkute, Clemens Mader, and Geoff Scott. New York: Palgrave Macmillan. Pp. 255–281.

Garcia, J. R.; and Zazueta, Aaron 2015. "Going beyond Mixed Methods to Mixed Approaches: A Systems Perspective for Asking the Right Questions." *IDS Bulletin* 46 (1):30–43.

Grafakos, Stelios; Zevgolis, Dimitrios; and Oikonomou, Vlasis. 2012. "Towards a Process for Eliciting Criteria Weights and Enhancing Capacity of Stakeholders in *ex ante* Evaluation of Climate Policies." In *Governance by Evaluation for Sustainable Development: Institutional Capacities and Learning*, edited by Michal Sedlacko and Andre Martinuzzi. Cheltenham, UK: Edward Elgar. Pp. 191–211.

Hailemichael Taye. 2013. "Evaluating the Impact of Agricultural Extension Programmes in Sub-Saharan Africa: Challenges and Prospects." *African Evaluation Journal* 1 (1):38–45.

Harvey, Lee. 2008. "Rankings of Higher Education Institutions: A Critical Review." *Quality in Higher Education* 14 (3):187–207.

Hazelkorn, Ellen. 2011. "Measuring World-Class Excellence and the Global Obsession with Rankings." In *Handbook on Globalization and Higher Education*, edited by Roger King, Simon Marginson, and Rajani Naidoo. Cheltenham, UK: Edward Elgar. Pp. 497–516.

Hazelkorn, Ellen. 2014. "Rankings and the Reconstruction of Knowledge during the Age of Austerity." In *Sustainable Development and Quality Assurance in Higher Education: Transformation of Learning and Society*, edited by Zinaida Fadeeva, Laima Galkute, Clemens Mader, and Geoff Scott. New York: Palgrave Macmillan. Pp. 25–48.

Holm, Tove; Sammalisto, Kaisu; Grindsted, Thomas S.; and Vuorisalo, Timo. 2015. "Process Framework for Identifying Sustainability Aspects in University Curricula and Integrating Education for Sustainable Development." *Journal of Cleaner Production* 106:164–174.

Hummelbrunner, Richard. 2012. "Process Monitoring of Impacts and Its Application in Structural Fund Programmes." In *Governance by Evaluation for Sustainable Development: Institutional Capacities and Learning*, edited by Michal Sedlacko and Andre Martinuzzi. Cheltenham, UK: Edward Elgar. Pp. 253–266.

Immonen, Sirkka; and Cooksy, Leslie L. 2014. "Using Performance Measurement to Assess Research: Lessons Learned from the International Agricultural Research Centres." *Evaluation* 20 (1):96–114.

Jones, Nicola; Bailey, Mark; and Lyytikäinen, Minna. 2007. *Research Capacity Strengthening in Africa: Trends, Gaps and Opportunities*. London: Overseas Development Institute.

Jost, Christine; Alvarez, Sophie; Baron, Deissy M.; Bonilla-Findji, Osana; Coffey, Kevin; Förch, Wiebke; Khatri-Chhetri, Arun; Moussa, Abdoulaye S.; Radeny, Maren; Richards, Meryl; Schuetz, Tonya; and Vasileiou, Ioannis. 2014. "Pathway to Impact: Supporting and Evaluating Enabling Environments for Outcomes in CCAFS." Paper presented at the 2nd International Conference on Evaluating Climate Change and Development, GEF Independent Evaluation Office, Washington, DC, 4–6 November.

Kruse, Stein-Erik. 2005. "Meta-evaluations of NGO Experience: Results and Challenges." In *Evaluating Development Effectiveness*, edited by George K. Pitman, Osvaldo N. Feinstein, and Gregory K. Ingram. World Bank Series on Evaluation and Development, Volume 7. New Brunswick, N.J.: Transaction Publishers. Pp. 109–127.

Lambrechts, Wim; and Ceulemans, Kim. 2013. "Sustainability Assessment in Higher Education: Evaluating the Use of the Auditing Instrument for Sustainability in Higher Education (AISHE) in Belgium." In *Sustainability Assessment Tools in Higher Education Institutions: Mapping Trends and Good Practices around the World*, edited by Sandra Caeiro, Walter L. Filho, Charbel Jabbour, and Ulisses M. Azeiteiro. Cham, Switzerland: Springer International Publishing. Pp. 157–174.

Mayne, John. 2008. *Contribution Analysis: An Approach to Exploring Cause and Effect*. ILAC Brief 16. Rome: Institutional Learning and Change Initiative, Biodiversity International.

Meyer, Wolfgang. 2012. "Should Evaluation Be Revisited for Sustainable Development?" In *Sustainable Development, Evaluation and Policy-Making: Theory, Practise and Quality Assurance*, edited by Anneke von Raggamby and Frieder Rubik. Cheltenham, UK: Edward Elgar. Pp. 37–54.

Miyaguchi, Takaaki; and Uitto, Juha I. 2015. *A Realist Review of Climate Change Adaptation Programme Evaluations: Methodological Implications and Programmatic Findings*. Occasional Paper Series. New York: United Nations Development Programme, Independent Evaluation Office.

Mohrman, Kathryn. 2010. "Educational Exchanges: What China Should Not Adopt from United States Higher Education." In *Crossing Borders in East Asian Higher Education*, edited by David W. Chapman, William K. Cummings, and Gerald A. Postiglione. Hong Kong: University of Hong Kong. Pp. 127–144.

National Academy for Academic Leadership (NAAL). n.d. "Assessment and Evaluation in Higher Education: Some Concepts and Principles." www.thenationalacademy.org/readings/assessandeval.html accessed 21 April 2016.

Nilsson, Måns. 2012. "Tools for Learning-Oriented Environmental Appraisal." In *Governance by Evaluation for Sustainable Development: Institutional Capacities and Learning*, edited by Michal Sedlacko and Andre Martinuzzi. Cheltenham, UK: Edward Elgar. Pp. 45–60.

Oketch, Moses; McCowan, Tristan; and Schendel, Rebecca. 2014. *The Impact of Tertiary Education on Development*. London: Institute of Education, University of London.

Olapade-Olaopa, Emiola O.; Baird, Sarah; Kiguli-Malwadde, Elsie; and Kolars, Joseph C. 2014. "Growing Partnerships: Leveraging the Power of Collaboration through the Medical Education Partnership Initiative." *Academic Medicine* 89, No. 8 (August Supplement):S19–S23.

Pain, Adam. 2009. "Economic Development and Sustainable Livelihoods." In *Higher Education and International Capacity Building: Twenty-Five Years of Higher Education Links*, edited by David Stephens. Oxford: Symposium Books. Pp. 95–114.

Pawson, Ray. 2013. *The Science of Evaluation: A Realist Manifesto*. London and Thousand Oaks: Sage.

Poister, Theodore H.; Aristigueta, Maria P.; and Hall, Jeremy L. 2015. *Managing and Measuring Performance in Public and Nonprofit Organizations: An Integrated Approach*, 2nd edition. San Francisco, CA: Jossey-Bass.

Popkin, Gabriel. 2016. "Update the Nobel Prizes." *New York Times*, 3 October, p. A23.

Powell, Steve; Molander, Joakim; and Celebicic, Ivona. 2012. "Assessment of Outcome Mapping as a Tool for Evaluating and Monitoring Support to Civil Society Organisations." In *Governance by Evaluation for Sustainable Development: Institutional Capacities and*

Learning, edited by Michal Sedlacko and Andre Martinuzzi. Cheltenham, UK: Edward Elgar. Pp. 215–232.

Rammel, Christian; Velazquez, Luis; and Mader, Clemens. 2016. "Sustainability Assessment in Higher Education Institutions: What and How?" In *Routledge Handbook of Higher Education for Sustainable Development*, edited by Matthias Barth, Gerd Michelsen, Marco Rieckmann, and Ian Thomas. London: Routledge. Pp. 331–346.

Ravetz, Joe. 2007. "The Role of Evaluation in Regional Sustainable Development." In *Impact Assessment and Sustainable Development: European Practice and Experience*, edited by Clive George and Colin Kirkpatrick. Cheltenham, UK: Edward Elgar. Pp. 65–89.

Razak, Dzulkifli A.; Sanusi, Zainal A.; Jegatesen, Govindran; and Khelghat-Doost, Hamoon. 2013. "Alternative University Appraisal (AUA): Reconstructing Universities' Ranking and Rating toward a Sustainable Future." In *Sustainability Assessment Tools in Higher Education Institutions: Mapping Trends and Good Practices around the World*, edited by Sandra Caeiro, Walter L. Filho, Charbel Jabbour, and Ulisses M. Azeiteiro. Cham, Switzerland: Springer International Publishing. Pp. 139–154.

Rodgers, Patricia J. 2011. "Implications of Complicated and Complex Characteristics for Key Tasks in Evaluation." In *Evaluating the Complex: Attribution, Contribution, and Beyond*, edited by Kim Forss, Mita Marra, and Robert Schwartz. New Brunswick, NJ, and London: Transaction Publishers. Pp. 33–52.

Roorda, Niko; and Martens, Pim. 2008. "Assessment and Certification of Higher Education for Sustainable Development." *Sustainability* 1 (1):41–53.

Sachs, Jeffrey D. 2015. *The Age of Sustainable Development*. New York: Columbia University Press.

Salter, Jonathan; Robinson, John; and Wiek, Arnim. 2010. "Participatory Methods of Integrated Assessment: A Review." *WIRES: Climate Change* 1:697–717.

Simon, Kathleen; and Haertle, Jonas. 2014. "Rio+20 Higher Education Sustainability Initiative (HESI) Commitments: A Review of Progress, October 2014." HESI. http://sustainabledevelopment.un.org/index.php?menu=1073

Sörlin, Sverker; and Vessuri, Hebe. 2007. "Introduction: The Democratic Deficit of Knowledge Economies." In *Knowledge Society vs. Knowledge Economy: Knowledge, Power, and Politics*, edited by Sverker Sörlin and Hebe Vessuri. Hampshire: Palgrave Macmillan. Pp. 1–33.

Sterling, Stephen; Warwick, Paul; and Wyness, Lynne. 2016. "Understanding Approaches to ESD Research on Teaching and Learning in Higher Education." In *Routledge Handbook of Higher Education for Sustainable Development*, edited by Matthias Barth, Gerd Michelsen, Marco Rieckmann, and Ian Thomas. London: Routledge. Pp. 89–99.

Stern, Elliot; Stame, Nicoletta; Mayne, John; Forss, Kim; Davies, Rick; and Befani, Barbara. 2012. *Broadening the Range of Designs and Methods for Impact Evaluations*. Working Paper 38. London: Department for International Development.

Stoecker, Randy. 2005. *Research Methods for Community Change: A Project-Based Approach*. Thousand Oaks, CA: Sage Publications.

Stromquist, Nelly P. 2013. "Higher Education and the Search for Excellence in US Universities." In *The Reorientation of Higher Education: Challenging the East-West Dichotomy*, edited by Bob Adamson, Jon Nixon, and Feng Su. Hong Kong: Comparative Education Research Centre, The University of Hong Kong. Pp. 165–183.

Szpaller, Keila. 2016. "Just How Did UM's Program Get to Be Tops?" *Missoulian*, 11 September, p. A10.

Taylor, Peter. 2008. "Introduction." In *Higher Education in the World 3: New Challenges and Emerging Roles for Human and Social Development*. GUNI Series on the Social Commitment of Universities 3. London: Palgrave Macmillan. Pp. xxiv–xxvii.

Thabrew, Lanka; Wiek, Arnim; and Ries, Robert. 2009. "Environmental Decision Making in Multi-Stakeholder Contexts: Applicability of Life Cycle Thinking in Development Planning and Implementation." *Journal of Cleaner Production* 17:67–76.

Thorp, Holden; and Goldstein, Buck. 2010. "How to Create a Problem-Solving Institution (and Avoid Organizational Silos)." *Chronicle of Higher Education*, 3 September, pp. A43–A44.

Uitto, Juha I. 2014. "Evaluating Environment and Development: Lessons from International Cooperation." *Evaluation* 20 (1):44–57.

Uitto, Juha I. 2016. "Evaluating the Environment as a Global Public Good." *Evaluation* 22 (1):108–115.

Urbanski, Monika; and Rowland, Paul. 2014. "STARS as a Multi-Purpose Tool for Advancing Campus Sustainability in US." In *Sustainable Development and Quality Assurance in Higher Education: Transformation of Learning and Society*, edited by Zinaida Fadeeva, Laima Galkute, Clemens Mader, and Geoff Scott. New York: Palgrave Macmillan. Pp. 153–182.

Vaessen, Jos; and Todd, David. 2008. "Methodological Challenges of Evaluating the Impact of the Global Environment Facility's Biodiversity Program." *Evaluation and Program Planning* 31:231–240.

Vaughter, Philip; Wright, Tarah; McKenzie, Marcia; and Lidstone, Lauri. 2013. "Greening the Ivory Tower: A Review of Educational Research on Sustainability in Post-Secondary Education." *Sustainability* 5:2252–2271.

Weaver, Paul; Rotmans, Jan; Turnpenny, John; Haxeltine, Alex; and Jordan, Andrew. 2007. "Methods and Tools for Integrated Sustainability Assessment (MATISSE): A New European Project." In *Impact Assessment and Sustainable Development: European Practice and Experience*, edited by Clive George and Colin Kirkpatrick. Cheltenham, UK: Edward Elgar. Pp. 149–163.

Weiss, Carol H. 1997. "Theory-Based Evaluation: Past, Present, and Future." *New Directions for Evaluation* 75 (1):41–55.

Wiek, Arnim; Bernstein, Michael J.; Foley, Rider; Cohen, Matthew; Forrest, Nigel; Kuzdas, Christopher; Kay, Braden; and Keeler, Lauren W. 2016. "Operationalising Competencies in Higher Education for Sustainable Development." In *Routledge Handbook of Higher Education for Sustainable Development*, edited by Matthias Barth, Gerd Michelsen, Marco Rieckmann, and Ian Thomas. London: Routledge. Pp. 241–260.

Wiek, Arnim; Withycombe, Lauren; and Redman, Charles L. 2011. "Key Competencies in Sustainability: A Reference Framework for Academic Program Development." *Sustainability Science* 6:203–218.

Wörlen, Christine; and Berg, Rob D. van den. 2014. "Blocked by No Change? Application Examples for the Theory of No Change." Paper presented at the 2nd International Conference on Evaluating Climate Change and Development, GEF Independent Evaluation Office, Washington, DC, 4–6 November.

Zazueta, Aaron. 2014. "Methodological Approach of the GEF IEO's South China Sea Impact Evaluation." Paper presented at the 2nd International Conference on Evaluating Climate Change and Development, GEF Independent Evaluation Office, Washington, DC, 4–6 November.

Zazueta, Aaron; and Negi, Neeraj. 2014. "Measuring Climate Change and Development Benefits of Project Interventions: Challenges and Prospects." Paper presented at the 2nd International Conference on Evaluating Climate Change and Development, GEF Independent Evaluation Office, Washington, DC, 4–6 November.

Zint, Michaela. 2011. "Evaluating Education for Sustainable Development Programs." In *World Trends in Education for Sustainable Development*, edited by Walter L. Filho. Frankfurt: Peter Lang. Pp. 329–347.

PART III

Framework for enhanced university sustainable-development evaluations

5

EVALUATIONS THAT MATTER

Universities and sustainable-development transitions

Part III of *Universities and the Sustainable Development Future* is tasked with con-structing a useful framework for evaluation that draws upon the multidimensional nature of urgent sustainable-development challenges illustrated in Chapter 2 along with insights regarding prevailing university-evaluation limitations and opportu-nities set forth in Part II. Chapter 5 makes a case for pursuing specific outcome and impact pathways and presents the overview picture of ways that higher-education evaluations can support sustainable-development transitions. The four follow-ing Part III chapters focus on curriculum, research, outreach, and partnering evaluations, respectively. Generic theories of change, best practices, appropriate methods, and practical guidance feature in each chapter's evaluation-framework presentation.

Our interest in *Universities and the Sustainable Development Future* is in evaluations that matter for sustainable development and not in paper or electronic exercises. To matter, university transnational-sustainable-development (TSD) evaluations need to adhere to certain guiding principles. Based on a new and replicable synthesis of accumulated research findings (see Rickinson and Reid, 2016, p. 143), this chap-ter identifies and justifies core guiding principles that contribute to a meaning-ful framework for sustainable-development evaluation. The core attributes that guide the framework we develop and apply involve comprehensiveness; outcome, impact, and process orientation; multiple methods; flexibility and adaptability; and evaluation-capacity building.

Evaluating university TSD performance is a complex and controversial under-taking. In the discussion that follows, we develop a novel framework for evaluating tertiary education's role in sustainable development. Our presentation is grounded in theory-based approaches and the realist tradition that emphasizes context and the non-linearity of outcomes and impacts (Pawson and Tilley, 1997) and is informed by an extensive literature on education and development evaluations.

The multidimensional nature of sustainable development necessitates an integrated transdisciplinary approach to evaluation (Weaver, et al., 2007, p. 149).

To provide additional practical guidance, we also draw upon field experiences with evaluating international-development programs. In particular, we take into consideration evidence that, in the international-development arena, approaches to evaluation are changing (see Eyben, 2013, 27; Thomas and Tominaga, 2013),[1] with increased emphasis on identifying "options and responsibilities for action" (Bakkes, 2012, p. 247) and on demonstrating the big picture of whether we are making a difference. There is a determined move from accounting for activities and outputs of programs and interventions to evaluating their outcomes (i.e., actual or intended changes in conditions that the intervention seeks to support) and impacts (actual or intended changes in human and ecosystem wellbeing). Outcomes and impacts are difficult to determine and attribute to a single intervention, and they always involve multiple reinforcing, negating, and synergizing actors interacting in a complex space (Thomas and Tominaga, 2013, pp. 60, 62). Among other intervening factors, climate change brings in new challenges and draws attention to risk and uncertainty (Picciotto, 2007; Uitto, 2016, p. 4).

Comprehensive treatment

Universities must be able to evaluate effectively where economic and social development and environmental protection meet. Theory-based evaluation is a useful approach for understanding diverse spatial, temporal, organizational, and value scales. Such understanding is necessary in order to identify the evaluation scope, appropriate units of analysis, and suitable approaches and methodologies in an iterative manner. However, modelling theories of change using the secessionist-causality concept (i.e., the traditional results chain) are not entirely satisfactory as university interventions operate in complex environments where they are part of a larger system with many unknowns (Deprez, 2012, p. 235; Rist, 2013, pp. 257–258). In higher-education TSD evaluations, an evaluation framework that embraces and interweaves the various elements of complexity is needed (Deprez, 2012, p. 235; Garcia and Zazueta, 2015).

Process, outcome, and impact orientation

Meaningful evaluations are designed to enhance learning about what works and what does not work. A holistic framework for evaluating higher-education TSD initiatives encompasses and integrates teaching, research, outreach, and partnering; treats environmental, economic, and social dimensions; and focuses on process, outcomes, and impacts. Successful process evaluations emphasize transformative learning; they are institution-wide, are collectively unit-based (see Togo and Lotz-Sisitka, 2013, p. 259; Rammel, Velazquez, and Mader, 2016, p. 341), and provide an entire-university picture of sustainability activity (Togo, 2015, pp. 36–39). In the absence of this guiding process orientation, "learning at the university level would be limited to cosmetic change and efficiency gains. It would be concerned primarily with doing things (even if unsustainable) better, but not with doing better things" (Rammel, Velazquez, and Mader, 2016, p. 341).

Addressing means as well as ends

Addressing means as well as ends is necessary in impact evaluations. Missing from sustainability evaluations focused on cost-benefit calculations are such important considerations as participant willingness to embrace uncertainty, the enthusiasm of community members when participating in development projects (Smillie, 2009, p. 226), the depth of commitment to boundary-spanning project objectives, and sustainability ethics (Ramos and Pires, 2013, p. 93).

Process plays a special role throughout means-shaped university sustainable-development evaluations. Thus, assessing the quality of the sustainability process itself constitutes a fundamental part of the TSD evaluation (Rammel, Velazquez, and Mader, 2016, p. 342). In impact-led monitoring, for instance, "understanding and observing the underlying processes provide an early indication as to whether a project/programme is on the right track" (Hummelbrunner, 2012, p. 264).[2]

Processes of interest are both externally and internally (institutionally) transforming (Meyer, 2007, pp. 38–39). Participatory practices that "affect the production of evaluation knowledge and the usefulness of the evaluation" (see Chouinard and Cousins, 2013, pp. 67–68) merit particular attention.[3] The conduct of a comprehensive stakeholder analysis is critical in evaluating the institution of higher learning's approach to sustainable development (Meyer, 2012, p. 46).

Holistic process evaluations inquire regarding the relationship of principles to criteria, indicators, and overall results.[4] Were core guiding principles of sustainable development articulated at the design stage? If so, evaluators should identify the criteria that would give concrete operational meaning to the selected core objectives and, therefore, guide the entire evaluation process. Were the selected core principles of sustainable development and education for sustainable development actually complied with throughout the process (Rammel, Velazquez, and Mader, 2016, pp. 334–336, 341–342)?

We find considerable value in the developmental-evaluation approach advanced by Brundiers and colleagues (2014, pp. 214–216, 218). Their developmental approach connects quality appraisal, theory-driven evaluation, and bottom-up participation among stakeholders who will utilize the information gathered as part of a continuous learning and improving process. In the process these authors envision, the development evaluator is "responsible for facilitating evaluative discussions, thinking and data-based reflection" as well as other sense-making activities.[5]

Following Meyer (2007, p. 36), process evaluations should encompass the three life-course phases of university-initiated undertakings: planning, implementing, and sustaining. Deliberative, continuous, and democratic evaluations help develop agreed-upon evaluation criteria (Ravetz, 2007, p. 76), deepen shared insights, and enhance outcomes and impacts. Community impacts are advanced to the extent that evaluation processes "help beneficiaries to formulate their own development strategies, encourage ownership and commitment, and help create a development consensus" (Stern, 2004, p. 39; also Jilke, 2013). All stakeholders benefit when diverse perspectives on problems, community needs, available expertise, and different services provided are continuously exchanged (Boydell and Rugkasa, 2007, p. 222; Sileshi, 2016, pp. 44–45). Peter Oakley (1991, p. 263) finds that "when the local people are involved in discussion, debate, analysis and interpretation of project activities, they come to share a common perspective and a shared commitment to action." In short, participatory evaluations promote community motivation and empowerment, directly address issues of relevance, identify pathways to local expertise, illuminate contextually appropriate development approaches, and facilitate coordinated action and continuous improvement (Crossley, et al., 2005, pp. 39–40; Boydell and Rugkasa, 2007, p. 223).[6]

In our approach, evaluators focus on determining how process is linked to outcome and impact additionalities. The mechanisms by which interventions create change in certain circumstances (see Miyaguchi and Uitto, 2015, pp. 4–5) are of special interest. The quality of interactions is the most important consideration when evaluating process from an outcome- and impact-additionality perspective (Ravetz, 2007, p. 83). "Radar diagrams" that offer a pictorial view of sustainable-development activity across units – complemented by triangulated data collected from interviews, documents, and observations – "make it easy to identify areas where the university is strong [has progressed] and where it is lacking in sustainability mainstreaming" (Togo, 2015, pp. 42–43; also see Togo and Lotz-Sisitka, 2013, pp. 270–273).

Are processes for stakeholder and public participation in the evaluation of university activity "in place and working effectively" (Gibson, 2005, p. 80)? How broad and diverse is the configuration of stakeholder participation in the selected sustainable-development challenge (Chouinard and Cousins, 2013, p. 68; Catley-Carlson, 2004, p. 22; Meyer, 2012, p. 48; Meyer, 2007, p. 44)? Have outliers and disparate viewpoints been incorporated (Catley-Carlson, 2004, p. 23; Gibson, 2005, p. 155)? To what extent did project leaders involve stakeholders at all stages of the development process (Thabrew, Wiek, and Ries, 2009, p. 74)? How have university personnel participated in community-based economic-development activities and/or embarked on and maintained collaborative relationships with domestic enterprises (Morfit and Gore, 2009, p. 16)? In Box 5.1, we provide additional illustrative examples of process-based inquiries that evaluators can pursue when evaluating higher-education sustainable-development curricula, research, and outreach interventions.

Beyond process and outputs

Sustainable-development evaluators are obliged to look beyond outputs of individual interventions to determine whether or not they are making a difference in terms of the health of the global environment and the wellbeing of people depending upon it.[7] Too many projects, programs, and policies have achieved

---

BOX 5.1 ILLUSTRATIVE PROCESS-FRAMEWORK QUESTIONS FOR EVALUATIONS OF CURRICULA, RESEARCH, AND OUTREACH

- Did participants reach early consensus on core sustainable-development and sustainable-development-education principles?
- Are planned sustainable-development interventions primarily outcome and impact-driven rather than activity or output-driven?
- Have interactive, experiential, and service- and distance-learning approaches been introduced or enhanced?
- How are faculty, administrative staff, and additional departments contributing to project activities?
- Which stakeholder and partner involvements increased, decreased, or remained consistent over the course of the undertaking? To what extent and why?
- How have curriculum reformers elicited, consulted, and incorporated the views, suggestions, and objectives of interested stakeholders?
- How deep is the actual level of each stakeholder's involvement in goal setting and in curriculum, research, and outreach activities?
- How are faculty, staff, and departments collaborating with community interests and other external stakeholders?
- Have evaluators shared results with all employees and stakeholders? Were findings reported in a timely and concise manner of strategic value to decision makers at all levels?
- To what extent have participants and beneficiaries engaged in responsible action based on adaptive learning?
- How strong is the evidence that senior university leaders concretely, visibly, consistently, and inclusively supported sustainable-development academic and outreach activity?

---

what they set out to accomplish, reached their objectives, but barely (if at all) made a dent in the big picture. Evaluators need to assess the benefits and risks and long-term sustainability of choices and actions that simultaneously affect natural and human systems.

Our ambitious goal in *Universities and the Sustainable Development Future* is to push the envelope of evaluation practice. Can universities measure beyond outputs and process? We think they can.

Moving beyond outputs to integrated-impact evaluations presents the greatest challenge. We will suggest pathways to this position – many of which are drawn from the leading evaluation work found in the international-development arena – that encompass university involvement in initiatives that address sustainable-development research, curriculum building, and community engagement. Rigorous and innovative approaches that incorporate mixed methods will be needed. Methodologies used in applied futures work (see Slaughter, 1995, p. 38) can be helpful. In addition, Big Data increasingly is available at low cost. Its proponents claim that it can change the way knowledge is produced and collected through a variety of means ranging from satellite images to data derived from consumer behavior and cell phone and internet usage. "Datafication" of everyday life is at the core of Big Data (Chandler, 2015, p. 837). We agree that techniques utilizing Big Data can be useful in certain circumstances. However, they do not replace more traditional data-collection methods for understanding sustainable-development outcomes and impacts.[8]

Outcome evaluation

We will find that moving from assessing outputs to evaluating outcomes is quite feasible. Outcomes frequently can be identified sequentially, ranging from initial through intermediate to long-term (Poister, Aristigueta, and Hall, 2015, p. 55). The theory-of-change approach can be helpful here. If the intended sustainable-development outcomes fail to materialize from higher-education activity, the underlying assumptions regarding intervention contributions and results are flawed (Poister, Aristigueta, and Hall, 2015, pp. 55, 58). The "harvesting" of multiple and reinforcing outcomes, on the other hand, can illuminate pathways to evaluating synergistic impacts.

Multiple and unintended outcomes are possible from university TSD interventions. The use of progress markers, progress-marker ladders, and outcome journals is helpful in determining "progression towards the ideal outcome challenge" in complex change-process situations (Deprez, 2012, pp. 240–241; Powell, Molander, and Celebicic, 2012, pp. 218–219, 223).[9] Outcome analysis folds into capacity development, the next subject for consideration.

Capacity-building evaluations

Evaluators look for evidence regarding critical dimensions of university development devoted to sustainable development. Here we focus on governance evaluation and on building evaluative capacity. Again, our primary interest is with outcomes.

Governance evaluation

From a process standpoint, the relationship of governance to new capacity building features in sustainable-development evaluations. What is the level of commitment to building sustainable-development capacity at top university-leadership levels? Are supportive institution-wide missions, policies, and budgets available? Are tailored-training resources available for building capacity for sustainable-development curriculum renewal, and to what extent have they been utilized?

Have promotion pathways encouraged curriculum, research, and outreach initiatives (Desha and Hargroves, 2014, pp. 103–104)? Have sustainable-development commitments been translated into enhanced expertise, faculty and student interest and involvement, internal collaborations, and external partnering?

Sustainable-development-capacity evaluations specifically address curricular and co-curricular outcomes. To what extent have the three pillars of sustainable development been embedded across the curriculum?[10] Are poverty, local and global resource consumption, values clarification, and human wellbeing adequately treated (see, for instance, Aklilu, 2015, pp. 195–199)? Do meaningful service-learning and community-collaboration opportunities exist?

Box 5.2 presents a suggestive list of questions that can be incorporated in institutional-capacity evaluation.

Other penetrating outcome criteria in the evaluation of university-governance-capacity building center on the breadth and depth of involvement in project-related research and community-development activities and on institutional credibility and influence. To what extent are faculty, staff, and additional departments

---

BOX 5.2 ILLUSTRATIVE INSTITUTIONAL-CAPACITY QUESTIONS: EVALUATIONS OF CURRICULA, RESEARCH, AND OUTREACH

- How has institutional capacity to transform curricula, course syllabi, internships, and service-learning opportunities changed?
- Has the university's annual operating budget devoted to sustainable-development activity increased? To what extent?
- Has there been an increase in the number of personnel hours devoted to sustainability-related professional development?[11]
- Has there been an increase in the number of position descriptions and recruitment advertisements with explicit reference to sustainable-development capabilities?[12]
- Has there been an increase in the number of new hires with sustainable-development competencies?
- Did the initiative strengthen and empower multiple academic programs?
- To what extent have sustainable-development contributions played a role in faculty-, researcher-, and staff-promotion pathways?
- Have university-community relationships resulted in improved capacity to exercise leadership in advancing sustainable development and in the adoption of useful innovations?
- What internal-evaluation and independent-external-evaluation processes have been put in place that utilize multiple-assessment methods to probe the sustainable capacity of higher-education personnel and communities to develop themselves across a range of activity?

contributing to sustainable-development activities? Did the initiative strengthen and empower multiple programs (Calder and Clugston, 2004, p. 257)? How have university human resources and involved stakeholders demonstrated capacity to respond to emerging TSD issues (Syed, et al., 2012)? Has there been an increase in media releases and stakeholder communiques regarding involvement in sustainable-development initiatives (Desha and Hargroves, 2014, p. 117; Thabrew, Wiek, and Ries, 2009, pp. 74–75)?

Evaluative capacity

Another important, but less frequently attended to, dimension of institutional-capacity assessment and sustainability involves the extent to which progress is achieved in developing and maintaining internal- and independent-measurement capacity (Hardi, 2007, p. 25). Too often, TSD-outcome evaluations neglect non-project interventions, including evaluation-capacity strengthening, advocacy, and education (Kruse, 2005, p. 113). *Evaluation-capacity development* must incorporate both the supply side and the equally important demand side.

Most often, the focus of evaluation-capacity development has been on individual and organizational ability to produce quality evaluations. These supply-side needs largely can be met by training evaluators to ensure that they are conversant in a variety of evaluation approaches and methodologies and possess a toolkit ranging from qualitative to quantitative methods that is useful in the design and conduct of process,[13] outcome, and impact evaluations.[14] For organizational learning about what works or does not work (and for whom)[15] to occur, evaluators also need to be able to *"explain* what has led to the impact" (Nilsson, 2012, p. 47 [emphasis in original]). Have the Bellagio principles of effective communication (plain and clear language, objective presentation, visual tools, and reliable and practicable detail) been used in disseminating evaluation results (Bakkes, 2012, p. 253; also Waas, et al., 2015, p. 94)? In addition, supply-side-capacity development aims to ensure adequate and sufficiently independent organizational structures to manage and disclose such evaluations.[16] Unlike independent evaluations, "when an internal evaluation unit challenges management the frequent response is to curtail the scope of the evaluation function, to control evaluation budgets, to undermine evaluation processes and/or to denigrate the methodologies of critical evaluations" (Naidoo, 2016; also see Steven A. Zyck, blog, 1 August 2016).

Until recently, the demand side received less attention in evaluation-capacity development (see, e.g., UNDP, 2012). The first step here is to create awareness of how evaluations can contribute to learning and the improvement of programs, strategies, and policies amongst users. There often is a need to create incentives and capacities to use evaluation findings – for instance, by clarifying the purpose of evaluation and rectifying the frequent misunderstanding of evaluation as criticism. Second, evaluation-capacity development on the demand side should institutionalize mechanisms and structures to commission evaluations and to receive regular feedback from them. Deep, or conceptual, learning revisits purposes, priorities, and strategies (Nilsson, 2012, p. 47). Third, since evaluations frequently are requested by the users, it is important to develop their capacity to commission relevant and professionally sound evaluations – including the ability to conceptualize evaluation questions and, in general, to act as competent contractors.[17]

Evaluating impact

Sustainable-development-impact evaluations aim to capture benefits, setbacks, risks, and promise across the three pillars of society, environment, and economy (Meyer, 2012, pp. 46, 48). For reasons set forth earlier in this book, impact assessments are the most challenging for sustainable-development evaluators. Evaluations of intended and unintended impacts integrate analysis of project interventions, institutional-capacity and human-capability outcomes, and contextual environmental influences (Meyer, 2007, pp. 39, 44).[18] For instance, we expect capacity development to play a catalytic role in sustainable-development impacts.

Comprehensive impact assessments include sector classifications, impact profiles, and differential impact weightings (see Blewitt, 2015, p. 256). Of utility in evaluating higher education's high, intermediate or neutral, and low sustainable-development impacts are components of the sustainability-assessment methodology developed at the Universiti Sains Malaysia (Koshy, et al., 2013, pp. 238, 240–241). In this approach to evaluating curricula and courses, research, and community-outreach initiatives, sectoral inquiries address water, energy, health, agriculture, and biodiversity laced with cross-sector analysis of priority sustainable-development concerns (e.g., "production-consumption, climate change-disaster risk management, and population-poverty").

Evaluating higher-education sustainable-development-impact pathways is made more complete by developing generic theories of change for curriculum, research, and outreach. Driver/barrier mapping offers another useful tool of impact analysis. Progress assessments must deal with the drivers of climate change and other environmental degradations in a broad contextual approach that includes co-benefits and cross-cutting issues that bear upon lasting benefits (Uitto, 2016, p. 111). Following identification of key driving and hindering factors, sustainable-development evaluators systematically collect holistic data on the positive, negative, and neutral impact of support strategies and interventions on the behavior and actions of key players in the change process (Deprez, 2012, pp. 245, 248). In situations where prevailing methods are expensive and technically challenging, rapid-impact evaluation offers a promising alternative (Rowe, 2016).

Probing the unintended, indirect, and secondary impacts of interventions in complex systems characterized by uncertainty and non-linearity requires a broad set of questions, a different approach to evaluation design and inquiry, and special attention to accelerating factors, to the catalytic effects of dynamic interactions, and to tracking and discerning *how* and *why* things happened (Batra, Uitto, and Cando-Noordhuizen, 2016, pp. 20, 22; Brundiers, et al., 2014, pp. 214–215). Developmental evaluators are challenged to "identify and acknowledge sources of uncertainty," to recognize and account for critical unexpected incidents, and to cope with ambiguity (Brundiers, et al., 2014, p. 214). Evaluations that are attentive to intermediate impacts help us begin to understand the unintended as well as intended consequences of university interventions.

Meaningful impact evaluation requires evidence that an intervention can be credibly linked to upstream or downstream sustainable-development results, including the reduction of environmental, economic, and social stressors and increased human wellbeing and security – without producing adverse effects in other areas. Did implemented development projects "encourage responsibility in long spatial and temporal scales by targeting [driving forces] and the root of a problem" (Fredericks, 2014, p. 120)? The identification of extended-impact chains (Thomas and Tominaga, 2013, pp. 58, 62) and attention to aggregating impacts, to scaling up and the replication of successful pilot initiatives (Uitto, 2016, p. 111), and to the duration of introduced impacts and risks can be helpful in this connection (Meyer, 2012, pp. 47, 49). Box 5.3 presents a suggestive list of queries that can be incorporated in higher-education impact-contribution evaluations.[19]

BOX 5.3 QUESTIONS THAT CAN BE ADDRESSED IN INTEGRATED HIGHER-EDUCATION-IMPACT EVALUATIONS

- Were the contextually selected core principles of sustainable development put into practice?
- How have program graduates exercised professional capabilities and transnational competence in ways that further sustainable development in economic, social, and/or ecological arenas?
- Has cross-institutional and/or cross-disciplinary research interaction produced synergies with positive effects for sustainable development?
- Do research results connect now with the future?
- Will future university research and outreach initiatives support community and regional priorities?
- Has the university provided technical and training support to public agencies, NGOs, and private firms?
- Is there evidence that university-led research or a university outreach project contributed to improvements in public service to local communities?
- Is there evidence that university-led research or a university-outreach project contributed to reductions in local social and economic inequality?
- Is there evidence that negative environmental, social, and economic impacts have been mitigated, at least in part, due to a university outreach project?
- Will people's wellbeing be maintained or enhanced?
- To what extent has the impetus for change strengthened over time?
- Have local cultural and social resources been enhanced or diminished? Why?
- Is there evidence of increases in local social, economic, and ecological

> innovations that can be plausibly attributed to a university-outreach project?
> - Are any locally and regionally adopted knowledge-based products that resulted from participatory research sustainable?
> - Is there evidence that university-led research or a university outreach project maintained or diminished habitats and biodiversity?
> - Have university research and/or outreach initiatives incurred public debt to be borne by future generations?
> - Did any university initiative produce negative impacts that will be difficult or impossible to reverse?
> - Does a full synthesis of evaluation results indicate that the net result of university activity will be positive or negative in the long-term?[20]
> - What risks or uncertainties remain?

Multiple methods

Evaluation as a professional field, especially in North America, has roots in social programs. Trail blazers developed many evaluation approaches and practices in the context of education. Drawing upon quantitative approaches used in sociology, social psychology, and medicine, contributors emphasized experimental and quasi-experimental methods. This emphasis has resulted in a rather narrow range of methodologies that are considered rigorous. For instance, in the much-vaunted *No Child Left Behind* program context, the US Department of Education determined that only quantitative methods, such as randomized controlled trials (RCTs), provided the "gold standard" in terms of evidence (Rallis, 2009, p. 170). We view this narrow range of approaches as misguided; it reduces evaluation to measuring easily quantifiable information and misses out on less obvious connections, unintended consequences, and the big picture.

Experience further indicates that the explanatory power and external validity of randomized controlled trials and similar experimental methods is low (Prichett and Sandefur, 2013). RCTs answer only a limited set of questions. Therefore, evaluators must be open to other approaches (Bickman and Reich, 2009, pp. 67–68). Since impact evaluations endeavor to link an intervention with multiple possible effects on beneficiaries, numerous possible designs and approaches should be in the evaluator's portfolio. The chosen designs should "match the evaluation question being asked and the attributes" of the programs being evaluated (Stern, et al., 2012, pp. 78–79).

Evaluation of international-development programs initially followed a path that focused on qualitative methods – largely due to the lack of systematic data and the nature and context of aid projects. As methodologies developed, evaluation became more rigorous, and quantitative approaches also made their way into the international-development sphere. Nevertheless, the emphasis has remained firmly on mixed methods that combine qualitative and quantitative approaches and on choosing methods based on the evaluation questions rather than vice versa. In an interesting convergence, recent environmental-education evaluations also draw increasingly on mixed methods (Zint, 2011, p. 337).

We believe that the higher-education sector has much to learn from the lessons and practices of evaluation in the international-development arena. In many instances, the established criteria of development effectiveness can be applied usefully to sustainable-development evaluations in higher education (Picciotto, 2013). In the chapters that follow, therefore, we combine lessons from recent educational evaluation[21] with those from evaluation in international development and from sustainable development more broadly (see, for instance, Uitto, 2016, pp. 110–111). These methodological lessons are incorporated in our elaborated comprehensive framework and applied in a novel way to university TSD-evaluation approaches.

Impact evaluation can be a particularly challenging and expensive proposition (Thomas and Tominaga, 2013, p. 62; Hailemichael, 2013, p. 43), particularly if one adheres to a narrow definition that uses experimental and quasi-experimental designs. Therefore, a broad range of impact-evaluation designs and methods[22] is widely recognized as essential (Stern, et al., 2012). For instance, an evaluation tool that is particularly useful for illuminating lagged effects is *biographical analysis*, which allows learners to trace educational outcomes and impacts over "however long a period seems appropriate" (Schuller, Hammond, and Preston, 2004, p. 189).

Interventions aimed at sustainable-development outcomes and impacts operate in complex environments where it is not easy to establish the specific contribution of any particular activity. Our framework allows multiple approaches and methods. The limitations of any single evaluation approach are mitigated by the use of multiple methods and data sources[23] to triangulate findings in search of establishing a "plausible contribution" for changes associated with a particular curricular, research, or community-outreach activity. As applied by the UNDP, the concept of triangulation in evaluation "refers to empirical evidence gathered through three major sources of information: perception, validation and documentation" (Uitto, 2011, p. 479). Furthermore, systematic triangulation can be used to ameliorate against challenges, such as the scarcity or unreliability of data from a single source or the complexity of comparing evidence across different disciplines (Carugi, 2016).

The cross-checking of findings through triangulated perspectives enriches evaluation as a meaningful explanatory exercise (Stern, 2004, pp. 38–39). A variety of forms of triangulation – including methodological, data, investigator, and theory triangulation – can be employed to increase confidence in university sustainable-development-evaluation findings (Green and Tones, 2010, p. 503; Meyer, 2007, pp. 34–35; Brundiers, et al., 2014, pp. 215–216; Kyburz-Graber, 2016, pp. 133–135).[24] Rapid-impact evaluation, for instance, triangulates assessments by three separate groups of experts to evaluate incremental change in results attributable to the intervention (Rowe, 2016). Unsurprisingly, therefore, most higher-education sustainable-development evaluations require transdisciplinarity (Scholz, et al., 2006, p. 231).

The Sustainability Assessment Methodology introduced at Universiti Sains Malaysia (see Koshy, et al., 2013) offers a useful and potentially holistic tool that can be adapted in evaluating the sustainable-development content of courses, research projects, and community initiatives along with changes over time. The Sustainability Assessment Methodology's simple sustainability-ranking system (total number of positive responses as a percentage of the total number of questions asked) will yield a high, medium, or low[25] sustainability classification (Koshy, et al., 2013, pp. 237–239, 242).

Backcasting begins with changes and trends (impacts) identified in a participatory manner. Then, backcasting endeavors to link observed changes directly and indirectly to project interventions (Strele, 2012, p. 175). An advantage of this approach is "identification of unintended effects of interventions by analyzing the impact situation in total without the limited focus on areas related to the intended effects" (Strele, 2012, p. 176). The time delay that often accompanies impacts limits the utility of backcasting for learning outside most project timeframes (Strele, 2012, p. 176).

Måns Nilsson (2012, pp. 52, 54, 57) presents a participatory toolkit of approaches that can be used meaningfully in participating public- and stakeholder-engaged evaluations. Based on pictorial visualization, concept mapping enables participants to "focus and develop a joint understanding in their own language." Carefully planned focus groups that address a predefined set of questions "capture the perceptions, knowledge and experience of participants." The goal-achievement-matrix approach uses "ranking and prioritization by asking experts, stakeholders or decision makers to assign numerical values to qualitative information" to identify complex impacts in a disaggregated manner.[26] When concerned community members "gather and record systematic observations about environmental or social conditions," evaluations are "potentially better equipped for identification of cumulative effects than [are] project-based approaches."

In a similar fashion, the evaluation design that guides the progress-marker approach involves extensive baseline and endline interviews with partners and beneficiaries coupled with customized-questionnaire data (Powell, Molander, and Celebicic, 2012, p. 224). This approach typically incorporates social-impact analysis based on structured interviews along with a questionnaire-based survey "administered to the population that is directly impacted" and to project stakeholders (Thabrew, Wiek, and Ries, 2009, p. 70); it can include risk assessment used in a participatory manner that combines stakeholder and community judgments in order to measure the probability of hazard occurrence and the magnitude of potential damage (Thabrew, Wiek, and Ries, 2009, p. 70).

Flexibility and adaptability

Within each TSD-evaluation dimension, evaluators can choose criteria and queries as elaborate or streamlined as they want, depending on the importance and complexity of the issue (for instance, see Bakkes, 2012, p. 245), stakeholder aspirations (Thabrew, Wiek, and Ries, 2009, p. 71), project attributes (Kruse, 2005, p. 125), available time and resources, and so forth. A purposive combination of evaluation approaches drawn from a well-stocked toolkit allows evaluators flexibility to make context-specific selections based on analytical, practical, and financial considerations (Nilsson, 2012, p. 57; Rammel, Velazquez, and Mader, 2016, p. 341; see Chapter 11 in this volume). An adaptive approach to sustainable-development evaluation that emphasizes patient probing, learning by observing, real-time feedback, immediate-response measures, and flexible designs and methods is particularly useful in dynamic circumstances replete with uncertainty as well as emerging and non-linear changes in interconnected conditions (Brundiers, et al., 2014, p. 214; Thomas and Tominaga, 2013, pp. 59–60, 63–64, 68; Becker, et al., 2013, p. 240).

Evaluating university sustainable-development activities

The evaluation framework for assessing sustainable-development education that we set forth in this chapter and will develop further in the rest of Part III addresses "the need to improve and strengthen the definition of key performance indicators" (Cloete, Bailey, and Maassen, 2011, p. xix).[27] Furthermore, in recognition of the lagged-effects phenomenon (Schuller, Hammond, and Preston, 2004, p. 188; Hummelbrunner, 2012, p. 255), our framework explicitly endeavors to capture the long-term as well immediate- and medium-time-range results of university activities (Africa-U.S. Higher Education Initiative, n.d., pp. 3–4; Stevens, 2012, pp. 57, 64; also see Derrick, 2013, pp. 52, 60).

We accept that to yield meaningful and useful insights, sustainable-development-education evaluations need to navigate beyond externally imposed measures, indicators, indices,[28] and global metrics. Although envisioning and promoting sustainable development is predominantly contextual and place-based, national and transnational facilitating and constraining forces also remain influential (Elliott, 2013, p. 305; Baker, 2016, p. 10). Therefore, the most rewarding evaluation frameworks integrate micro-, meso-, and macro-level territorial analysis (Meyer, 2007, p. 46). They operate at various scales, allowing aggregation and disaggregation while retaining local relevance (Hales and Prescott-Allen, 2002, p. 47).

We incorporate theory-based-evaluation principles (Funnell and Rogers, 2011) into our framework. The theory-of-change approach, which powerfully illuminates how and why activities shape outcomes and under which conditions, provides insights that can guide evaluative investigation of academic programs devoted to sustainable development (Kyburz-Graber, 2016, p. 134). By systematically identifying links among activities, context, driving forces, and outcomes (Connell and Kubisch, 1998, pp. 36–38; Gambone, 1998, pp. 159–160),

> [p]articipants engage in a process of theory generation in which they specify what outcomes they aim to achieve and how they expect their intended interventions to lead to their desired outcomes. They identify short- and medium-term goals and try to make explicit the links between them and long-term outcomes.
>
> (Boydell and Rugkasa, 2007, p. 219)[29]

Evaluators seek to explain the accuracy or inaccuracy of intervention-linkage predictions (Nilsson, 2012, pp. 47–48).

The theory-of-change approach is served by several useful analytical techniques. *Contribution analysis* is based on verifying the theory of change that the program or project is based on and, then, analyzing the intervening factors that might influence intended outcomes. This technique facilitates identification of particular program/project contributions based on reasonable levels of evidence (Mayne, 2008). *Scenario construction and assessment* generates guiding questions that can be fruitfully investigated through transdisciplinary case studies (Scholz, et al., 2006, p. 241). The *most-significant-change* technique involves reporting the changes caused by a project or intervention based on stories by stakeholders and identifying the most decisive ones (Davies and Dart, 2005).

Integrated assessments

In order to identify promising levers of organization change, starting points need to be defined (Hales and Prescott-Allen, 2002, p. 40), and "why" and "how" linkages among outputs, outcomes, and impacts need to be clarified (Vaessen and Todd, 2008; Shriberg, 2004, p. 73). Therefore, process evaluation features prominently in our tailored framework for evaluating higher education's sustainable-development activities.[30] Our approach to university TSD evaluation also is inclusive; it emphasizes transparency (see Waas, et al., 2015, p. 94), participation by key stakeholders, and the value of multiple and multidisciplinary perspectives (Crossley and Bennett, 2004, p. 222; Tikly, 2011, p. 10; Stevens, 2012, p. 57; Jacob, Hertin, and Volkery, 2007, p. 92). Integrated assessments, developed in participatory fashion, "help decisionmakers understand the linkages between short- and long-term needs and between apparently diverse goals by illuminating both connections and thresholds of impact" (Hales and Prescott-Allen, 2002, p. 40).

Our framework is built around an interconnected set of evaluative questions that are intended to encompass the range of academic sustainable-development activity that universities are prone to engage in. Specifically, framework questions relate to teaching (curricula), research, outreach, and partnering. Consistent with concern for sustainable development, the framework's overall outcome and impact foci are with improvements in livelihoods and current living conditions, advancing intra- and inter-generational equity and justice (see Gibson, 2005, p. 101), and preserving the ability of future generations in all world regions to meet their needs and realize their aspirations.[31]

Applications to teaching and curricula, research, partnering, and outreach

The framework elaborated above is set forth as a guide for analyzing current and promising approaches involving higher-education teaching and curricula, research, partnering, and outreach. We also have endeavored to ensure that the essential components of the articulated framework are consistent with the ten

Bellagio principles for assessing progress toward sustainable development (see Hales and Prescott-Allen, 2002, p. 41) and the African Evaluation Association's thirty African Evaluation Guidelines (Patel, 2013).

This chapter presented illustrative questions in-text and in Boxes 5.1, 5.2, 5.3. In the rest of Part III (Chapter 6 through Chapter 9), we draw on the framework outlined here for guidance in elaborating ways to improve evaluations of university involvement in sustainable-development undertakings.

Notes

1 One recently reported study found low use of indicators in European Commission impact assessments and a decline from 2006 to 2009 in efforts to quantify economic, social, and environmental impacts (Franz and Kirkpatrick, 2012, p. 79). Single indicators, used to represent a particular characteristic or property of a system (Hales and Prescott-Allen, 2002, p. 39), are unable to capture complexity, to encompass the diverse criteria used to judge sustainable development, or to "provide insights into why things happen" (Batra, Uitto, and Cando-Noordhuizen, 2016, p. 18; also Fredericks, 2014, pp. 63–64; Kruse, 2005, p. 123). Tomas Ramos and Sara Pires (2013, pp. 82, 85–86) maintain, however, that sustainability indicators "can improve the dialog with stakeholders, engaging them in sustainability matters and providing key relevant information for their decisions and aspirations." Thus, sustainability indicators can help broaden support for collective-sustainable-development actions.

2 Of course, the act of evaluating a process often at least subtly alters that process.

3 See Patton's (2008) broader discussion of utilization-focused evaluation, including process use.

4 A criterion can be distinguished from an indicator as "as standard by which something is judged . . . or 'something we want to achieve' without itself being a direct measure of performance." Indicators "infer the status of a particular criterion." A principle "provides the justification" for criteria (Rammel, Velazquez, and Mader, 2016, p. 334).

5 See the case example applying their development-evaluation framework at Dalhousie College of Sustainability (Brundiers, et al., 2014, pp. 216–221).

6 See the continuous, broadly participative, and integrated approach to evaluating ecological and socio-economic changes utilized by the Ni hat'ni community as reported in Gibson (2005, pp. 69–71).

7 It is important to recognize in this connection that overall personal-wellbeing evaluations are related to evaluations of particular aspects of life, including satisfaction with environmental conditions (OECD, 2013, pp. 30, 180).

8 There also are serious ethical questions pertaining to people's right to privacy.

9 Powell, Molander, and Celebicic (2012, p. 229) recommend that special efforts be made to ensure that progress markers and outcome challenges "overlap sufficiently with their [stakeholders'] own motivation and worldview, especially when targeting less powerful groups."

10 One capacity indicator of ESD penetration is "the percentage of units with sufficiently strong sustainability knowledge content for it to be visible in the unit description, learning outcome or other catalogue data." Individual student experience in encounters with educational programs offered by multiple units provides an outcome measure that merits probing (Tierney, Tweddell, and Willmore, 2015, pp. 513–514, 518–520).

11 See Desha and Hargroves (2014, p. 117).

12 See Desha and Hargroves (2014, p. 179).

13 Even the basic capacity to design projects so that they are evaluable often requires training.

14 For evaluations involving "Big Data," such as "massively collaborative" interventions involving public-health genomics, additional capacity building is needed in the "science

of whys" and the "science of hows" (Ozdemir, 2014, p. 83). In addition, new evaluation approaches need to be developed for climate-change-adaptation studies – that is, evaluating impacts on the vulnerability and resilience of people and infrastructure (Uitto, 2016, pp. 3–4).

15 Particularly for disadvantaged individuals, families, and communities (Batra, Uitto, and Cando-Noordhuizen, 2016, p. 17).

16 In contrast to assessments conducted by independent-evaluation units (such as German Technical Cooperation [GTZ] final reviews), Michaelowa and Borrmann (2006, pp. 321, 328) maintain that self-reports generated by internal staff should not be considered as actual evaluations.

17 When contracting with external providers, universities should "ensure that evaluators have few prior relationships with those they are evaluating, and they should take steps to limit the number of evaluations any one consultant can do . . . in given time period" (Steven A. Zyck, blog, 1 August 2016).

18 Environmental impacts occur at all life-cycle stages: extraction, production, usage, and afterlife (Blewitt, 2015, p. 256; Nilsson, 2012, p. 53). Life-cycle analysis enables evaluators to "comprehend and visualize a broader set of upstream and downstream consequences . . ." to map linkages among economic, social, and environmental impacts, and to identify who is advantaged and disadvantaged by sustainable-development at all stages (Thabrew, Wiek, and Ries, 2009, pp. 68, 71, 73–74). However, life-cycle assessment and life-cycle costing methodologies can "leave out critical social and community sustainability issues and do not explicitly incorporate externalities" (Cayuela, et al., 2013, p. 232).

19 Some of these questions are drawn from suggestions found in Morfit and Gore (2009, p. 16); Stevens (2012, pp. 65–67); Gibson (2005, p. 80); and Wiek, et al. (2013, p. 6).

20 For a useful set of fifteen generic questions for evaluating the significance of effects, see Gibson (2005, p. 173). The following questions drawn from Gibson's full set illustrate the value of incorporating specific questions of similar composition: "Could the effects add to stresses that might undermine socio-ecological integrity at any scale, in ways or to an extent that could damage important life support functions?" "Could the effects provide more economic and other opportunities for human well-being, especially for those now disadvantaged?"

21 Zint (2011, pp. 337–338) reports that evaluators "found qualitative measures more helpful in evaluating ESD program outcomes and impacts than quantitative measures."

22 Including case studies and stakeholder feedback (Thomas and Tominaga, 2013, p. 62).

23 Using multiple evaluation methods also allows a "nonproductive" approach to be "dropped without having to start data collection from scratch" (Palomba and Banta, 1999, p. 17).

24 Other types are time triangulation, place triangulation, and person (role) triangulation (see Collins, 2011, p. 60).

25 The Sustainability Assessment Methodology's cutoffs are 70 percent to 100 percent (high); 30 percent to 69 percent (medium); and 1 percent to 29 percent (low) (Koshy, et al., 2013, p. 242).

26 In a related participatory vein, a recommended method from the SIMPLE sustainability assessment "is to rank the potential positive and negative impacts" of an intervention "based on a checklist of agreed upon economic, environmental and social criteria using both qualitative judgments and available quantitative data" (Stevens, 2012, p. 64).

27 Evaluators select indicators based on reliability ("the extent to which a measure yields consistent results") and validity ("the extent to which an indicator actually captures the underlying concept that it purports to measure") (OECD, 2013, p. 13).

28 Indices, an aggregated collection of indicators, aim to simplify complex phenomena (Hales and Prescott-Allen, 2002, p. 39; Dietz and Hanemaaijer, 2012, p. 33). For an ethical analysis of existing sustainable-development indices, see Fredericks (2014, pp. 5, 58–59, 68–69, 123–127, 148–149, 155), who concludes (p. 169; also p. 177) that the foremost limitation of prevailing indexes "occurs with respect to the social dimension

of sustainability; it is understudied in comparison with other dimensions." Further, "priorities and conditions specific to local communities and ecosystems do not sufficiently influence national indexes" (Fredericks, 2014, pp. 184–185). In addition, "indicator/indices and product related assessment approaches . . . express a strong retrospective perspective for analysing the past and are not optimally designed for assessing long-term sustainability processes" (Rammel, Velazquez, and Mader, 2016, p. 337).

29 One drawback is that the theory-of-change approach is time-consuming and resource-intensive (Boydell and Rugkasa, 2007, p. 219).

30 For helpful procedural guidelines regarding the conduct of evaluations, see Poister, Aristigueta, and Hall (2015, pp. 426–427).

31 These overriding normative goals are conditioned by a subset of ethical principles for sustainability that are linked with technical considerations, including farsightedness, culturally and scientifically inclusive processes, careful use, responsibility, and feasible idealism (Fredericks, 2014, pp. 69–70, 100, 113–116).

Works cited

Africa-U.S. Higher Education Initiative. n.d. "Developing a Knowledge Center for the Africa-U.S. Higher Education Initiative: A Concept Paper." Association of Public and Land Grant Universities, Washington, DC.

Aklilu Dalelo. 2015. "Sustainability Issues in the Geography Curriculum for an Undergraduate Programme: The Case of Addis Ababa University, Ethiopia." In *Mainstreaming Environment and Sustainability in African Universities: Stories of Change*, edited by Heila Lotz-Sisitka, Gitile Naituli, Amanda Hlengwa, Mike Ward, Ayobami Salami, Akpezi Ogbuigwe, Mahesh Pradhan, Marie Neeser, and Sanne Lauriks. Grahamstown: Rhodes University Environmental Learning Research Centre. Pp. 185–199.

Baker, Susan. 2016. *Sustainable Development*, 2nd edition. London: Routledge.

Bakkes, Jan. 2012. "Bellagio Sustainability Assessment and Measurement Principles (BellagioSTAMP): Significance and Examples from International Environmental Outlooks." In *Sustainable Development, Evaluation and Policy-Making: Theory, Practise and Quality Assurance*, edited by Anneke von Raggamby and Frieder Rubik. Cheltenham, UK: Edward Elgar. Pp. 241–260.

Batra, Geeta; Uitto, Juha I.; and Cando-Noordhuizen, Lee. 2016. "Fron MDGs to SDGs: Evaluating Global Environmental Benefits." *Evaluation Matters* 1:16–23.

Becker, Anne; Motgi, Anjali; Weigel, Jonathan; Raviola, Giuseppe; Keshavjee, Salmaan; and Kleinman, Arthur. 2013. "The Unique Challenges of Mental Health and MDRTB: Critical Perspectives on Metrics of Disease." In *Reimagining Gloabal Health: An Introduction*, edited by Paul Farmer, Jim Jong Kim, Arthur Kleinman, and Matthew Basilico. Berkeley: University of California Press. Pp. 212–244.

Bickman, Leonard; and Reich, Stephanie M. 2009. "Randomized Controlled Trials: A Gold Standard with Feet of Clay?" In *What Counts as Credible Evidence in Applied Research and Evaluation Practice?* edited by Stewart I. Donaldson, Christina A. Christie, and Melvin M. Mark. Thousand Oaks and London: Sage. Pp. 51–77.

Blewitt, John. 2015. *Understanding Sustainable Development*, 2nd edition. London: Routledge.

Boydell, Leslie R.; and Rugkasa, Jorun. 2007. "Benefits of Working in Partnership: A Model." *Critical Public Health* 17 (3):217–228.

Brundiers, Katja; Savage, Emma; Mannell, Steven; Lang, Daniel J.; and Wiek, Arnim. 2014. "Educating Sustainability Change Agents by Design: Appraisals of the Transformative Role of Higher Education." In *Sustainable Development and Quality Assurance in Higher Education: Transformation of Learning and Society*, edited by Zinaida Fadeeva, Laima Galkute, Clemens Mader, and Geoff Scott. New York: Palgrave Macmillan. Pp. 196–229.

Calder, Wynn; and Clugston, Rick. 2004. "Lighting Many Fires: South Carolina's Sustainable Universities Initiative." In *Higher Education and the Challenge of Sustainability: Problematics, Promise, and Practice*, edited by Peter B. Corcoran and Arjen E. J. Wals. Dordrecht: Kluwer Academic Publishers. Pp. 249–262.

Carugi, Carlo. 2016. "Experiences with Systematic Triangulation at the Global Environment Facility." *Evaluation and Program Planning* 55:55–66.

Catley-Carlson, Margaret. 2004. "Foundations of Partnerships: A Practitioner's Perspective." In *Evaluation & Development: The Partnership Dimension*, edited by Andres Liebenthal, Osvaldo N. Feinstein, and Gregory K. Ingram. New Brunswick, NJ: Transaction Publishers. Pp. 21–27.

Cayuela, Alberto; Robinson, John B.; Campbell, Ann; Coops, Nicholas; and Munro, Alison. 2013. "Integration of Operational and Academic Efforts in Sustainability at the University of British Columbia." In *Sustainability Assessment Tools in Higher Education Institutions: Mapping Trends and Good Practices around the World*, edited by Sandra Caeiro, Walter L. Filho, Charbel Jabbour, and Ulisses M. Azeiteiro. Cham, Switzerland: Springer International Publishing. Pp. 223–236.

Chandler, David. 2015. "A World without Causation: Big Data and the Coming of Age of Posthumanism." *Millennium: Journal of International Studies* 43 (3):833–851.

Chouinard, Jill A.; and Cousins, J. Bradley. 2013. "Participatory Evaluation for Development: Examining Research-Based Knowledge from within the African Context." *African Evaluation Journal* 1 (1):66–74.

Cloete, Nico; Bailey, Tracy; and Maassen, Peter. 2011. *Universities and Economic Development in Africa: Pact, Academic Core, and Coordination*. Executive Summary of Synthesis Report. Wynberg, South Africa: Centre for Higher Education Transformation.

Collins, Christopher S. 2011. *Higher Education and Global Poverty: University Partnerships and the World Bank in Developing Countries*. Amherst, NY: Cambria Press.

Connell, James P.; and Kubisch, Anne C. 1998. "Applying a Theory of Change Approach to the Evaluation of Comprehensive Community Initiatives: Progress, Prospects, and Problems." In *New Approaches to Evaluating Community Initiatives*, edited by Karen Fulbright-Anderson, Anne C. Kubisch, and James P. Connell. Seward, NE: Concordia University Press. Pp. 15–44.

Crossley, Michael; and Bennett, J. Alexander. 2004. "Planning for Case Study Evaluation in Belize, Central America." In *Qualitative Educational Research in Developing Countries: Current Perspectives*, edited by Michael Crossley and Graham Vulliamy. New York: Garland Publishing. Pp. 221–243.

Crossley, Michael; Herriot, Andrew; Waudo, Judith; Mwirotsi, Miriam; Holmes, Keith; and Juma, Magdallen. 2005. *Research and Evaluation for Educational Development: Learning from the PRISM Experience in Kenya*. Oxford, UK: Symposium Books.

Davies, Rick; and Dart, Jess. 2005. "The 'Most Significant Change' Technique: A Guide to Its Use." Monitoring and Evaluation NEWS. www.mande.co.uk/docs/MSCGuide.pdf

Deprez, Steff. 2012. "Development of a Learning-Oriented Monitoring System for Sustainable Agriculture Chain Development in Eastern Indonesia." In *Governance by Evaluation for Sustainable Development: Institutional Capacities and Learning*, edited by Michal Sedlacko and Andre Martinuzzi. Cheltenham, UK: Edward Elgar. Pp. 233–252.

Derrick, Stephen. 2013. "Time and Sustainability Metrics in Higher Education." In *Sustainability Assessment Tools in Higher Education Institutions: Mapping Trends and Good Practices Around the World*, edited by Sandra Caeiro, Walter L. Filho, Charbel Jabbour, and Ulisses M. Azeiteiro. Cham, Switzerland: Springer International Publishing. Pp. 47–63.

Desha, Cheryl; and Hargroves, Karlson C. 2014. *Higher Education and Sustainable Development: A Model for Curriculum Renewal*. London: Routledge.

Dietz, Frank J.; and Hanemaaijer, Aldert H. 2012. "How to Select Policy-Relevant Indicators for Sustainable Development." In *Sustainable Development, Evaluation and Policy-Making: Theory, Practise and Quality Assurance*, edited by Anneke von Raggamby and Frieder Rubik. Cheltenham, UK: Edward Elgar. Pp. 21–35.

Elliott, Jennifer A. 2013. *An Introduction to Sustainable Development*, 4th edition. London: Routledge.

Eyben, Rosalind. 2013. "Uncovering the Politics of 'Evidence' and 'Results': A Framing Paper for Development Practitioners." www.bigpushforward.net

Franz, Jennifer; and Kirkpatrick, Colin. 2012. "Integrating Sustainable Development into Impact Assessments: How Effective Is the European Commission?" In *Governance by Evaluation for Sustainable Development: Institutional Capacities and Learning*, edited by Michal Sedlacko and Andre Martinuzzi. Cheltenham, UK: Edward Elgar. Pp. 63–85.

Fredericks, Sarah. 2014. *Measuring and Evaluating Sustainability: Ethics in Sustainability Indexes*. London: Routledge.

Funnell, Sue F.; and Rogers, Patricia J. 2011. *Purposeful Program Theory: Effective Use of Theories of Change and Logic Models*. San Francisco, CA: Jossey-Bass.

Gambone, Michelle A. 1998. "Challenges of Measurement in Community Change Initiatives." In *New Approaches to Evaluating Community Initiatives*, edited by Karen Fulbright-Anderson, Anne C. Kubisch, and James P. Connell. Seward, NE: Concordia University Press. Pp. 149–163.

Garcia, J. R.; and Zazueta, Aaron 2015. "Going beyond Mixed Methods to Mixed Approaches: A Systems Perspective for Asking the Right Questions." *IDS Bulletin* 46 (1):30–43.

Gibson, Robert B. 2005. *Sustainability Assessment: Criteria and Processes*. London: Earthscan.

Green, Jackie; and Tones, Keith. 2010. *Health Promotion: Planning and Strategies*, 2nd edition. Thousand Oaks, CA: Sage.

Hailemichael Taye. 2013. "Evaluating the Impact of Agricultural Extension Programmes in Sub-Saharan Africa: Challenges and Prospects." *African Evaluation Journal* 1 (1):38–45.

Hales, David; and Prescott-Allen, Robert. 2002. "Flying Blind: Assessing Progress toward Sustainability." In *Global Environmental Governance: Options & Opportunities*, edited by Daniel C. Esty and Maria H. Ivanova. New Haven, CT: Yale School of Forestry & Environmental Studies. Pp. 31–52.

Hardi, Peter. 2007. "The Long and Winding Road of Sustainable Development Evaluation." In *Impact Assessment and Sustainable Development: European Practice and Experience*, edited by Clive George and Colin Kirkpatrick. Cheltenham, UK: Edward Elgar. Pp. 15–30.

Hummelbrunner, Richard. 2012. "Process Monitoring of Impacts and Its Application in Structural Fund Programmes." In *Governance by Evaluation for Sustainable Development: Institutional Capacities and Learning*, edited by Michal Sedlacko and Andre Martinuzzi. Cheltenham, UK: Edward Elgar. Pp. 253–266.

Jacob, Klaus; Hertin, Julia; and Volkery, Axel. 2007. "Considering Environmental Aspects in Integrated Impact Assessment: Lessons Learned and Challenges Ahead." In *Impact Assessment and Sustainable Development: European Practice and Experience*, edited by Clive George and Colin Kirkpatrick. Cheltenham, UK: Edward Elgar. Pp. 90–106.

Jilke, Sebastian. 2013. "What Shapes Citizens' Evaluations of Their Public Officials' Accountability? Evidence from Local Ethiopia." *Public Administration and Development* 33 (5):389–403.

Koshy, Kanayathu C.; Nor, Norizan M.; Sibly, Suzyrman; Rahim, Asyirah A.; Jegatesen, Govindran; and Muhamad, Malik. 2013. "An Indicator-Based Approach to Sustainability Monitoring and Mainstreaming at Universiti Sains Malaysia." In *Sustainability Assessment Tools in Higher Education Institutions: Mapping Trends and Good Practices around the World*, edited by Sandra Caeiro, Walter L. Filho, Charbel Jabbour, and Ulisses M. Azeiteiro. Cham, Switzerland: Springer International Publishing. Pp. 237–258.

Kruse, Stein-Erik. 2005. "Meta-evaluations of NGO Experience: Results and Challenges." In *Evaluating Development Effectiveness*, edited by George K. Pitman, Osvaldo N. Feinstein, and Gregory K. Ingram. World Bank Series on Evaluation and Development, Volume 7. New Brunswick, N.J.: Transaction Publishers. Pp. 109–127.

Kyburz-Graber, Regula. 2016. "Case Study Research on Higher Education for Sustainable Development." In *Routledge Handbook of Higher Education for Sustainable Development*, edited by Matthias Barth, Gerd Michelsen, Marco Rieckmann, and Ian Thomas. London: Routledge. Pp. 126–141.

Mayne, John. 2008. *Contribution Analysis: An Approach to Exploring Cause and Effect*. ILAC Brief 16. Rome: Institutional Learning and Change Initiative, Biodiversity International.

Meyer, Wolfgang. 2007. "Evaluation of Sustainable Development: A Social Science Approach." In *Sustainable Development in Europe: Concepts, Evaluation and Applications*, edited by Uwe Schubert and Eckhard Stormer. Cheltenham, UK: Edward Elgar. Pp. 33–50.

Meyer, Wolfgang. 2012. "Should Evaluation Be Revisited for Sustainable Development?" In *Sustainable Development, Evaluation and Policy-Making: Theory, Practise and Quality Assurance*, edited by Anneke von Raggamby and Frieder Rubik. Cheltenham, UK: Edward Elgar. Pp. 37–54.

Michaelowa, Katharina; and Borrmann, Axel. 2006. "Evaluation Bias and Incentive Structures in Bi- and Multilateral Aid Agencies." *Review of Development Economics* 10 (2):313–329.

Miyaguchi, Takaaki; and Uitto, Juha I. 2015. *A Realist Review of Climate Change Adaptation Programme Evaluations: Methodological Implications and Programmatic Findings*. Occasional Paper Series. New York: United Nations Development Programme, Independent Evaluation Office.

Morfit, Christine; and Gore, Jane. 2009. *HED/USAID Higher Education Partnerships in Africa 1997–2007*. Washington, DC: Higher Education for Development.

Naidoo, Indran. 2016. "Forum: Is There a Trade-off between Accountability and Learning in Evaluation?" *Evaluation Connections* (European Evaluation Society) (February):12–17.

Nilsson, Måns. 2012. "Tools for Learning-Oriented Environmental Appraisal." In *Governance by Evaluation for Sustainable Development: Institutional Capacities and Learning*, edited by Michal Sedlacko and Andre Martinuzzi. Cheltenham, UK: Edward Elgar. Pp. 45–60.

Oakley, Peter. 1991. *Projects with People: The Practice of Participation in Rural Development*. Geneva: International Labor Office.

Organization of Economic Cooperation and Development (OECD). 2013. *OECD Guidelines on Measuring Subjective Well-Being*. Paris: OECD Publishing.

Ozdemir, Vural. 2014. "Public Health in the Age of Genomic, 'Big Data' and Massively Collaborative Global Science." In *Routledge Handbook of Global Public Health in Asia*, edited by Sian M. Griffiths, Jin Ling Tang, and Eng Kiong Yeoh. London: Routledge. Pp. 74–90.

Palomba, Catherine A.; and Banta, Trudy W. 1999. *Assessment Essentials: Planning, Implementing, and Improving Assessment in Higher Education*. San Francisco, CA: Jossey-Bass.

Patel, Mahesh. 2013. "African Evaluation Guidelines." *African Evaluation Journal* 1 (1):5–9.

Patton, Michael Q. 2008. *Utilization-Focused Evaluation*. 4th edition. Los Angeles, CA: Sage.

Pawson, Ray; and Tilley, Nick. 1997. *Realistic Evaluation*. London: Sage.

Picciotto, Robert. 2007. "The New Environment for Development Evaluation." *American Journal of Evaluation* 28 (4):509–521.

Picciotto, Robert. 2013. "The Logic of Development Effectiveness: Is It Time for the Broader Evaluation Community to Take Notice?" *Evaluation* 19 (2):155–170.

Poister, Theodore H.; Aristigueta, Maria P.; and Hall, Jeremy L. 2015. *Managing and Measuring Performance in Public and Nonprofit Organizations: An Integrated Approach*, 2nd edition. San Francisco, CA: Jossey-Bass.

Powell, Steve; Molander, Joakim; and Celebicic, Ivona. 2012. "Assessment of Outcome Mapping as a Tool for Evaluating and Monitoring Support to Civil Society Organisations." In *Governance by Evaluation for Sustainable Development: Institutional Capacities and Learning*, edited by Michal Sedlacko and Andre Martinuzzi. Cheltenham, UK: Edward Elgar. Pp. 215–232.

Prichett, Lant; and Sandefur, Justin. 2013. *Context Matters for Size: Why External Validity Claims and Development Practice Don't Mix*. Working Paper 336. Washington, DC: Center for Global Development.

Rallis, Sharon F. 2009. "Reasoning with Rigor and Probity: Ethical Premises for Credible Evidence." In *What Counts as Credible Evidence in Applied Research and Evaluation Practice?* edited by Stewart I. Donaldson, Chrisina A. Christie, and Melvin M. Mark. Thousand Oaks, CA: Sage Publications. Pp. 168–180.

Rammel, Christian; Velazquez, Luis; and Mader, Clemens. 2016. "Sustainability Assessment in Higher Education Institutions: What and How?" In *Routledge Handbook of Higher Education for Sustainable Development*, edited by Matthias Barth, Gerd Michelsen, Marco Rieckmann, and Ian Thomas. London: Routledge. Pp. 331–346.

Ramos, Tomas; and Pires, Sara M. 2013. "Sustainability Assessment: The Role of Indicators." In *Sustainability Assessment Tools in Higher Education Institutions: Mapping Trends and Good Practices around the World*, edited by Sandra Caeiro, Walter L. Filho, Charbel Jabbour, and Ulisses M. Azeiteiro. Cham, Switzerland: Springer International Publishing. Pp. 81–99.

Ravetz, Joe. 2007. "The Role of Evaluation in Regional Sustainable Development." In *Impact Assessment and Sustainable Development: European Practice and Experience*, edited by Clive George and Colin Kirkpatrick. Cheltenham, UK: Edward Elgar. Pp. 65–89.

Rickinson, Mark; and Reid, Alan. 2016. "Synthesis of Research in Higher Education for Sustainable Development." In *Routledge Handbook of Higher Education for Sustainable Development*, edited by Matthias Barth, Gerd Michelsen, Marco Rieckmann, and Ian Thomas. London: Routledge. Pp. 142–160.

Rist, Ray C. 2013. "Postscript – Evaluation and Turbulence: Beyond an Incremental View of the World." In *Evaluation and Turbulent Times: Reflections on a Discipline in Disarray*, edited by Jan-Eric Furubo, Ray C. Rist, and Sandra Speer. New Brunswick, NJ: Transaction Publishers. Pp. 255–262.

Rowe, Andy. 2016. "New Tools and a Use-Inspired Approach for Impact Evaluation." Paper presented at the 5th European Environmental Evaluators Network Forum: Evaluation for Better Regulation in Environment and Climate Policies – Lessons from Research and Practice, Copenhagen, 15–16 September.

Scholz, Roland W.; Lang, Daniel J.; Wiek, Arnim; Walter, Alexander I.; and Stauffacher, Michael. 2006. "Transdisciplinary Case Studies as a Means of Sustainability Learning: Historical Framework and Theory." *International Journal of Sustainability in Higher Education* 7 (3):226–251.

Schuller, Tom; Hammond, Cathie; and Preston, John. 2004. "Reappraising Benefits." In *The Benefits of Learning: The Impact of Education on Health, Family Life and Social Capital*, edited by Tom Schuller, John Preston, Cathie Hammond, Angela Brassett-Grundy, and John Bynner. London: RoutledgeFalmer. Pp. 179–193.

Shriberg, Michael. 2004. "Assessing Sustainability: Criteria, Tools, and Implications." In *Higher Education and the Challenges of Sustainability: Problematics, Promise, and Practice*, edited by Peter B. Corcoran and Arjen E. J. Wals. Dordrecht: Kluwer. Pp. 73–86.

Sileshi Sisaye. 2016. *Ecology, Sustainable Development and Accounting*. New York: Routledge.

Slaughter, Richard A. 1995. *The Foresight Principle: Cultural Recovery in the 21st Century*. Westport, CT: Praeger.

Smillie, Ian. 2009. "Backwards and in High Heels: NGO Leadership in Asia." In *Leadership for Development: What Globalization Demands of Leaders Fighting for Change*, edited by Dennis A. Rondinelli and John M. Heffron. Boulder, CO: Kumarian Press. Pp. 205–233.

Stern, Elliot. 2004. "Evaluating Partnerships." In *Evaluation & Development: The Partnership Dimension*, edited by Andres Liebenthal, Osvaldo N. Feinstein, and Gregory K. Ingram. New Brunswick, NJ: Transaction Publishers. Pp. 29–41.

Stern, Elliot; Stame, Nicoletta; Mayne, John; Forss, Kim; Davies, Rick; and Befani, Barbara. 2012. *Broadening the Range of Designs and Methods for Impact Evaluations*. Working Paper 38. London: Department for International Development.

Stevens, Candice. 2012. "A Basic Roadmap for Sustainability Assessments: The SIMPLE Methodology." In *Sustainable Development, Evaluation and Policy-Making: Theory, Practise and Quality Assurance*, edited by Anneke von Raggamby and Frieder Rubik. Cheltenham, UK: Edward Elgar. Pp. 57–72.

Strele, Martin. 2012. "Participatory Livelihoods System Appraisal: A Learning-Oriented Methodology for Impact Assessment." In *Governance by Evaluation for Sustainable Development: Institutional Capacities and Learning*, edited by Michal Sedlacko and Andre Martinuzzi. Cheltenham, UK: Edward Elgar. Pp. 173–190.

Syed, Shamsuzzoha B.; Dadwal, Viva; Rutter, Paul; Storr, Julie; Hightower, Joyce D.; Gooden, Rachel; Carlet, Jean; Nejad, Sepideh B.; Kelley, Edward T.; Donaldson, Liam; and Pittet, Didier. 2012. "Developed-Developing Country Partnerships: Benefits to Developed Countries?" *Globalization and Health* 8 (17). DOI: 10.1186/1744–8603–8–17

Thabrew, Lanka; Wiek, Arnim; and Ries, Robert. 2009. "Environmental Decision Making in Multi-Stakeholder Contexts: Applicability of Life Cycle Thinking in Development Planning and Implementation." *Journal of Cleaner Production* 17:67–76.

Thomas, Vinod; and Tominaga, Jiro. 2013. "Development Evaluation in an Age of Turbulence." In *Evaluation and Turbulent Times: Reflections on a Discipline in Disarray*, edited by Jan-Eric Furubo, Ray C. Rist, and Sandra Speer. New Brunswick, NJ: Transaction Publishers. Pp. 57–70.

Tierney, Aisling; Tweddell, Hannah; and Willmore, Chris. 2015. "Measuring Education for Sustainable Development: Experiences from the University of Bristol." *International Journal of Sustainability in Higher Education* 16 (1):505–522.

Tikly, Leon. 2011. "Towards a Framework for Researching the Quality of Education in Low-Income Countries." *Comparative Education* 47, No. 1 (February):1–23.

Togo, Muchaiteyi. 2015. "Development, Use and Significance of the Unit-Based Sustainability Assessment Tool for Universities in Africa and Asia." In *Mainstreaming Environment and Sustainability in African Universities: Stories of Change*, edited by Heila Lotz-Sisitka, Gitile Naituli, Amanda Hlengwa, Mike Ward, Ayobami Salami, Akpezi Ogbuigwe, Mahesh Pradhan, Marie Neeser, and Sanne Lauriks. Grahamstown: Rhodes University Environmental Learning Research Centre. Pp. 34–64.

Togo, Muchaiteyi; and Lotz-Sisitka, Heila. 2013. "The Unit-Based Sustainability Assessment Tool and Its Use in the UNEP Mainstreaming Environment and Sustainability in African Universities Partnership." In *Sustainability Assessment Tools in Higher Education Institutions: Mapping Trends and Good Practices around the World*, edited by Sandra Caeiro, Walter L. Filho, Charbel Jabbour, and Ulisses M. Azeiteiro. Cham, Switzerland: Springer International Publishing. Pp. 259–288.

Uitto, Juha I. 2011. "Sustainable Development of Natural Resources in Laos: Evaluating the Role of International Cooperation." *Asian Journal of Environment and Disaster Management* 3 (4):475–490.

Uitto, Juha I. 2016. "Implementing Climate Change Policy Evaluation." Paper presented at the National Institute of Ecology and Climate Change, Mexico City, 25 May.

UNDP. 2012. *Proceedings from the Second International Conference on National Evaluation Capacities: Use of Evaluation in Decision Making for Public Policies and Programmes.* New York: UNDP Evaluation Office.

Vaessen, Jos; and Todd, David. 2008. "Methodological Challenges of Evaluating the Impact of the Global Environment Facility's Biodiversity Program." *Evaluation and Program Planning* 31:231–240.

Waas, Tom; Huge, Jean; Verbruggen, Aviel; and Block, Thomas. 2015. "Navigating towards Sustainability: Essential Aspects of Assessment and Indicators." In *Sustainability: Key Issues*, edited by Helen Kopnina and Eleanor Shoreman-Ouimet. London: Routledge. Pp. 88–108.

Weaver, Paul; Rotmans, Jan; Turnpenny, John; Haxeltine, Alex; and Jordan, Andrew. 2007. "Methods and Tools for Integrated Sustainability Assessment (MATISSE): A New European Project." In *Impact Assessment and Sustainable Development: European Practice and Experience*, edited by Clive George and Colin Kirkpatrick. Cheltenham, UK: Edward Elgar. Pp. 149–163.

Wiek, Arnim; Talwar, Sonia; O'Shea, Meg; and Robinson, John. 2013. "Towards a Methodological Scheme for Capturing Societal Effects of Participatory Sustainability Research." Unpublished paper.

Zint, Michaela. 2011. "Evaluating Education for Sustainable Development Programs." In *World Trends in Education for Sustainable Development*, edited by Walter L. Filho. Frankfurt: Peter Lang. Pp. 329–347.

6

CURRICULAR EVALUATIONS THAT MATTER

From a beyond-outputs perspective, evaluating university sustainable-development curricula centers on teaching, learning outcomes, and action contributions. This chapter elaborates a framework for meaningful curricular evaluation that emphasizes process, outcomes, and impacts. Discussion begins with the teaching function.

Teaching sustainable development: an outcome-oriented-evaluation perspective

In the novel framework for evaluating university sustainable-development activity developed in *Universities and the Sustainable Development Future*, teaching-centered inquiries focus on the transformation of curricula and course syllabi and on connections with classroom and service-learning, faculty development, and, ultimately, individual human-capabilities enhancement. Core curriculum values are concern for the environment, commitment to sustainable development, justice, and equity, respect for diversity, and confidence that people can make a difference. The requisite knowledge, skills, and values draw heavily on non-economic social-science and humanities learning, areas that tend to be relatively neglected at many universities (Jones, Bailey, and Lyytikäinen, 2007, p. 25).

Curriculum transformation

The triple lens of required knowledge, skills, and values (Parker, Wade, and Atkinson, 2004) provides a common perspective for cutting into sustainable-development-curriculum transformation. Knowledge and understanding covers diversity; social justice and equity; interdependence; natural, human, and social capital; the current and future limits of dynamic human-nature interactions

(Ramos and Pires, 2013, p. 93; Disterheft, et al., 2013, p. 8); and peace and conflict. Required skills include cooperation (Fredericks, 2014, p. 34) and conflict
resolution (Sterling and Thomas, 2006, p. 364), learning from diverse peoples
and natural contexts, and critical thinking. Particularly relevant values include
natural-resource maintenance and restoration, poverty reduction, and the ability
to challenge injustice effectively. A sustainable-development curriculum focused
along these lines is likely to gain traction among students, particularly in the
South, because of the clear connection among "skills for work and skills for life"
(King and Palmer, 2013, p. 32).

Re-envisioned curricula that integrate sustainable development can be led
by different thematic frameworks. One promising approach balances cognitive-,
affective-, and psychomotor-learning objectives – that is, engages "head, hands
and heart." Higher-education courses and programs that satisfy these integrated-
learning objectives "exhibit an emergent property . . . termed transformative sustainability learning" (Sipos, Battisti, and Grimm, 2008, p. 68). The heads, hands,
and heart assessment schema for scoring sustainable-development curricula merits
inclusion in meaningful evaluations of curricula transformation.

In curricula-transformation evaluations, subject-level change must allow for
"the different starting points of academic disciplines, both conceptually and peda-
gogically" (Ryan and Cotton, 2013, p. 153). Basic process characteristics – including
whether university leaders and unit heads matched sustainable-development initiatives with commitments of adequate long-term budget provisions (Bekessy,
Samson, and Clarkson, 2007, p. 315; Desha and Hargroves, 2014, p. 179), how evaluations are recorded and disseminated, whether they are used only rhetorically or
lead to actions, and how internal[1] and external assessments are reconciled (Simon
and Knie, 2013, p. 403) – need to be taken into consideration. Did institutional-
sustainability managers succeed in working across disciplinary boundaries and in
initiating and coordinating curriculum innovations without personally shoulder-
ing excessive responsibilities (Vettori and Rammel, 2014, p. 61)? Did co-curricular
and extracurricular activities reinforce or undermine curricula initiatives (Fischer,
Jenssen, and Tappeser, 2015, p. 792)? Did a broad range of stakeholders participate
in developing sustainable-development curricula (Boer, 2013, p. 128)?

Sustainable-development curricular evaluations should explore cross-disciplinary
integration as well as the extent to which instructors have incorporated indigenous knowledges, ways of learning, and insights (Thaman, 2006, p. 181). To
what extent did curricula and syllabi link environmental, social, and economic
concerns; introduce local and global sustainability issues and challenges (Togo,
2015, p. 48);[2] enhance integrated thinking and analysis; and generate new synergies (Ospina, 2000, pp. 33–34)? Did faculty utilize in-depth case studies to reveal
why sustainable development unfolds or fails to unfold in particular ways under
certain circumstances? To what extent did instructors examine sustainability considerations in coursework assessments (Togo, 2015, p. 49)?

Did sustainable-development curricula incorporate core courses in natural
and social sciences, environmental sciences, health sciences, and management?[3]

Did the university integrate sustainability across all courses?[4] Does the program's sustainable-development curriculum make sense in its entirety (Palomba and Banta, 1999, p. 5)? Did new interdisciplinary degrees centered on sustainable development arise (Lotz-Sisitka, Agbedahin, and Hlengwa, 2015, pp. 29–33)? Did curriculum transformation impact student learning?

Service-learning

In sustainable-development education, are learning experiences integrated in "day to day personal and professional life" (Rammel, Velazquez, and Mader, 2016, p. 335)? To what extent did teachers consider sustainability issues when selecting service-learning and community-service opportunities and assessing student contributions? To what extent did educators integrate sustainability aspects in community-service and service-learning experiences (Togo and Lotz-Sisitka, 2013, p. 266)? To what extent have students been involved outside of class in sustainability issues and projects (Togo, 2015, pp. 53–55)? Did educators weave lessons from sustainable-development field experience into lectures, course assignments, mentoring, and teaching materials? To what degree are sustainability considerations addressed in instructor assessments of student-service-learning experiences (Togo, 2015, p. 50)?

Faculty development

Formal and informal educators need to "attain their own sustainability competencies alongside their students" (Rowe and Hiser, 2016, p. 328). The *Talloires Declaration*[5] expects that higher-education institutions will "create programs to develop the capability of university faculty to teach environmental literacy to all undergraduate, graduate, and professional school students" (cited in Wright, 2002, pp. 116–117).[6] The first step in evaluating faculty competence involves determining levels of understanding regarding meaningful sustainability-related attributes. Are program faculty at the "prepare," "explore," "test and pilot," or "integrate and implement learning pathways" stage (Desha and Hargroves, 2014, pp. 146, 148–149)? The next step involves the introduction of concerted efforts to train faculty across campus in the design and implementation of transnational-competency-based and sustainable-development-focused courses. Then, in the interest of further advancing sustainable-development education, faculty can be trained on "how to teach more project and problem-based courses (for example, coordinating learning activities with stakeholder partners)" (Wiek, et al., 2016, p. 258). Finally, faculty need to be prepared to direct specialized and individualized evaluations of student outcomes and impacts (Gruppen, Mangrulkar, and Kolars, 2012, p. 48).

Which of these steps have been undertaken? To what extent has faculty expertise in sustainable development increased? To what extent have faculty been willing to incorporate sustainable-development topics in their syllabi, classroom teaching, and assignments (Togo, 2015, p. 50) as well as in their research initiatives

(Lotz–Sisitka, Agbedahin, and Hlengwa, 2015, p. 23)? Have faculty successfully directed meaningful and comprehensive evaluations of student transnational-sustainable-development (TSD) skill learning and application?

Are clear tenure, promotion, and other performance-review benefits sought by and provided for faculty, particularly young and new recruits, who are committed to sustainable-development initiatives (Cayuela, et al., 2013, p. 234; Desha and Hargroves, 2014, p. 195)? How frequently and consistently have they been applied? Have internal incentives been awarded to experienced faculty who mentor younger colleagues in sustainable-development education (Cayuela, et al., 2013, p. 235)? Such questions measure the commitment of university administrators to promoting sustainable-development perspectives among faculty at the front lines of curricular transformation and student learning.

Outcome evaluations

In sustainable-development evaluations, curriculum and syllabi transformations, classroom and service learning, specific teaching objectives, and faculty development funnel down to human-capability building. Thus, needs assessments and learning outcomes feature in higher-education evaluations. Evaluating sustainable-development-learning outcomes is best served by a human-capabilities perspective.

Evaluating sustainable-development learning outcomes: a human-capabilities perspective

Competence-based education focuses on performance objectives – that is, what the learner should be able "to do" (Gruppen, Mangrulkar, and Kolars, 2012, p. 43). In the approach to evaluation elaborated here, core sustainable-development competencies provide the reference frame for evaluating learning outcomes (Wiek, Withycombe, and Redman, 2011, p. 204). Rather than relying on numerical output indicators such as the attainment of qualifications, human-capabilities evaluation should emphasize outcomes by connecting the graduate's demonstrated transnational competence (TC) (Koehn and Rosenau, 2010; Schuller and Desjardins, 2007, p. 41; Knight, 2008, p. 15) to sustainable-development pathways. Graduates of professional programs, in particular, should be able to demonstrate individual and transdisciplinary-team achievements consistently across all five transnational-competency domains and when confronted by differing TSD circumstances. Each skill domain is valuable and interacts with and influences the others.

As a predominantly skill-based initiative, authentic competency evaluations focus on behavioral demonstrations of skill-development (outcome and impact) expectations rather than on short-term and internal output facilitators such as personal knowledge acquisition[7] and attitudinal change (Koehn and Rosenau, 2010; also see Gruppen, Mangrulkar, and Kolars, 2012, pp. 43, 47; Pain, 2009, p. 110; Zint, 2011, pp. 335–336). Evaluators can distinguish individual levels of skill attainment: learn,[8] practice, and demonstrate (Desha and Hargroves, 2014, p. 143). Also helpful is the scoring scheme for identifying transformative-sustainability learning (not addressed, beginning, developing, accomplished, and exemplary) found in Sipos, Battisti, and Grimm (2008, pp. 76–81).

Human-capability outcomes can be usefully distinguished as intermediate-term (skill changes that enable transnational-sustainable-development behaviors) and long-term (expansion and continued enhancement and refinement of TSD skills and behaviors) (Brundiers, et al., 2014, p. 218). This approach to sustainable-development-competency evaluation requires baseline and near-graduation assessments as well as attention to near-term-direct and long-term outcomes (Colclough, 2012, p. 2). To facilitate meaningful evaluation, educators establish observable and measurable standards of activity and task performance that are representative of desired TSD competencies along with explicit criteria for measuring the extent to which skill-development outcomes are attained (Gruppen, Mangrulkar, and Kolars, 2012, p. 44).

Ideally, according to Gruppen, Mangrulkar, and Kolars (2012, p. 46), "students would have an opportunity to explore a menu of choices in learning activities and methods that could allow them to achieve [needed] competency." Drawing on input from stakeholders outside the university, evaluators' expectations regarding expected sustainable-development capabilities are linked to the program's contextually identified human needs and ecological challenges and are tailored to the student's individual-learning objectives (Gruppen, Mangrulkar, and Kolars, 2012, pp. 44–47). Among other advantages, external-stakeholder input provides "a means of validating the relevance of competencies and ensuring key domains are not neglected" (Gruppen, Mangrulkar, and Kolars, 2012, p. 45).

In the *analytic* realm, for instance, graduating practitioners should be evaluated based on a desired mix of generic and contextually tailored capabilities identified in Box 6.1. Advanced students should be versed in a relevant combination of structural analysis, cognitive mapping, quantitative modelling, causal-chain analysis, multi-criteria and impact assessment, social-network analysis, risk analysis, visioning methods (including backcasting), participatory-anticipatory approaches (e.g., Delphi), simulating dynamic-system developments (e.g., STELLA models), and the construction and appraisal of long-term forecasts (Wiek, et al., 2016, pp. 244–247, 252; Wiek, et al., 2011b, p. 6). In addition, they should be able to analyze critically practices from their discipline "in the context of principles of sustainable development" in order to identify potential impacts that would arise from the application of sustainability principles in situations that arise in their own field and contexts (Sterling and Thomas, 2006, pp. 364, 366; Rowe and Johnston, 2013, p. 49).

In assessing *emotional* competency, two dimensions that merit serious review are changes (if any) in the graduate's feelings of transnational efficacy (Schuller and Desjardins, 2007, p. 12) and in level of commitment to a sustainable future (Roorda, 2013, pp. 105–106; Sterling and Thomas, 2006, pp. 360–361, 363). What evidence exists of graduates' dedicated personal involvement in and passion for sustainable-development work (Roorda, Corcoran, and Weakland, 2012, p. 3350)?

BOX 6.1 DESIRABLE ANALYTIC-COMPETENCE CAPABILITIES FOR SUSTAINABLE-DEVELOPMENT GRADUATES

- Ability to recognize and be able to explain transboundary interconnections
- Demonstrated ability to identify and describe short-term and long-term tradeoffs among interdependent ecological, social, and economic factors (Desha and Hargroves, 2014, pp. 141–142; Remington-Doucette, et al., 2013, pp. 409–410)
- Ability to focus on sustainable futures and intergenerational equity while able to zoom in and out of short-term and long-term approaches (Roorda, 2013, pp. 105–107; Wiek, et al., 2016, pp. 244, 247–248; Rowe and Johnston, 2013, pp. 49, 52; Wiek, Withycombe, and Redman, 2011, p. 211)
- Adept at identifying triggering factors, feedback loops, and cascading effects through network thinking (Strele, 2012, p. 177; Wiek, et al., 2011b, p. 6)
- Ability to explain how distant events and trends connect to their community and the processes through which local actions contribute to or ameliorate geographically and temporally distant conditions
- Ability to distinguish non-linear processes and developments from linear ones (Roorda, Corcoran, and Weakland, 2012, p. 335)
- Analytic ability to "develop bridges between the technical and physical sciences and the humanities, for a more integrated multidisciplinary approach" (Sterling and Thomas, 2006, p. 362)
- Demonstrated fluency in "the complex interplay of natural and human systems, the risks of ignoring instabilities and tipping points, and the areas of leverage in human systems for maximum effect" (Dahl, 2014, p. 193; also Wiek, et al., 2016, p. 244).

Other bases for emotional-competence evaluation concern capacity to discern, and openness to, the values and perspectives of diverse others and flexibility in the face of uncertain and changing conditions (Roorda, 2013, pp. 105–106; Sterling and Thomas, 2006, p. 360).

Creative competency lends itself to developmental evaluation. Developmental evaluators look for evidence of adaptability, willingness to engage in social experimentation, and insights derived from systems thinking and boundary spanning that are sensitive to non-linear dynamics (Brundiers, et al., 2014, pp. 213–214; Roorda, 2013, p. 105; Rowe and Johnston, 2013, p. 52).

Communicative competence includes the ability to utilize knowledge and apply information interactively across boundaries (Sterling and Thomas, 2006, p. 359). Graduates should be skilled at cross-boundary inquiry and at attentive listening, and they should able to "communicate to diverse audiences, in written and oral formats, the results of sustainability-problem solving efforts" (Wiek, et al., 2016, pp. 250–251; also Rowe and Johnston, 2013, p. 51).

Evaluations of action-oriented (*functional*) competencies are at the "leading edge of outcomes assessment work" (Rowe and Hiser, 2016, p. 328). Functionally skilled graduates should demonstrate the TSD program's desired combination of capabilities set forth in Box 6.2. As part of the functional-capability-assessment process, educators across the curriculum design transboundary and socio-culturally diverse challenges that test the technical, interpersonal, sustainable-development-values internalization and expression (Dahl, 2014, p. 194)[9] and advocacy capabilities of a graduating professional.

In university TSD initiatives, participants and donors expect education to matter for individual agency and for societal change. After graduation, evaluators are interested in whether practitioners "actually do exercise their professional capabilities in ways that further social transformation" (Walker, et al., 2009, p. 568) rather than perpetuate or exacerbate inequities (Schuller and Desjardins, 2007, pp. 59, 114). For impact evaluations, the linked technical and interpersonal sustainable-development performance of graduated practitioners needs to be evaluated periodically over the long-term from multiple perspectives by socio-culturally diverse observers, collaborators, employers,[10] and community members. How do stakeholders rate the TSD-capacity-strengthening contributions of graduates (Dahl,

---

BOX 6.2 DESIRABLE FUNCTIONAL-COMPETENCE CAPABILITIES FOR SUSTAINABLE-DEVELOPMENT GRADUATES

- Ability "to work with people who define problems differently than they do" (Downey, 2005, p. 593)
- Adept at trust building, transnational collaboration across multiple teams, stakeholder engagement, and conflict management (Wiek, et al., 2016, pp. 250–251; Rowe and Johnston, 2013, p. 52; Remington-Doucette, et al., 2013, p. 410)
- Ability to leverage linking knowledge, critical reflection (Sileshi, 2016, p. 201), "future thinking" (Virtanen, 2010, pp. 234–235, 238–239), innovation, ethics, advocacy, and other generic TSD skills "into usable and accessible solutions" to specific sustainable-development challenges and opportunities (Wamae, 2011; also Tilbury, 2004, p. 105; Koehn and Rosenau, 2010, chapter 9; Wiek, et al., 2016, p. 242)
- Demonstrated ability to apply theory-of-change approaches, adaptation and mitigation strategies, and transition-management strategies and tactics (Wiek, et al., 2016, pp. 247–248)
- Demonstrated ability to act in situations characterized by uncertainty (Wiek, et al., 2011b, p. 7).

2014, pp. 190–191)? Eliciting the perceptions of poor and marginalized community members should be incorporated as a critical component of development-practitioner-competency evaluations (Jeffery, 2012, pp. 172–174).

Since human capabilities are not static, symmetrical-capability-building programs leave room for future skill development and life-long, life-wide personal and professional learning through the interactive effects of experience and continuously supportive training (Schuller and Desjardins, 2007, pp. 10, 18, 37, 68–69; Ashcroft and Raynor, 2011, p. 198; Blewitt, 2004, p. 26). Competencies developed or diminished after graduation or completion of a specific training program should be documented over the long-term through follow-up studies. Assessing the "cumulative and interactive impacts of learning that occur in multiple contexts (lifewide learning) over the lifespan (lifelong learning)" is a challenging task for university sustainable-development evaluators (Schuller and Desjardins, 2007, p. 37). Comprehensive assessments take into consideration the long-term cumulative impact of all trainees and learners by applying a multiplier to observed individual effects.

Human-capabilities-outcome assessment also includes such matters as the following: Is there evidence of improvement in the TSD-curriculum-design and experiential-education abilities of participating faculty members? Are "training the trainers" programs in place and working (Morfit and Gore, 2009, p. 16; also Gedde, 2009, p. 35)?

Finally, it is important that evaluations of human-capability building address the long-term sustainable-development and societal impacts of education and training initiatives. We expect capability development to play a catalytic role in impact analysis. In our era of brain drain and brain circulation, societal-impact analysis should include tracer studies that explore the country-of-origin and receiving-country(ies) TSD contributions of graduates. Carefully documented longitudinal-impact case studies that incorporate a justified multiplier for comparable situations are useful in this connection.

Impact evaluations that track behavioral change and real-world outcomes well after the intervention is over and the participants have scattered are particularly challenging and require special effort. Ongoing community-based evaluations of practitioner impact should integrate multiple data-collection methods that can include pre- and post-project needs-assessment exercises, statistical studies, structured and semi-structured interviews,[11] local government records and reports, geographic information systems (GIS) analysis, focus-group discussions (where culturally appropriate), periods of observation, end-user surveys, and analysis of personal and institutional life histories (see Jeffery, 2012, pp. 172–174; Fredericks, 2014, p. 174).

Box 6.3 presents a suggestive short list of questions that can be incorporated in human-capabilities evaluations. The outcome emphasis is on evidence of "behavioral additionality" (Ravetz, 2007, p. 83). Formative and summative evaluations that ask students to evaluate their overall sustainable-development learning gains are helpful in distinguishing additionality (Brundiers, et al., 2014, p. 224).[12]

BOX 6.3 QUESTIONS THAT CAN BE ASKED IN HUMAN-CAPABILITIES EVALUATIONS

- Are sustainable-development concepts accurately engaged by students across the core curriculum?
- Have indigenous knowledge and insights been linked to ecological literacy and TSD understanding?[13]
- How many degree programs offer progressive learning pathways to sustainable-development careers?[14]
- To what do students attribute their most powerful sustainability-learning gains? Why?
- What is the level of sustainable-development expertise possessed and demonstrated by teaching faculty?
- To what extent is learning linked to on-campus and community collaborations around contextually relevant issues of sustainable development?
- What opportunities have been provided for life-long and life-wide learning?
- What behavioral demonstrations of each domain of transnational competence can be identified?
- What added value and remaining skill shortcomings can be identified among graduates?
- Are conducive attitudes, values, and sustainable-development commitments sustained over time?
- How has human-capability development catalyzed short-, medium-, and long-term sustainable-development impacts?

In addressing these questions, evaluators also should seek to understand why change has or has not happened. Such understanding is key to allowing lessons to be learned and programs to be improved.

Individual-learning outcomes are best measured not in terms of qualifications awarded but in relation to asset building as reflected in "health, family life and social capital" (Schuller, Hammond, and Preston, 2004, p. 12; also Colclough 2012, pp. 10–11). These individual-learning assets can be used to generate "social outcomes that benefit others and future generations" (McMahon, 2009, p. 5, 38). Are TSD competencies increasingly viewed as a vital national asset (Cotton and Winter, 2010, p. 51)?

Positive- and negative-learning outcomes often emerge gradually, irregularly, and contextually over time (Colclough, 2012, p. 2). Such "lagged effects are inherently difficult to assess, but it is crucial to recognise that they do occur" (Schuller, Hammond, and Preston, 2004, p. 188). This understanding informs decisions to resist early pressures to evaluate in any decisive way (King and McGrath, 2004, p. 206). One qualitative-assessment tool for illuminating lagged effects is the biographical approach, which allows learners to trace educational impacts over "however long a period seems appropriate" (Schuller, Hammond, and Preston, 2004, p. 189).

Evaluating action contributions: an impact-oriented perspective

Curricula-impact evaluations that make a difference explore what graduates "do in the world" (Shriberg, 2004, p. 73; Wiek, et al., 2011b, p. 11). Evaluations of action contributions focus on how sustainable-development concepts across the core curriculum are applied and implemented by students (Sawahel, 2012; McFarlane and Ogazon, 2011, p. 100; Shriberg, 2004, p. 83; Tilbury, 2004, pp. 98, 104). To what extent are the teaching, research, and community-engagement components of sustainable development integrated (Moore, 2005, pp. 326, 331)? How adept were sustainability-prepared students at applying analytic insights regarding the social-ecological and cultural context and political, economic, and logistical constraints and opportunities to practical challenges of sustainable development?

Managing for sustainability specifically involves learning (1) how to maintain and enhance ecological and social diversity, adaptability, and renewal capacity, (2) means of incorporating and retaining redundancy, (3) how to activate leverage points that stimulate positive reinforcing feedback and neutralize inhibiting factors (Strele, 2012, p. 177), and (4) ways to retain flexibility and spread risks (Berkes, Colding, and Folke, 2003, p. 15; Folke, Colding, and Berkes, 2003, pp. 354, 356, 361). What post-graduation evidence exists of performance results or setbacks in these four crucial behavioral areas?[15] Were the action contributions of sustainable-development graduates enhanced over time by the multiplier effect?

Suggested enhancements for TSD curricular evaluations

In the concluding section of this chapter, we select particularly helpful and often tested suggestions (usually in the form of guiding questions) for enhancing sustainable-development curricular evaluations that are tied into the preceding discussion of best practices. We are particularly interested in lucid and verifiable lines of inquiry that yield data that capture contextual differences and complexities but are "specific enough to be calculable and comparable" (Shriberg, 2004, p. 74).

The overall purpose of focused evaluations of sustainability education is to mind the gap between intentions and implementing actions (Brundiers and Wiek, 2011, p. 122). Keeping meaningful-action contributions in mind, this section treats knowledge acquisition and understanding, pedagogy, process, and capabilities. Sterling and Thomas (2006, pp. 353–354) present a useful set of characteristics of education for sustainability that can be addressed when evaluating curricula transformation. We draw on their articulation in the framework and suggestions for evaluating sustainable-development curricula set forth below.

Acquisition of knowledge and understanding

With regard to enhanced TSD knowledge and understanding, we engage helpful theoretical work to construct a bank of probing questions that are useful in the curricula-evaluation process. These guiding questions are presented in Box 6.4.

BOX 6.4 HELPFUL GUIDING QUESTIONS IN TSD-CURRICULA EVALUATIONS

- To what extent do curricula address connectivity among social, economic, and environmental drivers and barriers across glocal levels (Brundiers and Wiek, 2011, p. 113; Sterling and Thomas, 2006, pp. 353–354; Sterling, 2013, p. 38; Mochizuki and Fadeeva, 2010, p. 393; Rowe and Johnston, 2013, p. 49; Waas, et al., 2015, p. 93; Lotz-Sisitka, Agbedahin, and Hlengwa, 2015, p. 22–23)?
- Do curricula incorporate harms that threaten socio-ecological integrity and viability (Brundiers and Wiek, 2011, p. 113) and/or tackle the unsustainability forces that need to be addressed (Sterling, 2009, pp. 110, 107)?
- Do curricula incorporate multiple contributors and barriers to sustainable development and celebrate place-based specificity (Brundiers and Wiek, 2011, p. 113; Sterling, 2009, p, 114; Blewitt, 2015, p. 309)?
- Do courses link local impact with global contributors and consequences (White, 2013, p. 173; Sterling, 2013, p. 38)?
- Did transformative learning occur that enabled participants to change their frame of reference regarding sustainable development (Sipos, Battisti, and Grimm, 2008, p. 71; Ralph and Stubbs, 2014, p. 71)?
- Did "anticipative education" utilize foresight and insight to address how emerging and evolving conditions and impacts are likely to play out for future generations (a minimum time period of twenty-five years) (Sterling, 2013, p. 28; Brundiers and Wiek, 2011, pp. 113, 115; Sterling and Thomas, 2006, pp. 353–354; Waas, et al., 2015, p. 93)?
- Are ethical responsibility toward present and future generations and natural systems and developing understanding of ways to promote a just and sustainable economy and society a central part of teaching across disciplines (Cortese, 2003, p. 19; Sterling and Thomas, 2006, p. 354; Rowe and Johnston, 2013, p. 46)?
- Do curricula recognize uncertainty (Waas, et al., 2015, p. 93), introduce alternative ways of knowing (Sterling, 2009, p, 114), and incorporate indigenous wisdom and values (Tilbury, 2013, p. 73)?

Framework for curricular evaluation: transnational competence for sustainable development

Higher-education sustainable-development initiatives need a conceptually derived and comprehensive set of core competencies to guide curricular and learning-outcome evaluations (Wiek, Withycombe, and Redman, 2011, p. 214). When constructing an evaluation plan, the ultimate concern is with impact – that is, the "degree to which graduates can improve sustainability in the world" (Wiek, Withycombe, and Redman, 2011, p. 214). In our sustainable-development-focused framework, evaluating the application of acquired skills constitutes the central component of human-capabilities analysis (see Box 6.5).

Useful outcome statements identify what graduating practitioners are and are not able to contribute to sustainable development across all five transnational-competency domains, are reported in "result-focused, observable, measurable, or inferable terms," and are developmental. Furthermore, they are "comprehensive and broad enough to be interdisciplinary," and they involve both formative and summative expectations, allowing the graduate continuously to build capacity and improve upon his/her performance (Martin-Kniep, 1997, pp. 104–105, 108; Gruppen, Mangrulkar, and Kolars, 2012, p. 43).

A diverse set of evaluation methods can be assigned for different competencies or even when assessing the same competency among multiple students (Gruppen, Mangrulkar, and Kolars, 2012, p. 47). Evaluators across the curriculum can design transboundary challenges that fall within the technical, interpersonal, and advocacy capacities of a graduating professional. In TC-guided sustainable-development programs, it is critical that students manifest multidimensional skills

---

BOX 6.5 HUMAN-CAPABILITIES EVALUATION: ACTION AND IMPACT DEMONSTRATIONS

- Do curricula link knowledge of transnational sustainable development with applied practice and action (Sterling, 2009, p, 114; White, 2013, p. 173)?
- What evidence is there of cross-fertilization of academic and operational contexts (Cayuela, et al., 2013, p. 224)?[16]
- Did professional practitioners and stakeholders weigh in on the various capabilities attained by individual students (Gruppen, Mangrulkar, and Kolars, 2012, p. 44)?
- Are student evaluations linked to actual sustainable-development contributions?[17]
- Do curricula emphasize "learning for life" (Sterling, 2009, p, 114)[18] and life-long learning (Sterling and Thomas, 2006, p. 354; Mochizuki and Fadeeva, 2010, p. 393; Roorda, 2013, p. 105)?

through their interactions in *multiple* socio-culturally diverse situations. Individual programs and professional accrediting bodies will determine levels of desired proficiency,[19] leaving room for future skill development, life-long learning, and long-term follow-up assessments.

Since in-class exercises and off-campus learning situations challenge students to demonstrate acquired skill-proficiency levels, such performance opportunities will play a major part in human-capability evaluations. Students' ability to apply sustainable-development skills also can be noninvasively observed via in-class and teamwork exercises that mirror plausible real-life professional challenges and through practice demonstrations, performance, and presentations in out-of-class experiential-learning situations (Martin-Kniep, 1997, pp. 101–104). Student portfolios that describe TSD-issue-oriented work, incorporate policy analysis, and demonstrate the application of each skill expectation in diverse and transnational contexts over time provide another performance-assessment format (see Parker, 1996, pp. 283–285; Martin-Kniep, 1997, p. 110).

Whenever possible, pre-training and post-training demonstrations should be documented by video for purposes of assessing skill gains, determining levels of goal attainment and transnational-task effectiveness, and analyzing and addressing weaknesses through performance repetitions. In TSD evaluations, the linked technical and interpersonal performance of graduating practitioners should be evaluated from multiple perspectives by socio-culturally diverse observers and participants. Multisource feedback, especially from stakeholders, promotes comprehensive-skill assessment and enables the graduating professional to grasp "both his or her personal strengths and areas in need of development" (Shuman, Besterfield-Sacre, and McGourty, 2005, p. 50). In all cases, evaluators recognize learners who demonstrate specific skills and support those who need to improve (Kuczewski, 2006, p. 194). Evaluators should emphasize discovery of the variable "strengths and weaknesses of students and . . . provide appropriate support to improve student performance" (Killick, 2007, p. 211). Continuous evaluation beyond graduation is recommended for impact analysis. Online surveys offer one method for tracking the impact of graduates. Collecting "most significant change stories" (Brundiers, et al., 2014, pp. 220–221) can be a particularly revealing means of identifying impacts.

Evaluators must recognize that students cannot be expected to master all required transnational-sustainable-development skills during their course of study (Stauffacher, et al., 2006, p. 267). The suggested "in-depth expertise in one or two . . . key competencies and a solid grounding in the others" (Wiek, Withycombe, and Redman, 2011, p. 214) expectation merits serious consideration by human-capabilities evaluators. The reality of limited time and exposure at the first-degree level also underscores the importance of more extensive post-graduate studies in sustainable development where degree candidates can be selected on the basis of pre-professional preparation. The learning processes incorporated in TSD programs need to build on valuable complementary first-degree and secondary-school attainments, particularly in the realm of communicative (additional-language) proficiency (Brademas, Kolb, and Mockett 2006, p. 26). Further, professional programs must be designed in ways that initiate, encourage, and facilitate processes of life-long learning.

Pedagogy

Generating valuable knowledge and understanding regarding sustainable development requires critical, complementary, and interactive pedagogical approaches that "flourish in the formal curriculum and through informal learning" (Ryan and Cotton, 2013, p. 164; also Sterling and Thomas, 2006, p. 352; Sterling, 2013, p. 38). Interdisciplinary sharing and collaboration is a common ingredient that encompasses a variety of pedagogical and innovative approaches (Cortese, 2003, p. 16; Cotton and Winter, 2010, p. 40; Mochizuki and Fadeeva, 2010, p. 393). Learning activities are explicitly and clearly connected to intended applied-learning outcomes (Rowe and Johnston, 2013, pp. 46, 50). Further, sustainable-development-focused pedagogical approaches emphasize participatory learning (Sterling and Thomas, 2006, p. 353; Sterling, 2013, p. 38).

Consideration of pedagogical applications and innovations constitutes an important component in a comprehensive TSD-curriculum evaluation. We present suggestions for guiding pedagogical questions in Box 6.6.

Curriculum transformation and evaluation processes

Conducted in an informed, sensitive, and symmetrical manner, intra- and inter-university evaluations can provide a powerful basis for curriculum changes (Shriberg, 2004, p. 71). Transformative and systemic changes are advanced by supportive processes (Sterling, 2004, p. 59). Inclusive leadership approaches that engage staff, students, and stakeholders provide critical initial indications that institutional-change possibilities exist (Tilbury, 2013, p. 74).

The extent to which participants demonstrated commitments of time and intellectual space to TSD-capability development constitutes particularly important process-evaluative dimensions (Sibbel, Hegarty, and Holdsworth, 2013, p. 397). Did senior university leadership demonstrate ownership and active involvement in curriculum transformation informed by sustainability research, and did they regularly communicate their endorsement (de la Harpe and Thomas, 2009, p. 77; Sterling, 2013, p. 43)? Did a guiding coalition of curriculum-transformation advocates "ensure that direction and momentum were sustained" (de la Harpe and Thomas, 2009, p. 82)? To what extent were critical support and inspiring incentives available (Ralph and Stubbs, 2014, p. 78)? Were capable and dedicated peer reviewers involved in evaluating curriculum transformation (Simon and Knie, 2013, p. 414)?

A number of additional useful guiding process questions can be employed in sustainable-development curricular evaluations (see Box 6.7). The starting point for success in higher-education-curricula transformation is participant understanding of the change process (de la Harpe and Thomas, 2009, p. 77).

BOX 6.6 PEDAGOGICAL QUESTIONS THAT CAN GUIDE SUSTAINABLE-DEVELOPMENT CURRICULA EVALUATIONS

- Did sustainable-development instruction and learning include rigorous interdisciplinary exposure to ecological, social, and economic dimensions (Ryan and Cotton, 2013, p. 152; Cortese, 2003, p. 18) and transdisciplinary inquiry (Sterling and Thomas, 2006, p. 353)?
- Did university educators introduce new and innovative pedagogical tools, materials, and approaches (e.g., Lotz-Sisitka, Agbedahin, and Hlengwa, 2015, p. 29)?
- Did students learn about sustainable development and develop methodological expertise through backcasting experience, case studies and incident/problem analysis, role plays, drama, games, debates, group discussions, values education, critical inquiry, ecological-footprint analysis, community-service learning, and visioning coupled with experiential testing and reflective accounting (Cotton and Winter, 2010, pp. 46–49; Wals and Blewitt, 2010, p. 58; Sterling, 2009, p. 114; Jones, Selby, and Sterling, 2010, p. 2; Moore, 2005, p. 331; Roorda, 2013, p. 105)?
- Did research/education endeavors allow for exploring innovative sustainability-problem-solving techniques (Brundiers and Wiek, 2011, p. 113)?
- Did students and experienced researchers possessing diverse but related expertise work in teams that addressed a sustainability challenge and produced a synthesis report?[20]
- Were available curricular pedagogies and co-curricular opportunities sufficient to cover the acquisition of core sustainable-development competencies (Rowe and Hiser, 2016, p. 317)?
- Did faculty members succeed in conveying TSD skills (Brundiers and Wiek, 2011, p. 120)?
- Which pedagogies proved most effective in teaching TSD competencies (Rowe and Hiser, 2016, p. 317)?

Evaluating TSD-program delivery and impacts

We also recommend that schools and programs be exposed to periodic review.[21] Internal and independent-external program evaluations should incorporate a variety of TSD-skill-expectation criteria, utilize multiple-assessment methods (particularly pre- and post-program self-efficacy surveys and student exit interviews), and include ongoing module, format, and pedagogy assessments (Killick, 2007, p. 2110; Deardorff, 2006, pp. 250–252, 257). Syllabi reviews[22] can be supplemented by direct evaluator observation of course delivery through

---

BOX 6.7 GUIDING PROCESS QUESTIONS IN TSD-CURRICULA EVALUATIONS

- Did academic and non-academic participants understand why change is needed and develop an agreed vision (de la Harpe and Thomas, 2009, pp. 77, 81)?
- Did they discern principal drivers and obstacles?
- Did they identify whom to involve and how, and broadly engage the campus community (de la Harpe and Thomas, 2009, p. 77)?
- To what extent was sustainability embedded across the entire university curriculum (Jones, Selby, and Sterling, 2010, p. 2; Cotton and Winter, 2010, p. 40; Desha and Hargroves, 2014, p. 117)?
- To what extent did curricula transformation provide new on-campus as well as overseas learning opportunities (including minors and certificates) (Peterson, 2015)?
- Did students make contributions to sustainable development beyond the campus and post-graduation (Cardwell, 2015, p. B2)?
- Were appropriate monitoring and evaluation systems and processes introduced and implemented (de la Harpe and Thomas, 2009, pp. 77, 81)?
- Did follow-up based on Monitoring and Evaluation (M&E) findings result in improved sustainable-development planning, policy decisions, activities, curriculum-change processes, and goal attainment (Moore, 2005, p. 331)?
- Did graduates collaborate with external stakeholders in evaluating programs and action plans (Wiek, et al., 2011b, p. 7)?

---

classroom lectures, seminars, assessments, and mentoring (Brundiers, et al., 2014, pp. 219–220; Desha and Hargroves, 2014, p. 155). Desha and Hargroves (2014, pp. 151, 154–155) suggest "auditing" existing courses "to identify the level of coverage of knowledge and/or skills assigned to them" and connections to desired learning outcomes.[23]

Evaluators should facilitate reflection on institution-wide program strengths and weaknesses (Desha and Hargroves, 2014, pp. 156, 158) as well as achievements and shortcomings (Wiek, Withycombe, and Redman, 2011, p. 214). When assessing the sustainable-development competence of university graduates, the extent of demonstrated improvement from the initial starting point ("added value") constitutes the principal component in programmatic evaluations (see Jamil Salmi, cited in Marshall, 2011). Educators should refer to skill gaps, opportunities, and threats revealed by critical evaluations when determining which competencies need to be enhanced and adapted in a particular sustainable-development program and context.

Tracking and systematic evaluation of short-term and long-term impacts asso-ciated with TSD-prepared versus non-TSD-prepared graduates provides valuable learning insights for curriculum reform. In this connection, curriculum review is facilitated by systematic feedback "in which graduates report back to the school the adequacy of their preparation in regard to the competencies and the need for modifications" (Gruppen, Mangrulkar, and Kolars, 2012, p. 45). To complete the picture, stakeholders need to be centrally involved in program-delivery and program-impact evaluations (Brundiers, et al., 2014, p. 224).

Concluding reflection

Evaluating TSD curricular reform engages a complex set of interacting factors and processes and is further complicated by the inability of a single person or collec-tive entity to control transformative efforts (Thomas, 2016, p. 68). We recognize that our framework sets a high and demanding bar for evaluating transnational-sustainable-development curricula and their outcomes and impacts. The extent to which the framework is implemented will determine how far along the path to credible evidence-based curricular evaluation a university is able to traverse. Chapter 11 aims, in part, to provide helpful, practical guidelines for implementing TSD curricular evaluations in academic contexts influenced by multiple actors with diverse backgrounds and interests.

Although curricula constitute the core of the academic enterprise, higher education also is distinguished by its research and outreach emphasis. The next chapters turn to research and outreach in the context of sustainable development, cognizant that outcomes and impacts in these areas tie back into the core educa-tional mission of universities around the world.

Notes

1 Internal checking by course instructors commonly ascertains whether students have attained subject-learning objectives (Desha and Hargroves, 2014, pp. 70, 143).
2 Togo (2015, pp. 47–48) suggests scoring according to the following guides: no information/don't know, none, a little, adequate, substantial, and a great deal.
3 See, for instance, www.hhh.umn.edu/masters-degrees/master-development-practice; ttps://www.macfound.org/press/publications/evaluation-masters-development-practice-initiative/
4 From their review of sustainability initiatives at 272 universities, Kathleen Simon and Jonas Haertle (2014, p. 4) found that only a small percentage of schools mandate a sus-tainability course in all programs and only a tiny minority integrate sustainability across all courses.
5 The *Talloires Declaration* is discussed in detail in the introduction to this book.
6 The University of South Carolina has undertaken an extensive program of faculty devel-opment in this connection (see Wright, 2002, p. 117).
7 Tests of knowledge gained are of limited utility in evaluations, given that even retained information becomes rapidly obsolete. Medical educators have found, moreover, that "quantitative performance on standardized tests by graduating students rarely correlates with the quality of care they provide" (Olapade-Olaopa, et al., 2014, p. 522).

8 As Gruppen and colleagues acknowledge (2012, p. 43), "learning objectives are often requisite but typically in and of themselves insufficient."

9 See the detailed intersubjective framework and measurement items for incorporating a values component to sustainable-development evaluations set forth in European Commission (2010).

10 "Fit to practice" competency should be assessed by public and private employers with an interest in beneficial sustainable-development impacts (Olapade-Olaopa, et al., 2014, pp. S20, S22).

11 Surveys and interviews "can track environmental economic and social insights from local ecological knowledge; assess people's access to information about environmental issues; register their ability to participate in decision making; and monitor their perceptions of injustices and local sustainability" (Fredericks, 2014, pp. 177–179).

12 Based on an idea presented by Desha and Hargroves (2014, p. xxvi), it would be interesting to conduct a multi-institutional, international, longitudinal behavioral-change study that compares sustainable-development curriculums and compares and contrasts the capability outcomes of graduates against a set of TSD competencies.

13 See, for instance, Gibson (2005, p. 70).

14 See Cayuela, et al. (2013, p. 228).

15 One promising tool for triangulated evaluations of behavioral changes over time is the alumni-results seminar (Lotz-Sisitka, Agbedahin, and Hlengwa, 2015, p. 21).

16 See, for instance, UBC's Sustainability Initiative (Cayuela, et al., 2013, pp. 227–228).

17 See, for instance, Mochizuki and Fadeeva (2010, p. 396).

18 Specifically, "life roles as family member, community member, consumer, and investor" (Rowe and Johnston, 2013, pp. 46, 51).

19 Also see Deardorff 2006, p. 257).

20 See www.icis.unimaas.info/icis-co-chair-of-new-international-network-on-sustainability-science/ (accessed 12 August 2015); also Brundiers and Wiek (2011, p. 116).

21 Downey (2005, p. 594) recommends that review teams be "trained to expect diversity" so that schools and departments can "develop and defend alternative ways in which their programmes meet outcomes criteria" (also see Desha and Hargroves, 2014, p. 153).

22 See Rodrigo Lozano and Mary Watson's (2013, pp. 359, 361–364) discussion of the STAUNCH tool for analyzing curriculum-sustainability content based on syllabi review that has been applied at the Georgia Institute of Technology and the University of Leeds.

23 See the course-classification options they set forth on page 156.

Works cited

Ashcroft, Kate; and Raynor, Philip. 2011. *Higher Education in Development: Lessons from Sub-Saharan Africa*. Charlotte, NC: Information Age Publishing.

Bekessy, S. A.; Samson, K.; and Clarkson, R. E. 2007. "The Failure of Non-Binding Declarations to Achieve University Sustainability: A Need for Accountability." *International Journal of Sustainability in Higher Education* 8 (3):301–316.

Berkes, Fikret; Colding, Johan; and Folke, Carl. 2003. "Introduction." In *Navigating Social-Ecological Systems: Building Resilience for Complexity and Change*, edited by Fikret Berkes, Johan Colding, and Carl Folke. Cambridge: Cambridge University Press. Pp. 1–25.

Blewitt, John. 2015. "Sustainability and Lifelong Learning." In *The Sustainability Curriculum: Facing the Challenge in Higher Education*, edited by John Blewitt and Cedric Cullingford. London: Earthscan. Pp. 24–42.

Boer, Pieternel. 2013. "Assessing Sustainability and Social Responsibility in Higher Education Assessment Frameworks Explained." In *Sustainability Assessment Tools in Higher Education Institutions: Mapping Trends and Good Practices around the World*, edited by Sandra Caeiro, Walter L. Filho, Charbel Jabbour, and Ulisses M. Azeiteiro. Cham, Switzerland: Springer International Publishing. Pp. 121–137.

Brademas, John; Kolb, Charles E. M.; and Mockett, Alfred T. 2006. *Education for Global Leadership: The Importance of International Studies and Foreign Language Education for U.S. Economic and National Security.* Washington, DC: Committee for Economic Development.

Brundiers, Katja; Savage, Emma; Mannell, Steven; Lang, Daniel J.; and Wiek, Arnim. 2014. "Educating Sustainability Change Agents by Design: Appraisals of the Transformative Role of Higher Education." In *Sustainable Development and Quality Assurance in Higher Education: Transformation of Learning and Society,* edited by Zinaida Fadeeva, Laima Galkute, Clemens Mader, and Geoff Scott. New York: Palgrave Macmillan. Pp. 196–229.

Brundiers, Katja; and Wiek, Arnim. 2011. "Educating Students in Real-World Sustainability Research: Vision and Implementation." *Innovative Higher Education* 36:107–124.

Cardwell, Diane. 2015. "Tackling Climate Change, One Class at a Time." *New York Times,* 1 July, pp. B1–B2.

Cayuela, Alberto; Robinson, John B.; Campbell, Ann; Coops, Nicholas; and Munro, Alison. 2013. "Integration of Operational and Academic Efforts in Sustainability at the University of British Columbia." In *Sustainability Assessment Tools in Higher Education Institutions: Mapping Trends and Good Practices around the World,* edited by Sandra Caeiro, Walter L. Filho, Charbel Jabbour, and Ulisses M. Azeiteiro. Cham, Switzerland: Springer International Publishing. Pp. 223–236.

Colclough, Christopher. 2012. "Investigating the Outcomes of Education: Questions, Paradigms and Methods." In *Education Outcomes and Poverty: A Reassessment,* edited by Christopher Colclough. London: Routledge. Pp. 1–15.

Cortese, Anthony D. 2003. "The Critical Role of Higher Education in Creating a Sustainable Future." *Planning for Higher Education* 2 (March–May):15–22.

Cotton, Debby; and Winter, Jennie. 2010. "It's Not Just Bits of Paper and Light Bulbs: A Review of Sustainability Pedagogies and Their Potential for Use in Higher Education." In *Sustainability Education: Perspectives and Practice across Higher Education,* edited by Paula Jones, David Selby, and Stephen Sterling. London: Earthscan. Pp. 39–55.

Dahl, Arthur L. 2014. "Sustainability and Values Assessment in Higher Education." In *Sustainable Development and Quality Assurance in Higher Education: Transformation of Learning and Society,* edited by Zinaida Fadeeva, Laima Galkute, Clemens Mader, and Geoff Scott. New York: Palgrave Macmillan. Pp. 185–195.

Deardorff, Darla K. 2006. "Identification and Assessment of Intercultural Competence as a Student Outcome of Internationalization." *Journal of Studies in International Education* 10, No. 3 (Fall):241–266.

Desha, Cheryl; and Hargroves, Karlson C. 2014. *Higher Education and Sustainable Development: A Model for Curriculum Renewal.* London: Routledge.

Disterheft, Antje; Caeiro, Sandra; Azeiteiro, Ulisses M.; and Filho, Walter L. 2013. "Sustainability Science and Education for Sustainable Development in Universities: A Way for Transition." In *Sustainability Assessment Tools in Higher Education Institutions: Mapping Trends and Good Practices around the World,* edited by Sandra Caeiro, Walter L. Filho, Charbel Jabbour, and Ulisses M. Azeiteiro. Cham, Switzerland: Springer International Publishing. Pp. 3–27.

Downey, Gary L. 2005. "Are Engineers Losing Control of Technology? From 'Problem Solving' to 'Problem Definition and Solution' in Engineering Education." *Chemical Engineering Research and Design* 83 (A6):583–595.

Elliott, Jennifer A. 2013. *An Introduction to Sustainable Development,* 4th edition. London: Routledge.

European Commission, Seventh Framework Programme. 2010. "Development of Indicators and Assessment Tools for CSO Projects Promoting Values-Based Education for Sustainable Development." www.esdinds.eu accessed 8 September 2015.

Fischer, Daniel; Jenssen, Silke; and Tappeser, Valentin. 2015. "Getting an Empirical Hold of the *Sustainable University*: A Comparative Analysis of Evaluation Frameworks across 12 Contemporary Sustainability Assessment Tools." *Assessment & Evaluation in Higher Education* 40 (6):785–800.

Folke, Carl; Colding, Johan; and Berkes, Fikret. 2008. "Synthesis: Building Resilience and Adaptive Capacity in Socio-Ecological Systems." In *Navigating Social-Ecological Systems: Building Resilience for Complexity and Change*, edited by Fikret Berkes, Johan Colding, and Carl Folke. Cambridge: Cambridge University Press. Pp. 352–387.

Fredericks, Sarah. 2014. *Measuring and Evaluating Sustainability: Ethics in Sustainability Indexes*. London: Routledge.

Gedde, Maia. 2009. *The International Health Links Manual: A Guide to Starting Up and Maintaining Long-Term International Health Partnerships*. London: Tropical Health and Education Trust.

Gibson, Robert B. 2005. *Sustainability Assessment: Criteria and Processes*. London: Earthscan.

Gruppen, Larry D.; Mangrulkar, Rajesh; and Kolars, Joseph C. 2012. "The Promise of Competence-Based Education in the Health Professions for Improving Global Health." *Human Resources for Health* 10:43–48.

Harpe, Barbara de la; and Thomas, Ian. 2009. "Curriculum Change in Universities: Conditions that Facilitate Education for Sustainable Development." *Journal of Education for Sustainable Development* 3 (1):75–85.

Jeffery, Roger. 2012. "Qualitative Methods in the RECOUP Projects." In *Education Outcomes and Poverty: A Reassessment*, edited by Christopher Colclough. London: Routledge. Pp. 170–189.

Jones, Nicola; Bailey, Mark; and Lyytikäinen, Minna. 2007. *Research Capacity Strengthening in Africa: Trends, Gaps and Opportunities*. London: Overseas Development Institute.

Jones, Paula; Selby, David; and Sterling, Stephen. 2010. "Introduction." In *Sustainability Education: Perspectives and Practice across Higher Education*, edited by Paula Jones, David Selby, and Stephen Sterling. London: Earthscan. Pp. 1–16.

Killick, Donald. 2007. "World-Wide Horizons: Cross-Cultural Capability and Global Perspectives – Guidelines for Curriculum Review." In *Internationalising Higher Education*, edited by Elspeth Jones and Sally Brown. London: Routledge. Pp. 201–220.

King, Kenneth; and McGrath, Simon. 2004. *Knowledge for Development? Comparing British, Japanese, Swedish, and World Bank Aid*. London: Zed Books.

King, Kenneth; and Palmer, Robert. 2013. *Post-2015 Agendas: Northern Tsunami, Southern Ripple? The Case of Education and Skills*. Working paper #4. Geneva: Network for International Policies and Cooperation in Education and Training (NORRAG).

Knight, Jane. 2008. "The Internationalization of Higher Education: Complexities and Realities." In *Higher Education in Africa: The International Dimension*, edited by Damtew Teferra and Jane Knight. Chestnut Hill, MA: Enter for International Higher Education, Boston College. Pp. 1–43.

Koehn, Peter H.; and Rosenau, James N. 2010. *Transnational Competence: Empowering Professional Curricula for Horizon-Rising Challenges*. Boulder, CO: Paradigm Publishers.

Kuczewski, Mark. 2006. "The Problem with Evaluating Professionalism." In *Professionalism in Medicine: Critical Perspectives*, edited by Delese Wear and Julie M. Aultman. New York: Springer. Pp. 185–198.

Lotz-Sisitka, Heila; Agbedahin, Adesuwa V.; and Hlengwa, Amanda. 2015. "Seeding Change: Developing a Change-Oriented Model for Professional Learning and ESD in Higher Education Institutions in Africa." In *Mainstreaming Environment and Sustainability in African Universities: Stories of Change*, edited by Heila Lotz-Sisitka, Gitile Naituli, Amanda Hlengwa, Mike Ward, Ayobami Salami, Akpezi Ogbuigwe, Mahesh Pradhan,

Marie Neeser, and Sanne Lauriks. Grahamstown: Rhodes University Environmental Learning Research Centre. Pp. 16–33.

Lozano, Rodrigo; and Watson, Mary K. 2013. "Assessing Sustainability in University Curricula: Case Studies from the University of Leeds and the Georgia Institute of Technology." In *Sustainability Assessment Tools in Higher Education Institutions: Mapping Trends and Good Practices around the World*, edited by Sandra Caeiro, Walter L. Filho, Charbel Jabbour, and Ulisses M. Azeiteiro. Cham, Switzerland: Springer International Publishing. Pp. 359–373.

Marshall, Jane. 2011. "UNESCO Debates Uses and Misuses of Rankings." *University World News* 172 (May).

Martin-Kniep, Giselle O. 1997. "Assessing Teachers for Learner-Centered Global Education." In *Preparing Teachers to Teach Global Perspectives: A Handbook for Teacher Educators*, edited by Merry M. Merryfield, Elaine Jarchow, and Sarah Picket. Thousand Oaks: Corwin Press. Pp. 99–122.

McFarlane, Donovan A.; and Ogazon, Agueda G. 2011. "The Challenges of Sustainability Education." *Journal of Multidisciplinary Research* 3, No. 3 (Fall):81–107.

McMahon, Walter W. 2009. *Higher Learning, Greater Good: The Private and Social Benefits of Higher Education*. Baltimore: Johns Hopkins University Press.

Mochizuki, Yoko; and Fadeeva, Zinaida. 2010. "Competences for Sustainable Development and Sustainability: Significance and Challenges for ESD." *International Journal of Sustainability in Higher Education* 11 (4):391–403.

Moore, Janet. 2005. "Seven Recommendations for Creating Sustainability Education at the University Level: A Guide for Change Agents." *International Journal of Sustainability in Higher Education* 6 (4):326–339.

Morfit, Christine; and Gore, Jane. 2009. *HED/USAID Higher Education Partnerships in Africa 1997–2007*. Washington, DC: Higher Education for Development.

Olapade-Olaopa, Emiola O.; Baird, Sarah; Kiguli-Malwadde, Elsie; and Kolars, Joseph C. 2014. "Growing Partnerships: Leveraging the Power of Collaboration through the Medical Education Partnership Initiative." *Academic Medicine* 89, No. 8 (August Supplement):S19–S23.

Ospina, Gustavo L. 2000. "Education for Sustainable Development: A Local and International Challenge." *Prospects* 30 (1):31–40.

Pain, Adam. 2009. "Economic Development and Sustainable Livelihoods." In *Higher Education and International Capacity Building: Twenty-Five Years of Higher Education Links*, edited by David Stephens. Oxford: Symposium Books. Pp. 95–114.

Palomba, Catherine A.; and Banta, Trudy W. 1999. *Assessment Essentials: Planning, Implementing, and Improving Assessment in Higher Education*. San Francisco, CA: Jossey-Bass.

Parker, Jenneth; Wade, Ros; and Atkinson, Hugh. 2004. "Citizenship and Community from Local to Global: Implications for Higher Education of a Global Citizenship Approach." In *The Sustainability Curriculum: Facing the Challenge in Higher Education*, edited by John Blewitt and Cedric Cullingford. London: Earthscan. Pp. 63–77.

Parker, Walter C. 1996. "Assessing Student Learning of an Issue-Oriented Curriculum." In *Handbook on Teaching Social Studies*, edited by Ronald W. Evans and David W. Saxe. Washington, DC: National Council for the Social Studies. Pp. 280–283.

Peterson, Patti M. [Presidential Advisor for Global Initiatives, American Council on Education] 2015. "A Flat Lens for a Round World?" Keynote address at the Defining a 21st Century Education for a Vibrant Democracy Conference, University of Montana, Missoula, 26 October.

Ralph, Meredith; and Stubbs, Wendy. 2014. "Integrating Environmental Sustainability into Universities." *Higher Education* 67:71–90.

Rammel, Christian; Velazquez, Luis; and Mader, Clemens. 2016. "Sustainability Assessment in Higher Education Institutions: What and How?" In *Routledge Handbook of Higher Education for Sustainable Development*, edited by Matthias Barth, Gerd Michelsen, Marco Rieckmann, and Ian Thomas. London: Routledge. Pp. 331–346.

Ramos, Tomas; and Pires, Sara M. 2013. "Sustainability Assessment: The Role of Indicators." In *Sustainability Assessment Tools in Higher Education Institutions: Mapping Trends and Good Practices around the World*, edited by Sandra Caeiro, Walter L. Filho, Charbel Jabbour, and Ulisses M. Azeiteiro. Cham, Switzerland: Springer International Publishing. Pp. 81–99.

Ravetz, Joe. 2007. "The Role of Evaluation in Regional Sustainable Development." In *Impact Assessment and Sustainable Development: European Practice and Experience*, edited by Clive George and Colin Kirkpatrick. Cheltenham, UK: Edward Elgar. Pp. 65–89.

Remington-Doucette, Sonya M.; Connell, Kim Y. H.; Armstrong, Cosette M.; and Musgrove, Sheryl L. 2013. "Assessing Sustainability Education in a Transdisciplinary Undergraduate Course Focused on Real-World Problem Solving: A Case for Disciplinary Grounding." *International Journal of Sustainability in Higher Education* 14 (4):404–433.

Roorda, Niko. 2013. "A Strategy and a Toolkit to Realize System Integration of Sustainable Development (SISD)." In *Sustainability Assessment Tools in Higher Education Institutions: Mapping Trends and Good Practices around the World*, edited by Sandra Caeiro, Walter L. Filho, Charbel Jabbour, and Ulisses M. Azeiteiro. Cham, Switzerland: Springer International Publishing. Pp. 101–119.

Roorda, Niko; Corcoran, Peter B.; and Weakland, Joseph P. 2012. *Fundamentals of Sustainable Development*. London: Routledge.

Rowe, Debra; and Hiser, Krista. 2016. "Higher Education for Sustainable Development in the Community and through Partnerships." In *Routledge Handbook of Higher Education for Sustainable Development*, edited by Matthias Barth, Gerd Michelsen, Marco Rieckmann, and Ian Thomas. London: Routledge. Pp. 315–330.

Rowe, Debra; and Johnston, Lucas F. 2013. "Learning Outcomes: An International Comparison of Countries and Declarations." In *Higher Education for Sustainability: Cases, Challenges, and Opportunities from across the Curriculum*, edited by Lucas F. Johnston. New York: Routledge. Pp. 45–59.

Ryan, Alex; and Cotton, Debby. 2013. "Times of Change: Shifting Pedagogy and Curricula for Future Sustainability." In *The Sustainable University: Progress and Prospects*, edited by Stephen Sterling, Larch Maxey, and Heather Luna. London: Routledge. Pp. 151–161.

Sawahel, Wagdy. 2012. "University Leaders Worldwide Sign Sustainability Declaration." *University World News* 223 (25 May).

Schuller, Tom; and Desjardins, Richard. 2007. *Understanding the Social Outcomes of Learning*. Paris: Organization for Economic Co-Operation and Development (OECD).

Schuller, Tom; Hammond, Cathie; and Preston, John. 2004. "Reappraising Benefits." In *The Benefits of Learning: The Impact of Education on Health, Family Life and Social Capital*, edited by Tom Schuller, John Preston, Cathie Hammond, Angela Brassett-Grundy, and John Bynner. London: RoutledgeFalmer. Pp. 179–193.

Shriberg, Michael. 2004. "Assessing Sustainability: Criteria, Tools, and Implications." In *Higher Education and the Challenges of Sustainability: Problematics, Promise, and Practice*, edited by Peter B. Corcoran and Arjen E. J. Wals. Dordrecht: Kluwer. Pp. 73–86.

Shuman, Larry J.; Besterfield-Sacre, Mary; and McGourty, Jack. 2005. "The ABET 'Professional Skills': Can They Be Taught? Can They Be Assessed?" *Journal of Engineering Education* 94 (1):41–53.

Sibbel, Anne; Hegarty, Kathryn; and Holdsworth, Sarah. 2013. "Action Research in Communities of Practice to Develop Curricula for Sustainability in Higher Education." In *Sustainability Assessment Tools in Higher Education Institutions: Mapping Trends and Good*

Practices around the World, edited by Sandra Caeiro, Walter L. Filho, Charbel Jabbour, and Ulisses M. Azeiteiro. Cham, Switzerland: Springer International Publishing. Pp. 387–404.

Sileshi Sisaye. 2016. *Ecology, Sustainable Development and Accounting*. New York: Routledge.

Simon, Dagmar; and Knie, Andreas. 2013. "Can Evaluation Contribute to the Organizational Development of Academic Institutions? An International Comparison." *Evaluation* 19 (4):402–418.

Simon, Kathleen; and Haertle, Jonas. 2014. "Rio+20 Higher Education Sustainability Initiative (HESI) Commitments: A Review of Progress, October 2014." HESI. http://sustainabledevelopment.un.org/index.php?menu=1073

Sipos, Yona; Battisti, Bryce; and Grimm, Kurt. 2008. "Achieving Transformative Sustainability Learning: Engaging Head, Hands, and Heart." *International Journal of Sustainability in Higher Education* 9 (1):68–86.

Stauffacher, Michael; Walter, Alexander I.; Lang, Daniel J.; Wiek, Arnim; and Scholz, Roland W. 2006. "Learning to Research Environmental Problems from a Functional Socio-Cultural Constructivism Perspective." *International Journal of Sustainability in Higher Education* 7 (3):252–275.

Sterling, Stephen. 2004. "Higher Education, Sustainability, and the Role of Systemic Learning." In *Higher Education and the Challenge of Sustainability: Problematics, Promise, and Practice*, edited by Peter B. Corcoran and Arjen E. J. Wals. Dordrecht: Kluwer Academic Publishers. Pp. 49–70.

Sterling, Stephen. 2009. "Sustainable Education." In *Science, Society, and Sustainability: Education and Empowerment for an Uncertain World*, edited by Donald Gray, Laura Colucci-Gray, and Elena Camino. New York: Routledge. Pp. 105–118.

Sterling, Stephen. 2013. "The Sustainable University: Challenge and Response." In *The Sustainable University: Progress and Prospects*, edited by Stephen Sterling, Larch Maxey, and Heather Luna. London: Routledge. Pp. 17–50.

Sterling, Stephen; and Thomas, Ian. 2006. "Education for Sustainability: The Role of Capabilities in Guiding University Curriculum." *International Journal of Innovation and Sustainable Development* 1 (4):349–369.

Strele, Martin. 2012. "Participatory Livelihoods System Appraisal: A Learning-Oriented Methodology for Impact Assessment." In *Governance by Evaluation for Sustainable Development: Institutional Capacities and Learning*, edited by Michal Sedlacko and Andre Martinuzzi. Cheltenham, UK: Edward Elgar. Pp. 173–190.

Thaman, Konai H. 2006. "Acknowledging Indigenous Knowledge Systems in Higher Education in the Pacific Island Region." In *Higher Education, Research, and Knowledge in the Asia-Pacific Region*, edited by V. Lynn Meek and Charas Suwanwela. Gordonsville, VA: Palgrave Macmillan. Pp. 175–184.

Thomas, Ian. 2016. "Challenges for Implementation of Education for Sustainable Development in Higher Education Institutions." In *Routledge Handbook of Higher Education for Sustainable Development*, edited by Matthias Barth, Gerd Michelsen, Marco Rieckmann, and Ian Thomas. London: Routledge. Pp. 56–71.

Tilbury, Daniella. 2004. "Environmental Education for Sustainability: A Force for Change in Higher Education." In *Higher Education and the Challenge of Sustainability: Problematics, Promise, and Practice*, edited by Peter B. Corcoran and Arjen E. J. Wals. Dordrecht: Kluwer Academic Publishers. Pp. 97–112.

Tilbury, Daniella. 2013. "Another World Is Desirable: A Global Rebooting of Higher Education for Sustainable Development." In *The Sustainable University: Progress and Prospects*, edited by Stephen Sterling, Larch Maxey, and Heather Luna. London: Routledge. Pp. 71–85.

Togo, Muchaiteyi. 2015. "Development, Use and Significance of the Unit-Based Sustainability Assessment Tool for Universities in Africa and Asia." In *Mainstreaming Environment and Sustainability in African Universities: Stories of Change*, edited by Heila

Lotz-Sisitka, Gitile Naituli, Amanda Hlengwa, Mike Ward, Ayobami Salami, Akpezi Ogbuigwe, Mahesh Pradhan, Marie Neeser, and Sanne Lauriks. Grahamstown: Rhodes University Environmental Learning Research Centre. Pp. 34–64.

Togo, Muchaiteyi; and Lotz-Sisitka, Heila. 2013. "The Unit-Based Sustainability Assessment Tool and Its Use in the UNEP Mainstreaming Environment and Sustainability in African Universities Partnership." In *Sustainability Assessment Tools in Higher Education Institutions: Mapping Trends and Good Practices around the World*, edited by Sandra Caeiro, Walter L. Filho, Charbel Jabbour, and Ulisses M. Azeiteiro. Cham, Switzerland: Springer International Publishing. Pp. 259–288.

Vettori, Oliver; and Rammel, Christian. 2014. "Linking Quality Assurance and ESD: Towards a Participative Quality Culture of Sustainable Development in Higher Education." In *Sustainable Development and Quality Assurance in Higher Education: Transformation of Learning and Society*, edited by Zinaida Fadeeva, Laima Galkute, and Clemens Mader, and Geoff Scott. New York: Palgrave Macmillan. Pp. 49–65.

Virtanen, Anne. 2010. "Learning for Climate Responsibility: Via Consciousness to Action." In *Universities and Climate Change*, edited by Walter L. Filho. Berlin: Springer. Pp. 231–240.

Waas, Tom; Huge, Jean; Verbruggen, Aviel; and Block, Thomas. 2015. "Navigating towards Sustainability: Essential Aspects of Assessment and Indicators." In *Sustainability: Key Issues*, edited by Helen Kopnina and Eleanor Shoreman-Ouimet. London: Routledge. Pp. 88–108.

Walker, Melanie; McLean, Monica; Dison, Arona; and Peppin-Vaughn, Rosie. 2009. "South African Universities and Human Development: Towards a Theorisation and Operationalisation of Professional Capabilities for Poverty Reduction." *International Journal of Educational Development* 29:565–572.

Wals, Arjen E. J.; and Blewitt, John. 2010. "Third-Wave Sustainability in Higher Education: Some (Inter)national Trends and Developments." In *Sustainability Education: Perspectives and Practice across Higher Education*, edited by Paula Jones, David Selby, and Stephen Sterling. London: Earthscan. Pp. 55–74.

Wamae, Watu. 2011. "Continent Needs Its Own Science Indicators." *University World News* 179 (July).

White, Rehema M. 2013. "Sustainability Research: A Novel Mode of Knowledge Generation to Explore Alternative Ways for People and Planet." In *The Sustainable University: Progress and Prospects*, edited by Stephen Sterling, Larch Maxey, and Heather Luna. London: Routledge. Pp. 168–191.

Wiek, Arnim; Withycombe, Lauren; and Redman, Charles L. 2011. "Key Competencies in Sustainability: A Reference Framework for Academic Program Development." *Sustainability Science* 6:203–218.

Wiek, Arnim; Withycombe, Lauren; Redman, Charles L.; and Mills, Sarah B. 2011b. "Moving Forward on Competence in Sustainability Research and Problem Solving." *Environment Magazine* 53, No. 2 (March–April):3–12.

Wiek, Arnim; and Bernstein, Michael J.; Foley, Rider; Cohen, Matthew; Forrest, Nigel; Kuzdas, Christopher; Kay, Braden; and Keeler, Lauren W. 2016. "Operationalising Competencies in Higher Education for Sustainable Development." In *Routledge Handbook of Higher Education for Sustainable Development*, edited by Matthias Barth, Gerd Michelsen, Marco Rieckmann, and Ian Thomas. London: Routledge. Pp. 241–260.

Wright, Tarah S. A. 2002. "Definitions and Frameworks for Environmental Sustainability in Higher Education." *Higher Education Policy* 12 (2):105–120.

Zint, Michaela. 2011. "Evaluating Education for Sustainable Development Programs." In *World Trends in Education for Sustainable Development*, edited by Walter L. Filho. Frankfurt: Peter Lang. Pp. 329–347.

7

RESEARCH EVALUATIONS THAT MATTER

This chapter is devoted to exploring prospects for meaningful research-evaluation approaches. This process-, outcome-, and impact-focused chapter treats evaluating transnational-sustainable-development (TSD) research activity in terms of the generation and application of knowledge and insight flows. Building off the framework for university sustainable-development evaluations presented in Chapter 5, we suggest promising lines of research-evaluation inquiry. The concluding section of this chapter is concerned with ways that enhanced university-research evaluations can contribute to deeper TSD outcomes and impacts in the post-2030 era.

"Research for sustainable development" is understudied in the field of sustainability and higher education. In an important breakthrough that helps inform the analysis presented in this chapter, Tom Waas, Aviel Verbruggen, and Tarah Wright (2010) identified prominent characteristics of the concept drawn from international declarations, workshop reports, and a literature search. Their synthesis consists of six content factors and sixteen process factors that characterize sustainable-development research. Content characteristics include physical scale (local to global; North and South), time scale (short, medium, and long), welfare-distribution considerations, multiple dimensions (economic, environmental, social, and institutional), and the precautionary principle (Waas, Verbruggen, and Wright, 2010, p. 633). Process characteristics encompass problem, action, and proactive orientations; international and cross-sector collaborations; multidisciplinarity and interdisciplinarity; knowledge transfer; participation (including local and indigenous insight contributions); interest in impacts; peer review; and transparency (Waas, Verbruggen, and Wright, 2010, pp. 633–634).

Process evaluation

Conducted in an informed, sensitive, and symmetrical manner, intra- and inter-university evaluations can provide a powerful basis for TSD-research advances (Shriberg, 2004, p. 71). The proactive evaluation plan sets forth the criteria and standards that will be employed in evaluating the attainment of research outcomes and impacts and their import. For the planning stage, evaluators also consider the data-gathering methods that participants decided to use to determine whether behavioral changes occurred. At the implementation stage, evaluators search for evidence of additionality and of change that "addresses underlying causes rather than symptoms" (Wahr and de la Harpe, 2016, p. 168). At the observing stage, evaluators analyze formative and summative data to determine how consistently researchers implemented the research plan, assess the extent to which university-research objectives were attained, and explore outcomes, impacts, and unintended consequences. Moreover, "when formative evaluation is combined with the involvement of local practitioners as research team members, feedback is directly built into the research process" (Crossley, et al., 2005, p. 106). The final stage of TSD-research evaluation involves "critical reflection on both the process and outcomes . . . in order to guide future decision-making and action, as well as to contribute to theory building" and to inform curriculum change (Wahr and de la Harpe, 2016, pp. 169, 175; also see Zimmermann, et al., 2014, p. 149).

Peer review remains a vital independent feature of every aspect of university evaluations (Simon and Knie, 2013, pp. 404–405, 416). Thorough, critical, and open peer review bolsters the credibility of research-intervention results (e.g., see Wahr and de la Harpe, 2016, p. 166). Capable and dedicated peer reviewers should be involved in evaluating research redirections (Simon and Knie, 2013, p. 414). Modified peer-review-based evaluation processes "take into account the institutional environment," address user and practitioner needs and otherwise peripheral or neglected themes, probe strengths and weaknesses in ways that move beyond data used in other evaluations, and "put explicit recommendations for further organizational development processes on the agenda" (Simon and Knie, 2013, pp. 406, 411–412, 414). However, Simon and Knie (2013, p. 414) caution that peer review can be preoccupied with technical standards "while neglecting other criteria, such as direct and indirect societal or economic benefits, or in general, usefulness." This caution needs to be kept in mind because the latter criteria are particularly important in evaluating sustainable development.

Process-oriented evaluation is particularly useful for sustainable-development-research contexts that span organizational and national boundaries (Simon and Knie, 2013, p. 406). To what extent did sustainability managers function successfully as interpreters and cross-disciplinary brokers among the university's diverse research subcultures (Vettori and Rammel, 2014, p. 61)? Did existing networks succeed in connecting Northern and Southern researchers around common and complementary TSD-research agendas (Jones, Bailey, and Lyytikäinen, 2007, p. 18)? Zimmermann and colleagues (2014, p. 149) contend that insight generation and mutual learning are "prerequisites for valuable sustainability research." Did stakeholder and transnational collaborations result in sharing of mutually rewarding insights?

Internally, to what extent were faculty and students in each academic unit involved in sustainable-development research and scholarship (Togo and Lotz-Sisitka,

2013, p. 278)? To what extent were student and faculty research undertakings linked around contextually relevant issues of sustainable development? To what degree did glocal sustainability issues feature in the selection and execution of these research undertakings (Togo and Lotz-Sisitka, 2013, p. 278; Roudometof, 2016, pp. 38–39)? Did research participants strategically identify and debate issues and queries that constitute meaningful candidates for research synthesis (Rickinson and Reid, 2016, p. 152)? Did the sustainable-development-research process "cultivate [additional] research donors and grant providers" (Desha and Hargroves, 2014, p. 104)?

Other process avenues of sustainability-evaluation inquiry focus on stakeholders. Did community members, practitioners, actors pursuing economic interests, environmentalists, university partners, and policy makers participate in defining the research question and initiating and designing the sustainability-research process (Brundiers and Wiek, 2011, p. 110; Talwar, Wiek, and Robinson, 2011, pp. 381, 383, 388; White, 2013, p. 173; Waas, et al., 2015, p. 94; Rowe and Hiser, 2016, p. 323)? If so, to what extent? Did stakeholders, practitioners, and policy makers work collaboratively with university personnel on conducting transacademic research aimed at creating results that address the identified sustainable-development challenge (Talwar, Wiek, and Robinson, 2011, p. 381; Brundiers and Wiek, 2011, pp. 110–111)? In the process of research education, did scholars and stakeholders "jointly negotiate, revise, and synthesize knowledge, and take decisions" (Brundiers and Wiek, 2011, p. 113)? Did the processes of negotiation and collaboration result in joint ownership (Brundiers and Wiek, 2011, p. 113)? Did stakeholders report that they "had been appropriately included in the process, adequately informed, and prepared for decision making" (Brundiers and Wiek, 2011, p. 116)?

Evaluators also should seek to know the following: Was the TSD-evaluation process understandable to all stakeholders (Shriberg, 2004, p. 74)? Did peer review result in products that "include strategies, plans, or recommendations for action agreed upon by all relevant stakeholders" (Brundiers and Wiek, 2011, p. 113)? To what degree did the collaborative-research process increase the capacity of each stakeholder to advance environmental stewardship, social justice, and human wellbeing (Mochizuki and Fadeeva, 2010, p. 393)? Did academics and non-academic users share control over the research process and acknowledge mutual dependence in ways that promoted ownership and implementation of results aimed at advancing sustainable development (Talwar, Wiek, and Robinson, 2011, pp. 384, 388)?

Outcome evaluation

In much of the Global South, institutions of higher learning and donors devote a relatively low level of spending to research-capacity building (see, for instance, Jones, Bailey, and Lyytikäinen, 2007, pp. 7, 12–13).[1] Capacity builders have been particularly prone to neglect the social sciences (other than economics) and the humanities (Jones, Bailey, and Lyytikäinen, 2007, pp. 8, 13, 15). This reality increases the importance of maximizing the capacity-building outcomes of limited investments in sustainability research.

Based on disappointing experience at Royal Melbourne Institute of Technology, Bekessy, Samson, and Clarkson (2007, p. 315) argue that universities that sign declarations or publicly commit to sustainable-development goals must swiftly assign "an appropriate long-term budget" that ensures the availability of sufficient resources to meet commitments. Did funding, mentorship, promotion schemes, and other incentives drive sustainable-development-research initiatives (Simon and Haertle, 2014, p. 5; Fischer, Jenssen, and Tappeser, 2015, p. 792)? The Alternative University Appraisal (AUA) assessment tool's Question 17 asks university respondents to "indicate incentive types, such as financial remuneration, appraisal mechanisms, infrastructure support, etc.," that are provided "to encourage and foster innovation as well as multidisciplinary collaboration" for sustainable-development research (Razak, et al., 2013, p. 150).

Independent evaluators play an important role in critical analyses of sustainable-development outcomes. Did evaluators begin with a theory of change for research-capacity and research-capability development (Jones, Bailey, and Lyytikäinen, 2007, p. 24)? What lessons can be drawn from the consistencies with and departures from the developed theory of change?

Research and problem-solving competencies also feature in learning-outcome evaluations. Were student-research-learning outcomes linked to key TSD competencies (Brundiers, et al., 2014, p. 203) and real-world challenges (Brundiers and Wiek, 2011, pp. 120–121)? Did students receive sufficient support to develop TSD-research competence (Brundiers, et al., 2014, p. 203)? Did students develop actionable options (Brundiers, et al., 2014, p. 203) with plausible potential to advance sustainable development? Did students and local partners jointly present research findings documenting their contributions to sustainable development and their insights regarding scaling-out and scaling-up sustainability initiatives (Mader, 2014, pp. 74, 80)? To what extent were specific TC skills and changes in sustainability behavior (Brundiers and Wiek, 2011, p. 113) connected with valuable sustainable-development-research capabilities and demonstrated contributions among students and graduated professionals?

Further, did sustainable-development capacity-building build on and strengthen research capabilities in ways that were linked to national, regional, and local development-policy priorities (Jones, Bailey, and Lyytikäinen, 2007, pp. 8–10, 21)? Did donors coordinate support for institutional-capacity strengthening initiatives and commit for long time periods (Jones, Bailey, and Lyytikäinen, 2007, p. 20)?

Box 7.1 lists illustrative evaluation questions for use in research-outcome evaluations focused on sustainable development. Additionality – the extent to which the identified outcomes would not have occurred without the intervention – is a central component of each line of evaluative inquiry. Interest in additionality moves evaluative approaches in the direction of "qualitative, embedded, sociocultural and process-based interactions" (Ravetz, 2007, p. 83).

BOX 7.1 ILLUSTRATIVE EVALUATION QUESTIONS FOR RESEARCH-OUTCOME EVALUATIONS FOCUSED ON SUSTAINABLE DEVELOPMENT

- Are tailored-training resources available for building capacity for TSD-research initiatives, and to what extent have they been utilized?
- Have sustainable-development researchers secured access to needed resources to conduct research?
- Did a cluster of competent scholars arise who were dedicated to conducting and coordinating TSD research (Simon and Haertle, 2014, p. 5)? Did the initiative succeed in mobilizing a critical multidisciplinary and transdisciplinary mass of competent sustainable-development researchers? Did research-capability-developing initiatives pursue gender balance (Jones, Bailey, and Lyytikäinen, 2007, pp. 19–20)?
- Is there evidence of improvement in the TSD-research capabilities of program participants?
- Did research-capability strengthening emphasize "in-depth understanding of the local context" and linkage with domestic- and transnational-sustainable-development priorities (Jones, Bailey, and Lyytikäinen, 2007, p. 20)?
- To what degree did the collaborative-research process increase the capacity of each stakeholder to advance environmental stewardship, social justice, and economic wellbeing (Mochizuki and Fadeeva, 2010, p. 393)?
- Were research initiatives linked to campus-operation sustainability undertakings?[2]
- How have research-management capacities – including institutional reward, sector coordination, findings dissemination, and end-use-uptake systems – improved (Jones, Bailey, and Lyytikäinen, 2007, pp. 7, 10, 15–16, 22)?
- Has the sustainability of research-capacity-building initiatives been promoted by ensuring that the local university (or universities) possesses a core ownership role in deciding TSD-research agendas, priorities, methods, and processes (Jones, Bailey, and Lyytikäinen, 2007, p. 10)?

Impact evaluation

Documenting the value of research is inherently challenging for numerous reasons, including its long-term, indirect, unnoticeable, and spin-off effects (see Bailey, 2010, p. 45). A place to start is by gathering evidence regarding the contributory and catalytic effects[3] of specific TSD-research and problem-solving projects (Wiek, et al., 2011b, p. 11). David Court (2008, p. 107) suggests that evaluative assessments should strive to secure (1) "clear documentation of the practice, quality, and developmental relevance of research partnerships"; (2) "detailed examples of success, and particularly failure"; and (3) "more assessment from the South." Court (2008, p. 107) recommends that evaluators provide in-depth case studies that analyze research-project successes and failures and discover what has worked and has not worked (Vromen, 2010, pp. 256–258).[4]

Evaluations of research impact, Walter McMahon (2009, p. 256) alerts us, should include its indirect professional and quality-of-life influence on collaborating students and their students along with the life-long contributions of both to society's needs. Diane Stone (2004, p. 155) cautions that "conventional indicators of academic excellence (such as academic citations and scholarly peer reviews) will not suffice, since they do not reliably indicate policy relevance or impact." In contrast to remote academic publications, influence over national and local policy has long-term multiplier effects. Were sustainable-development-research contributions linked to local policy and practice priorities (Jones, Bailey, and Lyytikäinen, 2007, pp. 8, 14, 18)?

Also missing from higher-education-research evaluations that are reduced to tracking outputs or cost-benefit analyses are such important considerations as demonstrated willingness to take on risk and pursue innovative approaches. Did research-project participants and evidence-based curriculum builders "welcome serendipity and unexpected developments" (Austin and Foxcroft, 2011, p. 130; also Beretz, 2012, pp. 144–147)?

In gaging the impact of TSD research, it is important to establish the extent to which studies are contextually appropriate and locally valuable. The conversion of scientific-research findings into policy interventions that support sustainable-development processes are critically important practical achievements and indications of the success or impact of specific university interventions. To what extent have disseminated research findings been utilized by stakeholders to enhance sustainable development?

Approaches used in assessing action-research interventions (Wahr and de la Harpe, 2016, p. 163) can be useful in evaluating the impact of all TSD-research activity. Did the activity lead to improvements in the research process? Did the research product enhance sustainable-development practices at one or more of the following levels of activity: improved individual-practitioner decision making when confronted by practical and contextual challenges of sustainable development; improved group-level collaboration on a shared sustainable-development challenge; improved community-level response to a specific small-scale economic, social, or ecological challenge; or improved national and/or transnational response to a sustainable-development challenge with cross-boundary claws?

Further, TSD-impact assessments should include the development, synthesis, and application of indigenous and practical knowledge and ways of learning. According to George Dei and Alireza Asgharzadeh (2006, p. 60), "a key tenet of indigenous knowings is that the worth of any knowledge can be measured when it enhances the capacity of local peoples to sustain their lives." Did sustainable-development-research efforts link knowledge to action (Brundiers and Wiek,

2011, p. 113) and engage structural and societal change (Disterheft, et al., 2013, p. 16)? Were non-academic stakeholders able to integrate sources of knowledge (including local and indigenous insights) about sustainability (Talwar, Wiek, and Robinson, 2011, p. 380; White, 2013, p. 173)?

How enhanced research evaluations can contribute to deeper sustainable-development outcomes and impacts in the post-2030 era

Why is it vitally important that research evaluations be meaningful and convincing? Moving the world toward sustainable development means exploring new frontiers and finding novel solutions to the pressing problems introduced in Chapter 2. Although research and innovation are indispensable for promoting TSD, it is precisely the traditional way of compartmentalizing phenomena into discreet disciplines that has led us down an unsustainable path – to cite only two examples of this problematic: (1) economics studies that consider environmental harm as an externality and (2) engineering approaches that concentrate on fixing things mechanically without addressing root causes.

Fortuitously, the *2030 Agenda for Sustainable Development*[5] adopted by world leaders in September 2015 recognizes the critical role of research in achieving the attendant Sustainable Development Goals (SDGs), whether they pertain to food security and nutrition, health, clean energy, industry, or conservation of marine resources. However, advancing the SDGs requires changes in the ways scholars conduct research. Integrating social, economic, and environmental perspectives across traditional academic disciplines demands new ways of thinking about and carrying out TSD research at Northern and Southern universities.[6] Such novelty calls for credible and comprehensive evaluations because we need to assess the results of new TSD-research initiatives and collaborations so that we can learn from these efforts and improve upon them in the future.

In short, credible research is essential if people's actions and policy interventions are to move in directions favorable to sustainable development. In order for research to contribute to innovative sustainability approaches and to drive change toward sustainable-development outcomes and impacts, we need to be able to document what works and why. For this reason, the learning dimension of research evaluation is a critical component of our framework. Cross-pollination from small-scale experiments over multiple contexts, including those that fail, can generate valuable insights into sustainable development. Thus, researchers accept and evaluators look for "safe to fail" outcomes and impacts.

TSD research also should be practically and societally relevant. Ultimately, therefore, the impact of sustainable-development research should be measured against whether it enhances prospects of sustainable development in the real world. This understanding underscores the connection of university-research initiatives to outreach activity – the subject of Chapter 8.

Notes

1 Although "capacity building for development research and research utilization is one of DfID's stated priorities," most of its support ends up at Northern institutions (Jones, Bailey, and Lyytikäinen, 2007, p. 9).
2 See, for instance, Cayuela, et al. (2013, p. 230).
3 The GEF's intervention logic, for instance, calls for "achieving impact through a catalytic effect" (Uitto, 2016, p. 109).
4 On the value of case studies as a research methodology in complex and contextual sustainable-development situations, particularly if combined with other methods, see Kyburz-Graber (2016, pp. 129, 133).
5 Resolution adopted by the General Assembly on 25 September 2015. 70/1. Transforming our world: the 2030 Agenda for Sustainable Development. United Nations.
6 For instance, integrated-TSD research on the SDGs can help shape the scientific agenda to meet the needs of people in Africa and elsewhere in the Global South, including women who are frequently bypassed by more traditional research efforts (Vesper, 2016).

Works cited

Austin, Ann E.; and Foxcroft, Cheryl. 2011. "Fostering Organizational Change and Individual Learning through 'Ground-Up' Inter-Institutional Cross-Border Collaboration." In *Cross-Border Partnerships in Higher Education: Strategies and Issues*, edited by Robin Sakamoto and David W. Chapman. New York: Routledge. Pp. 115–132.

Bailey, Tracy. 2010. "The Research-Policy Nexus: Mapping the Terrain of the Literature." Paper prepared for the Higher Education Research and Advocacy Network in Africa (HERANA). Wynberg, UK: Center for Higher Education Transformation.

Bekessy, S. A.; Samson, K.; and Clarkson, R. E. 2007. "The Failure of Non-Binding Declarations to Achieve University Sustainability: A Need for Accountability." *International Journal of Sustainability in Higher Education* 8 (3):301–316.

Beretz, Alain. 2012. "Preparing the University and Its Graduates for the Unpredictable and the Unknowable." In *Global Sustainability and the Responsibilities of Universities*, edited by Luc E. Weber and James J. Duderstadt. London: Economica. Pp. 143–151.

Brundiers, Katja; Savage, Emma; Mannell, Steven; Lang, Daniel J.; and Wiek, Arnim. 2014. "Educating Sustainability Change Agents by Design: Appraisals of the Transformative Role of Higher Education." In *Sustainable Development and Quality Assurance in Higher Education: Transformation of Learning and Society*, edited by Zinaida Fadeeva, Laima Galkute, Clemens Mader, and Geoff Scott. New York: Palgrave Macmillan. Pp. 196–229.

Brundiers, Katja; and Wiek, Arnim. 2011. "Educating Students in Real-World Sustainability Research: Vision and Implementation." *Innovative Higher Education* 36:107–124.

Cayuela, Alberto; Robinson, John B.; Campbell, Ann; Coops, Nicholas; and Munro, Alison. 2013. "Integration of Operational and Academic Efforts in Sustainability at the University of British Columbia." In *Sustainability Assessment Tools in Higher Education Institutions: Mapping Trends and Good Practices around the World*, edited by Sandra Caeiro, Walter L. Filho, Charbel Jabbour, and Ulisses M. Azeiteiro. Cham, Switzerland: Springer International Publishing. Pp. 223–236.

Court, David. 2008. "The Historical Effect of Partnerships in East Africa." *NORRAG News* 41 (December):105–107.

Crossley, Michael; Herriot, Andrew; Waudo, Judith; Mwirotsi, Miriam; Holmes, Keith; and Juma, Magdallen. 2005. *Research and Evaluation for Educational Development: Learning from the PRISM Experience in Kenya*. Oxford, UK: Symposium Books.

Dei, George J. S.; and Asgharzadeh, Alireza. 2006. "Indigenous Knowledges and Globalization: An African Perspective." In *African Education and Globalization: Critical Perspectives*, edited by Ali A. Abdi, Korbla P. Puplampu, and George J. S. Dei. Lanham, MD: Lexington Books. Pp. 53–78.

Desha, Cheryl; and Hargroves, Karlson C. 2014. *Higher Education and Sustainable Development: A Model for Curriculum Renewal.* London: Routledge.

Disterheft, Antje; Caeiro, Sandra; Azeiteiro, Ulisses M.; and Filho, Walter L. 2013. "Sustainability Science and Education for Sustainable Development in Universities: A Way for Transition." In *Sustainability Assessment Tools in Higher Education Institutions: Mapping Trends and Good Practices around the World*, edited by Sandra Caeiro, Walter L. Filho, Charbel Jabbour, and Ulisses M. Azeiteiro. Cham, Switzerland: Springer International Publishing. Pp. 3–27.

Fischer, Daniel; Jenssen, Silke; and Tappeser, Valentin. 2015. "Getting an Empirical Hold of the *Sustainable University*: A Comparative Analysis of Evaluation Frameworks across 12 Contemporary Sustainability Assessment Tools." *Assessment & Evaluation in Higher Education* 40 (6):785–800.

Jones, Nicola; Bailey, Mark; and Lyytikäinen, Minna. 2007. *Research Capacity Strengthening in Africa: Trends, Gaps and Opportunities.* London: Overseas Development Institute.

Kyburz-Graber, Regula. 2016. "Case Study Research on Higher Education for Sustainable Development." In *Routledge Handbook of Higher Education for Sustainable Development*, edited by Matthias Barth, Gerd Michelsen, Marco Rieckmann, and Ian Thomas. London: Routledge. Pp. 126–141.

Mader, Clemens. 2014. "The Role of Assessment and Quality Management in Transformations towards Sustainable Development: The Nexus between Higher Education, Society and Policy." In *Sustainable Development and Quality Assurance in Higher Education: Transformation of Learning and Society*, edited by Zinaida Fadeeva, Laima Galkute, Clemens Mader, and Geoff Scott. New York: Palgrave Macmillan. Pp. 66–83.

McMahon, Walter W. 2009. *Higher Learning, Greater Good: The Private and Social Benefits of Higher Education.* Baltimore: Johns Hopkins University Press.

Mochizuki, Yoko; and Fadeeva, Zinaida. 2010. "Competences for Sustainable Development and Sustainability: Significance and Challenges for ESD." *International Journal of Sustainability in Higher Education* 11 (4):391–403.

Ravetz, Joe. 2007. "The Role of Evaluation in Regional Sustainable Development." In *Impact Assessment and Sustainable Development: European Practice and Experience*, edited by Clive George and Colin Kirkpatrick. Cheltenham, UK: Edward Elgar. Pp. 65–89.

Razak, Dzulkifli A.; Sanusi, Zainal A.; Jegatesen, Govindran; and Khelghat-Doost, Hamoon. 2013. "Alternative University Appraisal (AUA): Reconstructing Universities' Ranking and Rating toward a Sustainable Future." In *Sustainability Assessment Tools in Higher Education Institutions: Mapping Trends and Good Practices around the World*, edited by Sandra Caeiro, Walter L. Filho, Charbel Jabbour, and Ulisses M. Azeiteiro. Cham, Switzerland: Springer International Publishing. Pp. 139–154.

Rickinson, Mark; and Reid, Alan. 2016. "Synthesis of Research in Higher Education for Sustainable Development." In *Routledge Handbook of Higher Education for Sustainable Development*, edited by Matthias Barth, Gerd Michelsen, Marco Rieckmann, and Ian Thomas. London: Routledge. Pp. 142–160.

Roudometof, Victor. 2016. *Glocalization: A Critical Introduction.* London: Routledge.

Rowe, Debra; and Hiser, Krista. 2016. "Higher Education for Sustainable Development in the Community and through Partnerships." In *Routledge Handbook of Higher Education for Sustainable Development*, edited by Matthias Barth, Gerd Michelsen, Marco Rieckmann, and Ian Thomas. London: Routledge. Pp. 315–330.

Shriberg, Michael. 2004. "Assessing Sustainability: Criteria, Tools, and Implications." In *Higher Education and the Challenges of Sustainability: Problematics, Promise, and Practice*, edited by Peter B. Corcoran and Arjen E. J. Wals. Dordrecht: Kluwer. Pp. 73–86, 315–330.

Simon, Dagmar; and Knie, Andreas. 2013. "Can Evaluation Contribute to the Organizational Development of Academic Institutions? An International Comparison." *Evaluation* 19 (4):402–418.

Simon, Kathleen; and Haertle, Jonas. 2014. "Rio+20 Higher Education Sustainability Initiative (HESI) Commitments: A Review of Progress, October 2014." HESI. http://sustainabledevelopment.un.org/index.php?menu=1073

Stone, Diane. 2004. "Research Partnerships and Their Evaluation." In *Evaluation & Development: The Partnership Dimension*, edited by Andres Liebenthal, Osvaldo N. Feinstein, and Gregory K. Ingram. New Brunswick, NJ: Transaction Publishers. Pp. 149–160.

Talwar, Sonia; Wiek, Arnim; and Robinson, John. 2011. "User Engagement in Sustainability Research." *Science and Public Policy* 38 (5):379–390.

Togo, Muchaiteyi; and Lotz-Sisitka, Heila. 2013. "The Unit-Based Sustainability Assessment Tool and Its Use in the UNEP Mainstreaming Environment and Sustainability in African Universities Partnership." In *Sustainability Assessment Tools in Higher Education Institutions: Mapping Trends and Good Practices around the World*, edited by Sandra Caeiro, Walter L. Filho, Charbel Jabbour, and Ulisses M. Azeiteiro. Cham, Switzerland: Springer International Publishing. Pp. 259–288.

Uitto, Juha I. 2016. "Evaluating the Environment as a Global Public Good." *Evaluation* 22 (1):108–115.

Vesper, Inga. 2016. "SDGs Could Boost Citizen Science in Africa." *SciDevNet*. www.scidev.net/global/sdgs/news/sdgs-citizen-science-africa.html

Vettori, Oliver; and Rammel, Christian. 2014. "Linking Quality Assurance and ESD: Towards a Participative Quality Culture of Sustainable Development in Higher Education." In *Sustainable Development and Quality Assurance in Higher Education: Transformation of Learning and Society*, edited by Zinaida Fadeeva, Laima Galkute, Clemens Mader, and Geoff Scott. New York: Palgrave Macmillan. Pp. 49–65.

Vromen, Ariadne. 2010. "Debating Methods: Rediscovering Qualitative Approaches." In *Theory and Methods in Political Science*, edited by David Marsh and Gerry Stoker. Basingstoke, UK: Palgrave Macmillan. Pp. 249–266.

Waas, Tom; Huge, Jean; Verbruggen, Aviel; and Block, Thomas. 2015. "Navigating towards Sustainability: Essential Aspects of Assessment and Indicators." In *Sustainability: Key Issues*, edited by Helen Kopnina and Eleanor Shoreman-Ouimet. London: Routledge. Pp. 88–108.

Waas, Tom; Verbruggen, Aviel; and Wright, Tarah. 2010. "University Research for Sustainable Development: Definition and Characteristics Explored." *Journal of Cleaner Production* 18, No. 7 (May):629–636.

Wahr, Fiona; and Harpe, Barbara de la. 2016. "Changing from within: An Action Research Perspective for Bringing about Sustainability Curriculum Change in Higher Education." In *Routledge Handbook of Higher Education for Sustainable Development*, edited by Matthias Barth, Gerd Michelsen, Marco Rieckmann, and Ian Thomas. London: Routledge. Pp. 161–180.

White, Rehema M. 2013. "Sustainability Research: A Novel Mode of Knowledge Generation to Explore Alternative Ways for People and Planet." In *The Sustainable University: Progress and Prospects*, edited by Stephen Sterling, Larch Maxey, and Heather Luna. London: Routledge. Pp. 168–191.

Wiek, Arnim; Withycombe, Lauren; Redman, Charles L.; and Mills, Sarah B. 2011b. "Moving Forward on Competence in Sustainability Research and Problem Solving." *Environment Magazine* 53, No. 2 (March–April):3–12.

Zimmermann, Friedrich M.; Raggautz, Andreas; Maier, Kathrin; Drage, Thomas; Mader, Marlene; Diethart, Mario; and Meyer, Jonas. 2014. "Quality System Development at the University of Graz: Lessons Learned from the Case of RCE Graz-Styria." In *Sustainable Development and Quality Assurance in Higher Education: Transformation of Learning and Society*, edited by Zinaida Fadeeva, Laima Galkute, Clemens Mader, and Geoff Scott. New York: Palgrave Macmillan. Pp. 131–152.

8

OUTREACH EVALUATIONS THAT MATTER

Sustainable development is flat out not possible without placing governments, community organizations, and other stakeholders, including the private sector, at the forefront of the 2030 Agenda. Therefore, advancing sustainable development necessitates that universities engage with societal actors, typically on a specific project basis. The focus of this chapter is on such change-directed collaborative initiatives. Although university-initiated sustainable-development projects are informed (and on occasion inspired) by research and teaching, they occur beyond the campus confines of institutions of higher learning and often involve multiple non-academic collaborators.

Tomorrow's sustainable-development breakthroughs will require spanning boundaries of place, socio-cultural context, and institutional delimiters. Although progress is discernable, most of the world's sustainability-committed universities need to be more proactive in moving beyond the Ivory Tower (see Collins, 2014, p. 949). At the same time that the multitude of unaddressed sustainable-development challenges are growing in number and complexity (see Chapter 2), there is room for considerably expanded societal engagement among higher-education institutions in both North and South. In the coming decades, decisive university-stakeholder collaborations in bringing about transnational sustainable development (TSD) will be a prime indicator of success for institutions of higher learning around the world.

Most Southern universities are disposed to broaden and deepen their public engagement (Lobera, 2008, p. 312; Johnson and Hirt, 2011). Indeed, resource-constrained countries depend on higher-education institutions to act as leading "development universities." In the Global South, one commonly encounters expectations among leaders and populations that the core mission of higher education includes promoting national and subnational development and societal well-being (Meek, 2006, p. 217). Julius Nyerere of Tanzania forcefully captured the prevailing sentiment of Africa's post-independence political leaders regarding the imperative of establishing the "development university." In Nyerere's unsparing words, "we in poor societies can only justify expenditure on a university – of any type – if it promotes real development of our people" (cited in Singh, 2007, p. 69). At the same time, university leaders and policy makers in Northern countries are searching for and endeavoring to demonstrate viable approaches to sustainable development that involve adjustments in prevailing systems of production, distribution, consumption, and disposal.

External stakeholders as key sustainable-development participants

Higher education's sustainable-development mission cannot progress without "relevant interaction with and commitment to" the university's "surrounding environment" (Lobera, 2008, p. 326). The term "public engagement" (Kellogg and Hervy, 2009, p. 8) fruitfully captures the context of sustainable-development initiatives involving higher-education institutions and the academic community acting in concert with stakeholders in their surrounding environments. In the sustainable-development context, university outreach to the external community consists of at least four themes: capacity-building partnerships with stakeholders, participation in awareness raising (Simon and Haertle, 2014, p. 6) and policy making, delivery of local and regional services (Fischer, Jenssen, and Tappeser, 2015, p. 792), and active transnational collaboration on projects and other initiatives aimed at glocal impacts.

Relevant stakeholders and beneficiaries, including national and local governments, professional associations, transnational diasporic and other non-governmental organizations, indigenous NGOs, community associations and their members, farmers,[1] entrepreneurs, and private-enterprise employers and employees (Ashcroft and Raynor, 2011, p. 40; Goddard and Vallance, 2011, pp. 425–428, 432; Brinkerhoff, 2007, pp. 193, 200) contribute critical resources and indispensable insights to the TSD challenges that universities opt to confront. Rather than being ignored and undermined, government agencies, communities, project beneficiaries, and other entities with responsibilities that drive and constrain sustainable development need to be consulted and centrally involved in university-societal collaborations. Jill Chouinard and J. Bradley Cousins (2013, p. 74) view this responsibility as a condition arising from horizontal accountability to state institutions and downward accountability to local actors and beneficiaries. And national and international declarations, including the Halifax Declaration,[2] urge members of university communities to enhance collaborative interactions with external organizations concerned with sustainable development (Wright, 2002, p. 116).

For maximum effect, moreover, "sustainability education must be situated in both the university and community environments" (Sipos, Battisti, and Grimm, 2008, p. 70). Public engagement embraces outreach, extension, and connections with community issues and contexts and captures an interactive relationship whereby faculty members and students "learn from people with whom they interact in society as well as impart knowledge and advice" (Vessuri, 2008, p. 128).

In most cases, university-public engagement occurs through a specific and identifiable sustainable-development intervention where resources are applied to uniquely defined and tangible objectives. In particular, public engagement on the part of university faculty and students needs to be connected to national and community intentions for sustainable development, including contextually determined initiatives aimed at poverty reduction and natural-resource conservation. The "rich [US] land grant tradition of providing practical assistance to communities" and linking university-research findings to complex local-development needs offers valuable lessons in this connection (Stephenson, 2011).

Establishing grassroots networks opens up opportunities to link with community members and other stakeholders in identifying structural barriers and local drivers affecting sustainable development (Dutta, 2007, p. 322). According to Philip Morgan, "no matter where you are in the food chain – policies, programs, projects, some would say even smaller than projects (operations) – you really do need to be looking for allies," not just for resource purposes, but for the basic "legitimacy of being able to conduct the work."[3]

The potential sustainable-development contributions universities can make through collaborating with societal institutions are manifold. They include human-capability-building outcomes among both involved students and community participants as well as short-term and long-term socio-economic and environmental impacts. Therefore, evaluating contributions toward desired sustainable-development effects can be especially rewarding for projects that engage stakeholders (Hummel-brunner, 2012, p. 265).

Collaborating with societal institutions also introduces new opportunities for linking university resources and expertise with crucial community-development initiatives. Most of these opportunities will present themselves at local or regional sites. Eugene Trani and Robert Holsworth (2010, p. 232) see higher-education institutions playing ever more vital roles in their neighborhoods and surrounding regions. Through the University of British Columbia's strategic-sustainability alliances, for instance, "private, public, and NGO sector partners can work with UBC to test solutions at an urban neighborhood scale, and then take those ideas out to the world" (Cayuela, et al., 2013, p. 232). Faculty and student researchers at Pennsylvania State University pursued "highly interactive [and participatory] outreach activities" in six regional municipalities aimed at inventorying local GHG-emissions sources and facilitating various context-specific mitigation approaches (Hillmer-Pegram, et al., 2012).

Evaluating university-society collaborations

Evaluating the outcomes and impacts of diverse forms of cross-sector university-society collaboration in the interest of TSD is challenging and important (Batra, Uitto, and Cando-Noordhuizen, 2016, p. 21), but rarely reflective and typically underreported (Mader, 2014, p. 78). Key issues in evaluations of university-stakeholder partnerships include the levels of higher-education and stakeholder commitment, cumulative impact,[4] and the presence or absence of symmetry and transparency as supporting process features.

Symmetrical-university-stakeholder collaborations are grounded in mutual respect, trust, influence, and responsibility. They encompass jointly determined and conceptualized project objectives pursued "through a shared understanding of the most rational division of labor based on the respective comparative advantages of each partner" (Brinkerhoff, 2002, pp. 14–18; also Hamann and Boulogne, 2008, p. 54). Universities are advantaged in developing symmetrical collaborations with other societal actors because they are recognized as neutral brokers with community interests at the core of their sustainable-development mission (Collins, 2011, p. 158).

Symmetry generates synergies – that is, outcomes that would not be individually or separately obtainable. Synergies emerge when two or more actors with different, but complementary, objectives and capabilities interact fruitfully on a common undertaking and all stakeholders share in project benefits. Thus, projects that engage Southern universities in symmetrical-community-service collaborations (Subotzky, 1999, pp. 426–428) are of particular interest in terms of outcome and impact evaluations.

Sustainable university-public engagements also embrace transparency and shared accountability for results (UNCTAD, 2008, p. 96). Therefore, evaluators are interested in the nature of financial arrangements and relations. To "quell any doubts about the ways in which funds are being used," budgets and financial reports should be open and shared among all stakeholders (Wanni, Hinz, and Day, 2010, p. 36).

Limitations of current stakeholder evaluations

University-stakeholder evaluations manifest most of the limitations attributed to sustainable-development evaluations generally in the introduction and in Chapter 4. In particular, there has been little success in moving beyond phase-one (supply-driven) evaluations focused on outputs (Jost, et al., 2014).[5]

When not-for-profit development initiatives are reviewed, moreover, "there is little systematic evaluation of whether they follow a process that encourages local ownership, transparency, accountability, and sustainable outcomes" (Srivastava and Oh, 2010). For instance, "the mechanical use" by NGOs in Ethiopia of donor-required monitoring and evaluation systems limited "organizational learning to immediate project outputs (e.g. progress, results, efficiency, etc. as defined by the indicators) rather than extending it to issues of power and power relationships within the project community" (Mebrahtu, 2002, p. 510; also see Platteau, 2005, p. 293). Furthermore, stakeholder training and education largely have been overlooked in evaluation practice (Chouinard and Cousins, 2013, p. 68). Consequently, many NGO evaluations have failed to generate improvements in practices or policies (Mebrahtu, 2002, p. 515; King and McGrath, 2004, p. 151) that impact sustainable development.

Promising approaches to participatory evaluation

Participatory evaluation involves the stakeholders of a program or project in the evaluation. Stakeholder involvement can take place at all or any stages of the evaluation, from evaluation design, data collection and analysis, to reporting.[6] Stakeholder involvement in university-outreach evaluations often carries the benefit of enriched triangulated perspectives.[7] In particular, evaluators appreciate the value of participant observations and treat the process as a mutual-learning experience (Joel Samoff, cited in Crossley, et al., 2005, p. 106; Jones, Bailey, and Lyytikäinen, 2007, p. 10) that continuously taps stakeholder perspectives on local outcomes and impacts (Oakley, 1991, pp. 263–266).

Ethnographic inquiries uncover indigenous and marginalized voices, pathways to sustainable development and desired social and economic changes, political and institutional connections and incentives that shape prospects for change (Mosse, 2004, pp. 656, 664), and grassroots impacts, including stakeholder empowerment (Powell, Molander, and Celebicic, 2012, p. 219; Platteau, 2005, pp. 290, 292), that are not fully recognized or revealed by quantitative methods (Crossley, et al., 2005, p. 107; Boydell and Rugkasa, 2007, p. 219; Schuller and Desjardins, 2007, p. 23). However, taking into consideration the influence of macro-contextual forces as well as micro-contextual dimensions is crucial because this holistic perspective "highlights the myriad challenges involved in developing collaborative relationships, in what are often complex and demanding contexts" (Chouinard and Cousins, 2013, p. 69).

The sections that follow are intended as a guiding framework for evaluating university-stakeholder outreach evaluations. We treat process evaluations first. Outreach-outcome and impact evaluations are considered in the next section of this chapter.

Improving university-society collaborative TSD evaluations through mutually invested processes

Symmetrical-outreach evaluations balance internal and independent reviews with participation by stakeholders. Combining forces can improve the quality of the evaluation process (Klitgaard, 2004, p. 51). The symmetrical approach to sustainable-development evaluations is participatory and inclusive (Tikly, 2011, p. 10). Involvement by all stakeholders (Crossley and Bennett, 2004, p. 222) and the value of multiple perspectives are emphasized when exploring economic, social, and environmental outcomes and impacts (Thabrew, Wiek, and Ries, 2009, pp. 68–69, 74). In symmetrical-sustainable-development evaluations, the participants in the process own the inquiry (Patton, 2008, p. 185). To reduce the risk of overloading and demotivating stakeholders, however, boundary partners should not be expected to participate in the evaluation process to a degree that is out of proportion to their investment in the overall project or is beyond their capacity (Powell, Molander, and Celebicic, 2012, p. 223).

An early stakeholder audit, followed up by mapping, delineates the full range of a university's multiple stakeholders (Poister, Aristigueta, and Hall, 2015, pp. 357–358). Comprehensive stakeholder mapping generates the foundation for systematic evaluations of (1) role performance, (2) the quality of interactions, (3) satisfaction with outreach-services provided by the university, and (4) the scope of collaborative impacts (Poister, Aristigueta, and Hall, 2015, p. 359; Thabrew, Wiek, and Ries, 2009, p. 73). Once evaluators have identified stakeholders, the insight-generating questions drawn from literature review and presented in Box 8.1 facilitate evaluation of critical collaborative-process features.

BOX 8.1 EVALUATING UNIVERSITY-STAKEHOLDER COLLABORATION: MEANINGFUL PROCESS QUESTIONS

- To what extent did university outreach managers involve potential beneficiaries in planning and task identification (Stern, 2004, p. 31)?
- Has everyone who can influence the selected sustainable-development challenge participated (Catley-Carlson, 2004, p. 22)? Have indigenous and international environmental NGOs with ecological-preservation missions been incorporated?
- Were specific stakeholder roles and required resources delineated and integrated (Thabrew, Wiek, and Ries, 2009, p. 68)?
- Did collaborating university actors and key stakeholders conduct a needs assessment that included identifying community vulnerabilities and assets (Rowe and Hiser, 2016, p. 323) and linking stakeholder objectives with specific evaluation criteria (Ravetz, 2007, p. 86)?
- To what extent did aspects of sustainable development drive the university's selection of community-engagement projects (Togo, 2015, p. 49)?
- Were project objectives consistent with community- and national-development priorities (Tikly, 2011, p. 10)?
- Did sufficient exchange of key information and ideas related to sustainable development occur among all outreach-project initiators and beneficiaries?
- Did project participants select appropriate methods for pursuing sustainable-development goals?
- Were the timeframes adopted for sustainable-development-project inputs, outputs, outcomes, and impacts feasible and flexible?
- Did periodic multi-stakeholder meetings occur where participants clarified roles and contributions and agreed on project interventions and revisions (Deprez, 2012, p. 245; Thabrew, Wiek, and Ries, 2009, p. 68)?
- Has project implementation been characterized by deep trust among all participants and by effective conflict management (Stern, 2004, p. 32)?[8]

Were program budgets transparent and shared? To what extent were budgets equitably distributed according to agreed-upon responsibilities? Were they modified as necessary (Stern, 2004, p. 31)?

- To what extent did each stakeholder demonstrate commitment to the sustainable-development undertaking? To what extent does a sense of joint ownership among universities and stakeholders exist?
- Evaluators also look for evidence of increased faculty and staff contributions to TSD undertakings, deeper involvement in development-policy circles (Morfit and Gore, 2009, p. 16), and contributions to action based on adaptive learning (Eyben, 2013, p. 14). To what extent are faculty, staff, and additional departments engaged with community associations? Have university personnel participated in community-based economic-development activities and/or embarked on and maintained collaborative relationships with domestic enterprises (Morfit and Gore, 2009, p. 16)? To what extent did increases occur in faculty and staff contributions to community-development undertakings and involvement in advocating policies that will advance sustainable development? Did participating faculty receive satisfying workload recognition for their outreach involvements (Desha and Hargroves, 2014, p. 195)?
- To what extent have the university's project components, strategies, and symmetrical collaborative arrangements been refined and improved based upon feedback from stakeholders?
- Have modifications in outreach approaches reflected consensus changes in initially identified ecological preservation, equity, and population well-being priorities?
- Did project directors resist imposing burdensome administrative procedures so that all participants were able to focus on the principal objectives of the outreach project?

The involvement of a large number of stakeholders from the start in university sustainable-development projects enhances prospects for "wider external changes in a shorter time" (Lotz-Sisitka, Agbedahin, and Hlengwa, 2015, p. 25). In addition to the breadth of stakeholder participation, however, evaluators are interested in exploring the depth or extent of commitment and the enthusiasm of community members when participating in partnered sustainable-development projects (Smillie, 2009, p. 226). Box 8.2 presents an additional set of specific process-related evaluative questions focused on the *extent* of stakeholder involvement in project planning, implementation, and maintenance. The recommended participatory process closely integrates evaluation with planning, implementation, and maintenance (also see Kruse, 2005, p. 126).

For the purpose of higher-education sustainable-development evaluations, the focus of each process inquiry listed in Box 8.2 is on stakeholder collaboration with university actors. Parallel inside-out inquiries (adapted from Togo, 2015, p. 49;

BOX 8.2 STAKEHOLDER INVOLVEMENT PROCESS QUESTIONS: PLANNING, IMPLEMENTATION, AND MAINTENANCE

Project Process	Evaluative Questions*
Planning	*Extent of stakeholder participation in proposing original idea?*
	Extent of stakeholder participation in project planning?
	Extent of stakeholder commitment to project?
	Extent to which local knowledge and understandings have informed evaluation designs, questions, methods, and processes?[9]
Implementation	*Extent of stakeholder financial contribution?*
	Extent of stakeholder participation in project implementation?
	Extent of reliance on indigenous versus external knowledge?
	Extent to which stakeholder owned the project?
	Extent of symmetry in stakeholder participation?
	Extent to which stakeholders influenced project redesigns?
Maintenance	*Extent of stakeholder participation in project maintenance and support for recurrent costs?*[10]
	Extent of reliance on indigenous versus external knowledge in project maintenance?
	Extent of stakeholder control of project facilities?
	Extent of stakeholder ownership of project maintenance?
	Extent to which project contributed to stakeholder empowerment?

*One useful reporting scale would range from "extensive," "considerable," "little," to "none."

Source: adapted from Oakley (1991, pp. 253–254).

Togo and Lotz-Sisitka, 2013, pp. 278–279) probe the extent of co-involvement by university participants. To what extent have sustainable-development issues and challenges constituted part of each department's community-engagement portfolio? To what extent have department members participated in community engagement in sustainable-development activity? What level of departmental-resource commitment has been devoted to TSD-outreach initiatives? To what extent have department members collaborated internally across disciplinary lines and externally with stakeholders in addressing sustainable-development challenges?

Outreach constitutes an integral component of the Alternative University Appraisal system and arguably is its principal contribution to education-for-sustainable-development evaluation. Box 8.3 presents a slightly modified set of ProSPER.Net's suggested BIQs (benchmark indicator questions) for assessing public engagement through four outreach-process subcategories: teaching, research, service, and support. Were all stages of particular process subcategories open to stakeholder participation? Was stakeholder involvement active or passive? Was it initiated from the top-down or bottom-up (Salter, Robinson, and Wiek, 2010, p. 704)?

BOX 8.3 BENCHMARKING INDICATOR QUESTIONS: UNIVERSITY-OUTREACH PROCESSES

Subcategory	BIQs
Teaching	*Is SD (sustainable development) action learning[11] a central part of student graduation requirements?*
	Did participants organize and offer SD seminars, conferences, and workshops?
	Does the community-engagement project offer SD training and other informal learning opportunities for community members?
	Does the university produce and disseminate brochures, media programming, and other non-academic publications related to SD?
Research	*Do stakeholders offer SD-research-connected attachments?*
	Are project participants engaged in joint SD-research collaborations with off-campus stakeholders?
	Are SD-research findings and innovations shared with community, government, and private-sector stakeholders?
	Are SD-research findings and innovations disseminated through accessible non-academic outlets?
Service	*Is SD service learning assessed as a valuable contribution by stakeholders?*
	Does the university provide SD-technical assistance and/or consultancies to off-campus stakeholders?
	Does the university provide SD training to off-campus stakeholders?
Support	*Are well-designed and valued mechanisms in place for collaborating with off-campus stakeholders?*
	Are specific staff dedicated to work specifically on SD-outreach activities?
	Are university finances allocated for SD-outreach initiatives?
	Are SD-outreach activities conducted with joint funding or other contributions from stakeholders?

Source: adapted from ProSPER.Net (2012, pp. 14–15).

As an evaluation tool, social mapping can illuminate degrees of participation and symmetry, identify interactive capabilities (Kruss, et al., 2015, p. 30), uncover central nodes, and reveal changes over time in the extent of collaboration (Walsh and Kahn, 2010, p. 67). Did external stakeholders join in project-related sustainable-development research and university-outreach activities (Calder and Clugston, 2004, p. 257; Yarime and Tanaka, 2012, p. 74; King, 2009, p. 44)? In all stages of symmetrical assessments, evaluators should be asking how participants addressed status, power, and resource discrepancies.

Another important criterion involves the extent to which intra-university and external stakeholders remain supportive of the collaboration. Did review result in products that "include strategies, plans, or recommendations for action agreed upon by all relevant stakeholders" (Brundiers and Wiek, 2011, p. 113)? Are non-university players (NGOs, government, for-profit firms, community members) committed to maintaining key project activities (Morfit and Gore, 2009, p. 16)? Did TSD-outreach activities continue beyond the termination of external funding (Stockmann, 2012, p. 8)? Did participants engage in a series of sustainability evaluations of long-term and spillover effects at intervals following exit by the catalyzing-university influence (Platteau, 2005, pp. 280–281, 294)?

The participatory-evaluation approach is distinguished by emphasis on co-construction and joint implementation by externally designated evaluators and diverse stakeholders (Chouinard and Cousins, 2013, p. 67). Therefore, outreach assessments should include the monitoring-and-evaluation process itself. Box 8.4 provides suggestive evaluation questions for review of the collaborative dimensions of the jointly conducted evaluation process.

BOX 8.4 QUESTIONS FOR EVALUATING CONDUCT OF THE COLLABORATIVE OUTREACH-EVALUATION PROCESS

- Who selected the stakeholders who participated in evaluation exercise (Chouinard and Cousins, 2013, pp. 69, 73)?
- Was the sustainable-development-evaluation process understandable to all stakeholders (Shriberg, 2004, p. 74)?
- Did the university's project managers facilitate bottom-up participatory evaluation, where the community members involved in specific sustainable-development projects joined in and took charge of key aspects of evaluation efforts?
- Did evaluators create conditions for the evaluation process that enabled stakeholders to learn through participating and to engage effectively throughout the process (Chouinard and Cousins, 2013, pp. 68–69, 72)?
- Did evaluators conduct monitoring-and-evaluation exercises at regular intervals, engage in bottom-up participatory evaluation, and continuously tap stakeholder perspectives on project impact and local outcomes?

- Have outliers and disparate viewpoints been incorporated (Catley-Carlson, 2004, p. 23)?
- To what extent did participants collaborate in the co-construction of the evaluation narrative (Chouinard and Cousins, 2013, p. 71)?
- Did beneficiaries affirm, adjust, discontinue, and redefine objectives and actions based on lessons drawn from participatory evaluations (Platteau, 2005, pp. 277–278, 293)?

Evaluating outreach outcomes and impacts

Treatment of process is essential in sustainable-development evaluation, but outcomes and impacts plausibly attributable to university-community-linkage initiatives also merit serious attention. Phase-2 (regional-priority-driven) international-development participatory evaluations focus on outcomes as a dynamic platform for the next decade (Jost, et al., 2014). This approach revolves around a collaborative process of identifying mutually desired outcomes and assigning evaluative responsibilities among stakeholders. A key phase-2 dimension is inclusion of boundary partners as well as the most active project collaborators (Jost, et al., 2014; Powell, Molander, and Celebicic, 2012, pp. 228–229). These lessons lend themselves to adaptation in evaluations of higher-education's TSD-outreach engagements.

Outcome evaluations feature stakeholder capacity and capabilities. Cumulatively, the multi-source evidence collected and analyzed helps evaluators assess whether collaborating has contributed in new, deeper, and durable ways to enhancing the capacity of targeted populations and community associations to sustain livelihoods and natural resources.[12] Has the university provided sustainable-development technical and training support to public agencies, NGOs, community groups, and private firms (Morfit and Gore, 2009, p. 16)? Have university-community relationships resulted in improved stakeholder capabilities to exercise leadership in advancing sustainable development and in the adoption and management of useful innovations (Calleson, 2005, pp. 319–320; Yarime, et al., 2012, p. 108)? Has the potential for sustained innovation been enhanced (Stockmann, 2012, p. 9)?

What progress or setbacks have been encountered in the three foundational-outcome categories that are critical for sustainable-development advocacy: strengthened organizational capacity, base of support, and alliances (Sutherland and Klugman, 2013, pp. 60, 64)? To what extent have stakeholders increased their awareness of and technical learning about TSD conditions, concerns, and governance (Cashmore, 2007, pp. 110–111)? Have durable relationships been built on the basis of "friendship, trust, and mutual respect" (Holm and Malete, 2010, p. 11)?

Impact evaluations aim to "generate a clearer understanding of the influence of a development project . . . on people's lives" (Crossley, et al., 2005, p. 38) and on the environment. On most sustainable-development-outreach projects, social impacts – including the creation of employment opportunities (Tarabini, 2010, p. 209), the reduction of poverty and inequality (Singh, 2007, p. 76; Bailey, 2010, p. 44), and contributions to the strengthening of civil society (Schuller and Desjardins, 2007, pp. 68, 88; McMahon, 2009, p. 34) – must be addressed. Favorable impacts reflect community-identified and stakeholder-defined needs (Nordtveit, 2010, p. 112), are "appropriate to the local situation (for example, in terms of technology)," are sustainable over the foreseeable future, and avoid imposing new and onerous financial burdens or other negative side effects (Smith, 2000, p. 216). Evaluations often are best served by targeting specific aspects of a public-engagement project that are perceived to be successful and unsuccessful and, then, identifying why (Smith, 2000, p. 217).

Sustainable-development-outreach evaluations allow for serendipity of outcomes and impacts. Evaluators are cognizant of situations when "too close an identification with project terms of reference and Logical Frameworks" stifles opportunities to respond to unexpectedly promising collaborative directions and to reap unintended benefits (Crossley, et al., 2005, p. 106). In particular, evaluators have to be open to looking beyond the individual intervention, to see the program or project in its broader context, and to be alert to unexpected impacts and spin-offs, both positive and negative.

Prospects for sustainability are enhanced when public engagement by universities in North and South incorporates evolving national and subnational priorities. What evidence is there that policy makers have recognized the social and economic contributions and wellbeing benefits of specific sustainable-development approaches and practices as a result of university-outreach activities? How often are participating universities called upon by external agencies for sustainable-development consultancies, research services, and training programs?

The conversion of university-generated research findings into policy interventions that support community sustainable-development processes is a compelling indication of successful impact. Is there evidence of improvements in public service to local communities that can be attributed, at least in part, to a sponsored outreach project (Morfit and Gore, 2009, p. 16; Newcomer, El Baradei, and Garcia, 2013, p. 77)? Are any locally and regionally adopted knowledge-based products that resulted from participatory research sustainable (Wiek, et al., 2013, p. 6)? Are university researchers participating in external-advisory bodies that shape sustainable-development-policy decisions?

Human and ecosystem wellbeing

Rather than concentrate on what is easily measurable, values-based-outreach evaluations emphasize achievements that matter most to beneficiaries (see Hoover, 2015). Amartya Sen (e.g., 1999) has long argued for broad definitions of development and wellbeing that include not simply access to resources and income. For Sen, life improvements are about expanding a person's functionings and capabilities – things they are able to "do" and "be" – and their set of available options. While commodities purchased with income certainly are important, these commodities are desired for their ability to add to a person's wellbeing. Many other factors, which are less related to income, also are important. For Peter Hardi (2007, p. 20), nature and biodiversity offer "the ultimate means necessary" to enjoy "happiness, respect and spiritual fulfillment." Sen (1999, p. 20) maintains that "precisely because income deprivations and capability deprivations often have considerable correlational linkages, it is important to avoid being mesmerized into thinking that taking note of the former would somehow tell us enough about the latter." In short, the capability to gain meaning and purpose in life and to function effectively in sustainable-development roles is independent of income level.

Martha Nussbaum (2000) posits a "universalist" list of capabilities with a threshold below which life would be too impoverished to be considered human. Her list includes respect and concern for other species, living to the end of a normal life, and being able to use one's senses. Adding subjective wellbeing to other measures of sustainable development (e.g., income levels and policy context) allows university-outreach evaluations to incorporate individual- and household-based assessments of the state and process of sustainable development.[13] Using responses to questions about personal and collective happiness, life satisfaction, care for nature and the physical environment, and subjective wellbeing (see Dahl, 2015, pp. 90–92)[14] allows researchers to gain insight into the types of goods, services, infrastructure, natural resources, education, and social networks that make people and the environment better off. In addition, meaningful values-driven collaborative-TSD evaluations address the extent to which participants demonstrated commitment to social justice and advocacy for those most in need. To what extent did university-outreach activities advance community empowerment in ways that promote environmental justice (Fredericks, 2014, pp. 178, 187)?

Useful outreach outcome- and impact-evaluation methods

Private-sector, government, and civil-society stakeholders are an integral part of societal-impact and outcome-centered-evaluation processes (Fadeeva and Mochizuki, 2010, pp. 254–255). Sustainable-development outcomes and impacts are evaluated periodically over the long-term from multiple perspectives by socio-culturally diverse observers, collaborators, and community members.

Moving beyond income and monetary measures requires both additional data and a more nuanced understanding of the components of wellbeing and the ways in which they are combined. For instance, it makes more sense from a wellbeing perspective to look at health outcomes (the ability to be healthy) instead of output spending on health care. The information required for an exploration of functionings, capabilities, and wellbeing certainly is more substantial than materialist measures that focus on income or expenditure (see Bookwalter and Koehn, 2014).

Participatory sustainable-livelihoods-systems appraisal (PSLSA) can be helpful in evaluating the impact of university-outreach interventions on population wellbeing and social justice. According to Martin Strele, a livelihood is a composite of assets (material and social resources) and personal capabilities. A sustainable livelihood "can be defined as one that can cope with and recover from stresses and shocks and maintain or enhance its capabilities and assets both now and in the future, while not undermining the natural resource base" (Strele, 2012, p. 177; also Platteau, 2005, p. 279). PSLSA, conducted by results-oriented facilitators working with heterogeneous local representatives and focus groups, includes identification of crucial livelihood factors, asset and trend analysis, attention to the ways in which different priority factors are interlinked (see Strele, 2012, pp. 178–188),[15] understanding links between policy decisions and household activities, and consideration of future generations' resource needs (Gapor, et al., 2014, pp. 262–263). PSLSA offers a valuable tool for identifying livelihood factors of relative high systemic influence and promising leverage points (Strele, 2012, pp. 187–188).

The Barometer of Sustainability offers a useful complementary tool for evaluating wellbeing. The Barometer of Sustainability measures "human and eco-system wellbeing together without submerging one in the other" in a way that further allows "analysis of people-ecosystem interactions." Levels of performance are identified for five human-wellness and five ecosystem-wellness criteria, with scores displayed on two axes (Hales and Prescott-Allen, 2002, pp. 43–45).

Approaches used in assessing action-research interventions (Wahr and de la Harpe, 2016, p. 163) also can be useful in evaluating the impact of university sustainable-development-outreach activity. Did the outreach initiative enhance sustainable-development practices at one or more of the following levels of activity: improved individual-practitioner decision making when confronted by practical and contextual challenges of sustainable development; improved group-level collaboration on a shared sustainable-development challenge; improved community-level response to a specific small-scale economic, social, or ecological challenge; or improved national and/or transnational response to a sustainable-development challenge with cross-boundary effects?

Mapping enables evaluators to view the blended evidence from various data-gathering techniques and to compare place-specific sustainable-development findings across locations (Fredericks, 2014, pp. 193, 186–188). In-depth case studies that analyze fruitful collaborative-project practices can contribute in valuable ways to illuminating impact pathways to sustainable development.

Finally, university actors and stakeholders treat the evaluation process as a mutual-learning experience. Project leaders should have communicated meaningful results convincingly to stakeholders, policy makers, and lay publics. Improvements are expected to be introduced iteratively based on evaluation results that span "a realistic time period – seldom less than 10–15 years" (Walt, Spicer, and Buse, 2009, p. 67). Although specific forms of community engagement and action will differ in line with unique local contexts (Fadeeva and Mochizuki, 2010, p. 253), participatory evaluations generally promote community empowerment, directly address relevant challenges, identify pathways to mobilizing local assets, illuminate contextually appropriate development approaches, and facilitate coordinated action and continuous improvement (Crossley, et al., 2005, pp. 39–40;

Boydell and Rugkasa 2007, p. 223). Peter Oakley (1991, p. 263) concludes that "when the local people are involved in discussion, debate, analysis and interpretation of project activities, they come to share a common perspective and a shared commitment to action."

To what extent were major shortcomings identified and reported by evaluators rectified by participants? Have stakeholders permanently adopted sustainable-development innovations (Stockmann, 2012, p. 8)? Is there evidence that community-based ownership has increased the likelihood of stakeholder self-generated sustainable-development narratives, initiatives, and replications (Miyaguchi and Uitto, 2015, p. 14)? Have benefits (intended and unintended, tangible and intangible, wanted and unwanted) outweighed the costs and difficulties of interacting and coordinating for all project participants?

Notes

1 Hailemichael (2013, p. 43) notes that the new agricultural-extension principles have shifted from treating farmers as beneficiaries to involving them as stakeholders.
2 See www.iau-hesd.net/sites/default/files/documents/rfl_727_halifax_2001.pdf
3 Telephonic interview with Philip Morgan conducted by Peter Koehn, 10 December 2007.
4 Establishing "uncontaminated" control groups for the evaluation of outreach-intervention impacts is both operationally and ethically challenging (Hailemichael, 2013, p. 41).
5 For instance, whether outputs have been consistent with plans and targets (Stern, 2004, p. 38).
6 Better Evaluation (http://betterevaluation.org/plan/approach/participatory_evaluation).
7 A detailed discussion of the mixed-method and triangulated-research approach utilized by the RECOUP project is found in Jeffery (2012).
8 Major perceptual differences on levels of trust among stakeholders suggest problems associated with asymmetrical management.
9 See Chouinard and Cousins (2013, pp. 67–69); Kruse (2005, p. 111).
10 Also see Platteau (2005, pp. 285, 289, 292).
11 See Roorda (2013, p. 105).
12 Newcomer, El Baradei, and Garcia (2013, p. 77) recommend that stakeholder contributions to outcome evaluations feature quantitative data supplemented by "qualitative assessments of outcomes, such as success stories and critical incidents."
13 Data from the 2009 Ethiopian Household Resources Survey illustrate the potential of this approach (see Bookwalter and Koehn, 2014).
14 An increasing body of evidence indicates that aspects of subjective wellbeing can be measured in valid and reliable surveys (see OECD, 2013, p. 10).
15 For simple matrix scoring, villagers or other stakeholders can rate the degree of influence of particular activities by placing stones, beans, or other available and accustomed indicators in boxes or holes (Strele, 2012, pp. 180, 182, 184).

Works cited

Ashcroft, Kate; and Raynor, Philip. 2011. *Higher Education in Development: Lessons from Sub-Saharan Africa.* Charlotte, NC: Information Age Publishing.
Bailey, Tracy. 2010. "The Research-Policy Nexus: Mapping the Terrain of the Literature." Paper prepared for the Higher Education Research and Advocacy Network in Africa (HERANA). Center for Higher Education Transformation, Wynberg, UK.

Batra, Geeta; Uitto, Juha I.; and Cando-Noordhuizen, Lee. 2016. "From MDGs to SDGs: Evaluating Global Environmental Benefits." *Evaluation Matters* 1:16–23.

Bookwalter, Jeffrey; and Koehn, Peter. 2014. "Post-Dependent Rural Development: Engaging and Assessing Subjective Wellbeing." In *Reflections on Development in Ethiopia: New Trends, Sustainability and Challenges,* edited by Dessalegn Rahmato, Meheret Ayenew, Asnake Kefale, and Birgit Habermann. Addis Ababa: Forum for Social Sciences, Addis Ababa University. Pp. 199–218.

Boydell, Leslie R.; and Rugkasa, Jorun. 2007. "Benefits of Working in Partnership: A Model." *Critical Public Health* 17 (3):217–228.

Brinkerhoff, Jennifer M. 2002. *Partnerships for International Development: Rhetoric or Results?* Boulder, CO: Lynne Reinner.

Brinkerhoff, Jennifer M. 2007. "Contributions of Digital Diasporas to Governance Reconstruction in Fragile States: Potential and Promise." In *Governance in Post-Conflict Societies: Rebuilding Fragile States,* edited by Derick W. Brickerhoff. London: Routledge. Pp. 185–203.

Brundiers, Katja; and Wiek, Arnim. 2011. "Educating Students in Real-World Sustainability Research: Vision and Implementation." *Innovative Higher Education* 36:107–124.

Calder, Wynn; and Clugston, Rick. 2004. "Lighting Many Fires: South Carolina's Sustainable Universities Initiative." In *Higher Education and the Challenge of Sustainability: Problematics, Promise, and Practice,* edited by Peter B. Corcoran and Arjen E. J. Wals. Dordrecht: Kluwer Academic Publishers. Pp. 249–262.

Calleson, Diane C. 2005. "Community-Engaged Scholarship." *Academic Medicine* 80 (April): 317–321.

Cashmore, Matthew. 2007. "The Contribution of Environmental Assessment to Sustainable Development: Toward a Richer Conceptual Understanding." In *Impact Assessment and Sustainable Development: European Practice and Experience,* edited by Clive George and Colin Kirkpatrick. Cheltenham, UK: Edward Elgar. Pp. 106–126.

Catley-Carlson, Margaret. 2004. "Foundations of Partnerships: A Practitioner's Perspective." In *Evaluation & Development: The Partnership Dimension,* edited by Andres Liebenthal, Osvaldo N. Feinstein, and Gregory K. Ingram. New Brunswick, NJ: Transaction Publishers. Pp. 21–27.

Cayuela, Alberto; Robinson, John B.; Campbell, Ann; Coops, Nicholas; and Munro, Alison. 2013. "Integration of Operational and Academic Efforts in Sustainability at the University of British Columbia." In *Sustainability Assessment Tools in Higher Education Institutions: Mapping Trends and Good Practices around the World,* edited by Sandra Caeiro, Walter L. Filho, Charbel Jabbour, and Ulisses M. Azeiteiro. Cham, Switzerland: Springer International Publishing. Pp. 223–236.

Chouinard, Jill A.; and Cousins, J. Bradley. 2013. "Participatory Evaluation for Development: Examining Research-Based Knowledge from within the African Context." *African Evaluation Journal* 1 (1):66–74.

Collins, Christopher S. 2011. *Higher Education and Global Poverty: University Partnerships and the World Bank in Developing Countries.* Amherst, NY: Cambria Press.

Collins, Christopher S. 2014. "Can Funding for University Partnerships between Africa and the US Contribute to Social Development and Poverty Reduction?" *Higher Education* 68:943–958.

Crossley, Michael; and Bennett, J. Alexander. 2004. "Planning for Case Study Evaluation in Belize, Central America." In *Qualitative Educational Research in Developing Countries: Current Perspectives,* edited by Michael Crossley and Graham Vulliamy. New York: Garland Publishing. Pp. 221–243.

Crossley, Michael; Herriot, Andrew; Waudo, Judith; Mwirotsi, Miriam; Holmes, Keith; and Juma, Magdallen. 2005. *Research and Evaluation for Educational Development: Learning from the PRISM Experience in Kenya.* Oxford, UK: Symposium Books.

Dahl, Arthur L. 2015. "Putting the Individual at the Center of Development: Indicators of Well-Being for a New Social Contract." In *Transitions to Sustainability*, edited by Francois Mancebo and Ignacy Sachs. New York: Springer. Pp. 83–103.

Deprez, Steff. 2012. "Development of a Learning-Oriented Monitoring System for Sustainable Agriculture Chain Development in Eastern Indonesia." In *Governance by Evaluation for Sustainable Development: Institutional Capacities and Learning*, edited by Michal Sedlacko and Andre Martinuzzi. Cheltenham, UK: Edward Elgar. Pp. 233–252.

Desha, Cheryl; and Hargroves, Karlson C. 2014. *Higher Education and Sustainable Development: A Model for Curriculum Renewal*. London: Routledge.

Dutta, Mohan J. 2007. "Communicating about Culture and Health: Theorizing Culture-Centered and Cultural Sensitivity Approaches." *Communication Theory* 17 (3):304–328.

Eyben, Rosalind. 2013. "Uncovering the Politics of 'Evidence' and 'Results': A Framing Paper for Development Practitioners." www.bigpushforward.net

Fadeeva, Zinaida; and Mochizuki, Yoko. 2010. "Higher Education for Today and Tomorrow: University Appraisal for Diversity, Innovation and Change towards Sustainable Development." *Sustainability Science* 5:249–256.

Fischer, Daniel; Jenssen, Silke; and Tappeser, Valentin. 2015. "Getting an Empirical Hold of the *Sustainable University*: A Comparative Analysis of Evaluation Frameworks across 12 Contemporary Sustainability Assessment Tools." *Assessment & Evaluation in Higher Education* 40 (6):785–800.

Fredericks, Sarah. 2014. *Measuring and Evaluating Sustainability: Ethics in Sustainability Indexes*. London: Routledge.

Gapor, Salfarina A.; Aziz, Abd M. A.; Razak, Dzulkifli A.; and Sanusi, Zainal A. 2014. "Implementing Education for Sustainable Development in Higher Education: Case Study of Albukhary International University, Malaysia." In *Sustainable Development and Quality Assurance in Higher Education: Transformation of Learning and Society*, edited by Zinaida Fadeeva, Laima Galkute, Clemens Mader, and Geoff Scott. New York: Palgrave Macmillan. Pp. 255–281.

Goddard, John; and Vallance, Paul. 2011. "Universities and Regional Development." In *Handbook of Local and Regional Development*, edited by Andy Pike, Andres Rodriguez-Pose, and John Tomaney. London: Routledge. Pp. 425–437.

Hailemichael Taye. 2013. "Evaluating the Impact of Agricultural Extension Programmes in Sub-Saharan Africa: Challenges and Prospects." *African Evaluation Journal* 1 (1):38–45.

Hales, David; and Prescott-Allen, Robert. 2002. "Flying Blind: Assessing Progress toward Sustainability." In *Global Environmental Governance: Options & Opportunities*, edited by Daniel C. Esty and Maria H. Ivanova. New Haven, CT: Yale School of Forestry & Environmental Studies. Pp. 31–52.

Hamann, Ralph, and Boulogne, Fleur. 2008. "Partnerships and Cross-Sector Collaboration." In *The Business of Sustainable Development in Africa: Human Rights, Partnerships, Alternative Business Models*, edited by Ralph Hamann, Stu Woolman, and Courtenay Sprague. Pretoria: Unisa Press. Pp. 54–82.

Hardi, Peter. 2007. "The Long and Winding Road of Sustainable Development Evaluation." In *Impact Assessment and Sustainable Development: European Practice and Experience*, edited by Clive George and Colin Kirkpatrick. Cheltenham, UK: Edward Elgar. Pp. 15–30.

Hillmer-Pegram, Kevin C.; Howe, Peter D.; Greenberg, Howard; and Yarnal, Brent. 2012. "A Geographic Approach to Facilitating Local Climate Governance: From Emissions Inventories to Mitigation Planning." *Applied Geography* 34:76–85.

Holm, John D.; and Malete, Leapetsewe. 2010. "The Asymmetries of University Partnerships between Africa and the Developed World: Our Experience in Botswana." Paper delivered at the 2010 Going Global 4 – The British Council's International Education Conference, London, 24–26 March.

Hoover, Elona. 2015. "Starting from Values: Evaluating Intangible Legacies of Community-University Research Projects." www.esdinds.eu

Hummelbrunner, Richard. 2012. "Process Monitoring of Impacts and Its Application in Structural Fund Programmes." In *Governance by Evaluation for Sustainable Development: Institutional Capacities and Learning*, edited by Michal Sedlacko and Andre Martinuzzi. Cheltenham, UK: Edward Elgar. Pp. 253–266.

Jeffery, Roger. 2012. "Qualitative Methods in the RECOUP Projects." In *Education Outcomes and Poverty: A Reassessment*, edited by Christopher Colclough. London: Routledge. Pp. 170–189.

Johnson, Ane T.; and Hirt, Joan B. 2011. "Reshaping Academic Capitalism to Meet Development Priorities: The Case of Public Universities in Kenya." *Higher Education* 61 (4):483–499.

Jones, Nicola; Bailey, Mark; and Lyytikäinen, Minna. 2007. *Research Capacity Strengthening in Africa: Trends, Gaps and Opportunities*. London: Overseas Development Institute.

Jost, Christine; Alvarez, Sophie; Martinez Baron, Deissy; Bonilla-Findji, Osana; Coffey, Kevin; Förch, Wiebke; Khatri-Chhetri, Arun; Moussa, Abdoulaye S.; Radeny, Maren; Richards, Meryl; Schuetz, Tonya; and Vasileiou, Ioannis. 2014. "Pathway to Impact: Supporting and Evaluating Enabling Environments for Outcomes in CCAFS." Paper presented at the 2nd International Conference on Evaluating Climate Change and Development, GEF Independent Evaluation Office, Washington, DC, 4–6 November.

Kellogg, Earl D.; and Hervy, Anne-Claire. 2009. "Contributions of Higher Education Investments to Development and Implications for African Higher Education." Paper presented at the Conference on Reshaping Human and Institutional Capacity Building through Higher Education Partnerships, Accra, Ghana, 26 August.

King, Kenneth. 2009. "Higher Education and International Cooperation: The Role of Academic Collaboration in the Developing World." In *Higher Education and International Capacity Building: Twenty-Five Years of Higher Education Links*, edited by David Stephens. Oxford, UK: Symposium Books. Pp. 33–49.

King, Kenneth; and McGrath, Simon. 2004. *Knowledge for Development? Comparing British, Japanese, Swedish, and World Bank Aid*. London: Zed Books.

Klitgaard, Robert. 2004. "Evaluation of, for, and through Partnerships." In *Evaluation & Development: The Partnership Dimension*, edited by Andres Liebenthal, Osvaldo N. Feinstein, and Gregory K. Ingram. New Brunswick, NJ: Transaction Publishers. Pp. 43–57.

Kruse, Stein-Erik. 2005. "Meta-evaluations of NGO Experience: Results and Challenges." In *Evaluating Development Effectiveness*, edited by George K. Pitman, Osvaldo N. Feinstein, and Gregory K. Ingram. World Bank Series on Evaluation and Development, Volume 7. New Brunswick, N.J.: Transaction Publishers. Pp. 109–127.

Kruss, Glanda; McGrath, Simon; Petersen, Il-haam; and Gastrow, Michael. 2015. "Higher Education and Economic Development: The Importance of Building Technological Capabilities." *International Journal of Educational Development* 43:22–31.

Lobera, Josep. 2008. "Delphi Poll – Higher Education for Human and Social Development." In *Higher Education in the World 3: New Challenges and Emerging Roles for Human and Social Development*. London: Palgrave Macmillan. Pp. 307–327.

Lotz-Sisitka, Heila; Agbedahin, Adesuwa V.; and Hlengwa, Amanda. 2015. "Seeding Change: Developing a Change-Oriented Model for Professional Learning and ESD in Higher Education Institutions in Africa." In *Mainstreaming Environment and Sustainability in African Universities: Stories of Change*, edited by Heila Lotz-Sisitka, Gitile Naituli, Amanda Hlengwa, Mike Ward, Ayobami Salami, Akpezi Ogbuigwe, Mahesh Pradhan,

Marie Neeser, and Sanne Lauriks. Grahamstown: Rhodes University Environmental Learning Research Centre. Pp. 16–33.

Mader, Clemens. 2014. "The Role of Assessment and Quality Management in Transformations towards Sustainable Development: The Nexus between Higher Education, Society and Policy." In *Sustainable Development and Quality Assurance in Higher Education: Transformation of Learning and Society*, edited by Zinaida Fadeeva, Laima Galkute, Clemens Mader, and Geoff Scott. New York: Palgrave Macmillan. Pp. 66–83.

McMahon, Walter W. 2009. *Higher Learning, Greater Good: The Private and Social Benefits of Higher Education*. Baltimore: Johns Hopkins University Press.

Mebrahtu, Esther. 2002. "Perceptions and Practices of Monitoring and Evaluation: International NGO Experiences in Ethiopia." *Development in Practice* 12 (August):501–517.

Meek, V. Lynn. 2006. "Research Management in the Postindustrial Era: Trends and Issues for Further Investigation." In *Higher Education, Research, and Knowledge in the Asia-Pacific Region*, edited by V. Lynn Meek and Charas Suwanwela. Gordonsville, VA: Palgrave Macmillan. Pp. 213–234.

Miyaguchi, Takaaki; and Uitto, Juha I. 2015. *A Realist Review of Climate Change Adaptation Programme Evaluations – Methodological Implications and Programmatic Findings*. Occasional Paper Series. New York: United Nations Development Programme, Independent Evaluation Office.

Morfit, Christine; and Gore, Jane. 2009. *HED/USAID Higher Education Partnerships in Africa 1997–2007*. Washington, DC: Higher Education for Development.

Mosse, David. 2004. "Is Good Policy Unimplementable? Reflections on the Ethnography of Aid Policy and Practice." *Development and Change* 35 (4):639–671.

Newcomer, Kathryn; El Baradei, Laila; and Garcia, Sandra. 2013. "Expectations and Capacity of Performance Measurement in NGOs in the Development Context." *Public Administration and Development* 33:62–79.

Nordtveit, Bjorn. 2010. "Development as a Complex Process of Change: Conception and Analysis of Projects, Programs and Policies." *International Journal of Education and Development* 30:110–117.

Nussbaum, Martha C. 2000. *Women and Human Development: The Capabilities Approach*. Cambridge: Cambridge University Press.

Oakley, Peter. 1991. *Projects with People: The Practice of Participation in Rural Development*. Geneva: International Labor Office.

Organization for Economic Cooperation and Development (OECD). 2013. *OECD Guidelines on Measuring Subjective Well-Being*. Paris: OECD Publishing.

Patton, Michael Q. 2008. *Utilization-Focused Evaluation*, 4th edition. Los Angeles, CA: Sage.

Platteau, Jean-Philippe. 2005. "Institutional and Distributional Aspects of Sustainability in Community-Driven Development." In *Evaluating Development Effectiveness*, edited by George K. Pitman, Osvaldo N. Feinstein, and Gregory K. Ingram. World Bank Series on Evaluation and Development, Volume 7. New Brunswick, NJ: Transaction Publishers. Pp. 275–297.

Poister, Theodore H.; Aristigueta, Maria P.; and Hall, Jeremy L. 2015. *Managing and Measuring Performance in Public and Nonprofit Organizations: An Integrated Approach*, 2nd edition. San Francisco, CA: Jossey-Bass.

Powell, Steve; Molander, Joakim; and Celebicic, Ivona. 2012. "Assessment of Outcome Mapping as a Tool for Evaluating and Monitoring Support to Civil Society Organisations." In *Governance by Evaluation for Sustainable Development: Institutional Capacities and Learning*, edited by Michal Sedlacko and Andre Martinuzzi. Cheltenham, UK: Edward Elgar. Pp. 215–232.

ProSPER.Net (Promotion of Sustainability in Postgraduate Education and Research Network). 2012. *Alternative University Appraisal Model for ESD in Higher Education Institutions*, Version 1.2. Hokkaido: AUA Secretariat, Hokkaido University.

Ravetz, Joe. 2007. "The Role of Evaluation in Regional Sustainable Development." In *Impact Assessment and Sustainable Development: European Practice and Experience*, edited by Clive George and Colin Kirkpatrick. Cheltenham, UK: Edward Elgar. Pp. 65–89.

Roorda, Niko. 2013. "A Strategy and a Toolkit to Realize System Integration of Sustainable Development (SISD)." In *Sustainability Assessment Tools in Higher Education Institutions: Mapping Trends and Good Practices around the World*, edited by Sandra Caeiro, Walter L. Filho, Charbel Jabbour, and Ulisses M. Azeiteiro. Cham, Switzerland: Springer International Publishing. Pp. 101–119.

Rowe, Debra; and Hiser, Krista. 2016. "Higher Education for Sustainable Development in the Community and through Partnerships." In *Routledge Handbook of Higher Education for Sustainable Development*, edited by Matthias Barth, Gerd Michelsen, Marco Rieckmann, and Ian Thomas. London: Routledge. Pp. 315–330.

Salter, Jonathan; Robinson, John; and Wiek, Arnim. 2010. "Participatory Methods of Integrated Assessment: A Review." *WIRES: Climate Change* 1:697–717.

Schuller, Tom; and Desjardins, Richard. 2007. *Understanding the Social Outcomes of Learning*. Paris: Organization for Economic Co-Operation and Development (OECD).

Sen, Amartya. 1999. *Development as Freedom*. New York: Anchor Books.

Shriberg, Michael. 2004. "Assessing Sustainability: Criteria, Tools, and Implications." In *Higher Education and the Challenges of Sustainability: Problematics, Promise, and Practice*, edited by Peter B. Corcoran and Arjen E. J. Wals. Dordrecht: Kluwer. Pp. 73–86.

Simon, Kathleen; and Haertle, Jonas. 2014. "Rio+20 Higher Education Sustainability Initiative (HESI) Commitments: A Review of Progress, October 2014." HESI. http://sustainabledevelopment.un.org/index.php?menu=1073

Singh, Mala. 2007. "Universities and Society: Whose Terms of Engagement?" In *Knowledge Society vs. Knowledge Economy: Knowledge, Power, and Politics*, edited by Sverker Sörlin and Hebe Vessuri. Hampshire: Palgrave Macmillan. Pp. 53–78.

Sipos, Yona; Battisti, Bryce; and Grimm, Kurt. 2008. "Achieving Transformative Sustainability Learning: Engaging Head, Hands, and Heart." *International Journal of Sustainability in Higher Education* 9 (1):68–86.

Smillie, Ian. 2009. "Backwards and in High Heels: NGO Leadership in Asia." In *Leadership for Development: What Globalization Demands of Leaders Fighting for Change*, edited by Dennis A. Rondinelli and John M. Heffron. Boulder, CO: Kumarian Press. Pp. 205–233.

Smith, Harvey. 2000. "Transforming Education through Donor-Funded Projects: How Do We Measure Success?" In *Globalisation, Educational Transformation and Societies in Transition*, edited by Teame Mebrahtu, Michael Crossley, and David Johnson. Oxford: Symposium Books. Pp. 207–218.

Srivastava, Prachi; and Oh, Su-Ann. 2010. "Private Foundations, Philanthropy, and Partnership in Education and Development: Mapping the Terrain." *International Journal of Educational Development* 30 (5):460–471.

Stephenson, Max Jr. 2011. "Conceiving Land Grant University Community Engagement as Adaptive Leadership." *Higher Education* 61 (1):95–108.

Stern, Elliot. 2004. "Evaluating Partnerships." In *Evaluation & Development: The Partnership Dimension*, edited by Andres Liebenthal, Osvaldo N. Feinstein, and Gregory K. Ingram. New Brunswick, NJ: Transaction Publishers. Pp. 29–41.

Stockmann, Reinhard. 2012. "Understanding Sustainability Evaluation and Its Contributions to Policy – Making." In *Sustainable Development, Evaluation and Policy-Making:*

Theory, Practise and Quality Assurance, edited by Anneke von Raggamby and Frieder Rubik. Cheltenham, UK: Edward Elgar. Pp. 3–20.

Strele, Martin. 2012. "Participatory Livelihoods System Appraisal: A Learning-Oriented Methodology for Impact Assessment." In *Governance by Evaluation for Sustainable Development: Institutional Capacities and Learning*, edited by Michal Sedlacko and Andre Martinuzzi. Cheltenham, UK: Edward Elgar. Pp. 173–190.

Subotzky, George. 1999. "Alternatives to the Entrepreneurial University: New Modes of Knowledge Production in Community Service Programs." *Higher Education* 38 (4):401–440.

Sutherland, Carla; and Klugman, Barbara. 2013. "Finding Common Ground: A Participatory Approach to Evaluation." *African Evaluation Journal* 1 (1):56–65.

Tarabini, Aina. 2010. "Education and Poverty in the Global Development Agenda: Emergence, Evolution and Consolidation." *International Journal of Education and Development* 30 (2):204–212.

Thabrew, Lanka; Wiek, Arnim; and Ries, Robert. 2009. "Environmental Decision Making in Multi-Stakeholder Contexts: Applicability of Life Cycle Thinking in Development Planning and Implementation." *Journal of Cleaner Production* 17:67–76.

Tikly, Leon. 2011. "Towards a Framework for Researching the Quality of Education in Low-Income Countries." *Comparative Education* 47, No. 1 (February):1–23.

Togo, Muchaiteyi. 2015. "Development, Use and Significance of the Unit-Based Sustainability Assessment Tool for Universities in Africa and Asia." In *Mainstreaming Environment and Sustainability in African Universities: Stories of Change*, edited by Heila Lotz-Sisitka, Gitile Naituli, Amanda Hlengwa, Mike Ward, Ayobami Salami, Akpezi Ogbuigwe, Mahesh Pradhan, Marie Neeser, and Sanne Lauriks. Grahamstown: Rhodes University Environmental Learning Research Centre. Pp. 34–64.

Togo, Muchaiteyi; and Lotz-Sisitka, Heila. 2013. "The Unit-Based Sustainability Assessment Tool and Its Use in the UNEP Mainstreaming Environment and Sustainability in African Universities Partnership." In *Sustainability Assessment Tools in Higher Education Institutions: Mapping Trends and Good Practices around the World*, edited by Sandra Caeiro, Walter L. Filho, Charbel Jabbour, and Ulisses M. Azeiteiro. Cham, Switzerland: Springer International Publishing. Pp. 259–288.

Trani, Eugene P.; and Holsworth, Robert D. 2010. *The Indispensible University: Higher Education, Economic Development, and the Knowledge Economy*. Lanham, MD: Rowman & Littlefield.

United Nations Conference on Trade and Development (UNCTAD). 2008. *The Least Developed Countries Report 2008: Growth, Poverty and the Terms of Development Partnership*. New York: United Nations.

Vessuri, Hebe. 2008. "The Role of Research in Higher Education: Implications and Challenges for an Active Contribution to Human and Social Development." In *Higher Education in the World 3: New Challenges and Emerging Roles for Human and Social Development*. GUNI Series on the Social Commitment of Universities 3. London: Palgrave Macmillan. Pp. 119–129.

Wahr, Fiona; and Harpe, Barbara de la. 2016. "Changing from Within: An Action Research Perspective for Bringing about Sustainability Curriculum Change in Higher Education." In *Routledge Handbook of Higher Education for Sustainable Development*, edited by Matthias Barth, Gerd Michelsen, Marco Rieckmann, and Ian Thomas. London: Routledge. Pp. 161–180.

Walsh, Lorraine; and Kahn, Peter. 2010. *Collaborative Working in Higher Education: The Social Academy*. New York: Routledge.

Walt, Gill; Spicer, Neil; and Buse, Kent. 2009. "Mapping the Global Health Architecture." In *Making Sense of Global Health Governance: A Policy Perspective*, edited by Kent Buse, Wolfgang Hein, and Nick Dragger. London: Palgrave Macmillan. Pp. 47–71.

Wanni, Nada; Hinz, Sarah; and Day, Rebecca. 2010. *Good Practices in Educational Partnerships Guide: UK-Africa Higher & Further Education Partnerships.* London: ACU, Africa Unit.

Wiek, Arnim; Talwar, Sonia; O'Shea, Meg; and Robinson, John. 2013. "Towards a Methodological Scheme for Capturing Societal Effects of Participatory Sustainability Research." Unpublished paper.

Wright, Tarah S. A. 2002. "Definitions and Frameworks for Environmental Sustainability in Higher Education." *Higher Education Policy* 12 (2):105–120.

Yarime, Masaru; and Tanaka, Yuko. 2012. "The Issues and Methodologies in Sustainability Assessment Tools for Higher Education Institutions: A Review of Recent Trends and Future Challenges." *Journal of Education for Sustainable Development* 6 (1):63–77.

Yarime, Masaru; Trencher, Gregory; Mino, Takashi; Scholz, Roland W.; Olson, Lennart; Ness, Barry; Frantzeskaki, Niki; and Rotmans, Jan. 2012. "Establishing Sustainability Science in Higher Education Institutions: Towards an Integration of Academic Development, Institutionalization, and Stakeholder Collaborations." *Sustainability Science* 7 (Supplement 1):101–113.

9

EVALUATING TRANSNATIONAL-HIGHER-EDUCATION PARTNERSHIPS FOR SUSTAINABLE DEVELOPMENT

In this chapter, we focus on evaluating transnational higher-education partnerships (THEPs) that possess sustainable-development objectives.[1] THEPs that involve teaching, research, and/or community-outreach initiatives are increasingly favored arrangements by universities around the world for mobilizing and integrating mutually supportive approaches to challenges of sustainable development (see Jowi, Knight, and Sehoole, 2013, pp. 16–21). A book on contemporary sustainable-development evaluations would not be complete without treating THEPs. We treat horizontal partnering for transnational sustainable development (TSD) in this chapter and suggest pathways to improving process, outcome, and impact evaluations.

Partnering for sustainable development

Today, international education is "as much a process of joining broader alliances as it is one of promoting the interests of single institutions" (Sutton, Egginton, and Favela, 2012, p. 148; also Peterson, 2015). Higher-education institutions partner for sustainable development with foundations, ministries, private firms, NGOs, communities, and local governments (Ackah, 2008, p. 40; Tandon, 2008, p. 149; Angula, 2009, pp. 24–25; Yusuf, Saint, and Nabeshima, 2009, p. xxiii; Brown, 2008, p. 154) as well as with other universities. "In a typical flagship university in Africa," for instance, "the list and diversity of international partnerships are quite staggering" (Damtew, 2009, p. 156).

Among universities in the North and the South, sustainable development has emerged as a popular, adaptable, and encompassing (McFarlane and Ogazon, 2011, pp. 84–85) framework for transnational collaboration. THEPs are necessary because the challenges of sustainable development that knowledge leaders tackle cannot be meaningfully addressed in singular fashion (Rist, 2013, p. 259; de-Graft Aikins, et al., 2012, p. 29). Partnering enables institutions of higher learning worldwide to mobilize transdisciplinary expertise and professionals with the capability to navigate and connect the global and the local and to apply knowledge from diverse sources for the benefit of TSD. For these and other reasons, the *Swansea Declaration* obliges signatory universities to "co-operate with one another and with all segments of society in the pursuit of practical and policy measures to achieve sustainable development and thereby safeguard the interests of future generations" (cited in Wright, 2002, p. 116). The World Conference on Sustainable Development and the Bonn Declaration also emphasized the importance of higher-education-partnerships for sustainable development, especially North-South-South and South-South arrangements (Fadeeva and Mochizuki, 2010, p. 255). At the regional level, the African Union has emphasized that the revitalization of Africa's universities to play their critical role in sustainable development "will require partnerships not only with local and regional actors and stakeholders, but also with the universities, businesses and governments of the developed world" (NEPAD, 2005, p. 21).

In advance of the 2012 UN Conference on Sustainable Development, the United Nations Environmental Programme (UNEP) launched the multicontinental Global Universities Partnership on Environment and Sustainability (GUPES) in an effort to encourage transnational-university networking and joint-research projects – particularly South-South collaborations that will address twenty-first-century TSD challenges. GUPES' five-hundred-plus intercontinental university network builds on the prior organization of eighty-five African universities in thirty countries called Mainstreaming Environment and Sustainability in African University Partnerships (MESA) formed in 2004 with support from UNEP, UNESCO, and the Association of African Universities (Sharma, 2012; Wals and Blewitt, 2010, p. 64; Pradhan, Waswala-Olewe, and Ayombi, 2015, pp. 5, 7–9).[2] In line with the focus of this book, "the MESA partnership holds that mainstreaming SD [in current and future priorities] encompasses all three core functions of a university: teaching, research and community engagement, and also includes management and extramural partnerships" (Wals and Blewitt, 2010, pp. 64–65; also see Mukuna, 2015, pp. 245–250). MESA further strives to promote the long-term public engagement of students and young professionals in sustainability activity and provides a platform for inter-university dialog on sustainable development (Pradhan, Waswala-Olewe, and Ayombi, 2015, pp. 6, 8–9).

The Promotion of Sustainability in Postgraduate Education and Research network (ProSPER.Net) is a consortium of nineteen Asia-Pacific higher-education institutions under the auspices of the United Nations University Institute of Advanced Studies "launched with funding support from the Ministry of Environment, Japan," that jointly "undertake a variety of projects ranging from capacity development for the policy makers to poverty and ESD" (Fadeeva and Mochizuki, 2010, pp. 249, 253, 255). The Alternative University Appraisal project initiated by ProSPER.Net in 2009 (ProSPER.Net, 2012, p. 4) is the subject of considerable attention later in this chapter.

Mutual benefits

Many higher-education institutions in low-income countries continue to confront acute financial, capacity-building, political-stability, and connectivity needs (Bloom, 2003, p. 145; Juma and Yee-Cheong, 2005, p. 90). Tertiary-level institutions are in a particularly precarious and neglected position in sub-Saharan Africa (Damtew, 2003, pp. 129–130). Confronted with massification and other extreme pressures, most public and private universities in Africa can afford to devote few of their meager domestic resources to promising research undertakings or community-engagement projects (Jowi, 2009, pp. 272–273; Samoff and Carrol, 2004, p. 136; Jowi, Knight, and Sehoole, 2013, p. 27). Partnerships offer higher-education institutions in the South prospects of tapping into an expanded array of useful resources, relationships, and skills (Brinkerhoff, 2002, p. 16; Francisconi, Grunder, and Mulloy, 2011, p. 19; Olapade-Olaopa, et al., 2014).

For universities in the North, there are numerous potential benefits of partnership that fall within the purview of sustainable-development evaluations. Northern institutions of higher education currently face competing internal agendas, increasing operational costs, and revenue and accountability constraints that condition their involvement in cross-border sustainable-development ventures. Many fiscally challenged Northern universities are searching for novel pathways to sustainable development. Northern academic institutions concerned with these issues can learn from and build upon the experience Southern universities have gained in coping with the political, economic, and social impacts of structural-adjustment programs, dealing with inequities and poverty, operating under severe financial constraints (Forster, 1999, p. 44), and collaborating across boundaries (Olapade-Olaopa, et al., 2014, pp. S19, S23).

While THEPs carry transaction costs, they can pool and share assembled essential resources, spread risks, bring multiple perspectives and complementary core competencies to bear on TSD issues, enhance the reputation and social capital of reliable participants, and facilitate the leveraging of contributions and support from non-academic sources. Thus, transnational-higher-education partnerships offer Northern as well as Southern universities one cost-effective way to respond to escalating demands for increased higher-education capacity and performance to address wicked problems without diminishing the quality of academic programs (Johnstone and Marcucci, 2010, p. 26; Eckel and Hartley, 2011, p. 199). In short, THEPs open mutually beneficial opportunities for new creativity that is focused on sustainable development and community outreach.

However, economic and epistemic asymmetries between Northern and Southern countries are enormous and difficult to overcome. If the goals of reducing knowledge asymmetries; strengthening teaching, research, and outreach capacity; and restoring the academic profession to its position at the "front line of social and economic development" (Enders and de Weert, 2009, p. 270) are to be realized in the South, higher-education leaders will need to pursue symmetrical transnational-partnership initiatives (see Koehn and Obamba, 2014). Designed properly, THEPs promise to remedy prevailing North-South power asymmetries and resource imbalances. Symmetrical THEPs can play leading roles in rectifying existing transcontinental-institutional imbalances (see Koehn and Obamba, 2014; Olapade-Olaopa, et al., 2014, pp. S19, S23). Thus, near-symmetry as a THEP-process objective is a consistent theme in our sustainable-development-evaluation approach.

THEPs are of considerable interest in sustainable-development evaluations because governments and foundations channel hundreds of millions of dollars and euros to research and community-outreach projects that are initiated, carried out, and assessed by universities. Indeed, a number of bilateral-donor agencies that fund international-development assistance and scientific research have insisted that Northern researchers identify partners in the Global South (Habermann, 2008; Olsson, 2008). Since THEPs typically are financed, at least in part, by external bodies, donor involvement also is included for scrutiny in our framework. Enhancing institutional and human resources in the South; pooling scientific and financial resources through various forms of North-South, South-South, and North-South-South university partnering; expanding access to and sharing of knowledge that is available in the North and in the South; and applying collaborative-research insights and practical experiences to glocal challenges of sustainable development present some of the strategies pursued to counter prevailing imbalances that constitute core subjects for evaluation.

Transnational research and societal engagement

Today's transnationally partnered university undertakes collaborative-research and community-outreach initiatives in diverse contexts on multiple continents. Many of today's most exciting TSD-knowledge breakthroughs are emerging from trans-disciplinary research along the edges of intersecting boundaries. The twenty-first-century research university must be transnational in scope, with faculty and staff collaborating across porous boundaries through team-based, cross-disciplinary partnerships. Transnational research at the interface of science, technology, and international relations, for instance, facilitates "progress on otherwise intractable transboundary conflicts" (Juma and Yee-Cheong, 2005, p. 157).

Research, the igniter of knowledge with sustainable-development applications, is an expensive endeavor that outstretches the limited resources available in low-income countries (Damtew, 2009, p. 156; Damtew and Altbach, 2003, p. 6). Fortunately, widespread academic interconnectivity, both within the global network of universities and at other research sites, inspires transformations in the organizational and epistemic structure of knowledge production and transmission. Mobility and transdisciplinarity have created vast opportunities and scope for scientific partnering among researchers in the South and North.

The scale of inter-university collaboration ranges from a team of two or more researchers working independently of higher authorities on a narrowly focused project of mutual interest to multinational consortia of universities operating under agreements managed at the highest institution-wide levels. For instance, engaging actionable perspectives on greenhouse-gas-emissions mitigation and adaptation to climatic change must "include a large-scale, multinational and multidisciplinary effort, including engineers, climate scientists, economists, political scientists, sociologists, economic and environmental planners, and policy makers, and it would require the integral participation and guidance of scholars and policy makers [and community/group members] from the global South" (Roberts and Parks, 2007, pp. 233, 213–218, 231, 235, 241). Ambitious and complex partnerships connect consortia of universities that pursue multiple, even multi-continental, projects. One example of the latter is Universitas 21, an association of higher-education institutions from thirteen countries with four regional nodes engaged in multidisciplinary undertakings aimed at addressing innovative strategies for urban-water systems, water reclamation and re-use, and sustainable-waterfront development.[3] Another active partnership consortium is the Medical Education Partnership Initiative (MEPI). MEPI – devoted to physician retention, capacity building, relevant research, and sustainability – currently involves collaborative activity on the part of nearly 25 percent of all medical schools in sub-Saharan Africa and twenty-three US higher-education institutions (Olapade-Olaopa, et al., 2014, pp. S20–S22, especially Figures 1 & 2; also see Larkan, et al., 2016, p. 18).

The sustainable-development function of basic and applied research often is ignored when assessing the contribution of THEPs (Crewe and Young, 2002, p. v). From a foundational perspective, technological and informational imbalance, marginalization, and dependence can only be redressed when scholars in the South possess in-depth understanding of change processes and the facilities and incentives that enable innovative and contextually appropriate breakthroughs. As Samoff and Carrol (2004, p. 151) point out, "the conduct of basic research and the opportunity for original thought are in the last resort the only means by which societies can take control of their destiny. Such a function is not a luxury . . . , but an integral part of the development process itself." Equitable and beneficiary-oriented transnational-partnership research, including insights based on indigenous knowledge and Southern scholarship, plays a critical role in evidence-based policy making aimed at advancing widely shared sustainable-development goals such as reducing poverty and hunger, protecting life-support systems, and enhancing wellbeing (e.g., Afsana, et al., 2009, pp. 4, 9).

For decades, Northern funding agencies and scholars have controlled the agenda of TSD research and practice.[4] From the Southern vantage point, universities have encountered manifestations of asymmetric relationships and benefit distributions across a wide range of North-South research and sustainable-development-outreach activities.[5] In Northern-dominated divisions of higher-education labor, for instance, "research agenda setting, activity planning, fund management, data interpretation, results dissemination and basic research components are taken on by Northern researchers, while their Southern counterparts are in charge of data gathering and the more applied research components" (Gutierrez, 2008, p. 21; also

Samoff and Carrol, 2004, p. 147; Samoff and Assie-Lumumba, 2003, p. 321; Chege, 2008, p. 103; Afsana, et al., 2009, pp. 9, 12; Anderson, et al., 2014, p. 1125).

In addition, Vessuri (2007, p. 164) laments that "solutions based on modern science have been used in situations where indigenous or local knowledge could have offered a better response, but . . . was not even considered as an option." The unique and useful sustainable-development synergy often generated by multiple ways of knowing and by linking specific local contexts with transnational challenges argues for additional creative syntheses of science and technology with indigenous insights and practices (see Crossley and Watson, 2003, p. 102; Okolie, 2003, p. 250; Dei and Asgharzadeh, 2006, pp. 59–60, 67; Vessuri, 2007, pp. 168, 172).

Transnational-institution building and human-capability development allows all partners to develop innovative approaches to complex problems and crises of sustainable development and to move on to higher levels of collaboration. In the design and execution of projects and the dissemination of results, developing and practicing skills in interacting with academic collaborators of diverse nationality and across specialization boundaries are especially pivotal for research partners intent on addressing emerging interdependent challenges.

Limitations of current THEP-evaluation approaches

Notwithstanding the widely acknowledged and growing scientific and geopolitical importance of academic partnering worldwide, there have been relatively few independent and systematic studies of the patterns and dynamics of transnational-higher-education collaboration in research and development undertakings (Drake, et al., 2000, p. 2; Wanni, Hinz, and Day, 2010, p. 62; Collins, 2014, p. 943). Ironically, studies of research and sustainable-development partnerships in the African university context are especially rare even though African countries are heralded as the greatest beneficiary or victim of much of the transcontinental-collaborative effort (Court, 2008).[6]

Among other limitations, the societal benefits of university research often are underestimated in both North and South. In addition to direct economic spin offs, Walter McMahon (2009, p. 256) reminds us that "research keeps the faculty in touch with new technologies and knowledge developed worldwide, which is then embodied in master's, PhD, and professional students at the research universities and elsewhere who then teach undergraduates, and leave to teach at other colleges or to fill research and administrative positions in firms, in government, and abroad."

Higher-education rankings

Higher-education rankings that rely on bibliometrics and indicators of recognition like Nobel Prizes awarded to faculty members and alumni (see Badat, 2010, pp. 122–124; Mohrman, 2010, p. 133), including the Shanghai Jiao Tong Institute of Higher Education (SJTIHE)[7] and the Times Higher Education-Quacquarelli

Symonds (THE-QS)[8] listings, assume prestige goals that are not relevant to Southern institutions focused on sustainable development and on developing locally relevant and useful curricula (Taylor, 2008, p. 99). Such rankings only encourage costly and imprudent races for world-class reputations.

In addition, rankings such as the SJTIHE and THE-QS are "underpinned by questionable social science, arbitrarily privilege particular indicators and use shallow [quantitative] proxies as correlates of quality" (Badat, 2010, pp. 136, 125, 127, 131; also Harvey, 2008, p. 189; Labi, 2010, p. A20; Hazelkorn, 2011, pp. 500–501). They also privilege "the physical, life, and medical sciences because these disciplines publish frequently with multiple authors" (Hazelkorn, 2011, p. 502). They "concentrate on past performance rather than potential" and fail to account for diverse "contexts and missions" (Hazelkorn, cited in Marshall, 2011) and internationalization efforts (Deardorff and van Gaalen, 2012, p. 167). Even more importantly, these rankings "completely ignore the value of community engagement" (Badat, 2010, pp. 131, 126; Downing, 2012, p. 37), each university's unique strengths and self-determined objectives (Thorp and Goldstein, 2010, p. A44), indicators of partnership symmetry (Stromquist, 2013, p. 178), and research relevance (Jamil Salmi, cited in Marshall, 2011) – particularly in terms of local- and regional-development needs and the indispensable non-monetary assets that Southern partners contribute to collaborative-knowledge generation (Damtew, 2009, p. 165).

A more useful approach in examining South-North collaboration initially focuses on *process*: how the research agenda is constructed and managed and how the knowledge-production process unfolds. Under this formulation, assessments of transnational-research collaboration emphasize "the creation of common vocabularies or conceptual bridges that allow for new ways of thinking or new combinations of existing thought" through the encounter of ideas from more than one source (Drake, et al., 2000, p. 4). Online and open-access publishing offers one promising means of promoting the transnational circulation of ideas and leveling opportunities to access research findings in Southern places (Metcalfe, Esseh, and Willinsky, 2009, p. 93).

Additional defining criteria of consequential scholarly collaboration are undertaking partnered initiatives that address societal needs and national-sustainable-development priorities, building research capacity within collaborating institutions and among community stakeholders in the South, and contributing to the unique mission and TSD responsibilities of participating universities (Chapter 8; Badat, 2010, pp. 130, 136–137). Evaluating societal relevance and impact is at least as important as traditional peer-review methods (Hemlin and Rasmussen, 2006, pp. 187–188, 174–175, 177, 183). According to Sven Hemlin and Soren Rasmussen (2006, pp. 176, 182, 186–187, 191), the social appropriateness and research-application aspects of academic-quality monitoring "will bring new peers to judge the knowledge process and results because traditional peers do not possess the competence to evaluate all social and organizational issues of knowledge claims. This makes it necessary to involve users, management consultants, and even lay persons as peers."

THEP-evaluation weaknesses

Although THEPs aimed at attaining sustainable-development objectives have expanded rapidly in number and scope, evaluators, evaluation efforts, and evaluation products have lagged behind in determining "how collaboration is working (or not), and how shared responsibility is to be understood and measured" (Rist, 2013, p. 260). Meta-analysis indicates that Northern-designed evaluations of the effectiveness of development assistance to education "concentrate on assessing the delivery of inputs rather than assessing the extent to which intended outcomes were actually achieved" (Chapman and Moore, 2010, pp. 555, 557, 562; also Srivastava and Oh, 2010). Northern funders also are prone to promote "ever-widening standardization" of evaluation metrics internationally (Taylor, 2008, p. 99; Neave, 2012, pp. 5–7). Further, donors are inclined to limit their perceptions of success to timeliness, cost containment, and requisite specifications for short-term deliverables (Smith, 2000, pp. 214–215; Neave, 2012, p. 207).

Donors have favored the use of predefined quantitative indicators in learning, research, and development evaluations. Exclusive donor determinations of project indicators and baselines against which achievements are measured leads to asymmetric evaluations (Crossley, et al., 2005, p. 37). Pressure to borrow standardized, externally determined, indicators narrows opportunities to conduct contextually based evaluations and increases "power asymmetries in many [Southern] HEIs" (Taylor, 2008, p. 99; also Esther, 2002, p. 510).

The asymmetrical nature of Northern-designed development evaluations is further revealed by the disproportionate attention paid to monitoring performance and assessing results on only the Southern side of transnational partnerships (van den Berg and Feinstein, 2009, p. 35). Benefits that accrue to Northern institutions and societies often fall outside the purview of TSD evaluations (see Syed, et al., 2012). The positive influence of transnational collaborations on Northern higher-education institutions merits increased attention. In short, growing recognition of the power of THEP development linkages and the diversity of pursued and secured benefits among partners "adds a new dimension to evaluation" (Thomas and Tominaga, 2013, pp. 58–59).

While project designs tend to emphasize impacts, evaluations concentrate on immediate and readily quantifiable inputs and outputs (such as the number of partnerships entered, courses developed, professionals trained, reports issued, workshops conducted, and staff exchanged) (Stone, 2004, p. 157; Stephens, 2009, p. 20; Chapman and Moore, 2010, pp. 557, 563; Deardorff and van Gaalen, 2012, p. 167). With regard to higher-education partnerships with non-university stakeholders, Robert Marten and Jan Witte (2008, p. 21) found that "few foundations invest in monitoring and evaluation, and even fewer conduct thorough impact evaluations." Moreover, when key data are unavailable, important variables are excluded from analysis, "leading to bias and ambiguity of results" (Colclough, 2012b, p. 6).

Reforming THEP evaluations

Looking ahead, Robert Klitgaard (2004, p. 45) foresaw the following at the start of the new millennium:

> We will be doing more evaluations of partnerships. We will be doing more evaluations for partnerships. And we will be engaging in more partnerships to do our evaluations.

In that future, we need to make sure that we produce THEP evaluations that matter.

The core impact of a THEP devoted to sustainable-development undertakings can be defined as "the contributions that it makes in terms of significant and lasting changes in the well-being of populations in the South" (Obamba, Mwema, and Riechi, 2011, p. 2) along with the benefits derived for adaptation and application in the North and globally. The impact dimension of the sustainable-development-process evaluation is tied to systemic changes in the way institutions of higher learning in the North and South are connected with societal institutions and policy centers (Wals and Blewitt, 2010, p. 65).

We recognize the complexities involved in efforts to link partnerships to social and development impacts and do not presume to identify perfectly reliable evaluation methodologies. Our more modest objective is to identify a flexible and adaptable approach, along with promising measurement possibilities, that will illuminate processes that are connected to outcomes and impacts (also see Colclough, 2012b, p. 4). Progress in the framework-building direction will enable the results of THEP-evaluation exercises to be communicated meaningfully and convincingly to educational leaders, partnership participants, and other stakeholders (Stone, 2004, p. 156; Schuller and Desjardins, 2007, p. 18).

One of the major challenges involved in evaluating THEP-research collaboration is the difficulty of defining all its components and measuring its impacts. To yield meaningful process, outcome, and impact insights, development-education evaluations need to be broadened beyond externally imposed quantitative measures. As Steve Fuller (2006, p. 369) has noted, "metrics need to be developed that present universities as producers of more than simply paper (i.e., academic publications, patents and diplomas) in order to capture the full extent of their governance functions [and influence]." The inclusion of qualitative measures facilitates the cross-checking of findings through triangulated perspectives, thereby enriching evaluation as a meaningful explanatory exercise (Stern, 2004, pp. 38–39).

Although sustainable development is predominantly contextual and place-based, facilitating and constraining forces beyond the local level exert influence over process, outcomes, and impacts (Elliott, 2013, p. 305). The comparative ethnographic case study is particularly illuminating, therefore, when conducted vertically as well as horizontally. In the context of THEP analysis, vertical comparisons involve ethnographic tracing of mutual influence across local, regional, national, and transnational levels (Bartlett and Vavrus, 2009, pp. 9–11). Multisited vertical-case studies encompass donor comparisons. Horizontal-case studies elaborate intra-institutional and national dynamics.

One issue peculiar to THEP-research and outreach evaluations involves the extent to which the partnership meets mutual objectives. Thus, in symmetrical-THEP evaluations, evaluators seek to identify individual and social benefits and costs on all sides of the partnership. Interest in symmetrical evaluations also focuses attention on contextual indicators of achievements and vulnerabilities rather than on global metrics.

In addition to inputs, objectives, outputs, outcomes, and impacts, evaluations of partnerships need to consider *processes and pathways*. Too often, "the dynamics of partnerships, both positive and negative, are underemphasized" (Klitgaard, 2004, p. 52). Process-oriented evaluation is particularly useful for research contexts that span organizational and national boundaries (Simon and Knie, 2013, p. 406). Did partners agree at the start on the relevance of the problem, on research objectives, and on methods of inquiry (Brundiers, et al., 2014, p. 203)?

Applying the Alternative University Appraisal model in THEP evaluations

ProSPER.Net's Alternative University Appraisal approach offers tested components that can be adapted to improve THEP evaluations of sustainable-development-curricular reform (Tanaka, et al., 2013, pp. 6, 64) as well as governance, research, and outreach[9] activity (Fadeeva and Mochizuki, 2010, p. 253). With the goal of encouraging higher-education institutions to develop contextually appropriate combinations of practices rather than imposing predetermined or generic options (Fadeeva and Mochizuki, 2010, p. 253), Alternative University Appraisal involves suggested self-awareness questions (SAQs), benchmarking indicator questions (BIQs), and dialogue (sharing education-for-sustainable-development concerns, lessons, and best practices) (Tanaka, et al., 2013, pp. 62, 64). SAQs are "subjective and qualitative questions" dealing with specific designated fields of education-for-sustainable-development activity while BIQs are "objective and quantitative questions about the overall maturity of the university" (ProSPER.Net, 2012, pp. 6, 9).

The Alternative University Appraisal's benchmarking-indicator questions are relevant and helpful for conducting a holistic evaluation of higher-education-partnership dynamics. THEP partners must first agree that the collection of comparative performance data (both within and beyond the partnership) is worthwhile and commit to the evaluation exercise (Poister, Aristigueta, and Hall, 2015, p. 391).

Box 9.1 presents a slightly modified set of ProSPER.Net's suggested process-oriented BIQs for assessing the five governance subcategories of policies, management, operations, incentives, and monitoring/evaluation. Among other considerations, the governance indicators address institutional recognition of the importance of sustainable development, policy and budgetary support, training, incentives, and accountability.

BOX 9.1 BENCHMARKING INDICATOR QUESTIONS: THEP GOVERNANCE

Subcategory	BIQs
Policies	*Is sustainability explicitly stated in each university's mission/vision?*
	Is sustainability included in each university's programs/plans?
Management	*Does each partner have an office dedicated to sustainable development?*
	Does each partner have an independent standing committee for SD?
	Does each university participate in an in-country network for SD?
	Does each university participate in an international network for SD?[10]
	Does the THEP offer SD-capacity-building programs for faculty and staff?
	Does each partner earmark internal resources for SD?
	Has the THEP mobilized government and non-governmental resources for SD?
Operations	*Does each university operate SD-promotional/awareness activities?*
	Does each university conduct itself as a living laboratory for SD?
Incentives	*Does each partner operate a functional award/reward system based on SD performance?*
M&E	*Are SD activities and results regularly reported in transparent fashion to university authorities, partners, donors, and stakeholders?*
	Does each university operate an internal M&E system for SD activities?
	Does each university possess an external-evaluation system actively engaged in assessing SD outcomes and impacts?

Source: adapted from ProSPER.Net (2012, pp. 11–12).

Box 9.2 presents a slightly modified set of ProSPER.Net's suggested outcome-oriented BIQs for assessing the three education subcategories of resources, curriculum,[11] and process. ProSPER.Net's education indicators call attention to the importance of developing faculty and staff expertise, to interdisciplinary sustainable-development course offerings, to stakeholder involvement in learning, to peer reviews and course evaluations, to societal-impact assessment, and to broad-based information dissemination.

BOX 9.2 BENCHMARKING INDICATOR QUESTIONS: THEP EDUCATIONAL PROCESSES

Subcategory	BIQs
Resources	*Does each partner have faculty and staff with SD expertise/experience?*
	Does each partner call upon stakeholder SD expertise/experience for student learning?
Curriculum	*Is SD specifically featured in teaching/learning activities?*
	Are community, government, and private-sector stakeholders involved in SD curriculum development?
	Are interdisciplinary courses, undergraduate minors, and graduate specializations available for SD enrichment?
	Are service-learning SD opportunities widely provided?
	Are students of diverse abilities and backgrounds encouraged to participate in SD learning?
	Is student learning of SD issues and skills specifically assessed?
	Do partners have a system in place that assesses learning for long-term SD impact?
Process	*Are sustainable-development considerations explicitly included in assessment policies and procedures?*
	Does each partner make glocal SD information resources widely available?

Source: adapted from ProSPER.Net (2012, pp. 12–13).

ProSPER.Net's subcategories for research benchmarking include output, scholarly impact, quality, and awards. Rather than list specific BIQs that could be adapted to THEP evaluations, the model refers users to the United Nations University's Global Research Benchmarking System (ProSPER.Net, 2012, pp. 13–14). Outreach subcategories and BIQs, addressed in detail in Chapter 8, also constitute key components of the holistic Alternative University Appraisal system.

Additional evaluation enhancements

The limitations of summative evaluations that focus on outputs underscore the value of the qualitative and formative dimensions of THEP evaluations (see Crossley and Bennett, 2004, p. 222). Qualitative evaluations emphasize context and culture over global metrics (see Coxon and Munce, 2008, pp. 147, 162). This provides an important advantage because "context is central to understanding" the relationship of transnational education to development (McGrath and Badroodien, 2006, p. 492; Colclough, 2012a, pp. 160, 167). Ethnographic inquiries and narrative studies, for instance, uncover key interpersonal and inter-institutional relationships (see Pelto, 2013). To yield meaningful insights, therefore, THEP evaluations need to be broadened beyond externally imposed quantitative measures and global metrics. A variety of forms of triangulation – including methodological, data, investigator, time, space, person, and theory triangulation – can be employed to increase confidence in partnership evaluations (Green and Tones, 2010, p. 503; Collins, 2014, pp. 947–948).

An inclusive THEP-evaluation framework provides for sustained observations over the long-term. Capacity development and societal impacts are long-term-investment propositions that require time for mutual respect, trust, and complementary working relations to develop among higher-education partners (Jones, Bailey, and Lyytikäinen, 2007, p. 24; Collins, 2014, p. 954; Afsana, et al., 2009, p. 12). A minimum of ten years often is heralded as the gold standard for externally financed tertiary-level partnerships, particularly those that incorporate an institutional-capacity-building component and are committed to sustainable outcomes and impacts (Kellogg, Hervy, and Teshome, 2008; de-Graft Aikins, et al., 2012, pp. 39–40; also see Olapade-Olaopa, et al., 2014, p. S23). Among others, the APLU-led Africa-U.S. Higher Education Initiative (n.d., pp. 3–4) explicitly recognizes the need to "develop new indicators of impact that will assess longer term [fundamental] results" of THEPs. In the interest of capturing long-term results, evaluators "need to develop a more holistic, imaginative and generous attitude to education's benefits" (Schuller, Hammond, and Preston, 2004, p. 192). In this connection, the framework presented here devotes special attention across all partnership dimensions to formative and ongoing evaluations.

Symmetrical THEP-sustainable-development evaluations balance external reviews with participation by the higher-education partners (Van de Water, Green, and Koch, 2008, p. 52). Team members pursue mixed-method and complementary evaluation strategies and collect qualitative and quantitative data (Singh, 2007, p. 76). The use of mixed methods "generates important synergies" and "provides additional layers of explanation and insight that single-method studies are denied" (Colclough, 2012b, p. 6; also Jeffery, 2012, pp. 172–174). Establishment of a flexible time frame for the symmetrical-evaluation process reduces prospects that accountability demands will outweigh learning objectives (Crossley, et al., 2005, p. 107).

Step-by-step THEP sustainable-development evaluations

In this section, we endeavor to build on lessons learned from past THEP-evaluation weaknesses and from the above review of suggested enhancements. Specifically, we set forth a step-by-step series of formative and summative inquiries that collectively are designed to provide a framework for assessing the life-course curricula, research, and outreach components of sustainable-development initiatives undertaken via transnational-university partnerships and collaborations. To ensure sustainability, process considerations feature prominently in our approach.

Evaluating the life course of a THEP can be distinguished by phases.[12] Partnership and project design and planning are featured during the inception phase. The management or implementation phase is followed by the closing or internal-sustainability interval (see Meyer, 2007, pp. 36–37, 42, 44–45; Koehn and Obamba, 2014, chapters 4–7). Interwoven across temporal process evaluations are core considerations of sustainable-development linkages, outcomes, and impacts.

Partnership inception: design and planning

The first evaluative criteria to be applied in assessing sustainable-development-partnership design should specifically consider whether or not the reasons advanced for adopting the transnationally collaborative approach outweighed the arguments in favor of unilateral implementation (Catley-Carlson, 2004, p. 22). Equitable inclusion and the pursuit of mutually beneficial relations feature front and center (Larkan, et al., 2016, pp. 20, 23). To what extent was the partnership proposal initiated by the Southern university (Jones, Bailey, and Lyytikäinen, 2007, p. 21)? Did each partner articulate a best-case and a worst-case scenario for the partnership (Afsana, et al., 2009, p. 15)? Did partners share the same sustainable-development vision of what they aimed to achieve (Stern, 2004, p. 32)? Did partners jointly decide on research objectives (de-Graft Aikins, et al., 2012, pp. 31, 37)? Did each partner identify what they planned to give and hoped to get from the collaboration (Afsana, et al., 2009, p. 12)? Did each partner have a clear and accurate understanding of the contributions that each collaborator would bring to the enterprise as a whole (Catley-Carlson, 2004, p. 21)? Were initial expectations on the part of one or more partners unrealistically high (Samoff and Carrol, 2004, p. 130; Chapman and Moore, 2010, p. 563)? Are alternative partnership arrangements likely to generate superior results (Klitgaard, 2004, pp. 45, 52)?

Further along these lines, evaluators explore the extent to which project objectives were supportive of community- and national-development priorities (Tikly, 2011, p. 10). The 2008 *Accra Agenda for Action*, a product of the *Paris Declaration on Aid Effectiveness* of 2005, provides a monitorable expression of the basic principles of the development-partnership approach – namely, country ownership of national-development strategies, harmonization and alignment of external involvement with those strategies, and mutual accountability (Gore, 2008).

The design of partnership governance also requires evaluation. Did the partners establish a formal governance structure (Afsana, et al., 2009, p. 15)? How symmetrical was participation in establishing the governance arrangements? How inclusive, balanced, and transparent (Stone, 2004, p. 157) was the original design and any subsequent iterations? Did partners jointly negotiate a charter-like agreement that set forth consensus principles that would guide the sustainable-development collaboration and serve as a "touchstone" for future initiatives (see, for instance, Anderson, et al., 2014, pp. 1125–1129)?

Did key administrators at all partner universities endorse the sustainable-development initiative (Calder and Clugston, 2004, p. 256)? Did it involve all those in each institution's core and periphery who needed to cooperate in planning and project implementation (Stern, 2004, p. 31; Walsh and Kahn, 2010, p. 39)? Were project responsibilities differentiated in ways that minimized confusion (Stern, 2004, p. 32)? Did participants agree on strategies for managing and minimizing conflicts that might arise over the course of the THEP (Larkan, et al., 2016, p. 23)?

Did each university's reward system "encourage partnership modes of working" (Jones, Bailey, and Lyytikäinen, 2007, p. 10)? To what extent were the incentives for each partner symmetrically aligned during the design phase (Catley-Carlson, 2004, p. 24; Jones, Bailey, and Lyytikäinen, 2007, p. 21)? Were the rewards and risks "equitably shared" (Stern, 2004, p. 35)? Did the "distribution of risks take account of the different abilities of partners to carry them" (Stern, 2004, p. 35)? Were incentives aligned with performance (Klitgaard, 2004, p. 48)? Have the initially perceived benefits of transnational collaboration been maintained or modified by each partner?

THEPs devoted to sustainable development evaluate relationship dynamics as well as the partnership design (Walsh and Kahn, 2010, p. 45). Were the champions of sustainable development credible and highly regarded at all partner universities (Calder and Clugston, 2004, p. 256)? To what extent did each institution demonstrate commitment to the partnership? Did participants, including senior officers, across the relevant units of partner institutions and external entities enthusiastically engage in project activities and take initiatives or "exhibit a fatalistic orientation to collaborative working" (Walsh and Kahn, 2010, p. 45; also Boydell and Rugkasa, 2007, p. 222)?

Were the timeframes adopted for learning and research inputs, outputs, outcomes, and impacts feasible and flexible? The key lesson here is remaining context sensitive and not bound to rigid "Western notions of efficiency" (Crossley, et al., 2005, p. 97).

To what extent did TSD-research plans incorporate specific and broad-based dissemination and adoption pathways (Jones, Bailey, and Lyytikäinen, 2007, p. 22)? Did partners look toward the end of the partnership? Did the partners formulate a preliminary exit strategy at the partnership-formation stage (Larkan, et al., 2016, p. 20)? Did they agree in advance on a "closing plan" (Afsana, et al., 2009, p. 18)?

Partnership management

In the interest of promoting and sustaining THEPs devoted to sustainable development, management issues also require comprehensive attention during the evaluation process. Face-to-face and virtual visits and meetings are important partnership lubricants. Were meetings productive? Who participated? Did senior managers interact with project staff and community constituents (Bailey, 2010, p. 44)? Were the number and quality of contacts sufficient? Did physical conditions, agendas, and the use of technology promote the exchange of aspirations, ideas, and memories and generate a range of perspectives, insights, and contributions (Walsh and

Kahn, 2010, p. 39)? Did sufficient exchange of key information and ideas related to sustainable development occur among the partners (King, 2009, p. 44)? To what extent did THEP managers and stakeholders jointly analyze the data collected (Walsh and Kahn, 2010, p. 67)? To what extent were visits and meeting decisions followed up with action(s) that addressed identified problems and obstacles (Gedde, 2009, p. 35)?

Budgeting constitutes a key dimension of THEP management. Did senior managers allocate adequate staffing, resources, and rewards? Were program budgets transparent and shared? To what extent were TSD budgets equitably distributed among transnational partners according to agreed-upon responsibilities? Were they modified as necessary (Stern, 2004, p. 31)? How deeply was control over funds devolved (Jones, Bailey, and Lyytikäinen, 2007, p. 21)? Did sponsoring agencies play a transparent and facilitative role (Hoppers, 2001, p. 469)? To what extent is each partner satisfied with the allocation of resources (Afsana, et al., 2009, p. 19)?

Did managers concentrate on principal partnership objectives and sustainable-development needs (Smith, 2000, p. 216)? To what extent were they sidetracked by competing interests? Did they resist imposing burdensome administrative procedures so that all partners were free to focus on the principal objectives of the partnership (Catley-Carlson, 2004, p. 26)? Did they select appropriate methods for pursuing partnership goals (Catley-Carlson, 2004, p. 25)? To what extent did Southern-university partners participate in all stages of research (Jones, Bailey, and Lyytikäinen, 2007, p. 21)?

Mutual trust and respect is a defining aspect of effective North-South THEP management (see, for instance, Jones, Bailey, and Lyytikäinen, 2007, p. 8). Trust has interpersonal, inter-group, and inter-institutional dimensions (Schuller and Desjardins, 2007, p. 70). Has partnership management been characterized by deep trust among all partners and by effective conflict management (Stern, 2004, p. 32)? Specifically, were disagreements and incidents that might have derailed the partnership openly discussed and resolved in ways that strengthened the THEP (Boydell and Rugkasa, 2007, p. 224)? Evaluating trust typically rests on subjective assessments. Major perceptual differences on levels of trust among partners suggest problems associated with unbalanced management.

The symmetrical-management process involves collaborative monitoring and evaluation. Have the partnership managers conducted agreed-upon monitoring and evaluation exercises at regular intervals (Wanni, Hinz, and Day, 2010, p. 58)? Further, as Klitgaard (2004, p. 51) maintains, "evaluation partnerships must be managed in a way that tries to value and preserve dissenting perspectives" rather than by stifling diversity and creativity by insisting on consensus. Ensuring that diverse perspectives are accorded a central role often requires that the Southern partner be granted additional financial and human resources that enhance their members' evaluation capabilities (Whitaker, 2004, p. 25; Tikly, 2011, p. 10).

To document partnership obstacles and accomplishments, the symmetrical plan for monitoring and evaluation initially negotiated at the partnership-formation stage should be set in motion by project leaders (Wanni, Hinz, and Day, 2010, pp. 58–59). It is not helpful to measure symmetry in THEP-management processes primarily by relying on quantitative indicators. Subjective perceptions are determinative. When all partners trust that management issues are subject to mutual decision making, interaction in decision-making processes and structures and research and curriculum innovation will be smoother, and transaction costs will be lower (Mochizuki and Fadeeva, 2010, p. 399). However, symmetrical collaboration to achieve a shared TSD goal does not mean that each and every aspect of the collaborative project has to be carried out together or equally by all partners (KEFPE, 2012). What often matters most in partnership management are transparency and receptivity to mutual-learning processes, where "interdependencies are explicitly acknowledged" and addressed by reliance on each partner's comparative advantage (Brinkerhoff, 2002, p. 22; Collins, 2011, p. 166). Did the THEP function as a learning organization that profited from inevitable mistakes and miscalculations by focusing on the application of lessons learned to newly arising challenges?

Regular monitoring of key aspects of the partnership arrangement is essential to ensure that overall aims are "still synergized" (Wanni, Hinz, and Day, 2010, p. 58) and participants are utilizing key data related to capacity-building and performance criteria (Cloete, Bailey, and Maassen, 2011, p. xix). Have outputs been consistent with plans and targets (Stern, 2004, p. 38)? Have the partners jointly modified the design to reflect changes in priorities (Walsh and Kahn, 2010, p. 66)? Do design modifications reflect any changes in initially identified sustainable-development priorities (e.g., curriculum insights, research breakthroughs, partnership sustainability) and desired tradeoffs among incentives (Ingram, 2004, pp. xviii–xix)? To what extent have project components, strategies, and symmetrical arrangements been refined and improved (Wanni, Hinz, and Day, 2010, p. 58) based upon feedback from and reflection by all partners (Stern, 2004, p. 38)?

Partnership linkages

In common with individual university research and outreach (treated in Chapters 7 and 8), interaction with other stakeholders is critical for successful TSD-partnership initiatives. For instance, the universite Nationale du Rwanda partnership with Texas A&M and Michigan State universities (PEARL, or Partnership for Enhancing Agriculture in Rwanda through Linkages) emphasized community-based development. PEARL partners and stakeholders linked "farmers in rural communities with researchers and faculty members" in ways that strengthened value-chain development and empowered "growers to employ new agribusiness techniques and thus make their farms more sustainable" (Collins, 2011, pp. 147, 155–160, 168–169, 184–185).

Thus, the university-community-linkage dimensions of sustainable-development projects also merit serious attention in THEP-process evaluations. All partners can benefit when diverse perspectives on problems, community needs, available expertise, and different services provided are continuously exchanged (Boydell and Rugkasa, 2007, p. 222). Participatory approaches to evaluating university-society collaborations are treated in detail in Chapter 5. A useful transnational-partnership question drawn from the Unit-Based Sustainability Assessment Tool (Togo and Lotz-Sisitka, 2013, pp. 278, 271, 273) is this: to what extent did each department collaborate with other university units, partner institutions, and stake-holders in addressing challenges of sustainable development?

Another essential relationship-evaluation issue involves *accountability* to exter-nal stakeholders. Did partnership members agree on a plan for involving relevant stakeholders in research and outreach undertakings (Afsana, et al., 2009, p. 17)? Were stakeholders involved in guiding project management, monitoring progress, and evaluating outcomes (Stern, 2004, p. 31)? Have university governing bod-ies, donors, and community constituencies received progress reports (Stern, 2004, p. 38)? Do external stakeholders remain supportive of the partnership?

Partnership outcomes

Transnational-university partnerships offer opportunities for simultaneously building the capabilities of Northern and Southern researchers, teaching faculty (e.g., Collins, 2011, p. 163), and students (Bradley, 2008). To ensure the success of collaborative endeavors, THEP-research and outreach initiatives involving part-ners situated in low-income places commonly combine results-directed scholarly activity with support for individual-capability and institutional-capacity building.

To what extent have researcher skills and research-management capabilities been enhanced (Jones, Bailey, and Lyytikäinen, 2007, p. 18)? How has the part-nership contributed to the creation of a broad-based sustainable-development community of teaching faculty, researchers, and students at participating universi-ties (Sterling, 2013, p. 44)? Did the partnership build capabilities in humanities and non-economic social sciences as well as in other fields (Jones, Bailey, and Lyytikäinen, 2007, p. 7; de-Graft Aikins, et al., 2012, p. 32)? Are continuous skill-updating opportunities provided? How has commitment to the training of train-ers been demonstrated? To what extent did the partnership enhance capacity for innovation at individual and institutional levels (Meyer, 2007, p. 43)?

In sustainable-development partnerships that aspire to be symmetrical, insti-tutional capacity should be judged, in part, on the extent to which faculty and administrators place a premium on social justice and advocate for those most in need. Thus, evaluators explore the extent to which learning opportunities are equitable and benefits are extended to persons who lack access to higher educa-tion (Walker, et al., 2009, p. 567). Further, they look for evidence of increased faculty and staff contributions to poverty-reduction undertakings and involve-ment in sustainable-development-policy circles (Calleson, 2005; Morfit and Gore, 2009, p. 16).

Box 9.3 extends institutional-capacity evaluation to cover the fruits of North-South faculty collaborations.

BOX 9.3 EVALUATING NORTH-SOUTH FACULTY COLLABORATIONS

- Have additional faculty members at the Southern partner institutions learned the value of transnational collaboration with Northern colleagues?
- What lessons have participating Northern universities learned from research and development collaboration with Southern partners that have been applied in their own communities or regions?
- Have additional faculty members at the Northern partner institutions learned the value of transnational collaboration with Southern colleagues?

The Southern university's capacity to engage in sustainable development is dramatically enhanced when partners simultaneously initiate efforts to strengthen the institutional capacity of collaborating domestic businesses, indigenous NGOs, and community associations. Did university partners build symmetrical and sustained linkages with sustainable-development stakeholders (Jones, Bailey, and Lyytikäinen, 2007, p. 10)?

In an outcome typology employed to evaluate transnational-health partnerships that has TSD applicability, Edwards and colleagues (2015, p. 3) merge organizational capacity and individual capabilities.[13] Partnerships that emphasize both infrastructure strengthening and generic skills that are transferable across a number of tasks have the highest probability of being associated with long-term outcomes (Edwards, et al., 2015, pp. 51–52).

THEP impacts

Evaluations that concentrate on identifying *contributions toward* impact objectives are particularly well-suited for partnership initiatives (Hummelbrunner, 2012, p. 265). Catalytic impacts on transformation processes and rule-making systems shaping sustainable development merit exploration in this connection.

Do tracer studies illuminate the chain of impact by university graduates and community trainees (Jones, Bailey, and Lyytikäinen, 2007, p. 18)? Did THEP interventions contribute in unintended ways to sustainable-development impacts? What intended and unintended sustainable-development-impact contributions are revealed by the chain of impact?

THEP-research impacts rest in large measure on stakeholder follow-through. To what extent have various stakeholders (academics, government personnel, NGO and community members, donors) received and acted upon partnership-research findings related to sustainable development (Afsana, et al., 2009, p. 21)?

Meaningful partnership evaluations also involve determinations of *sustainable external impacts*. Did the partners, in conjunction with stakeholders, set in motion continuing and durable activities that generate sustainability innovations and advance sustainable development in societal contexts (Meyer, 2007, pp. 45, 47)?

Partnership sustainability

THEP sustainability requires mutual perception that the partnership will enrich institutional environments (and, in the case of sustainable-development initiatives, enhance human wellbeing) over the long run and, consequently, should be continued in some form. We agree with Wanni, Hinz, and Day (2010, p. 58), therefore, that "evaluation of the partnership itself, not just of outputs and deliverables, has to be built into the partnership."

The Partnership Assessment Toolkit (PAT) offers a useful set of practical inquiries regarding the actualization of plans for "good endings and new beginnings." How will any remaining resources be (re)allocated? How will staff be redeployed or transitioned? How will biological and intellectual property be handled (Afsana, et al., 2009, p. 23)? Wrap-up debriefing sessions ask all partners to contribute their views on the "three most beneficial aspects of this collaboration" and the "three aspects of the collaboration that should be improved for the future" (Afsana, et al., 2009, p. 24).

In TSD evaluations, it is particularly "fruitful to focus on the ways in which partnerships create [or fail to create] the conditions that make change possible" (Boydell and Rugkasa, 2007, p. 225). Thus, process and sustainability indicators play a key part in overall THEP assessments. THEP evaluators look for tangible and intangible evidence of shared understandings, strengthened trust, deepened connections, and mutual-asset building among participants (Boydell and Rugkasa, 2007, pp. 219, 222; Eddy, 2010, pp. 2, 11). Have firm and sustainable relationships been established (Syed, et al., 2012)?

Evaluators also seek to discover change-promoting and change-resisting factors and forces (Nordtveit, 2010, p. 111). How has the THEP morphed over time (Wanni, Hinz, and Day, 2010, p. 62; de-Graft Aikins, et al., 2012, pp. 38–39)? Have sustainable-development learning objectives, research-project components, and management changes been replicated and become institutionalized (Morfit and Gore, 2009, p. 16)? Have stakeholders been organized and energized to maintain, enhance, and carry forward the sustainable-development initiatives introduced by the partnership?[14] Have the partners made plans to "invest in the partnership's own organizational memory" (Stern, 2004, p. 31) and monitoring-and-evaluation capacity?

THEP sustainable-development evaluations based on "learning, capabilities and interaction enable the identification of weaknesses" that lie within organizations, are related to their capabilities, or are found externally within the partnership system itself, "including misalignment between networks, missing organizations and critical blockages of flows of knowledge and resources" (Kruss, et al., 2015, p. 30). Have plans been agreed upon, based in part on assessment of partnership strengths and weaknesses, complementarities and synergies, for specific future collaborations (Klitgaard, 2004, pp. 46, 51; Wanni, Hinz, and Day, 2010, p. 59) that would engage new opportunities (Van de Water, Green, and Koch, 2008, p. 52)?

Other critical THEP-sustainability considerations relate to the ability partners demonstrate to leverage additional funding for TSD from external sources that would enable durable change (Boydell and Rugkasa, 2007, p. 223; Pain, 2009, p. 112; Biermann, et al., 2012, p. 74; Olapade-Olaopa, et al., 2014, p. S21; de-Graft Aikins, et al., 2012, pp. 33–34). Did partners actively search for additional resources (Collins, 2014, p. 957)? To what extent were they successful? Did ownership result to the extent that collaborative-research and sustainable-development activities among all or some of the partners continued beyond the termination of external funding (Catley-Carlson, 2004, p. 21; King 2009, p. 35; Morfit and Gore, 2009, p. 16; Meyer, 2007, p. 44)? If so, how far can the THEP progress based on the "ongoing commitment and application of its own resources" (Crossley, et al., 2005, p. 89)?

Another outcome indicator of THEP sustainability needs to be introduced at this stage. Specifically, we are concerned with the ability of both Northern and Southern universities to maintain legitimacy with their core constituencies. Stern (2004, p. 36) warns that "the consequence of partnerships not managing . . . balance between constructing distinctive understandings and visions and remaining in touch with their natural hinterland is loss of 'reach' . . . [and] reduced ability to carry with them a wider constituency." Thus, evaluators need to ask: has the transnational partnership "constrained the independence of partners more than it has enhanced their capabilities" (Stern, 2004, p. 36)? What lessons have participating Northern universities learned from research and development collaboration with Southern partners that have been applied in their own communities or regions?

In his review of development-partnership evaluations, Klitgaard (2004, pp. 52, 45) finds that costs, including opportunity costs, are "downplayed" and that some of the "most important" benefits are ignored. Useful THEP evaluations explore whether partnership benefits (both intended and unintended, tangible and intangible) outweigh the costs and difficulties of interacting, coordinating, and partnering for all partners (Klitgaard, 2004, pp. 45, 47, 51; Boydell and Rugkasa, 2007, pp. 221–223, 226–227)? Are the combined transaction benefit and cost outcomes of the THEP greater than what it would cost to engage in such transnational-sustainable-development work outside of the partnership (Sutton, Egginton, and Favela, 2012, pp. 159–160)?

Working with donors

Sustainable-development evaluations of THEP relations with key donors devote special attention to the role of Southern universities. Of particular interest in this connection are the extent of Southern involvement in proposal initiation and resource allocation within the partnership (Jones, Bailey, and Lyytikäinen, 2007, p. 10). From Sida's perspective, for instance, the context of research and development activity is of great importance. Therefore, all participants are presumed to bring knowledge to the table (King and McGrath, 2004, pp. 45–46, 147). One of DfID's (UK Department for International Development) most substantial long-term funding programs for competitively funded collaborative-development research and capacity building is the flagship *Research Programme Consortium* (DfID, 2009). RPCs (research-program consortia) are clusters of research institutions acting as centers of specialization that focus around a particular high-priority research or policy theme broadly relevant to international development, capacity building, and global poverty reduction. The overriding requirements are that each consortium must contribute to research-capacity building in the South, engage with policymakers, and develop a comprehensive strategy for communicating research outcomes as widely as possible. Each consortium is made up of between four and six research-partner organizations – at least three of which must be from the South. The lead-consortium institution can be from either the South or the North (DfID, 2009).

Another important consideration in THEP sustainable-development evaluations is donor concern for capacity and capability development within Southern universities. Prospects for symmetrical partnerships are enhanced when donors support long-term enhancements to Southern "research management and knowledge management skills" (Jones, Bailey, and Lyytikäinen, 2007, p. 24).[15] Too many partnership evaluations are conducted "informally with minimal financial and staffing inputs" (Wanni, Hinz, and Day, 2010, p. 58). There have been moves in the enabling direction. For instance, the multi-foundation Partnership for Higher Education in Africa directly awarded "resources necessary for activities that may increase the effectiveness of international linkages" in an effort to build the capacity of African higher-education institutions to "be more equal partners in collaborative projects" (Whitaker, 2004, p. 25; Lewis, Friedman, and Schoneboom, 2010). Support from the Gates Foundation and the William and Flora Hewlett Foundation led to establishment of the International Initiative for Impact Evaluation (see www.3ieimpact.org).

Additional process concerns focus on the nature of external requirements. From the vantage point of Southern partners that can be the recipient of allocations for projects from multiple donors, evaluations should center on patterns of resource distributions among Northern and Southern universities (Collins, 2014, p. 950) and avoidance of excessive process complexity and onerous reporting and accounting obligations (Jones, Bailey, and Lyytikäinen, 2007, p. 19; Collins, 2014, pp. 950–953, 956).

Holistic evaluations

The presence of multiple partners and stakeholders underscores the importance of common evaluation approaches and transparency of methods and findings (see Olapade-Olaopa, et al., 2014, p. S20).[16] To fulfill these objectives, our sustainable-development-centered framework provides for holistic evaluations. Although holistic evaluations encompass all of the phases treated above, they need not proceed in strict linear fashion. Back and forth applications can be revealing. Did, for instance, planning for "good endings and new beginnings" start during the inception phase (Afsana, et al., 2009, p. 14)?[17]

At the summative point, evaluators integrate the separate assessment results related to all sustainable-development THEP projects and phases based on multiple-evaluation methods and identify the measures by which curricular, research, and action initiatives have succeeded and failed (Catley-Carlson, 2004, p. 26; Walsh and Kahn, 2010, p. 69; Yarime and Tanaka, 2012, p. 75). In the interests of THEP symmetry, one should encounter mutual, although not identical, benefits in partnership design, partnership management, institutional-capacity and human-capability building, partnership sustainability, and research and development processes, outcomes, and impacts.[18]

Addressing means as well as ends is necessary in holistic sustainability evaluations. Research and evaluation findings suggest that a sense of *joint ownership* among partnered universities and communities is likely to be associated with favorable partner and partnership-sustaining outcomes (Fukuda-Parr, Lopes, and Malik, 2002, p. 14). THEP objectives are advanced to the extent that evaluation processes "help beneficiaries to formulate their own development strategies, encourage ownership and commitment, and help create a development consensus" (Stern, 2004, p. 39; Jilke, 2013). Missing from evaluations that are reduced to financial calculations are such important considerations as participant willingness to take on risk and pursue innovative approaches. Did participants "welcome serendipity and unexpected developments" (Austin and Foxcroft, 2011, p. 130)?

Holistic THEP evaluations are rare, and "few comprehensive and accessible accounts of international education development projects exist in the available literature" (Crossley, et al., 2005, p. 55). Reflective case studies help fill this void (Crossley, et al., 2005, p. 56). Klitgaard (2004, p. 54) recommends the study of outrageous partnership success stories and of outrageous failures (also Chapman and Moore, 2010, p. 563).[19] Further, he suggests that we seek to "identify superb cases of evaluations for partnerships, where the way the evaluation was done and presented helped each partner and helped the partnership as a whole" (Klitgaard, 2004, p. 54). The next section offers detailed case studies of THEPs devoted to sustainable development involving Southern higher-education institutions along with analysis of key dimensions of process and structural symmetry and mutually promising outcomes and impacts.

African partnership case studies

African universities must play a pivotal role if *Agenda 2030*'s SDGs are to be attained (Jowi, Knight, and Sehoole, 2013, p. 27). In this section, we draw upon published case studies of higher-education partnerships involving African universities to demonstrate the utility of symmetrical approaches to TSD evaluation. In particular, we highlight strengths and weaknesses of several VLIR-UOS (Flemish Interuniversity Council [Belgium]) evaluation processes and suggest symmetry-based advancements based on the framework elaborated above. An organization of Flemish universities, VLIR-UOS supports partnerships among universities in Flanders, Belgium, and developing countries, with the explicit objective of looking for innovative responses to global and local challenges. The overall objective of the institutional university cooperation (IUC) program is to empower the Southern university as an institution to fulfill its role as a development actor in society.

VLIR-UOS uses a systematic approach to evaluating cooperation at the university level that includes conducting both mid-term and final evaluations. Of the nine evaluations of university collaboration it has conducted in sub-Saharan Africa, we focus on three final evaluations of comprehensive research and development partnerships. These evaluations covered partnerships with Mekelle University in Ethiopia (van Baren and Alemayehu, 2013), University of Nairobi in Kenya (de Nooijer and Abagi, 2009), and University of the Western Cape in South Africa (Vander Weyden and Livni, 2014). The three full-term evaluations had almost identical objectives[20] and similar scope.[21]

The evaluation methodologies mainly involved qualitative inquiries, including document analysis, interviews, debriefing meetings, and visits to project sites. The evaluations used standard criteria of quality, efficiency, effectiveness, impact, development relevance, and sustainability (also see de Nooijer and Siakanomba, 2008, p. 7) which were applied to the key results areas (research, teaching, extension and outreach, management, human-resources development, infrastructure, and mobilization of additional resources). Then, evaluators scored each IUC partnership on a five-point scale used to judge the results in quantitative terms and to evaluate the performance of projects.

Although evaluations were tailored to the specific cases, all of them accounted for traditional collaboration outputs, including the generation and strengthening of academic research, published research papers, numbers of graduates, and curriculum development. Largely based on citation counts for instance, the University of Western Cape evaluation detected an "incredible transformation" from a teaching to a research-based academic university with a high academic impact. On the outcome front, the evaluation of the IUC with Mekelle University found that the program had established a research culture in an institution that was highly teaching driven and that the teaching program had been strengthened by introduction of new curricula and integration of research findings.

The reviewed evaluations also attempted to assess the societal impact of the programs through links established with government authorities and with communities for extension and outreach. Here, evaluators typically relied upon anecdotal observations. In the Mekelle case, for instance, the evaluation team reported observing positive examples of implementation of research results for improved livelihoods, transfer of techniques, and support in marketing, which enabled communities to improve the management of ground-and-surface-water resources and micro dams, cultivate apples, and increase income.

Although the three cases involved serious efforts to conduct comprehensive THEP evaluations, we can observe important limitations. For instance, making broad claims about the transformation of the universities from teaching-based to research-oriented ones based on the numbers of graduates, papers, and citations alone is not justifiable. At minimum, such outcome-based evaluations need to include measures of relevance to local sustainable-development needs. Assessing and attributing community-level changes in resource management and livelihoods to the IUC program in question also is impossible without application of a comprehensive framework. As recognized in the South Africa evaluation, it proved difficult to analyze actual impact within the limited framework of the evaluation (Vander Weyden and Livni, 2014, p. 21).

Process shortcomings occurred as well. The VLIR-UOS-funded partnerships adopted a structured, generic, and bureaucratic approach to partnership initiation. In an earlier VLIR-UOS final evaluation of the IUC with the University of Zambia, the authors acknowledge that "an evaluation mission of 6 working days to assess a 10-year programme almost 1 year after it has come to an end is bound to be affected by lack of time to fully grasp the evolution of the programme and its constituent projects" (de Nooijer and Siakanomba, 2008, p. 7).

The VLIR-UOS evaluations also demonstrated certain asymmetries, starting with the fact that monitoring and evaluation of the IUC programs was explicitly the responsibility of the Northern partner. Other evaluation weaknesses are attributable to failure to take into consideration the presence or absence of symmetry in "evaluation as design." Examples of fruitful initial-design questions in our comprehensive framework not addressed include: "how symmetrical was participation in the process of establishing governance arrangements?" and "did the THEP involve all core and periphery stakeholders who needed to cooperate in planning and project implementation?"

A number of unasked questions regarding "evaluation as management" would have provided depth of understanding regarding drivers of and barriers to change. These questions include: "did top higher-education managers concentrate on principal partnership objectives and sustainable-development needs or were they sidetracked by competing interests?"; "what was the degree of each academic stakeholder's involvement in overseeing project management?"; and "were partner budgets equitably distributed according to agreed-upon responsibilities?" The VLIR-UOS partnerships granted African researchers holding PhD degrees substantive autonomy to formulate their own research projects in ways that are relevant to local-development challenges. However, none of the projects proposed by the African researchers could materialize without the approval and conceptual support of the senior Northern researchers (also see Barrett, Crossley, and Dachi's, 2011 study of the EdQual research partnership between two UK and four African universities). In contrast, and in line with our framework recommendations, every research project in Kenya's AMPATH-partnership program involving Moi University–Indiana University Purdue University Indianapolis entailed joint leadership by Northern and Southern researchers (Koehn and Obamba, 2014, p. 193). This management practice offers a promising pathway for improving VLIR-UOS THEP implementation and in designing future partnerships.

Other unasked evaluation questions in our framework that reveal the extent of institutional-capacity and human-capability development are: "what evidence is there that policy makers have officially recognized the social and economic benefits of specific sustainable-development approaches and practices as a result of THEP activities?" and "how have program graduates exercised professional capabilities and transnational competence in ways that further sustainable development?" Filling these and other capacity-building-information gaps would enable evaluators to address outcomes in greater depth (see Mukuna, 2015, pp. 251–261, 267–269).

Further, one THEP feature intended to promote financial autonomy and mutual symmetry is the practice of decentralizing financial management to African partner institutions. This strategy potentially provides opportunities to strengthen capacity for financial management and technology transfer. In the VLIR-UOS partnerships, however, financial decentralization co-existed with a tight, rigid, and asymmetric regime of budgetary rules and rigidities determined by the Belgian partners and donors. It is important that evaluations capture such asymmetric relationships so that these can be corrected in future program design.

In a different partnership model, grant funds from the multi-university Medical Education Partnership Initiative (MEPI) "flow to the primary investigator (PI) at the core universities in Sub-Saharan Africa, who in turn distribute funds to co-PIs at medical schools in the United States" (Olapade-Olaopa, et al., 2014, p. S19). Internal assessment concluded that this reversal in the prevailing partnership-funding arrangement resulted in "profound outcomes." Specifically, "the PIs in Sub-Saharan Africa are now clearly driving an agenda that they have established, with innovations and approaches that likely would not have been envisioned by their counterparts in the North" (Olapade-Olaopa, et al., 2014, p. S21).

Viewing the three VLIR-UOS evaluations in the context of our comprehensive framework for assessing North-South university partnerships revealed existing asymmetries. Some of the most important asymmetries identified for discussion here relate to financial management and accountability. The potential for fiscal mismanagement and corruption remains a legitimate concern that would undermine other partnership aims and tarnish accomplishments. Within an overall context of fiscal decentralization and symmetry-enhancement pathways, we learned that THEPs would be particularly well-served by devoting further attention to building North-South trust through enhanced transparency, budgetary flexibility, financial-management-capacity development, and the progressive removal of Northern constraints.

Asian partnership case studies

We also looked into several Asian-university-partnership evaluations commissioned by the United States Agency for International Development (Tate, et al., 2014). The evaluations covered three US-Indonesian sustainable-development-related THEPs:

(1) Smart Strategic Coalition for Sustainable Agricultural and Economic Development in Indonesia (SSCSAEDI) (partners: Institut Pertanian Bogor, Indonesian Institute of Science, Bogor, and Washington State University).

(2) Enhancing Behavior Change through Conservation (partners: Universitas Mulawarman, Rare, and the University of Texas El Paso).
(3) Climate Change Mitigation Capacity Program (CCMCP) (partners: University of Indonesia and Columbia University).

The common purposes of these evaluations covered six objectives: (i) assess the extent of the knowledge and skills transfer that occurred between the lead US university and the Indonesian partner(s); (ii) determine the extent or level of the capacity building within the partnerships; (iii) assess the effectiveness of the project interventions by the partners to improve teaching and research services; (iv) assess whether the projects achieved their objectives and are sustainable; (v) secure lessons learned from the partnerships that can be applied to the future direction of the program; and (vi) demonstrate how institutions have achieved measurable improvements in the quality and relevance of their teaching and research (Tate, et al., 2014, p. 7). Thus, the evaluation purposes were forward-looking and formative. The assumptions behind the evaluations clearly indicated a one-directional flow of knowledge, skills, and capacity from the US universities to their Indonesian partners.

USAID provided five key evaluation questions to be covered for all three partnership programs (Tate, et al., 2014, pp. 7–8):

(1) What specific knowledge and skills and institutional-capacity building have occurred as a result of the partnership?
(2) What project interventions were effective between the participating universities?
(3) What unintended results have occurred?
(4) What are the lessons learned from the partnership that may be replicated in future programs?
(5) What are the strengths and weaknesses of the partnerships?

The donor agency formulated the five key questions in an open manner that allowed for evaluators to explore them from multiple angles. From the perspective of the framework articulated here, we find it encouraging that the Indonesian THEP evaluations explicitly posed the question of unintended results as one of the key queries and that the process incorporated evaluation of the partnerships themselves.

The USAID-commissioned evaluation relied almost exclusively on document review and interviews with personnel and students from the three Indonesian-partnership institutions. After examining a variety of reports, the evaluators visited all partner institutions in Indonesia and conducted semi-structured interviews with project and university management, technical-advisory groups, faculty and students, provincial- and district-level officials, and key agency stakeholders as well as personnel of the US partner universities. Evaluators endeavored to quantify their qualitative data by applying a simple ratings scale (4 = excellent, 3 = very good, 2 = average, 1 = poor) to interviewee perceptions of partnership strengths and weaknesses. At the end of the evaluation team's work in Indonesia, a workshop brought together all Indonesian-university partners. Nevertheless, the short time allocated for in-country work limited the scope and depth of the evaluations.

A positive process feature in these partnership evaluations is the balance of Indonesian nationals on the team. While the team leader was a US expert, the two specialists and the logistics coordinator were Indonesian. The team went about its business in a systematic manner, covering all the evaluation questions for each of the partnerships. They clearly used the project documents as guides for their questioning. While justifiable, this approach did result in a somewhat mechanistic undertaking with certain limitations.

Although the three projects pursued ambitious objectives in terms of strengthening and building sustainable capacity among the universities,[22] the evaluations largely relied on the indicators identified in the project document, which reduced the effort to measuring outputs and expressing findings in numerical terms – e.g., number of students trained, number of institutions involved in networks, number of linkages to existing extension networks (and their perceived value and strength);[23] at least fifteen academic-journal articles published, fifteen conference papers to be presented, and at least ten teaching workshops to be given on campus;[24] number of curricula developed; number of workshops, courses, and executive programs; number of students registered; number of participants targeted; etc.[25] This approach often led the evaluators to focus on the fulfilment of target numbers, rather than on assessing the broader outcomes of the partnerships. In fairness, the evaluators themselves identified this as an issue. One of the key recommendations of the evaluation to all of the partners is that the quality of the indicators should be enhanced and that they should clearly show the linkages of inputs and outputs to the more important outcomes (Tate, et al., 2014, p. 32).

As mentioned above, the fact that the evaluation sought to identify unanticipated results constitutes a positive feature. In practice, most of the unanticipated consequences cannot be attributed to actions or inactions by the partner institutions. For example, SSCSAEDI was affected by the Indonesian government's sudden budget cuts. While unanticipated, this was not a result of the partnership program. In the case of CCMCP, however, the evaluation identified a late realization that a demonstration-project site was inappropriate, leading to difficulties in implementing that particular part of the program, as an unanticipated development. This unanticipated consequence resulted from inadequate project preparation.

The evaluation also highlighted financial and management problems in the case of the Conservation Partnership and in CCMCP. Evaluators found financial and management shortcomings to be particularly debilitating in the case of the partnership between UNMUL (Universitas Mulawarman, Rare, Indonesia) and the University of Texas. The evaluation report is so telegrammatic in its treatment of the subject that it is impossible to conclude whether these problems resulted from the ways in which partners implemented the program or resulted from insufficient capacity assessment that would have revealed that the partner universities needed prior training to be able to handle the financial, cooperative, and contractual arrangements required by USAID.[26]

In responding to the open question about the strengths and the weaknesses of the partnerships, the evaluators demonstrated insights that went beyond enumerating outputs and identifying constraints. They highlighted that building such a partnership program is a long-term process, which cannot be accomplished in a program that lasts for only a few years (four years, in the case of CCMCP). The evaluation also paid attention to the inclusiveness of the partnerships in terms of, for instance, gender balance, as well as the importance of long-standing relationships and commitment to collaboration. Only in the CCMCP case, however, did evaluators explicitly identify the "perceived equality of the partner institutions" (Tate, et al., 2014, p. 29) as a specific process strength.

Overall, the evaluation of the three partnership programs involving US and Indonesian universities systematically assessed whether the programs were reaching their objectives in terms of their outputs. The evaluators' recommendations were based on evidence and presented in a practical manner that facilitated their implementation. From the point of view of a comprehensive transnational-sustainable-development THEP evaluation, however, the three products were lacking on several fronts. Most notably, they typically failed to extend beyond outputs to understanding the potential outcomes and impacts of the partnerships in terms of the universities' triple mission of research, education, and outreach. For instance, one of the partnerships had as a stated collaborative goal to "improve conservation and development impact,"[27] while another one foresaw as a societal-engagement outcome "reaching different audiences and making clear the importance of reduced forest conversion, the use of market mechanisms in motivating forest conservation, and the value of forests to promoting the health and economic well-being of Indonesians."[28] None of the evaluations endeavored to assess behavioral changes in the direction of partnership-impact goals.

In addition, the authors presented the evaluation report in a succinct manner that did not allow for exploration of key factors that could have explained success and/or failure. Application of the TSD-evaluation framework presented in Part III of *Universities and the Sustainable Development Future* would enable a more comprehensive and richly rewarding evaluation process.

Concluding observations

In practice, THEPs are fluid and malleable organizational arrangements that stretch across geographic, socio-cultural, political, disciplinary, and epistemological boundaries. Relations among Northern and Southern universities are etched with contestations and imbalances intensified by the forces of globalization and the rise of the knowledge economy. Given the extensive socio-cultural, economic, political, and epistemological differences that exist among countries, universities, and individual researchers, transnational-academic collaboration involves a complex and fragmented set of relationships whose sustainable-development pathways and outcomes can be both convoluted and unexpected.

A developing consensus treats THEPs as opportunities for mutually construct-ing knowledge generation and knowledge application rather than benevolent ven-tures designed to assist weak Southern universities and researchers (McGrath and King, 2004, pp. 177, 179; Salmi, Hopper, and Bassett, 2009, pp. 102–103; Koehn, 2012). Mutual-capacity building and the conversion of scientific-research findings into policy interventions that support sustainable-development processes are criti-cally important practical achievements and indicators of the successful impact of specific transnational partnerships (Bradley, 2007, p. 208).

Although THEPs primarily are about building institutional capacity, enhanc-ing human capabilities, strengthening networks of professional communication, and supporting sustainable-development efforts in low-income countries (King, 2008), thoughtful analysts have observed that they must simultaneously build capacity in the North as well as in the South (Bradley, 2008; Habermann, 2008). In many transnationally linked fields of study, local discovery provides the key to learning and to the generation of valuable community and global innovations (Crossley and Holmes, 2001, p. 396). Contemporary Northern institutions of higher learning are porous institutions in which "knowledge comes from engage-ment from beyond the institution as much as it does from work within it" (Sutton, Egginton, and Favela, 2012, p. 160). In such TSD undertakings, "a strong com-mitment to valuing different forms of knowledge is required to promote learning that challenges and rethinks traditional practice within global systems" (Syed, et al., 2012). This understanding "makes clear the contextual nature of knowledge and the importance of exchange and joint creation of knowledge rather than its transfer" (King and McGrath, 2004, pp. 141, 209).

For instance, Colclough (2012b, p. 10), reflecting on the multi-institutional RECOUP THEP, reports that "learning by the Northern collaborators was also deep and extensive. The experience of working with colleagues from different Southern cultures and contexts led directly to innovations in teaching qualita-tive research methods in at least one of the Northern partner institutions." More widely, an evaluation study of twelve USAID-funded partnerships between Afri-can and US institutions reported concrete examples of how the improved skills and knowledge of academic faculty, staff, and students resulted in strengthened institutional capacity, new degree programs, revised curricula, and outreach in both the United States and partner countries (Gore and Odell, 2009, p. 3).

A study of sixty-five articles published in English between 1990 and 2010 is particularly encompassing and detailed in terms of "reverse innovation." The authors identify multiple health-care lessons in each of the WHO's six "building blocks of health systems" based on initiatives and experiences in poor countries that rich countries have benefitted from through transnational partnering. For instance, a US-based AIDS program seeking to increase patient follow-up treat-ment found inspiration from a community- and patient-centered project under-taken in Zambia as part of a University of Alabama at Birmingham partnership initiative (Syed, et al., 2012). The investigators conclude by identifying ten areas of health care where Northern countries have the most to learn from Southern practice: providing services to remote areas; skills substitution; decentralization of management; creative problem solving; education for communicable-disease control; innovation in mobile phone use; low-tech simulation training; local-product manufacture; health financing; and social entrepreneurship (Syed, et al., 2012).

In THEPs devoted to sustainable development, partner benefits are largely attributable to the very diversity that drives the collaboration. As Samoff and Carrol (2004, p. 115; also Samoff, 2009, p. 129; Wanni, Hinz, and Day, 2010, p. 18) have captured the concept, "a partnership must involve a collaboration that can reasonably be expected to have mutual (though not necessarily identical) benefits, that will contribute to the development of institutional and individual capacities at both institutions, and that is self-empowering, enabling both [all] partners to specify goals, chart [transformative] directions, create appropriate governance strategies, employ effective administrative routines, and focus human, material, and financial resources on high priority objectives." These principles, which are consistent with Articles 15 and 17 of the *1998 UNESCO World Declaration on Higher Education for the Twenty-First Century: Vision and Action*, should drive evaluations of THEPs devoted to sustainable development.

Notes

1 Chapter 9 draws, in part, on Koehn and Uitto (2015).
2 See also http://web.unep.org/training/mainstreaming-environment-and-sustainability-africa-mesa-universities-partnership
3 See www.universitas21.com/news/details/182/u21-connect-april-2015
4 The Northern-directed approach to delivering assistance for development was founded on the notion of the unidirectional vertical transfer of knowledge, skills, resources, practices, and policies from donors to recipients or beneficiaries. The asymmetrical Northern-inspired model of development assistance and transnational collaboration reigned supreme until as recently as the 1990s, and "donor-recipient" attitudes still persist in reduced and veiled form even though the approach has been heavily criticized by experts for its tendency to reproduce relationships of material dependency and unequal North-South power relations (Gore, 2008; Samoff, 2009, p. 138; Colclough, De, and Webb, 2012, p. 150).
5 Educational systems in small states are "particularly vulnerable to the influence of international agendas" (Crossley and Holmes, 2001, p. 402).
6 The evaluation studies of Christopher Collins (2011, 2012, 2014) constitute an exception to this generalization.
7 Across the entire African continent, only a couple of South African HEIs have been included in the SJTIHE ranking of the world's top-five-hundred universities (Sörlin and Vessuri 2007, p. 20).
8 In 2010, Times Higher Education ended its collaboration with Quacquarelli Symonds Ltd. and introduced a revised evaluation scheme (Labi 2010, p. A20).
9 For an adapted version of ProSPER.Net's university-outreach-process indicator questions, see Chapter 8.
10 See, for instance, Lotz-Sisitka, Agbedahin, and Hlengwa (2015, p. 33).
11 By 2015, thirty-five African and Asian universities had utilized MESA's *Unit-Based Sustainability Tool* as a basis for revising sustainability curriculum, reorienting courses toward sustainable development, and adapting teaching approaches (see Togo, 2015, pp. 43–44,

58–64; Togo and Lotz-Sisitka, 2013, pp. 273–277; Pradhan, Waswala-Olewe, and Ayombi, 2015, p. 8).

12 Our suggestions for partnership evaluation in each phase incorporate research-focused questions and exercises drawn from the Southern-inspired Partnership Assessment Toolkit (PAT). The PAT is an ongoing interactive tool designed to self-evaluate research-partnership principles and outcomes through an equity lens. The PAT "encourages in-depth discussion among partners at all stages of the partnership" that lead to "concrete actions to improve equity, effectiveness and sustainability in partnerships" (Afsana, et al., 2009, pp. 4, 6, 12).

13 Jones, Bailey, and Lyytikäinen (2007, p. 7) found that bilateral donors support individual training and university-capacity development whereas multilateral donors prefer to invest in independent-research organizations and thematic networks.

14 See, for instance the "communities of practice" (essentially stakeholder partnerships) launched by MEPI universities and welcomed by African ministries of health (Olapade-Olaopa, et al., 2014).

15 However, most bilateral donors restrict external support to time periods far short of the ten-year "gold standard" required for THEPs that pursue sustainable-development objectives (Koehn and Obamba, 2014; Collins, 2014, pp. 950, 953–954).

16 MEPI partner institutions have developed common performance metrics based on core themes and activities that are organized into logic models and collectively tracked (Olapade-Olaopa, et al., 2014, p. S22).

17 Backcasting from impacts also offers a useful approach to partnership evaluation.

18 Cross-THEP-evaluation comparisons are practically nonexistent. Broadly, the concept of sensitive dependence on initial conditions helps us understand how THEPs that start with similar features and missions end up with many different and unanticipated outcomes. Due in part to sensitive dependence on initial conditions, chaotic behavior can be distinguished from random behavior. This means that when chance enters chaotic systems that initially are similar, the outcomes will not be entirely random although they will be uncertain and substantially divergent (Elliott and Kiel, 1996, p. 6). While each of the intervening forces that impact initial conditions can be minuscule, they "amplify exponentially as their effects unfold so the end result bears little resemblance to the beginning" (Murphy, 1996, p. 97).

19 For instance, application of MESA's Unit-Based Sustainability Assessment Tool at the University of Swaziland resulted in the following curriculum, research, and partnering findings: "integration of sustainability in the Department of Consumer Sciences was found to be very low. There is little sustainability content in the curriculum and there were no research initiatives in sustainable development. . . . There were also no sustainable development partnerships between the department and other universities and/or other stakeholders. Most of the indicators were rated 1 (a little) and the average indicator score was also 1" (Togo and Lotz-Sisitka, 2013, pp. 268–269). A self-reported case study of the UK-Africa Academic Partnership on Chronic Disease identified "major success in creating a platform for research dissemination through international meetings [the partnership website] and publications. Other [less output-centered] goals, such as engaging in collaborative research and training postgraduates, were not as successfully realized." Further, "we did not build appropriate monitoring and evaluation processes into our policy goal. Therefore, . . . it is difficult to make any claims about the transfer of knowledge into policymaking" (de-Graft Aikins, et al., 2012, pp. 29, 35–36).

20 Principal objectives included (1) measurement of actual results of the IUC program; (2) formulation of recommendations for ongoing and future collaboration; (3) identification of strengths and weaknesses of each collaboration; (4) identification of departments and/or research groups that have received substantive support and thus can present proposals for the post-IUC program focus; (5) identification of possible themes and partnerships for possible network programs for the future of the involved projects in view of establishing sustainability; and (6) formulation of recommendations to all stakeholders in terms of the follow-up plan that has been elaborated by the Northern and Southern project leaders.

21 Scope of the evaluations addressed (1) the present implementation of the program (state of implementation; activities, intermediate results, meeting the objectives); (2) quality, efficiency, efficacy, impact, development relevance, and sustainability; (3) position of the IUC program within the international cooperation activities of the partner university in comparison to other donor cooperation programs (added value); (4) management of the program both in Flanders and locally (recommendations for improvement); (5) cooperation among all parties involved; (6) follow-up plan to achieve sustainability among institutions and involved research groups; and (7) embedment and impact of the university on development processes in surrounding community, province, and country.

22 In the case of CCMCP, the objectives included strengthening the capacity of Indonesia's private, public, and civil-society sectors to implement REDD (Reducing Emissions from Deforestation and Forest Degradation) and other similar market mechanism projects throughout the Indonesian archipelago. REDD is a market-based model to combat climate change through incentives for forest conservation (see http://redd.unfccc.int).

23 SSCSAEDI.

24 Conservation program.

25 CCMCP.

26 The overall recommendations of the evaluation suggest the latter.

27 Conservation program.

28 CCMCP.

Works cited

Ackah, Kofi (chief rapporteur). 2008. *Developing and Retaining the Next Generation of Academics: Report of the Second University Leaders' Forum Held in Accra, Ghana, 22–25 November.* New York: Partnership for Higher Education in Africa.

Africa-U.S. Higher Education Initiative. n.d. *Developing a Knowledge Center for the Africa-U.S. Higher Education Initiative: A Concept Paper.* Washington, DC: Association of Public and Land Grant Universities.

Afsana, Kaosar; Demissie Habte; Hatfield, Jennifer; Murphy, Jill; and Neufeld, Victor. 2009. *Partnership Assessment Toolkit.* Wakefield, QC, Canada: Canadian Coalition for Global Health Research.

Anderson, Frank; Donkor, Peter; de Vries, Raymond; Appiah-Denkyira, Ebenezer; Dakpallah, George F.; Rominski, Sarah; Hassinger, Jane; Lou, Airong; Kwansah, Janet; Moyer, Cheryl; Rana, Gurpreet K.; Lawson, Aaron; and Ayettey, Seth. 2014. "Creating a Charter of Collaboration for International University Partnerships: The Elmina Declaration for Human Resources for Health." *Academic Medicine* 89:1125–1132.

Angula, Nahas A. 2009. "The New Dynamics for Higher Education in Africa." *UNESCO in Africa* 1 (July):21–25.

Austin, Ann E.; and Foxcroft, Cheryl. 2011. "Fostering Organizational Change and Individual Learning through 'Ground-Up' Inter-Institutional Cross-Border Collaboration." In *Cross-Border Partnerships in Higher Education: Strategies and Issues*, edited by Robin Sakamoto and David W. Chapman. New York: Routledge. Pp. 115–132.

Badat, Saleem. 2010. "Global Rankings of Universities: A Perverse and Present Burden." In *Global Inequalities and Higher Education: Whose Interests Are We Serving?*, edited by Elaine Unterhalter and Vincent Carpentier. Hampshire: Palgrave Macmillan. Pp. 117–141.

Bailey, Tracy. 2010. "The Research-Policy Nexus: Mapping the Terrain of the Literature." Paper prepared for the Higher Education Research and Advocacy Network in Africa (HERANA). Center for Higher Education Transformation, Wynberg, UK.

Baren, Ben van; and Alemayehu Assefa. 2013. *Final Evaluation of the IUC Partner Programme with Mekelle University, Ethiopia.* Brussels: VLIR-UOS.

Barrett, Angeline M.; Crossley, Michael; and Dachi, Hillary A. 2011. "International Collaboration and Research Capacity Building: Learning from the EdQual Experience." *Comparative Education* 47 (1):25–43.

Bartlett, Lesley; and Vavrus, Frances. 2009. "Introduction: Knowing Comparatively." In *Critical Approaches to Comparative Education: Vertical Case Studies from Africa, Europe, the Middle East, and the Americas*, edited by Frances Vavrus and Lesley Bartlett. New York: Palgrave Macmillan. Pp. 1–18.

Berg, Rob D. van den; and Feinstein, Osvaldo. 2009. "Evaluating Climate Change and Development." In *Evaluating Climate Change and Development*, edited by Rob D. van den Berg and Osvaldo Feinstein. New Brunswick, NJ: Transaction Publishers. Pp. 1–40.

Biermann, Frank; Chan, Sander; Mert, Aysem; and Pattberg, Phillip. 2012. "The Overall Effects of Partnerships for Sustainable Development: More Smoke Than Fire?" In *Public-Private Partnerships for Sustainable Development: Emergence, Influence and Legitimacy*, edited by Phillip Pattberg, Frank Biermann, Sander Chan, and Aysem Mert. Cheltenham, UK: Edward Elgar. Pp. 69–87.

Bloom, David E. 2003. "Mastering Globalization: From Ideas to Action on Higher Education Reform." In *Universities and Globalization: Private Linkages, Public Trust*, edited by Gilles Breton and Michel Lambert. Paris: UNESCO Publishing. Pp. 140–149.

Boydell, Leslie R.; and Rugkasa, Jorun. 2007. "Benefits of Working in Partnership: A Model." *Critical Public Health* 17 (3):217–228.

Bradley, Megan. 2007. *North-South Research Partnerships: Challenges, Responses and Trends, A Literature Review and Annotated Bibliography*. Canadian Partnerships Working Paper # 1. Ottawa, ON: IDRC.

Bradley, Megan. 2008. "North-South Research Partnerships: Lessons from the Literature." *NORRAG News* (41).

Brinkerhoff, Jennifer M. 2002. *Partnerships for International Development: Rhetoric or Results?* Boulder, CO: Lynne Reinner.

Brown, L. David. 2008. "Practice-Research Engagement for Human and Social Development in a Globalizing World." In *Higher Education in the World 3: New Challenges and Emerging Roles for Human and Social Development*. London: Palgrave Macmillan. Pp. 152–156.

Brundiers, Katja; Savage, Emma; Mannell, Steven; Lang, Daniel J.; and Wiek, Arnim. 2014. "Educating Sustainability Change Agents by Design: Appraisals of the Transformative Role of Higher Education." In *Sustainable Development and Quality Assurance in Higher Education: Transformation of Learning and Society*, edited by Zinaida Fadeeva, Laima Galkute, Clemens Mader, and Geoff Scott. New York: Palgrave Macmillan. Pp. 196–229.

Calder, Wynn; and Clugston, Rick. 2004. "Lighting Many Fires: South Carolina's Sustainable Universities Initiative." In *Higher Education and the Challenge of Sustainability: Problematics, Promise, and Practice*, edited by Peter B. Corcoran and Arjen E. J. Wals. Dordrecht: Kluwer Academic Publishers. Pp. 249–262.

Calleson, Diane C. 2005. "Community-Engaged Scholarship." *Academic Medicine* 80 (April):317–321.

Catley-Carlson, Margaret. 2004. "Foundations of Partnerships: A Practitioner's Perspective." In *Evaluation & Development: The Partnership Dimension*, edited by Andres Liebenthal, Osvaldo N. Feinstein, and Gregory K. Ingram. New Brunswick, NJ: Transaction Publishers. Pp. 21–27.

Chapman, David W.; and Moore, Audrey S. 2010. "A Meta-Look at Meta-Studies of the Effectiveness of Development Assistance to Education." *International Review of Education* 56:547–565.

Chege, Fatuma. 2008. "Experiences of Partnerships from Kenya: North-South and South-South." *NORRAG News* 41 (December):103–105.

Cloete, Nico; Bailey, Tracy; and Maassen, Peter. 2011. *Universities and Economic Development in Africa: Pact, Academic Core, and Coordination.* Executive Summary of Synthesis Report. Wynberg, SAf: Centre for Higher Education Transformation.

Colclough, Christopher. 2012a. "Education Outcomes Reassessed." In *Education Outcomes and Poverty: A Reassessment,* edited by Christopher Colclough. London: Routledge. Pp. 154–169.

Colclough, Christopher. 2012b. "Investigating the Outcomes of Education: Questions, Paradigms and Methods." In *Education Outcomes and Poverty: A Reassessment,* edited by Christopher Colclough. London: Routledge. Pp. 1–15.

Colclough, Christopher; De, Anuradha; and Webb, Andrew. 2012. "The Practice of Partnership: Aid and Education Policy in India and Kenya." In *Education Outcomes and Poverty: A Reassessment,* edited by Christopher Colclough. London: Routledge. Pp. 138–153.

Collins, Christopher S. 2011. *Higher Education and Global Poverty: University Partnerships and the World Bank in Developing Countries.* Amherst, NY: Cambria Press.

Collins, Christopher S. 2012. "Land-Grant Extension as a Global Endeavor: Connecting Knowledge and International Development." *Review of Higher Education* 36 (1):91–124.

Collins, Christopher S. 2014. "Can Funding for University Partnerships between Africa and the US Contribute to Social Development and Poverty Reduction?" *Higher Education* 68:943–958.

Court, David. 2008. "The Historical Effect of Partnerships in East Africa." *NORRAG News* 41 (December):105–107.

Coxon, Eve; and Munce, Karen. 2008. "The Global Education Agenda and the Delivery of Aid to Pacific Education." *Comparative Education* 44 (2):147–165.

Crewe, Emma; and Young, John. 2002. *Bridging Research and Policy: Context, Evidence and Links.* Working Paper 173. London: Overseas Development Institute.

Crossley, Michael; and Bennett, J. Alexander. 2004. "Planning for Case Study Evaluation in Belize, Central America." In *Qualitative Educational Research in Developing Countries: Current Perspectives,* edited by Michael Crossley and Graham Vulliamy. New York: Garland Publishing. Pp. 221–243.

Crossley, Michael; Herriot, Andrew; Waudo, Judith; Mwirotsi, Miriam; Holmes, Keith; and Juma, Magdallen. 2005. *Research and Evaluation for Educational Development: Learning from the PRISM Experience in Kenya.* Oxford, UK: Symposium Books.

Crossley, Michael; and Holmes, Keith. 2001. "Challenges for Educational Research: International Development, Partnerships and Capacity Building in Small States." *Oxford Review of Education* 27 (3):395–409.

Crossley, Michael; and Watson, Keith. 2003. *Comparative and International Research in Education: Globalisation, Context and Difference.* London: RoutledgeFalmer.

Damtew Teferra. 2003. "Scientific Communication and Research in African Universities: Challenges and Opportunities in the Twenty-First Century." In *African Higher Education: An International Reference Handbook,* edited by Damtew Teferra and Philip G. Altbach. Bloomington, IN: Indiana University Press. Pp. 128–142.

Damtew Teferra. 2009. "Higher Education in Africa: The Dynamics of International Partnerships and Interventions." In *International Organizations and Higher Education Policy: Thinking Globally, Acting Locally?* edited by Roberta M. Bassett and Alma Maldonado-Maldonado. London: Routledge. Pp. 155–173.

Damtew Teferra, and Altbach, Philip G. 2003. "Trends and Perspectives in African Higher Education." In *African Higher Education: An International Reference Handbook,* edited by Damtew Teferra and Philip G. Altbach. Bloomington: Indiana University Press. Pp. 3–14.

Deardorff, Darla K.; and van Gaalen, Adinda. 2012. "Outcomes Assessment in the Internationalization of Higher Education." In *The Sage Handbook of International Higher Education*, edited by Darla K. Deardorff, Hans de Wit, John Heyl, and Tony Adams. Los Angeles, CA: Sage. Pp. 167–190.

de-Graft Aikins, Ama; Arhinful, Daniel K.; Pitchforth, Emma; Ogedegbe, Gbenga; Allotey, Pascale; and Agyemang, Charles. 2012. "Establishing and Sustaining Research Partnerships in Africa: A Case Study of the UK-Africa Academic Partnership on Chronic Disease." *Globalization and Health* 8:29–41.

Dei, George J. S.; and Asgharzadeh, Alireza. 2006. "Indigenous Knowledges and Globalization: An African Perspective." In *African Education and Globalization: Critical Perspectives*, edited by Ali A. Abdi, Korbla P. Puplampu, and George J. S. Dei. Lanham, MD: Lexington Books. Pp. 53–78.

de Nooijer, Paul; and Abagi, Okwach. 2009. *Final Evaluation of the IUC Partner Program with the University of Nairobi (UoN), Kenya*. Gent: VLIR-UOS.

de Nooijer, Paul; and Siakanomba, Bornwell. 2008. *Final Evaluation of the IUC Partnership with the University of Zambia (UNZA)*. Brussels: VLIR-UOS.

Department for International Development (DfID). 2009. *Research Program Consortia: Terms of Reference*. London: UK Department for International Development.

Downing, Kevin. 2012. "Do Rankings Drive Global Aspirations at the Expense of Regional Development?" In *Going Global: The Landscape for Policy Makers and Practitioners in Tertiary Education*, edited by Mary Stiasny and Tim Gore. London: Emerald Group. Pp. 31–39.

Drake, Paul; Ludden, David; Nzongola-Ntalaia, Georges; Patel, Sujata; and Shevtsova, Lilia (editors). 2000. *International Scholarly Collaboration: Lessons From the Past*. New York: The Social Science Research Council.

Eckel, Peter D.; and Hartley, Matthew. 2011. "Developing Academic Strategic Alliances: Reconciling Multiple Institutional Cultures, Policies, and Practices." In *Higher Education: Major Themes in Education*, Volume 4, edited by Malcolm Tight. London: Routledge. Pp. 199–222.

Eddy, Pamela L. 2010. *Partnerships and Collaborations in Higher Education*. San Francisco, CA: Jossey-Bass.

Edwards, Suzanne; Ritman, Dan; Burn, Emily; Dekkers, Natascha; and Baraitser, Paula. 2015. "Towards a Simple Typology of International Health Partnerships." *Globalization and Health* 11:49–55.

Elliott, Euel; and Kiel, L. Douglas. 1996. "Introduction." In *Chaos Theory in the Social Sciences: Foundations and Applications*, edited by L. Douglas Kiel and Euel Elliott. Ann Arbor: University of Michigan Press. Pp. 1–19.

Elliott, Jennifer A. 2013. *An Introduction to Sustainable Development*, 4th edition. London: Routledge.

Enders, Jurgen; and de Weert, Egbert. 2009. "Towards a T-Shaped Profession: Academic Work and Career in the Knowledge Society." In *The Changing Face of Academic Life: Analytical and Comparative Perspectives*, edited by Jurgen Enders and Egbert de Weert. Hampshire: Palgrave Macmillan. Pp. 251–272.

Esther Mebrahtu. 2002. "Perceptions and Practices of Monitoring and Evaluation: International NGO Experiences in Ethiopia." *Development in Practice* 12 (August):501–517.

Fadeeva, Zinaida; and Mochizuki, Yoko. 2010. "Higher Education for Today and Tomorrow: University Appraisal for Diversity, Innovation and Change towards Sustainable Development." *Sustainability Science* 5:249–256.

Forster, Jacques. 1999. "The New Boundaries of International Development Co-Operation." In *Changing International Aid to Education: Global Patterns and National Contexts*, edited by Kenneth King and Lene Buchert. Paris: UNESCO. Pp. 31–45.

Francisconi, Cheryl; Grunder, Alyson; and Mulloy, Maura. 2011. *Building Sustainable U.S.-Ethiopian University Partnerships: Findings from a Higher Education Conference.* New York: Institute for International Education White Paper.

Fukuda-Parr, Sakiko; Lopes, Carlos; and Malik, Khalid. 2002. "Overview." In *Capacity for Development: New Solutions to Old Problems,* edited by Sakiko Fukuda-Parr, Carlos Lopes, and Khalid Malik. London: Earthscan Publications. Pp. 1–21.

Fuller, Steve. 2006. "Universities and the Future of Knowledge Governance from the Standpoint of Social Epistemology." In *Knowledge, Power and Dissent: Critical Perspectives on Higher Education and Research in Knowledge Society,* edited by Guy Neave. Paris: UNESCO Publishing. Pp. 345–370.

Gedde, Maia. 2009. *The International Health Links Manual: A Guide to Starting Up and Maintaining Long-Term International Health Partnerships.* London: Tropical Health and Education Trust.

Gore, Charles. 2008. "Improving the Terms of Development Partnership." *NORRAG News* (December):13–15.

Gore, Jane S.; and Odell, Malcolm J. Jr. 2009. *Higher Education Partnerships in Sub-Saharan Africa: An Impact Assessment of 12 Higher Education Partnerships.* Washington, DC: USAID, Bureau for Economic Growth, Agriculture and Trade (EGAT).

Green, Jackie; and Tones, Keith. 2010. *Health Promotion: Planning and Strategies,* 2nd edition. Thousand Oaks, CA: Sage.

Gutierrez, David. 2008. "Beyond Disappointment: Transforming Ideology and Practice in North-South Research Partnerships." *NORRAG News* 41:19–21.

Habermann, Birgit. 2008. "Research Partnership: Charity, Brokerage, Technology Transfer or Learning Alliance?" *NORRAG News* 41:33–37.

Harvey, Lee. 2008. "Rankings of Higher Education Institutions: A Critical Review." *Quality in Higher Education* 14 (3):187–207.

Hazelkorn, Ellen. 2011. "Measuring World-Class Excellence and the Global Obsession with Rankings." In *Handbook on Globalization and Higher Education,* edited by Roger King, Simon Marginson, and Rajani Naidoo. Cheltenham, UK: Edward Elgar. Pp. 497–516.

Hemlin, Sven; and Rasmussen, Soren B. 2006. "The Shift in Academic Quality Control." *Science, Technology, & Human Values* 31 (2):173–198.

Hoppers, Wim. 2001. "About How to Reach the Truth in Development Co-Operation: ODA/DFID's Education Papers." *International Journal of Educational Development* 21:463–470.

Hummelbrunner, Richard. 2012. "Process Monitoring of Impacts and Its Application in Structural Fund Programmes." In *Governance by Evaluation for Sustainable Development: Institutional Capacities and Learning,* edited by Michal Sedlacko and Andre Martinuzzi. Cheltenham, UK: Edward Elgar. Pp. 253–266.

Ingram, Gregory K. 2004. "Overview." In *Evaluation & Development: The Partnership Dimension,* edited by Andres Liebenthal, Osvaldo N. Feinstein, and Gregory K. Ingram. New Brunswick, NJ: Transaction Publishers. Pp. xi–xxi.

Jeffery, Roger. 2012. "Qualitative Methods in the RECOUP Projects." In *Education Outcomes and Poverty: A Reassessment,* edited by Christopher Colclough. London: Routledge. Pp. 170–189.

Jilke, Sebastian. 2013. "What Shapes Citizens' Evaluations of Their Public Officials' Accountability? Evidence from Local Ethiopia." *Public Administration and Development* 33 (5):389–403.

Johnstone, D. Bruce; and Marcucci, Pamela N. 2010. *Financing Higher Education Worldwide: Who Pays? Who Should Pay?* Baltimore: Johns Hopkins University Press.

Jones, Nicola; Bailey, Mark; and Lyytikäinen, Minna. 2007. *Research Capacity Strengthening in Africa: Trends, Gaps and Opportunities.* London: Overseas Development Institute.

Jowi, James O. 2009. "Internationalization of Higher Education in Africa: Developments, Emerging Trends, Issues and Policy Implications." *Higher Education Policy* 22 (3):263–281.

Jowi, James O.; Knight, Jane; and Sehoole, Chika. 2013. "Internationalisation of African Higher Education: Status, Challenges and Issues." In *Internationalisation of African Higher Education: Towards Achieving the MDGs*, edited by Chika Sehoole and Jane Knight. Rotterdam: Sense Publishers. Pp. 11–31.

Juma, Calestous; and Yee-Cheong, Lee. 2005. *Innovation: Applying Knowledge in Development*. London: Earthscan.

Kellogg, Earl D.; Hervy, Anne-Claire; and Teshome Yizengaw. 2008. "Africa-U.S. Higher Education Initiative: Empowering African Higher Education for Africa's Transformation." *IIE Networker* (Fall):36–38.

KEFPE (Swiss Commission for Research Partnerships with Developing Countries). 2012. *A Guide for Transboundary Research Partnerships: 11 Principles*. Bern: Swiss Commission for Research Partnerships with Developing Countries.

King, Kenneth. 2008. "The Promise and Peril of Partnership." *NORRAG News* 41:5–6.

King, Kenneth. 2009. "Higher Education and International Cooperation: The Role of Academic Collaboration in the Developing World." In *Higher Education and International Capacity Building: Twenty-Five Years of Higher Education Links*, edited by David Stephens. Oxford, UK: Symposium Books. Pp. 33–49.

King, Kenneth; and McGrath, Simon. 2004. *Knowledge for Development? Comparing British, Japanese, Swedish, and World Bank Aid*. London: Zed Books.

Klitgaard, Robert. 2004. "Evaluation of, for, and through Partnerships." In *Evaluation & Development: The Partnership Dimension*, edited by Andres Liebenthal, Osvaldo N. Feinstein, and Gregory K. Ingram. New Brunswick, NJ: Transaction Publishers. Pp. 43–57.

Koehn, Peter H. 2012. "Turbulence and Bifurcation in North-South Higher-Education Partnerships for Research and Sustainable Development." *Public Organization Review* 12 (4):331–355.

Koehn, Peter H.; and Obamba, Milton O. 2014. *The Transnationally Partnered University: Insights from Research and Sustainable Development Collaborations in Africa*. Gordonsville, VA: Palgrave Macmillan.

Koehn, Peter H.; and Uitto, Juha I. 2015. "Beyond Outputs: Pathways to Symmetrical Evaluations of University Sustainable-Development Partnerships." *Development Studies Research* 2 (1):1–19.

Kruss, Glanda; McGrath, Simon; Petersen, Il-haam; and Gastrow, Michael. 2015. "Higher Education and Economic Development: The Importance of Building Technological Capabilities." *International Journal of Educational Development* 43:22–31.

Labi, Aisha. 2010. "'Times Higher Education' Releases New Rankings, but Will They Appease Skeptics?" *Chronicle of Higher Education*, 24 September, p. A21.

Larkan, Fiona; Uduma, Ogenna; Lawal, Saheed A.; and van Bavel, Bianca. 2016. "Developing a Framework for Successful Research Partnerships in Global Health." *Globalization and Health* 12:17–25.

Lewis, Suzanne G.; Friedman, Jonathan; and Schoneboom, John. 2010. *Accomplishments of the Partnership for Higher Education in Africa, 2000–2010; Report on a Decade of Collaborative Foundation Investment*. New York: Partnership for Higher Education in Africa.

Lotz-Sisitka, Heila; Agbedahin, Adesuwa V.; and Hlengwa, Amanda. 2015. "'Seeding Change': Developing a Change-Oriented Model for Professional Learning and ESD in Higher Education Institutions in Africa." In *Mainstreaming Environment and Sustainability in African Universities: Stories of Change*, edited by Heila Lotz-Sisitka, Gitile Naituli, Amanda Hlengwa, Mike Ward, Ayobami Salami, Akpezi Ogbuigwe, Mahesh Pradhan,

Marie Neeser, and Sanne Lauriks. Grahamstown: Rhodes University Environmental Learning Research Centre. Pp. 16–33.

Marshall, Jane. 2011. "UNESCO Debates Uses and Misuses of Rankings." *University World News* 172 (May).

Marten, Robert; and Witte, Jan M. 2008. *Transforming Development? The Role of Philanthropic Foundations in International Development Cooperation.* GPPi Research Paper Series No. 10. Berlin: Global Public Policy Institute.

McFarlane, Donovan A.; and Ogazon, Agueda G. 2011. "The Challenges of Sustainability Education." *Journal of Multidisciplinary Research* 3, No. 3 (Fall):81–107.

McGrath, Simon; and Badroodien, Azeem. 2006. "International Influences on the Evolution of Skills Development in South Africa." *International Journal of Educational Development* 26 (5):483–494.

McGrath, Simon; and King, Kenneth. 2004. "Knowledge-Based Aid: A Four Agency Comparative Study." *International Journal of Educational Development* 24:167–181.

McMahon, Walter W. 2009. *Higher Learning, Greater Good: The Private and Social Benefits of Higher Education.* Baltimore: Johns Hopkins University Press.

Meyer, Wolfgang. 2007. "Evaluation of Sustainable Development: A Social Science Approach." In *Sustainable Development in Europe: Concepts, Evaluation and Applications,* edited by Uwe Schubert and Eckhard Stormer. Cheltenham, UK: Edward Elgar. Pp. 33–50.

Metcalfe, Amy S.; Esseh, Samuel; and Willinsky, John. 2009. "International Development and Research Capacities: Increasing Access to African Scholarly Publishing." *Canadian Journal of Higher Education* 39 (3):89–109.

Mochizuki, Yoko; and Fadeeva, Zinaida. 2010. "Competences for Sustainable Development and Sustainability: Significance and Challenges for ESD." *International Journal of Sustainability in Higher Education* 11 (4):391–403.

Mohrman, Kathryn. 2010. "Educational Exchanges: What China Should *Not* Adopt from United States Higher Education." In *Crossing Borders in East Asian Higher Education,* edited by David W. Chapman, William K. Cummings, and Gerald A. Postiglione. Hong Kong: University of Hong Kong. Pp. 127–144.

Morfit, Christine; and Gore, Jane. 2009. *HED/USAID Higher Education Partnerships in Africa 1997–2007.* Washington, DC: Higher Education for Development.

Mukuna, Truphena E. 2015. "Championing a Green Future through Higher Education: Initiatives of Selected Regional Research Organizations in Africa." In *Milestones in Green Transition and Climate Compatible Development in Eastern and Southern Africa,* edited by Truphena E. Mukuna and Christopher A. Shisanya. Addis Ababa: Organization for Social Science Research in Eastern and Southern Africa. Pp. 231–277.

Murphy, Priscilla. 1996. "Chaos Theory as a Model for Managing Issues and Crises." *Public Relations Review* 22 (2):95–113.

Neave, Guy. 2012. *The Evaluative State, Institutional Autonomy and Re-Engineering Higher Education in Western Europe: The Prince and His Pleasure.* London: Palgrave Macmillan.

New Partnership for Africa's Development (NEPAD). 2005. "Renewal of Higher Education in Africa: Report of AU/NEPAD Workshop." NEPAD, Johannesburg, 27–28 October.

Nordtveit, Bjorn. 2010. "Development as a Complex Process of Change: Conception and Analysis of Projects, Programs and Policies." *International Journal of Education and Development* 30:110–117.

Obamba, Milton O.; Mwema, Jane K.; and Riechi, Andrew R. 2011. *University Partnerships Can Reduce Poverty.* ANIE Policy Brief. Accra: Association of African Universities.

Okolie, Andrew C. 2003. "Producing Knowledge for Sustainable Development in Africa: Implications for Higher Education." *Higher Education* 46 (2):235–260.

Olapade-Olaopa, Emiola O.; Baird, Sarah; Kiguli-Malwadde, Elsie; and Kolars, Joseph C. 2014. "Growing Partnerships: Leveraging the Power of Collaboration through the Medical Education Partnership Initiative." *Academic Medicine* 89, No. 8 (August Supplement):S19–S23.

Olsson, Berit. 2008. "Symmetry and Asymmetry in Research Partnerships: Lessons from 20 Years Experience." *NORRAG News* 41:78–80.

Pain, Adam. 2009. "Economic Development and Sustainable Livelihoods." In *Higher Education and International Capacity Building: Twenty-Five Years of Higher Education Links*, edited by David Stephens. Oxford: Symposium Books. Pp. 95–114.

Pelto, Pertti. 2013. *Applied Ethnography: Guidelines for Field Research.* Walnut Creek, CA: Left Coast Press.

Peterson, Patti M. [Presidential Advisor for Global Initiatives, American Council on Education]. 2015. "A Flat Lens for a Round World?" Keynote address at the Defining a 21st Century Education for a Vibrant Democracy Conference, University of Montana, Missoula, 26 October.

Poister, Theodore H.; Aristigueta, Maria P.; and Hall, Jeremy L. 2015. *Managing and Measuring Performance in Public and Nonprofit Organizations: An Integrated Approach*, 2nd edition. San Francisco, CA: Jossey-Bass.

Pradhan, Mahesh; Waswala-Olewe, Brian M.; and Ayombi, Mariam. 2015. "Introducing the UNEP Mainstreaming Environment and Sustainability in African Universities Partnership Programme." In *Mainstreaming Environment and Sustainability in African Universities: Stories of Change*, edited by Heila Lotz-Sisitka, Gitile Naituli, Amanda Hlengwa, Mike Ward, Ayobami Salami, Akpezi Ogbuigwe, Mahesh Pradhan, Marie Neeser, and Sanne Lauriks. Grahamstown: Rhodes University Environmental Learning Research Centre. Pp. 5–15.

Promotion of Sustainability in Postgraduate Education and Research Network (ProSPER. Net). 2012. *Alternative University Appraisal Model for ESD in Higher Education Institutions*, Version 1.2. Hokkaido: AUA Secretariat, Hokkaido University.

Rist, Ray C. 2013. "Postscript – Evaluation and Turbulence: Beyond an Incremental View of the World." In *Evaluation and Turbulent Times: Reflections on a Discipline in Disarray*, edited by Jan-Eric Furubo, Ray C. Rist, and Sandra Speer. New Brunswick, NJ: Transaction Publishers. Pp. 255–262.

Roberts, J. Timmons; and Parks, Bradley C. 2007. *A Climate of Injustice: Global Inequality, North-South Politics, and Climate Policy.* Cambridge: MIT Press.

Salmi, Jamil; Hopper, Richard; and Bassett, Roberta M. 2009. "Transforming Higher Education in Developing Countries: The Role of the World Bank." In *International Organizations and Higher Education Policy: Thinking Globally, Acting Locally?* edited by Roberta M. Bassett and Alma Maldonado-Maldonado. London: Routledge. Pp. 99–112.

Samoff, Joel. 2009. "Foreign Aid to Education: Managing Global Transfers and Exchanges." In *South-South Cooperation in Education and Development*, edited by Linda Chisholm and Gita Steiner-Khamsi. New York: Teachers College Press. Pp. 123–156.

Samoff, Joel; and Assie-Lumumba, N'Dri T. 2003. "Analysis, Agendas and Priorities in African Education." In *Education, Society and Development: National and International Perspectives*, edited by Jandhyala B. G. Tilak. New Delhi: APH Publishing. Pp. 307–322.

Samoff, Joel; and Carrol, Bidemi. 2004. "The Promise of Partnership and Continuities of Dependence: External Support to Higher Education in Africa." *African Studies Review* 47 (1):67–199.

Schuller, Tom; and Desjardins, Richard. 2007. *Understanding the Social Outcomes of Learning.* Paris: Organization for Economic Co-Operation and Development (OECD).

Schuller, Tom; Hammond, Cathie; and Preston, John. 2004. "Reappraising Benefits." In *The Benefits of Learning: The Impact of Education on Health, Family Life and Social Capital*, edited by Tom Schuller, John Preston, Cathie Hammond, Angela Brassett-Grundy, and John Bynner. London: RoutledgeFalmer. Pp. 179–193.

Sharma, Yojana. 2012. "New Global Universities Partnership on the Environment Launched." *University World News* 226 (16 June).

Simon, Dagmar; and Knie, Andreas. 2013. "Can Evaluation Contribute to the Organizational Development of Academic Institutions? An International Comparison." *Evaluation* 19 (4):402–418.

Singh, Mala. 2007. "Universities and Society: Whose Terms of Engagement?" In *Knowledge Society vs. Knowledge Economy: Knowledge, Power, and Politics*, edited by Sverker Sörlin and Hebe Vessuri. Hampshire: Palgrave Macmillan. Pp. 53–78.

Smith, Harvey. 2000. "Transforming Education through Donor-Funded Projects: How Do We Measure Success?" In *Globalisation, Educational Transformation and Societies in Transition*, edited by Teame Mebrahtu, Michael Crossley, and David Johnson. Oxford: Symposium Books. Pp. 207–218.

Sörlin, Sverker; and Vessuri, Hebe. 2007. "Introduction: The Democratic Deficit of Knowledge Economies." In *Knowledge Society vs. Knowledge Economy: Knowledge, Power, and Politics*, edited by Sverker Sörlin and Hebe Vessuri. Hampshire: Palgrave Macmillan. Pp. 1–33.

Srivastava, Prachi; and Oh, Su-Ann. 2010. "Private Foundations, Philanthropy, and Partnership in Education and Development: Mapping the Terrain." *International Journal of Educational Development* 30 (5):460–471.

Stephens, David. 2009. "Introduction and Overview: Twenty-Five Years of Higher Education and International Capacity-Building Partnerships." In *Higher Education and International Capacity Building: Twenty-Five Years of Higher Education Links*, edited by David Stephens. Oxford: Symposium Books. Pp. 15–31.

Sterling, Stephen. 2013. "The Sustainable University: Challenge and Response." In *The Sustainable University: Progress and Prospects*, edited by Stephen Sterling, Larch Maxey, and Heather Luna. London: Routledge. Pp. 17–50.

Stern, Elliot. 2004. "Evaluating Partnerships." In *Evaluation & Development: The Partnership Dimension*, edited by Andres Liebenthal, Osvaldo N. Feinstein, and Gregory K. Ingram. New Brunswick, NJ: Transaction Publishers. Pp. 29–41.

Stone, Diane. 2004. "Research Partnerships and Their Evaluation." In *Evaluation & Development: The Partnership Dimension*, edited by Andres Liebenthal, Osvaldo N. Feinstein, and Gregory K. Ingram. New Brunswick, NJ: Transaction Publishers. Pp. 149–160.

Stromquist, Nelly P. 2013. "Higher Education and the Search for Excellence in US Universities." In *The Reorientation of Higher Education: Challenging the East-West Dichotomy*, edited by Bob Adamson, Jon Nixon, and Feng Su. Hong Kong: Comparative Education Research Centre, The University of Hong Kong. Pp. 165–183.

Sutton, Susan B.; Egginton, Everett; and Favela, Raul. 2012. "Collaborating on the Future: Strategic Partnerships and Linkages." In *The Sage Handbook of International Higher Education*, edited by Darla K. Deardorff, Hans de Wit, John Heyl, and Tony Adams. Los Angeles, CA: Sage. Pp. 147–166.

Syed, Shamsuzzoha B.; Dadwal, Viva; Rutter, Paul; Storr, Julie; Hightower, Joyce D.; Gooden, Rachel; Carlet, Jean; Nejad, Sepideh B.; Kelley, Edward T.; Donaldson, Liam; and Pittet, Didier. 2012. "Developed-Developing Country Partnerships: Benefits to Developed Countries?" *Globalization and Health* 8 (17). DOI: 10.1186/1744-8603-8-17

Tanaka, Aurea; Shimura, Ayako; Dirksen, Anna; and Tabucanon, Mario (editors). 2013. *ProSPER.Net: Developing a New Generation of Leaders 2008–2013*. Yokohama: United Nations University, Institute of Advanced Studies.

Tandon, Rajesh. 2008. "Civil Engagement in Higher Education and Its Role in Human and Social Development." In *Higher Education in the World 3: New Challenges and Emerging Roles for Human and Social Development*. GUNI Series on the Social Commitment of Universities 3. London: Palgrave Macmillan. Pp. 142–152.

Tate, Sean A.; Dwatmadji; Ali, Mohammad R.; and Kusuma, Wardhani. 2014. *Evaluation of the Indonesia University Partnership Program: Phase Four – Partnerships 9-11*. Final Report. Washington, DC: United States Agency for International Development.

Taylor, Peter. 2008. "Introduction." In *Higher Education in the World 3: New Challenges and Emerging Roles for Human and Social Development*. GUNI Series on the Social Commitment of Universities 3. London: Palgrave Macmillan. Pp. xxiv–xxvii.

Thomas, Vinod; and Tominaga, Jiro. 2013. "Development Evaluation in an Age of Turbulence." In *Evaluation and Turbulent Times: Reflections on a Discipline in Disarray*, edited by Jan-Eric Furubo, Ray C. Rist, and Sandra Speer. New Brunswick, NJ: Transaction Publishers. Pp. 57–70.

Thorp, Holden; and Goldstein, Buck. 2010. "How to Create a Problem-Solving Institution (and Avoid Organizational Silos)." *Chronicle of Higher Education*, 3 September, pp. A43–A44.

Tikly, Leon. 2011. "Towards a Framework for Researching the Quality of Education in Low-Income Countries." *Comparative Education* 47, No. 1 (February):1–23.

Togo, Muchaiteyi. 2015. "Development, Use and Significance of the Unit-Based Sustainability Assessment Tool for Universities in Africa and Asia." In *Mainstreaming Environment and Sustainability in African Universities: Stories of Change*, edited by Heila Lotz-Sisitka, Gitile Naituli, Amanda Hlengwa, Mike Ward, Ayobami Salami, Akpezi Ogbuigwe, Mahesh Pradhan, Marie Neeser, and Sanne Lauriks. Grahamstown: Rhodes University Environmental Learning Research Centre. Pp. 34–64.

Togo, Muchaiteyi; and Lotz-Sisitka, Heila. 2013. "The Unit-Based Sustainability Assessment Tool and Its Use in the UNEP Mainstreaming Environment and Sustainability in African Universities Partnership." In *Sustainability Assessment Tools in Higher Education Institutions: Mapping Trends and Good Practices around the World*, edited by Sandra Caeiro, Walter L. Filho, Charbel Jabbour, and Ulisses M. Azeiteiro. Cham, Switzerland: Springer International Publishing. Pp. 259–288.

van Baren, Ben; and Alemayehu Assefa. 2013. *Final Evaluation of the IUC Partner Programme with Mekelle University, Ethiopia*. Brussels: VLIR-UOS.

Vander Weyden, Patrick; and Livni, Leah. 2014. *Final Evaluation of the Institutional University Cooperation with the University of the Western Cape (UWC), South Africa*. Brussels: VLIR-UOS.

Van de Water, Jack; Green, Madeline F.; and Koch, Kimberly. 2008. *International Partnerships: Guidelines for Colleges and Universities*. Washington, DC: American Council on Education.

Vessuri, Hebe. 2007. "The Hybridization of Knowledge: Science and Local Knowledge in Support of Sustainable Development." In *Knowledge Society vs. Knowledge Economy: Knowledge, Power, and Politics*, edited by Sverker Sörlin and Hebe Vessuri. Hampshire: Palgrave Macmillan. Pp. 158–173.

Walker, Melanie; McLean, Monica; Dison, Arona; and Peppin-Vaughn, Rosie. 2009. "South African Universities and Human Development: Towards a Theorisation and Operationalisation of Professional Capabilities for Poverty Reduction." *International Journal of Educational Development* 29:565–572.

Wals, Arjen E. J.; and Blewitt, John. 2010. "Third-Wave Sustainability in Higher Education: Some (Inter)national Trends and Developments." In *Sustainability Education: Perspectives and Practice across Higher Education*, edited by Paula Jones, David Selby, and Stephen Sterling. London: Earthscan. Pp. 55–74.

Walsh, Lorraine; and Kahn, Peter. 2010. *Collaborative Working in Higher Education: The Social Academy.* New York: Routledge.

Wanni, Nada; Hinz, Sarah; and Day, Rebecca. 2010. *Good Practices in Educational Partnerships Guide: UK-Africa Higher & Further Education Partnerships.* London: ACU, Africa Unit.

Whitaker, Beth E. 2004. *U.S.-South African Research and Training Collaborations.* New York: Social Science Research Council.

Wright, Tarah S. A. 2002. "Definitions and Frameworks for Environmental Sustainability in Higher Education." *Higher Education Policy* 12 (2):105–120.

Yarime, Masaru; and Tanaka, Yuko. 2012. "The Issues and Methodologies in Sustainability Assessment Tools for Higher Education Institutions: A Review of Recent Trends and Future Challenges." *Journal of Education for Sustainable Development* 6 (1):63–77.

Yusuf, Shahid; Saint, William; and Nabeshima, Kaoru. 2009. *Accelerating Catch-Up: Tertiary Education for Growth in Sub-Saharan Africa.* Washington, DC: The World Bank.

10

ENHANCING *AGENDA 2030*– EVALUATION CAPACITY AT NORTHERN AND SOUTHERN UNIVERSITIES

We have seen that transnational-sustainable-development (TSD) evaluations are complex undertakings. Currently, most Northern and Southern universities are hard-pressed to conduct rudimentary output-focused exercises. The rigorous outcome- and impact-oriented curricular, research, outreach, and partnership evaluations called for in *Universities and the Sustainable Development Future* require urgent attention to enhanced higher-education-evaluation capacity. Given that our framework incorporates external participation in sustainable-development evaluation, we also treat stakeholder and independent professional capacity in Chapter 10.

Internal and independent capacity for contemporary TSD evaluation merits special attention in light of personpower shortages and weak evaluation systems. This chapter is devoted to ways to enhance the evaluation capabilities of key staff at local institutions of higher learning who are not in a position to carry out meaningful evaluation "selfies" and to addressing the need to improve university monitoring and evaluation systems. Strong and reliable evaluation capacity is crucial in order for universities to be positioned to demonstrate institutional, behavioral, and societal TSD outcomes and impacts.

Developing *Agenda 2030*-evaluation capacity at institutions of higher learning and among external evaluators typically involves several interrelated and interdependent dimensions. Evaluators will be expected to demonstrate sensitivity to symmetrical and asymmetrical, positive and negative, outcomes and impacts (unanticipated, indirect, and discontinuous as well as intended and direct); to take into consideration multiple and diverse perspectives; to be adept at multiple methodologies; to be able to deal with context complexity, public-policy impacts, and links to bigger pictures; and to be skilled at dealing with complexity and non-linearity. Skills needed to apply innovative methodologies and to estimate counterfactuals will be at a premium. Training in theory-of-change approaches, participatory evaluation, stakeholder identification and involvement, and stream-lined responding to funder requests also is likely to be especially helpful.

Evaluating evaluation capacity

Before university TSD-evaluation structures and processes can be improved, it is necessary to identify institutional and human strengths and weaknesses. In line with the themes of this book, capacity and capability evaluations would encompass curricula, research, outreach, and partnering. The goal is for contextually derived findings from systematic-capacity evaluation to drive enhanced analyses and evaluations of intervention outcomes and impacts.

Given the demanding nature of the comprehensive-evaluation framework for evaluating higher-education sustainable-development activity proposed in *Universities and the Sustainable Development Future*, we expect that shortcomings in existing evaluation systems, personnel, and approaches will be encountered. Identification of shortcomings provides an essential step forward toward addressing deficiencies.

In spite of their considerable experience with sustainable development, development-agency evaluations continue to suffer from capacity and capability weaknesses. A systematic review of impact-evaluation reports in ten sub-Saharan African countries attributed the fact that the overwhelming positive assessments of agricultural-extension impacts are out of sync with lagging growth in agricultural productivity in the region to insufficient field capacity "to conduct rigorous impact evaluations" (Hailemichael, 2013, pp. 38–39; also see Kruse, 2005, p. 113) – due in part to the serious shortage of qualified personpower to evaluate in general and to carry out "impact evaluation in particular." In addition, impact evaluations are underfunded; there is "poor capacity to collect and store quality data"; and impact evaluators rush to finish their studies by using small samples within short periods of time conducted by less competent professionals (Hailemichael, 2013, pp. 42–43).

Based on international-development-agency experience, we will recommend that universities in the North and South consider certain critical system features in order to maximize the value of their capacity and capability assessments. Each feature should be evaluated from a sustainable-development-capacity perspective separately for curriculum, research, outreach, and partnering and, then, integrated into an institution-wide assessment.

Not all evaluation capacities are the same

When one considers evaluation capacity, it often is assumed that we are concerned with the technical capabilities of conducting an evaluation with sound and credible methodologies. Although technical considerations are important, they fail to provide the full picture. The first International Conference on National Evaluation Capacities sponsored by the United Nations Development Programme (UNDP) with the Government of the Kingdom of Morocco clearly distinguished capacities for managing, conducting, and using evaluations (UNDP, 2011b). Managing an evaluation requires a broad understanding of evaluation without necessitating the specific skills needed to conduct it. Conducting an evaluation requires specific skills in carrying out the study and in disseminating its findings. Using an evaluation again calls for separate skill sets given that the users usually are decision makers and sometimes policy makers (UNDP, 2011, pp. 9–10).

Consequently, TSD-evaluation capacity must be "unbundled" (Feinstein, 2011). Not everyone involved in evaluating university initiatives needs the same skill sets or technical capacities. It is particularly important to recognize the differences between the capacities needed for managing and conducting evaluations as there is not complete overlap between the two (Feinstein, 2011, p. 130). University managers basically need the capacity to act as competent contractors without needing to possess the ability to conduct evaluations. On the other hand, persons who conduct evaluations also must be competent in disseminating and communicating their findings to evaluation users and other stakeholders. As for evaluation users, they must be aware of the benefits of conducting an evaluation as an available tool for improved decision making regarding university policies, programs, and projects.

Critical features for university sustainable-development evaluation capacity

The utility of university-evaluation contributions rests on both demand and supply of evaluation and depends upon the capacities to manage, conduct, and use evaluations. These crucial attributes all require both internal and external capacity.

Internal

The internal capacity to initiate evaluations of university sustainable-development curricular, research, outreach, and partnering undertakings starts with understanding the value added by evaluation. This capacity can be unbundled into various components, the first of which relates to evaluation demand. Internal university decision makers must be able to create demand for evaluative knowledge and to indicate how it can be used to improve planning, programming, and performance.

Once university decision makers have created such demand, it needs to be used to shape perspectives on what to evaluate. Evaluations should not be initiated and conducted for their own sake or as pro-forma requirements. As evaluations come with costs, as well as benefits, in terms of staff, time, and monetary resources, it is important to determine where the benefits from evaluative knowledge are needed and where evaluations can answer critical questions about program performance, management effectiveness, lessons learned, and so forth. Utility is one of the general norms for evaluation in the international arena. "In commissioning and conducting an evaluation," according to the United Nations Evaluation Group (UNEG), "there should be a clear intention to use the resulting analysis, conclusions or recommendations to inform decisions and actions" (UNEG, 2016, norm 2, p. 10). Furthermore, "evaluations should be designed to ensure that they provide timely, valid and reliable information that will be relevant to the subject being assessed and should clearly identify the underlying intentionality" (UNEG, 2016, standard 4.1, p. 21).

The relevance, timeliness, and quality of the TSD evaluation obviously affect its use, but capacity gaps can still be there as a hindrance. There is a further "need to develop human capabilities to use evaluations, to distill their findings and lessons learned, and the political will to ensure effective evaluation use" (UNDP, 2012, p. 13). Thus, the next step is to ensure that there is capacity to commission and manage evaluations as well as to receive findings and recommendations. This capacity encompasses human and financial resources along with institutional support. For university staff, it is important to have the ability to define the scope of the evaluation and to write the terms of reference (TOR). The scope of the evaluation and how it will be conducted (e.g., methodology; internal vs. external evaluators; stakeholder involvement; etc.) will determine the budget. Although they need not possess capabilities to conduct the TSD evaluation or apply all the methodologies, university participants also should be able to make informed judgments regarding alternative-evaluation approaches and methodologies, stakeholder participation, the quality of the evaluation process, and the final report. Kathryn Newcomer and colleagues (2013, p. 77) contend that "guidance on how to analyse performance data in order to make connections to improve both program management and . . . planning and redesign should be given high priority in capacity building training."

Internal capacity to conduct actual TSD evaluations depends on a number of factors, such as the purpose, the type, and the scope of the evaluation. A large variety of both quantitative- and qualitative-data-collection and analysis tools might or might not be needed for a particular university sustainable-development evaluation, including remote sensing, geographical-information-system, social-network analysis, risk analysis, and time-series-data analysis. Although the whole range is likely not to be required for any specific evaluation, ideally multiple-methods capabilities should be available and employable for those conducting the evaluation (see Chapter 5). It is important to select the methods to be used based on the evaluation questions and not vice versa. Too often, familiarity with certain methods is allowed to determine which to use irrespective of their suitability to answering core questions. This decision point is where both the evaluation managers and the conductors need the ability to make informed choices about methodology. Another critical determinant involves the type of evaluation (e.g., curricular, research, outreach, partnering). Process, outcome, and impact evaluations also require different approaches, methodologies, and data.[1]

Another internal dimension pertains to student evaluations. While implementing sustainable-development-research projects, students should be prepared to "assess impact on a small scale" and to envision "next steps towards scaling the solution to the societal level" (Rowe and Hiser, 2016, p. 327). Training in this area also would enhance student understanding of the goals and processes of TSD evaluation and their ability to conduct systematic evaluations. A prerequisite for realizing these learning objectives is the active involvement of faculty who themselves possess the requisite capabilities and training and mentoring abilities.

Additional challenges are likely to be faced when moving up the scale from individual initiatives or unit interventions. Specifically, cross-campus coordination can be challenging in large-scale TSD evaluations involving multiple transdisciplinary partners. Comprehensive curricular, research, and public-engagement evaluations seek to provide an overview of the achievements and performance of a program, fund, institution, or organization (see van den Berg, 2012).[2] They can become contested. It is important, therefore, that all participants in a particular evaluation effort have the same understanding of the need for the evaluation, its purpose, key questions asked, approach, and methodology.

It is obvious from the above that multiple internal-evaluation capabilities need to be placed in order for the kind of comprehensive, principle-based, TSD-evaluation framework and practical guidelines called for in *Universities and the Sustainable Development Future* to play a transforming role in a university. While it is far from clear that these capabilities are present in most Northern universities, resource shortcomings are likely to require special attention to and additional support for capacity-development efforts at Southern universities (e.g., Newcomer, El Baradei, and Garcia, 2013, p. 63).

External

The external dimensions of TSD-evaluation capacity arise, in part, from how universities and their sustainable-development initiatives interact with audiences and partners outside their own institutional realm or "campus." Chapter 8 is devoted to university-outreach efforts focused on transnational sustainable development. Stakeholders include community members in areas where university sustainable-development programs operate – both the intended beneficiaries of such programs and people otherwise affected because of their physical location or their position in society. Although stakeholder skills form an important aspect of capacity to conduct an external TSD evaluation, they can by no means be taken as given. In terms of building this dimension of external-evaluation capacity, there are questions to be asked about stakeholder facilitation and involvement. Did faculty members (or other program proponents) enhance fruitful stakeholder engagement in the evaluation process?

It is important, therefore, that university-outreach programs incorporate the development by program participants (and even non-participants who may be affected by the intervention) of capabilities to evaluate how the TSD intervention is affecting their lives and wellbeing. Positive and negative unintended or unanticipated consequences plausibility connected to the university's initiatives must be included in stakeholder-TSD evaluations. In this regard, building community participatory monitoring and evaluation (M&E) capabilities is particularly valuable. In the words of proponents of the practice in China, the integration of participatory M&E has "strengthened the learning, accountability, and effectiveness of the research efforts . . . in particular through the realization that what matters is not only *what* is assessed, but *who* does the measuring and assessing" (Vernooy, Sun, and Xu, 2003, p. 3, emphasis in original).

Different challenges regarding external-evaluation capacity can arise when multiple partners are involved. For instance, evaluations of THEPs involving universities in the North and South are further complicated when they involve non-university partners or donors that fund the collaborative TSD initiative – such as multilateral or bilateral aid agencies, foundations, or NGOs. Coordination among a multiplicity of donors, partners, and stakeholders with diverse evaluation mandates and evaluation capacities requires special efforts (see, for instance, Porter and Goldman, 2013, p. 14; Newcomer, El Baradei, and Garcia, 2013, p. 74).[3]

Donors often also employ independent-evaluation systems either by hiring private consulting firms or using their own internal-independent-evaluation units, where such exist, that look for evidence of results – particularly with regard to THEP sustainable-development initiatives. Such independent evaluations typically focus on accountability for the proper use of funds and the effectiveness of the intervention rather than on participatory evaluation that emphasizes downward accountability to the intended beneficiaries and affected people. Many evaluators working for consulting firms and in independent-evaluation units have been trained in conducting accountability-focused evaluations and may not be well-versed in more participatory, learning-oriented evaluations. Consequently, they would benefit from being exposed to these approaches. Similarly, the commissioners and users of Northern independent evaluations should understand that accountability, effectiveness, and efficiency must be seen in the context of whether the partnerships lead to desired behavioral change rather than only attempting to analyze how much was produced per dollar invested. By the same token, focusing attribution narrowly on the inputs of a single donor risks missing the point when one evaluates THEPs in which change is produced, by definition, by the combined actions of several actors. In terms of capacity for use, commissioning/management, and conduct of evaluation, such situations call for coordination and harmonization of expectations from a diverse range of external and internal evaluations.

Enhancing evaluation capacity

In sum, universities require strengthened and streamlined capabilities to demand, use, design, commission, manage, conduct, and communicate evaluations. They also need capacity to "address multiple funders' reporting requirements, involve stakeholders in a meaningful and valuable manner, develop capabilities of staff within the providers to collect data, assess the quality of data, analyse data and use the data internally to improve service and enhance learning" (Newcomer, El Baradei, and Garcia, 2013, p. 73). Drawing on experience with international-development evaluation and insights derived from the prior chapters of this book, the next sections of this chapter set forth specific recommendations for improving internal and external university TSD-evaluation capacity.

Intra-institutional capacity

In terms of evaluations of university contributions to TSD, the foundational task is to build a culture supportive of evaluation. This capability-developing undertaking first involves creating understanding among university authorities of the utility of evaluative evidence and, consequently, the importance of demand for it. Second, there is distinct need to ensure the existence of capabilities to commission and manage evaluations that respond effectively to the demand – i.e., evaluations that are relevant, intentional, timely, and of high quality. The evaluation commissioners and managers must possess the capabilities to scope the evaluations in a realistic manner and to judge their quality.

Evaluation questions with regard to capacity to demand, use, commission, and manage evaluations should include:

- Does the university have the capacity to demand and use evaluation that is strategic from the point of view of utility, intentionality, and timeliness?
- Does the university have the capacity realistically to scope an evaluation and to write its terms of reference?
- Are adequate funds available for commissioning an independent evaluation of adequate scope and quality?
- Does the university have the capacity to judge the validity of the evaluation findings based on the approach and methodology used?
- Are institutional channels in place to ensure that evaluation findings and recommendations are communicated and disseminated in an effective manner to decision makers, partners, donors, and stakeholders?

Should the answer to any of these questions be negative, an institutional-capacity-development need is identified. For similar purposes, the same questions should be addressed in the context of the capabilities present in each TSD-involved university unit participating in the curriculum, research, and/or outreach evaluation.

The needed capacities to conduct intra-institutional TSD evaluations will vary and depend on the specific situations and types of evaluations. However, they start with ensuring that the intervention design is evaluable and that the monitoring process can be linked with the evaluation plan. To link design with evaluation and monitoring means that program or project proponents be trained upfront to identify success factors for their intervention and how to measure them. Success factors include indicators for monitoring progress. However, indicators are not sufficient for evaluation. Given that the purpose of evaluation is not only to measure achievement of milestones but to provide explanations for success or failure, to identify what works, for whom, under what circumstances and why, and to be alert for unintended or unanticipated consequences, it is fundamentally important that internal evaluators be able to articulate program theories that will provide a basis against which meaningful process (Brundiers, et al., 2014, p. 203), outcome, and impact evaluations can be conducted.

Early training in data processing and analytic support (Poister, Aristigueta, and Hall, 2015, p. 420) will be needed in certain situations. Evaluation-capacity needs are expanded when we move from evaluating the outcomes of individual programs or projects to evaluating the catalytic impact of interventions on broader adoption and behavioral change in the long-term interest of sustainable development (Uitto, 2016b, p. 109). Evaluating transformational change requires a more holistic way of looking at the context in which the intervention takes place. Understanding outcome to impact pathways in complex systems can be facilitated by theory-based approaches that identify the assumptions and risks that will affect how interventions lead to lasting change (GEF, 2009). In international-development evaluation, there is a growing understanding that evaluations must start by identifying the broader system in which the intervention takes place, what the system boundaries are, the components, and the emergent properties (Garcia and Zazueta, 2015). Training in these areas will enhance university TSD evaluations as well.

Furthermore, sustainable-development evaluation places a premium on evaluating the (intergenerational) nexus between environment and human wellbeing (Uitto, 2016a). This can be challenging because of the differing time horizons and spatial scales of natural and human phenomena as well as possible discrepancies in the goals and orientations of various actors (for instance, conservationists and developers). Further complexity is added by climate change, which increases risk and uncertainty. To counter complexity challenges, Andy Rowe (2012) proposes a two-system evaluand that would explicitly take into account the differences in time and space between natural and human systems and potentially different values among stakeholder groups (say, those wishing to exploit and those wishing to conserve natural resources). Exploring these and other transboundary interlinkages requires diverse expertise (Thomas and Tominaga, 2013, p. 66) and training in multi-source analysis and collaboration.

To respond to such challenges, evaluators must first understand how systems (both natural and human) work and how they change. For university evaluators, this may be easier than for many others as they can draw upon institutionally available and partnership-based scientific knowledge. Still, it is important that they are guided to be cognizant of this factor when they design and conduct evaluations.

As established earlier in this chapter, facilitation of stakeholder participation is particularly important in sustainable-development evaluations (Strele, 2012, p. 188). The capacity-building question to ask is: did the project leaders train stakeholders in collaborative and participatory evaluation practices and, if not, why not?

The ability to utilize evaluation results is critically important (Brundiers, et al., 2014, p. 203). First of all, institutional structures need to be put in place to ensure that evaluation findings and recommendations reach the intended users. Too many evaluation reports gather dust in archives and on bookshelves without having made a contribution to change. However, even if reports reach their target audiences, it is not a given that they will be understood and acted upon. There is a need to provide time and training on how to interpret and utilize (performance) evaluation data (Newcomer, El Baradei, and Garcia, 2013, p. 74). Frequently, there also is a need to work on how to counter inertia and resistance to change so that participants in TSD initiatives understand how evaluations provide opportunities to improve the performance and impact of the evaluand (i.e., the object of the evaluation, be it a program, project, policy, or organization).

Evaluation commissioners, managers, and users also benefit from the ability to monitor and evaluate the evaluation process (Stevens, 2012, p. 62) to ensure its validity and reliability. Training in meta-evaluation – that is, how to conduct "an evaluation of an evaluation, as a critical assessment of the strengths and weaknesses of an evaluation" (Ramos and Pires, 2013, p. 87) – can be quite useful in this connection.

Stakeholder training

Lack of skills is one of the principal constraints on community involvement in participatory M&E. Okechukwu Ukaga and Chris Maser (2004, pp. 124–125) have identified several ways of addressing the lack of capacity in communities to engage in participatory M&E: (1) letting the more skilled persons in the group coordinate the process and coach others; (2) rotating responsibilities as a way of drawing on a wider range of abilities; (3) using people who may not be highly skilled but who have the interest and ability to learn; (4) providing specialized training to participants in relevant areas, such as facilitation, data analysis, and documentation to enhance their abilities and confidence; and (5) using information in books to build skills within a community, project, or organization.

At times, it will be useful to address the need to provide additional capacity for technical and scientific learning (Cashmore, 2007, p. 111). Following the principle of learning by doing, engaging in the practice of participatory evaluation offers "an indirect approach to evaluation capacity building" (Chouinard and Cousins, 2013, pp. 67, 72–73).

Enhancing the capabilities of external evaluators

Not all of those who design and conduct external evaluations have had sufficient education or field experience. Moreover, university interventions differ from the kinds of initiatives that international-development evaluators are accustomed to. Therefore, attention also is needed to external-evaluator training. In particular, evaluators working in the university TSD domain should have the ability to understand local conditions and to link them to the bigger context. They should be competent in dealing with complexity and non-linearity where traditional causal models may not apply. Consequently, they must have a good understanding and be able to apply theory-of-change approaches and risk analysis to university curricular, research, and outreach evaluations.

External THEP evaluators need sensitivity to symmetrical and asymmetrical situations and related outputs, outcomes, and impacts (intended and unintended) – particularly in situations where the power relations among partners and stakeholders are less than equal. This requires openness to multiple perspectives. Power-relation issues often arise in evaluations pertaining to higher-education partnerships between universities in the North and South. Transnational-competence education can be particularly helpful in developing THEP-evaluation capabilities.

Additional capacity-development initiatives for external TSD evaluators can be determined depending on situational needs and contextual interventions. Training in qualitative comparative analysis (QCA) and other technical fields can be called for in certain circumstances. Various types of meta-analysis also belong in the evaluators' toolkit. These techniques are useful when existing evaluations or related research products already exist and can be analyzed to glean information and lessons to improve program design and performance. Scientific approaches that can be utilized include, for instance, realist synthesis (Pawson, et al., 2004) and systematic reviews (Duvendack, et al., 2012; Mallett, et al., 2012). As these methods have clearly established procedures, their application will require training.

External evaluators also should also be adept at multiple methodologies so that they will be able to select and apply the approaches and methods that are most suitable for the evaluation questions that require answering. Situations where the available methodologies dictate the evaluation approach must be avoided.

Concluding observations

In this chapter, we have made a case for enhanced evaluation capabilities across the board for university sustainable development evaluations; our recommendations range from generating demand for evaluation, to commissioning and managing evaluations, to evaluation use. Institutionally, it is crucial that universities ensure a culture supportive of professional TSD evaluation. Capacity building should be attended to consistently from the initial-design effort on and should include progress markers. Most universities will opt to commission and conduct selective studies that provide a credible attribution/contribution story supported by case evidence regarding performance.

The target groups for TSD-evaluation-capacity development include both internal (university administrators and faculty) and external (evaluators, stakeholders) participants. Intra-university capability strengthening should encourage participants to remain cognizant of unit and disciplinary identity while evaluating university-wide transformation (Simon and Knie, 2013, p. 416).

The goal of capacity development is to perceive and treat TSD evaluation as a way to increase understanding of performance issues and direct changes toward enhanced outcomes and impacts rather than as a compliance response to critical reviews. Ultimately, universities should strive to implement Hailemichael's (2013, p. 43) recommendation, based on agricultural-development-impact evaluations, to shift from "proving impact" to "improving impact." Developing proactive-evaluation capabilities primarily would be concerned with "how to improve practice and develop internal learning systems, with a focus on qualitative data and use of participative tools" (Hailemichael, 2013, p. 43).

With regard to higher-education-TSD interventions, especially in the case of North-South university partnerships, there is a clear need to enrich capacity for ongoing institutional and stakeholder learning about ways to engage in civic deliberations and to conduct fruitful sustainable-development evaluations (Gibson, 2005, p. 155). This outcome depends, in part, on expanded donor-community investments in building sound higher-education evaluation capacity and in results dissemination (also see Jones, Bailey, and Lyytikäinen, 2007, pp. 24–25; Newcomer, El Baradei, and Garcia, 2013, pp. 74–75). Unfortunately, evaluation-capacity development has rarely been a priority in development cooperation, although there are positive indications that it is gaining prominence (see, e.g., LaRovere and Soares, 2014). In this chapter, we have shown why it is important that internal and external commitment to enhancing TSD-evaluation capacity be extended to universities and their evaluation-process partners in the North and South.

Notes

1 To encourage university-wide-capacity improvements, including staff capabilities in performance measurement and analysis, completion of each unit's needs-assessment process could be employed as a criteria for determining eligibility for new or renewed support (Newcomer, El Baradei, and Garcia, 2013, p. 75).
2 On the international-development scene, the relatively few comprehensive evaluations conducted thus far have tended to be expensive, prolonged, and complex. Most often, they were linked to a reform or a replenishment process of an organization or fund (van den Berg, 2012).
3 Donor-evaluation mandates frequently emphasize accountability toward the funders or tax payers.

Works cited

Berg, Rob D. van den. 2012. "Comprehensive Evaluations of International Institutions: A First Synthesis." Paper presented at the European Evaluation Society Biennial Conference, Helsinki.

Brundiers, Katja; Savage, Emma; Mannell, Steven; Lang, Daniel J.; and Wiek, Arnim. 2014. "Educating Sustainability Change Agents by Design: Appraisals of the Transformative Role of Higher Education." In *Sustainable Development and Quality Assurance in Higher Education: Transformation of Learning and Society*, edited by Zinaida Fadeeva, Laima Galkute, Clemens Mader, and Geoff Scott. New York: Palgrave Macmillan. Pp. 196–229.

Cashmore, Matthew. 2007. "The Contribution of Environmental Assessment to Sustainable Development: Toward a Richer Conceptual Understanding." In *Impact Assessment and Sustainable Development: European Practice and Experience*, edited by Clive George and Colin Kirkpatrick. Cheltenham, UK: Edward Elgar. Pp. 106–126.

Chouinard, Jill A.; and Cousins, J. Bradley. 2013. "Participatory Evaluation for Development: Examining Research-Based Knowledge from within the African Context." *African Evaluation Journal* 1 (1):66–74.

Duvendack, Maren; Garcia Hombrados, Jorge; Palmer-Jones, Richard; and Waddington, Hugh. 2012. "Assessing 'What Works' in International Development: Meta-Analysis for Sophisticated Dummies." *Journal of Development Effectiveness* 4 (3):456–471.

Feinstein, Osvaldo. 2011. "National Evaluation Capacity: Lessons Learned and a Conceptual Scheme." In *National Evaluation Capacities 2009.* Proceedings from the International Conference on National Evaluation Capacities, Casablanca, Kingdom of Morocco, 15–17 December 2009. New York: UNDP Evaluation Office. Pp. 130–135.

Garcia, Jeneen R.; and Zazueta, Aaron. 2015. "Going beyond Mixed Methods to Mixed Approaches: A Systems Perspective for Asking the Right Questions." *IDS Bulletin* 45 (1):30–43.

Gibson, Robert B. 2005. *Sustainability Assessment: Criteria and Processes.* London: Earthscan.

Global Environmental Facility (GEF). 2009. *The ROtI Handbook: Towards Enhancing the Impacts of Environmental Projects.* The Fourth Overall Performance Study of the GEF, Methodological Paper #2. Washington, DC: Global Environment Facility Evaluation Office.

Hailemichael Taye. 2013. "Evaluating the Impact of Agricultural Extension Programmes in Sub-Saharan Africa: Challenges and Prospects." *African Evaluation Journal* 1 (1):38–45.

Jones, Nicola; Bailey, Mark; and Lyytikäinen, Minna. 2007. *Research Capacity Strengthening in Africa: Trends, Gaps and Opportunities.* London: Overseas Development Institute.

Kruse, Stein-Erik. 2005. "Meta-evaluations of NGO Experience: Results and Challenges." In *Evaluating Development Effectiveness*, edited by George K. Pitman, Osvaldo N. Feinstein, and Gregory K. Ingram. World Bank Series on Evaluation and Development, Volume 7. New Brunswick, N.J.: Transaction Publishers. Pp. 109–127.

LaRovere, Roberto; and Soares, Ana R. 2014. "Evolution of UNDP's Approach to National Evaluation Capacity Development." *European Evaluation Society Connections*, July, p. 13.

Mallett, Richard; Hagen-Zanker, Jessica; Slater, Rachel; and Duvendack, Maren. 2012. "The Benefits and Challenges of Using Systematic Reviews in International Development Research." *Journal of Development Effectiveness* 4 (3):445–455.

Newcomer, Kathryn; El Baradei, Laila; and Garcia, Sandra. 2013. "Expectations and Capacity of Performance Measurement in NGOs in the Development Context." *Public Administration and Development* 33:62–79.

Pawson, Ray; Greenhalgh, Trisha; Harvey, Gill; and Walshe, Kieran. 2004. *Realist Synthesis: An Introduction.* RMP Methods Paper 2/2004. ESRC Research Methods Programme, Manchester, UK: University of Manchester.

Poister, Theodore H.; Aristigueta, Maria P.; and Hall, Jeremy L. 2015. *Managing and Measuring Performance in Public and Nonprofit Organizations: An Integrated Approach*, 2nd edition. San Francisco, CA: Jossey-Bass.

Porter, Stephen; and Goldman, Ian. 2013. "A Growing Demand for Monitoring and Evaluation in Africa." *African Evaluation Journal* 1 (1):10–18.

Ramos, Tomas; and Pires, Sara M. 2013. "Sustainability Assessment: The Role of Indicators." In *Sustainability Assessment Tools in Higher Education Institutions: Mapping Trends and Good Practices around the World*, edited by Sandra Caeiro, Walter L. Filho, Charbel Jabbour, and Ulisses M. Azeiteiro. Cham, Switzerland: Springer International Publishing. Pp. 81–99.

Rowe, Andy. 2012. "Evaluation of Natural Resource Interventions." *American Journal of Evaluation* 33 (3):382–392.

Rowe, Debra; and Hiser, Krista. 2016. "Higher Education for Sustainable Development in the Community and through Partnerships." In *Routledge Handbook of Higher Education for Sustainable Development*, edited by Matthias Barth, Gerd Michelsen, Marco Rieckmann, and Ian Thomas. London: Routledge. Pp. 315–330.

Simon, Dagmar; and Knie, Andreas. 2013. "Can Evaluation Contribute to the Organizational Development of Academic Institutions? An International Comparison." *Evaluation* 19 (4):402–418.

Stevens, Candice. 2012. "A Basic Roadmap for Sustainability Assessments: The SIMPLE Methodology." In *Sustainable Development, Evaluation and Policy-Making: Theory, Practise and Quality Assurance*, edited by Anneke von Raggamby and Frieder Rubik. Cheltenham, UK: Edward Elgar. Pp. 57–72.

Strele, Martin. 2012. "Participatory Livelihoods System Appraisal: A Learning-Oriented Methodology for Impact Assessment." In *Governance by Evaluation for Sustainable Development: Institutional Capacities and Learning*, edited by Michal Sedlacko and Andre Martinuzzi. Cheltenham, UK: Edward Elgar. Pp. 173–190.

Thomas, Vinod; and Tominaga, Jiro. 2013. "Development Evaluation in an Age of Turbulence." In *Evaluation and Turbulent Times: Reflections on a Discipline in Disarray*, edited by Jan-Eric Furubo, Ray C. Rist, and Sandra Speer. New Brunswick, NJ: Transaction Publishers. Pp. 57–70.

Uitto, Juha. 2016a. "The Environment-Poverty Nexus in Evaluation: Implications for the Sustainable Development Goals." *Global Policy* 7 (3):441–447.

Uitto, Juha I. 2016b. "Evaluating the Environment as a Global Public Good." *Evaluation* 22 (1):108–115.

Ukaga, Okechukwu; and Maser, Chris. 2004. *Evaluating Sustainable Development: Giving People a Voice in Their Destiny*. Sterling, VA: Stylus Publishing.

United Nations Development Programme (UNDP). 2011. "Main Outcomes of the International Conference on National Evaluation Capacities." In *National Evaluation Capacities 2009*. Proceedings from the International Conference on National Evaluation Capacities, Casablanca, Kingdom of Morocco, 15–17 December 2009. New York: UNDP Evaluation Office. Pp. 8–11.

United Nations Development Programme (UNDP). 2012. "Conceptual Note." In *National Evaluation Capacities 2011*. Proceedings from the Second International Conference on National Evaluation Capacities: Use of Evaluation in Decision Making for Public Policies and Programmes, Johannesburg, South Africa, 12–14 September 2011. New York: UNDP Evaluation Office. Pp. 2–21.

United Nations Evaluation Group (UNEG). 2016. *Norms and Standards for Evaluation*. New York: United Nations Evaluation Group.

Vernooy, Ronnie; Sun Qiu; and Xu Jiangchu (editors). 2003. *Voices for Change: Participatory Monitoring and Evaluation in China*. Kunming: Yunnan Science & Technology Press and International Development Research Centre.

PART IV

Sustainable development and enhanced university process, outcome, and impact evaluations

11

PRACTICAL GUIDELINES FOR UTILIZING THE SUSTAINABLE-DEVELOPMENT-EVALUATION FRAMEWORK

Part III provided a comprehensive framework for evaluating university sustainable-development initiatives. This chapter offers practical guidelines for applying the framework.

In real-world situations, evaluators (including university evaluators) often operate under severe time, budget, data, and political constraints that need to be dealt with in scoping, designing, and executing their studies (Bamberger, Rugh, and Mabry, 2012). It is important to avoid situations where so much of participants' time is "being devoted to performance measurement and reporting against targets to the detriment of time spent actually doing their job" (Eyben, 2013, p. 13; also Collins, 2014, p. 953; Powell, Molander, and Celebicic, 2012, p. 230). Further, as Peter Hopkinson and Peter James (2013, p. 250) discovered at Ecoversity, "progress towards sustainability is always likely to vary over time, with some periods of rapid progress, and others of stasis or even some backwards movement."

In this chapter, we recognize that universities will employ variable and tailored applications of any framework for sustainable-development evaluation. Although the ideal version elaborated in *Universities and the Sustainable Development Future* is unlikely to be fully utilized, we expect that its components will be applied by committed universities to a greater or lesser extent. To avoid haphazard applications, we will suggest here a core set of illustrative evaluation guidelines that can serve as a practical foundation with widespread utility in the North and South. However, before presenting core questions for university sustainable-development evaluations, we need to revisit critical process features. Meaningful evaluations depend in the first instance on getting multiple process components right (Gibson, 2005, p. 142).

Critical process features

Attention to process has been a recurring theme of *Universities and the Sustainable Development Future*. In the preceding chapters, we referred often to key evaluation-process considerations. The centrality of supportive and principled processes to the success of university sustainable-development evaluations requires that a set of best practices be followed across the board. Process cannot be compromised, and vital process guidelines cannot be treated as optional.

This section presents a critical, arguably essential and contextually universal (Gibson, 2005, p. 11), distillation of process guidelines for university sustainable-development evaluations. "We may debate how far to go with generic criteria and standard processes," Robert Gibson (2005, p. 12) maintains, "but . . . we have enough experience to consolidate into a useful basic package of overall guidance." Box 11.1 lists ten foundational process-guiding principles we have culled from best evaluation practices identified in prior chapters. These broadly defined process principles should be followed in all university sustainable-development evaluations, although some tweaking will be necessary in certain circumstances (Gibson, 2005, pp. 145, 182).[1]

It is important that university sustainable-development evaluations start off on a solid process footing. Interest in and support for evaluating at top university levels and throughout the hierarchy is a key ingredient. Teams of independent (external) as well as internal evaluators with diverse, transboundary[2] expertise (Thomas and Tominaga, 2013, p. 69) need to be assembled, engaged, and supplied

---

BOX 11.1 UNIVERSITY SUSTAINABLE-DEVELOPMENT EVALUATIONS: PROCESS PRINCIPLES

(1) Ensure top-level commitment and support
(2) Allocate sufficient resources to formative and summative, internal and external, evaluation practice
(3) Evaluation should encompass curricula, research, outreach, and partnerships and be linked to campus operations
(4) Move beyond outputs; incorporate process, outcome, and impact assessments
(5) Impact evaluation should encompass all three pillars of sustainable development, be contextually centered, and be near-term and long-term
(6) Utilize multiple methods and triangulate whenever possible; evaluation questions must drive the choice of appropriate methods rather than vice versa
(7) Engage stakeholders and partners in a near-symmetrical-evaluation process
(8) Implement lessons learned; promote organizational learning
(9) Ensure evaluation-process transparency and wide dissemination of findings (share results with all employees and stakeholders). Report findings in a timely and concise manner of strategic value to decision makers at all levels
(10) Identify and secure recognition for contextual and generic attainments and pursue external certification.

with material and staff resources that enable successful implementation of the practical evaluation plan.[3]

The framework for evaluation articulated in *Universities and the Sustainable Development Future* requires particular attention to curricula, research, outreach, and partnerships and encompasses connections with estate management. The suggested multi-level evaluation process builds from unit-focused to institution-wide to stakeholder and partner encompassing.

Evaluators are challenged to emphasize integrated outcome and impact assessments. Systematic-university evaluations progress from process to outcomes and, then, from local to transnational (glocal) impacts. The conduct of integrated evaluations addresses near-term and inter-generational ecological, economic, and social impacts; the process is contextually driven but cognizant of common criteria. The needed evaluation response to specific framework inquiries determines the research methods that evaluators use and the triangulation possibilities pursued.

All university-evaluation initiatives should aim to involve key stakeholders from the beginning in the evaluation process. Stakeholder involvement can take different forms at different stages of evaluation. It is, however, important to engage stakeholders in setting the evaluation questions and criteria in order to ensure that the evaluation addresses questions that are relevant and of use to the stakeholders. Similarly, the stakeholders should have an opportunity to review evaluation conclusions and recommendations before they are finalized so that what is suggested is realistic and implementable.

Strategic feedback, continuous learning, and transformational change are central features of meaningful higher-education approaches to evaluating sustainable-development activity. Transparency suffuses all stages of the evaluation process. As Thomas and Tominaga (2013, p. 66) point out, "consolidating evaluative findings from diverse perspectives into integrated recommendations is vital." Evaluation findings are disseminated internally, among stakeholders and partners, to other educators, and to the evaluation community. Shortcomings are identified; contextual and generic attainments become part of the university's reputation and are included in applications for external recognition and/or certification.[4]

Practical evaluation applications

The full evaluation of university contributions to sustainable development is attained by implementing the comprehensive framework based on extensive scholarship and international-development experience that we developed in Part III of *Universities and the Sustainable Development Future*. Of course, we would like to see all evaluations proceed in such an informed, detailed, and encompassing manner. Evaluations with ambitious objectives possess the highest potential for inspiring major changes (Gibson, 2005, p. 24). However, the downside to comprehensiveness and a vast list of evaluation questions is its time-consuming and expensive nature. In addition, the dissemination of abundant information, particularly if provided in complex formulations, can "overwhelm users" (Fredericks, 2014, p. 64).

Our objective in this section, therefore, is to encourage wide application of feasible evaluation guidelines among universities in the South and North. Focusing on a limited number of agreed upon pre-identified core criteria and adoption of a pre-analysis plan enables time-constrained evaluators to complete a meaningful assessment with modest resources and to avoid selective data mining.

At the same time, sustainable-development evaluators understand that context matters and that "uncertainty demands flexibility" (Gibson, 2005, pp. 11–12, 33). Therefore, "any useful guidance for future sustainability assessments must incorporate adaptive flexibility and respect the specifics of context" (Gibson, 2005, p. 11; also Razak, et al., 2013, p. 152). Our approach to practical university sustainable-development evaluations further embraces the humble position articulated by Robert Gibson in *Sustainability Assessment* (p. 93):

> The intent is not imposition of one grand agenda. Realistically, there is no serious prospect of one set of core criteria winning widespread adoption. Nor is any one set of criteria likely to be found satisfactory for long. As sustainability assessment practice expands and experience increases, any initial set of criteria will be found wanting. Revisions of approaches, categories and formulations will be needed again and again.

The contextual nature of university sustainable-development evaluations requires that project participants and stakeholders identify their most critical shared process, outcome, and impact objectives (Gibson, 2005, p. 84; Hummelbrunner, 2012, p. 255). To promote rough consistency in approach, internal and external evaluators choose and adapt relevant questions from those provided in the generic evaluation framework, identify issues for in-depth attention, and concentrate on progress or setbacks.[5] If the framework articulated in Part III provides the decision-making underpinning for common reference by university evaluators, applying contextually based core questions will facilitate a series of partial cross-context parameter comparisons (Razak, et al., 2013, p. 153) and generate insights and supplemental guidance for reaching compromises, determining tradeoffs (Gibson, 2005, pp. 93, 177–178), and identifying promising pathways to sustainable development that can be more widely adapted in situations where conditions and challenges are similar.

The rest of this section of Chapter 11 is devoted to illustrating a manageable and meaningful sustainable-development-evaluation scheme that follows the process guidelines set forth above and, by tailoring the framework to their needs and means, can be applied by universities with limited commitments of money and time. The illustrative scheme presented here can be used as guidelines or as a checklist when conducting an evaluation of university involvement in sustainable development. The suggested scheme draws upon particularly salient questions we selected from the comprehensive framework developed in Part III. The questions require probing responses rather than simple "yes" or "no" answers.[6] Evaluators are encouraged to focus on initiatives or combinations of undertakings that universities designate as most important and that scoping suggests involve the greatest potential for major gains or serious losses in human and environmental wellbeing (Gibson, 2005, pp. 146, 152–154).

Actual applications might prefer different core questions, further narrow inquires found in the menu presented here, and tailor evaluation probes and methods to fit unique contextual conditions. In common, however, will be focus on a short list of key questions regarding process, outcome, capacity, impact, and evaluation[7] as well as care and rigor in executing integrated evaluations that will still encompass new and expanded objectives and criteria (Gibson, 2005, pp. 93, 115).

Process questions: the conduct of university interventions

The process dimension of the practical-evaluation framework is concerned with the conduct of university TSD interventions. Assessing the nature of the sustainability process itself constitutes an essential component in practical evaluations. In the practical approach to sustainable-development evaluations, evaluators focus on determining how process is linked to outcome and impact additionalities. Process evaluations should encompass the three life-course phases of university-initiated undertakings: planning, implementing, and sustaining. Key questions in this connection are contained in Box 11.2.

BOX 11.2 ILLUSTRATIVE CORE QUESTIONS FOR EVALUATING UNIVERSITY SUSTAINABLE-DEVELOPMENT PROCESSES

- How strong is the evidence that senior university leaders concretely, visibly, consistently, and inclusively supported sustainable-development academic and outreach activity?
- To what degree did TSD issues feature in the selection and execution of the university's research and outreach undertakings?
- Did collaborating university actors and key stakeholders conduct a needs assessment that included identifying community vulnerabilities and assets and linking stakeholder objectives with specific evaluation criteria?
- To what extent did community members, stakeholders, practitioners, and policy makers participate in defining and refining the principal research questions and initiating and designing the sustainability-research process? Did periodic multi-stakeholder meetings occur where participants clarified roles and contributions and agreed on project interventions and revisions?
- How broad and diverse was the configuration of stakeholder participation in the selected sustainable-development challenge? To what extent were stakeholders involved in all stages of the sustainable-development undertaking? How deep was the actual level of each stakeholder's involvement in goal setting and in curriculum, research, and outreach

activities? Did stakeholders report that they "had been appropriately included in the process, adequately informed, and prepared for decision making" (Brundiers and Wiek, 2011, p. 116)?

- To what extent were budgets equitably distributed among departments, stakeholders, and transnational partners according to agreed-upon responsibilities?
- To what extent are the teaching, research, and community-engagement components of sustainable development integrated?
- What evidence is there of cross-fertilization of academic and estate-management contexts?
- What level of departmental-resource commitment has been devoted to sustainable-development curricular, research, and outreach initiatives?
- To what extent have department members collaborated internally across disciplinary lines? How many and what types of departments collaborated (e.g., natural and social sciences, humanities, engineering, health)?
- To what extent have university-program participants collaborated externally with stakeholders in addressing sustainable-development challenges?
- Have academic-promotion pathways encouraged TSD-curriculum, research, outreach, and transnational-partnering initiatives?
- To what extent were sustainable-development interventions primarily outcome- and impact-driven rather than activity- or output-driven?
- Were the selected core principles of sustainable development and education for sustainable development actually complied with throughout the process?
- Did project directors resist imposing burdensome administrative procedures so that all participants were able to focus on the principal objectives of the sustainable-development initiative?
- To what extent have disseminated research findings been utilized by stakeholders to enhance sustainable development?
- Did the process result in continuing "experimentation for learning and adjustment" (Gibson, 2005, p. 84)?

Outcome questions

We now turn to a practical set of outcome questions. Box 11.3 presents an illustrative short list of queries that lend themselves to meaningful and manageable higher-education outcome evaluations.

Capacity building is an outcome feature that merits consideration in its own right. Box 11.4 provides an illustrative list of questions that lend themselves to meaningful and manageable higher-education sustainable-development capacity-building evaluations.

BOX 11.3 ILLUSTRATIVE CORE QUESTIONS FOR EVALUATING UNIVERSITY SUSTAINABLE-DEVELOPMENT-OUTCOME CONTRIBUTIONS

- To what extent do curricula address glocal connectivity among social, economic, and environmental drivers and barriers? To what extent have faculty been willing to incorporate the three pillars of sustainable-development in their syllabi, classroom teaching, and assignments and in their research undertakings? Are academic-program faculty at the "pre-pare," "explore," "test and pilot," or "integrate and implement learning pathways" stage?
- To what extent did educators integrate sustainability aspects in community-service and service-learning experiences?
- To what extent did the initiative strengthen and empower multiple academic programs?
- Did a guiding coalition of curriculum-transformation advocates "ensure that direction and momentum were sustained" (de la Harpe and Thomas, 2009, p. 82)?
- Did a cluster of competent scholars arise who were dedicated to conducting and coordinating sustainable-development research?
- To what extent did the sustainable-development initiative result in symmetrical and beneficial partnership outcomes?
- How have university human resources and involved stakeholders demonstrated capacity to respond to emerging sustainability issues?
- How often are participating universities called upon by external agencies for sustainable-development consultancies, research services, and training programs?

Impact questions

Box 11.5 presents an illustrative short list of queries that lend themselves to meaningful and manageable higher-education impact-contribution evaluations. These core questions address both immediate and long-term contributions and impacts. Additional in-depth and ongoing inquiries attend to complex issues, "especially scientific uncertainty and cumulative effects," with a dose of humility (Gibson, 2005, pp. 16, 32–33).

Evaluation questions

Finally, we offer an illustrative set of core questions concerning the evaluation process that lend themselves to practical application. Box 11.6 incorporates these questions.

BOX 11.4 ILLUSTRATIVE CORE QUESTIONS FOR EVALUATING UNIVERSITY SUSTAINABLE-DEVELOPMENT CAPACITY-BUILDING CONTRIBUTIONS

- To what extent has faculty expertise in sustainable development increased?
- What behavioral demonstrations of each domain of transnational competence for sustainable development can be identified?
- Is there evidence of improvement in the sustainable-development-research capabilities of program participants?
- Did research-capability strengthening emphasize "in-depth understanding of the local context" and linkage with domestic and TSD priorities?
- What evidence is there that the initiative enhanced capacity for innovation at individual and institutional levels?
- Did enhanced local capabilities include indigenous knowledge and insights?
- Did sustainable-development capacity building build on and strengthen local capabilities in ways that were linked to national, regional, and local development-policy priorities?
- To what degree did the research process increase the capacity of each stakeholder to advance environmental stewardship, social justice, and economic wellbeing?
- How do beneficiaries rate the sustainable-development capacity-strengthening contributions of graduates?
- Has the university provided sustainable-development technical and training support to public agencies, NGOs, community groups, and private firms?

BOX 11.5 ILLUSTRATIVE CORE QUESTIONS FOR EVALUATING UNIVERSITY SUSTAINABLE-DEVELOPMENT IMPACT CONTRIBUTIONS

- How have program graduates exercised professional capabilities and transnational competence in ways that further sustainable development in economic, social, and/or ecological arenas?
- Were the action contributions of sustainable-development graduates enhanced over time by the multiplier effect?
- To what extent did the university-research or outreach initiative enhance sustainable-development practice at one or more of the following levels of activity: improved individual-practitioner decision making when confronted by practical and contextual challenges of sustainable development; improved group-level collaboration on a shared TSD challenge; improved community-level response to a specific small-scale economic, social, or ecological challenge; or improved national and/or transnational response to a sustainable-development challenge with cross-boundary effects?

- Is there evidence of increases in sustainable social, economic, and eco- logical innovations that can be plausibly attributed to the university research or outreach project?
- Is there evidence that university-led research or a university-outreach project contributed to improvements or reductions in public service to local communities?
- Is there evidence that university-led research or a university-outreach project contributed to reductions or increases in local social and eco- nomic inequality?
- Is there evidence that university-led research or a university-outreach project contributed to advances or setbacks in human wellbeing?
- Is there evidence that university-led research or a university-outreach project maintained or diminished habitats and biodiversity?
- What tradeoffs did interventions catalyze among economic, ecological, and social aspirations, between immediate and long-term benefits, and among beneficiaries (Gibson, 2005, p. 85)?
- Are any locally and regionally adopted knowledge-based products that resulted from participatory research sustainable?
- What intended and unintended sustainable-development-impact contri- butions are revealed by the chain of impact?
- What evidence is there that policy makers have recognized the social and economic contributions and wellbeing benefits of specific sustainable- development approaches and practices as a result of university-outreach activities?
- How did exogenous pressures, opportunities, and facilitating and con- straining factors influence local impacts (Gibson, 2005, p. 85)?
- Did sustainable-development-research and outreach activities continue beyond the termination of external funding?
- Are non-university players (NGOs, governments, for-profit firms, community members) committed to maintaining key project activities? Is there evidence that community-based ownership has increased the likelihood of stake- holder self-generated sustainable-development initiatives and replications?

BOX 11.6 ILLUSTRATIVE CORE QUESTIONS FOR EVALUATING UNIVERSITY SUSTAINABLE- DEVELOPMENT EVALUATION PROCESSES

- What internal- and independent-external-evaluation processes have been put in place that utilize multiple-assessment methods to probe the sustainable capacity of higher-education personnel and communities to develop themselves across a range of sustainable-development activity?
- Did the evaluation explore "competing options for positive action" (Gib- son, 2005, p. 84)?

- Did the evaluation consider alternative futures (Gibson, 2005, p. 84)?
- Did evaluators explore mutually reinforcing contributions as well as "avoidance or mitigation of negative effects" (Gibson, 2005, p. 146)?
- Did the project leaders train stakeholders in collaborative-evaluation practices?
- Did the evaluation process emphasize "open discussion and participative engagement of local residents" (Gibson, 2005, p. 84)?
- Did external evaluators working in the university TSD domain possess the ability to understand local conditions and to link them to the bigger context?
- Were findings reported in a timely and concise manner of strategic value to decision makers at all levels?

Practical evaluations and the 2030 Agenda

As we approach 2030, universities increasingly will be expected by attentive publics, scholars, accrediting agencies, national governments, concerned NGOs, and the international community to demonstrate their local and transnational contributions to sustainable development. The practical guidelines for evaluating illustrated in this chapter offer a foundation to build upon in the interest of conducting meaningful evaluations that focus on higher-education initiatives and move beyond outputs. Practical applications are likely to be of special value to resource-constrained institutions of higher education in the South, where "there is strong growth in evaluation" (Naidoo, 2016).

Although the most impressive evaluations embrace comprehensiveness in scope, more limited approaches that adhere to core-process principles and incorporate key framework questions contribute vital insights and understandings regarding the role of universities in our sustainable-development voyage. At the same time, working within a common-evaluation framework enables individual institutions of higher education to document their contributions to sustainable development in ways that receive external recognition, generate internal gratification, and result in enhanced motivation.

Notes

1 In cases of resource scarcity or limited institutional capacity, for instance, "sophistication of criteria elaboration, range of alternatives, depth of analysis, extent of consultation, detail of design . . . might be constrained without serious loss" (Gibson, 2005, p. 145).
2 Transboundary in this context refers to the ability to bridge disciplines, political jurisdictions, natural and human interfaces, interacting challenges, and other places where diverse edges meet.
3 Steven Zyck (blog, 1 August 2016) cautions that minimal funding for independent evaluations ensures that "your evaluation will be cursory in nature, include minimal field work, and will uncover few if any faults."
4 The lead author is grateful to Scott Whittenburg, University of Montana Vice President for Research and Creative Scholarship, for bringing the importance of this point to his attention on 25 August 2016.

5 One important aim here is to provide a foundation for consolidating the current diversity of approaches to evaluating sustainable-development activity encountered at universities around the world (also see Gibson, 2005, p. 115).
6 At times, evaluators will encounter incomplete information and be unable to determine positive or negative effects (see Gibson, 2005, p. 119).
7 Alternative versions that adhere to our process principles and retain the framework's core insights can "serve at least as adequately as a foundation for [evaluation] decision making" (Gibson, 2005, p. 115).

Works cited

Bamberger, Michael; Rugh, Jim; and Mabry, Linda. 2012. *RealWorld Evaluation: Working under Budget, Time, Data and Political Constraints*, 2nd edition. Thousand Oaks, CA: Sage.

Brundiers, Katja; and Wiek, Arnim. 2011. "Educating Students in Real-World Sustainability Research: Vision and Implementation." *Innovative Higher Education* 36:107–124.

Collins, Christopher S. 2014. "Can Funding for University Partnerships between Africa and the US Contribute to Social Development and Poverty Reduction?" *Higher Education* 68:943–958.

Eyben, Rosalind. 2013. "Uncovering the Politics of 'Evidence' and 'Results': A Framing Paper for Development Practitioners." www.bigpushforward.net

Fredericks, Sarah. 2014. *Measuring and Evaluating Sustainability: Ethics in Sustainability Indexes*. London: Routledge.

Gibson, Robert B. 2005. *Sustainability Assessment: Criteria and Processes*. London: Earthscan.

Harpe, Barbara de la; and Thomas, Ian. 2009. "Curriculum Change in Universities: Conditions that Facilitate Education for Sustainable Development." *Journal of Education for Sustainable Development* 3 (1):75–85.

Hopkinson, Peter; and James, Peter. 2013. "Whole Institutional Change towards Sustainable Universities: Bradford's Ecoversity Initiative." In *The Sustainable University: Progress and Prospects*, edited by Stephen Sterling, Larch Maxey, and Heather Luna. London: Routledge. Pp. 235–255.

Hummelbrunner, Richard. 2012. "Process Monitoring of Impacts and Its Application in Structural Fund Programmes." In *Governance by Evaluation for Sustainable Development: Institutional Capacities and Learning*, edited by Michal Sedlacko and Andre Martinuzzi. Cheltenham, UK: Edward Elgar. Pp. 253–266.

Naidoo, Indran A. 2016. "Forum Section." *Evaluation Connections* (European Evaluation Society), February, p. 15.

Powell, Steve; Molander, Joakim; and Celebicic, Ivona. 2012. "Assessment of Outcome Mapping as a Tool for Evaluating and Monitoring Support to Civil Society Organisations." In *Governance by Evaluation for Sustainable Development: Institutional Capacities and Learning*, edited by Michal Sedlacko and Andre Martinuzzi. Cheltenham, UK: Edward Elgar. Pp. 215–232.

Razak, Dzulkifli A.; Sanusi, Zainal A.; Jegatesen, Govindran; and Khelghat-Doost, Hamoon. 2013. "Alternative University Appraisal (AUA): Reconstructing Universities' Ranking and Rating toward a Sustainable Future." In *Sustainability Assessment Tools in Higher Education Institutions: Mapping Trends and Good Practices around the World*, edited by Sandra Caeiro, Walter L. Filho, Charbel Jabbour, and Ulisses M. Azeiteiro. Cham, Switzerland: Springer International Publishing. Pp. 139–154.

Thomas, Vinod; and Tominaga, Jiro. 2013. "Development Evaluation in an Age of Turbulence." In *Evaluation and Turbulent Times: Reflections on a Discipline in Disarray*, edited by Jan-Eric Furubo, Ray C. Rist, and Sandra Speer. New Brunswick, NJ: Transaction Publishers. Pp. 57–70.

12

CONCLUSION

Evaluation and higher-education contributions to the 2030 Agenda

If universities around the world are to contribute in ways that matter to the 2030 Agenda, it is incumbent upon them to move forward with enhanced evaluations of their curricula, research, and outreach initiatives. Evaluation has multiple ramifications for higher-education contributions to transnational sustainable development (TSD). Systematic and informed curricular, research, and outreach evaluations enable participants in sustainable-development initiatives to distinguish outcomes and impacts from mere outputs. They enrich institutional and individual learning from successes and shortfalls in ways that enable enhanced short-term and long-term contributions (see Wright, 2002, p. 118). They allow participants to share the insights that emerge about addressing challenges of sustainable development with local stakeholders, transnational partners, and attentive publics. And principled evaluations help demonstrate to supportive stakeholders and skeptics alike that university undertakings can contribute in decisive ways to the pressing global challenge of sustainable development illustrated in Chapter 2. Furthermore, higher-education centrality rather than marginality on the global sustainable-development stage is advanced by trusted outcome and impact evaluations.

In Stephen Sterling's (2013, p. 19, emphasis in original) words, the contemporary academic enterprise is challenged "to integrate *higher education into the wider societal context of sustainability.*" Integrative transformation requires action and reaction by universities in local, national, and transnational spaces (Sipos, Battisti, and Grimm, 2008, p. 70). Evaluation encourages universities to be more proactive and interactive in ensuring that the 2030 Agenda actions and contributions they generate are useful to and applied by stakeholders and compliant with international protocols concerned with transnational sustainable development.

To conclude treatment of universities and the sustainable-development future, we focus attention on the challenges involved in evaluating outcomes and impacts.

We begin by revisiting the keys to improved outcome- and impact-evaluation approaches. The next section presents our vision of the internal and external actors and roles that can move meaningful university process, outcome, and impact evaluation forward. The parting section looks to the future.

A comprehensive approach to evaluating university outcomes and impacts

In *Universities and the Sustainable Development Future*, we have approached evaluation through a comprehensive approach that recognizes the importance of teaching, research, outreach, and transnational partnering. Across these interconnected domains,[1] we have developed an elaborate framework for sustainable-development evaluations that emphasizes process, outcomes, and impacts. We advocate adherence to fundamental process principles and contextually designed applications of the guiding framework.

On the process front, it is advisable that Northern and Southern universities design a contextually driven and resource-smart evaluation strategy from the beginning. Top-level support for all stages of the comprehensive approach to evaluation is an essential ingredient. Internal and external evaluators with transboundary expertise need to be engaged and supplied with resources and incentives that will enable successful implementation of the evaluation plan.

Systematic-university evaluations progress from process to outcomes (unit-focused, institution-wide, and stakeholder-inclusive) and, then, from local to transnational (glocal) impacts and from near-term to inter-generational ecological, economic, and social impacts. The needed evaluation response to specific framework inquiries determines the research methods that evaluators use.

At outcome- and impact-concerned universities, sustainable-development-evaluation initiatives will involve key stakeholders from the beginning of the evaluation process. Transparency will characterize all stages. Evaluation findings will be distributed broadly across campus, among stakeholders and interested members of the public, to other educators, and to the evaluation community.

Part III of the book is devoted to developing a comprehensive framework for university evaluations of TSD activities. The framework's relevant-question-centered focus is on curricular, research, outreach, and partnership outcomes and impacts. The extensive and integrated set of specific guiding questions provided in these chapters can be drawn upon by evaluators in the North and South. More advanced applications will move from demonstrating sustainable-development contributions to improving inter-generational payoffs.

We also deemed it helpful to suggest a shorter list of core questions that can guide sustainable-development evaluations involving universities in resource- and time-constrained contexts. We present these action-process, outcome, impact, and evaluation-process questions in Chapter 11 as a practical application of the guiding framework. By focusing on manageable objectives, innovative place-based methods for evaluating outcome and impact contributions, developing the institutional capacity and human capabilities needed to adopt and adapt the book's framework (the subject of Chapter 10), and streamlined reporting of results, it is possible to realize compelling advancements in sustainable-development evaluations.

Moving meaningful evaluation processes forward

How might the world's universities gain a central role in influencing the sustainable-development agenda in the wake of the Decade of Education for Sustainable Development? We believe that systematic evaluation provides an important part of the answer to this question. Moving meaningful evaluation processes forward offers an available pathway for increased influence. By demonstrating that higher education is in the forefront in terms of evidence- and insight-generation, pedagogy, process, and learning, transparent outcome and impact evaluations of curriculum change, research initiatives, and community-outreach undertakings can earn the attention and respect of international policy makers concerned with maintaining biodiversity, climate stabilization, wellbeing, and the other sustainable-development issues treated in Chapter 2.

Moving forward with university evaluations will not come easily. Impact evaluations remain particularly challenging. While promising breakthroughs are emerging and on the horizon, the best impact evaluations are uncertain and contestable (Cashmore, 2007, p. 121).[2] The confounding factors become less manageable as impact inquiries probe deeper in time. We view these challenges as calls for increased higher-education initiative and innovation rather than as reason for despair. To achieve immediate progress, we urge evaluators to keep front and center the big picture of sustainable development traced in Chapter 2. We recognize that individual universities will place priority on particular *Agenda 2030* goals. Therefore, we have constructed the evaluation guidelines set forth in Part III of this book in a way that can be applied on a project-by-project basis, while linking plausible contextual university contributions and shortfalls to big-picture outcomes and impacts.

In an immediate sense, moving meaningful evaluations forward also depends on committed and influential advocates. Who will read *Universities and the Sustainable Development Future* and step forward on behalf of utilizing its framework, process guidelines, and practical applications? What contribution can each reader make?

The next sections grapple with the "who" question. We will look both internally and externally for advocates or champions of meaningful sustainable-development, evaluating who can play vital instrumental and supportive roles. Our search for internal champions and external drivers is largely interest-based on the grounds that prospective beneficiaries are most likely to take the lead in advocating meaningful evaluations. We expect each champion to make diverse and contextually relevant contributions to transformative evaluating. For this reason, it is important to cast a wide net.

Internal transformative-evaluation champions

Evaluation practices cannot be transformed through unfunded mandates. Overt or covert resistance to change on the part of administrators, faculty, staff, and students often is linked to resource issues. Resources, primarily financial support, need to be matched specifically with comprehensive university TSD-evaluation initiatives.

Part of the answer to the resource conundrum lies in internal transfers and incentives, but most universities will need to find additional external sources of funding to support their internal- and independent-evaluation needs. These resource-mobilizing roles require executive-level champions, including the top university administrator and the officer in charge of research and development. In an age when advancing sustainable development is at the forefront of governing board, funder, public, employer, and professional-association expectations for institutions of higher learning, and effectively addressing contextual contributors to economic disparities in sustainable fashion constitutes a central part of the forward-looking university's strategic agenda and pressing responsibilities (Rowland, 2012, p. x), top-level administrators will find it useful to support the conduct of credible evaluations.

Internally, the next step is to recruit strong and credible dean-level[3] and faculty advocates who can convince their colleagues of the relevance, utility, and viability of comprehensive-sustainability evaluations. Sustained high-level administrative commitment and encouragement greatly improves prospects for buy-in by deans and faculty members.

Faculty buy-in

Internal sustainable-development evaluations will not be transformed unless faculty commit to the comprehensive process. In the initial stages of TSD evaluation, evaluators are likely to encounter professors who are *disinterested* in participating in the comprehensive-evaluation process, *unprepared* to adopt its novel and heavily interactive features, and/or *unwilling* to incorporate new evaluation approaches and methods (see, for instance, Biddle, 2002, p. 60). Fortunately, it is within the reach of evaluation champions to address each of these faculty-related constraints. The rest of this "faculty-buy-in" discussion is devoted to suggesting feasible approaches to overcoming faculty disinterest, incapacity, and unwillingness to change.

Addressing disinterest

One place to begin raising faculty interest in the sustainable-development-evaluation framework is with collegial assessment of the skills that will be needed by graduating practitioners over the next half a century. Reaching agreement on the importance of outcome and impact evaluations for learners, professionals, and society will go a long way toward generating and sustaining faculty enthusiasm for transformative-evaluation practices.

Involvement in constructing the specific details of the contextually informed evaluation design encourages the emergence of program champions and gives participating faculty a vested interest in its successful execution. Faculty are most likely to take ownership of the curriculum-, research-, and outreach-evaluation process when it engages them at the heart of their intellectual interests. In arranging evaluation responsibilities, therefore, every effort should be made to tap the academic passions of collaborating faculty.

Addressing perceived incapacity

A fundamental requirement for successful internal evaluations is the availability of faculty who are confident about their ability to engage in the process. In most academic programs, the adoption and sustained implementation of the sustainable-development-evaluation processes highlighted in this book will require attention to faculty development. Faculty-development opportunities should be framework-focused, attend to process principles, and be regarded as rewarding by participants.

A number of valuable mechanisms are available for enhancing the capacity of faculty to participate effectively in comprehensive sustainable-development evaluations. Learning opportunities include internal workshops, external peer-support networks, and establishing long-term insight-sharing relationships with fellow educators around the world. Designation of comprehensive sustainable-development evaluation as an institutional priority often paves the way for securing the additional resources needed to inspire faculty to undertake any needed retooling.

Addressing unwillingness to change

Although a critical mass of faculty advocates is required for professional-program-transformative evaluation to occur, some professors will not "*need* global education personally or professionally" (Case and Werner, 1997, pp. 203, 205 [emphasis in original]) or be convinced that evaluating TSD should be a priority. We recognize and value the autonomy that university professors exercise over how they devote their time and intellectual energy. Rather than mandate particular evaluation approaches, we recommend emphasis on sustained opportunities and inducements (also see Case and Werner, 1997, pp. 204, 206).

The drag of competing demands on their time is likely to be a major factor blocking faculty willingness to engage in innovative sustainable-development evaluating. This obstacle can be overcome, but success requires compelling emotional and material incentives (Case and Werner, 1997, p. 202). For some faculty, buy-in will require compensation or released time to support participation in demanding evaluation exercises.

In addition, personal intellectual rewards and the dedication of additional resources usually are motivating (Biddle, 2002, p. 61). Linking transformative evaluation to a faculty member's research interests and inherent desire to excel professionally offers a particularly promising approach. Participating faculty can be expected to discover that the requisite transboundary stretching is intellectually exciting and that making an important difference in students' careers/lives and a sustained contribution in multiple societal contexts is professionally rewarding. In a clear signal of institutional commitment, the willingness of a faculty member to engage effectively in comprehensive sustainable-development evaluating would constitute a major positive consideration in tenure, promotion, special recognition, and merit-award decisions (also see Wiek, et al., 2014, p. 432).[4]

Student demand

In higher education, student demand is influenced by the perceived quality and long-term utility of an academic course of study. To an increasing extent, informed and committed undergraduate and post-graduate students at Southern and Northern universities will seek out educational programs and research opportunities that demonstrate success in linking technical expertise with relevant TSD skills in an experiential learning environment that is both stimulating and richly rewarding. University and external financial support for students to enhance learning by engaging in sustainable-development evaluations with community stakeholders will further encourage participation. We expect growing student demand to be an important internal impetus for moving toward transformative-sustainable-development evaluations.

External drivers

In evaluation, as well as other matters, universities respond to external influence. Numerous potential sustainable-development-evaluation drivers are present in the active environment that surrounds higher-education institutions. Among these drivers are bodies equipped to conduct external evaluations and community stakeholders poised to participate in the sustainable-development-evaluation process. Both types of participants possess vested interest in conducting comprehensive and systematically designed evaluations of university sustainable-development undertakings. Moreover, stakeholder engagement in developing recommendations based on evaluations is a key factor in generating buy-in that leads to stronger use and influence of the evaluation.

Other interested external collectivities also can be mobilized to play instrumental and supportive roles in the evaluation process. Many of the organizations treated in Chapter 3's landscape review of Northern and Southern bodies that engage in university assessment are likely to be interested in drawing upon the framework for evaluating university sustainable-development activity elaborated in Part III of *Universities and the Sustainable Development Future*. Accrediting associations and various professional bodies with sustainable-development missions could be in the forefront in adopting, adapting, and applying the framework.

Increasingly, the associations that university leaders around the world interact in are called upon to engage sustainable-development issues. To be persuasive, the messages they convey regarding these issues must be supported by evaluative evidence. In the United States, for instance, prospective levers for systematic university evaluation include the Disciplinary Associations Network for Sustainability (DANS) and the Higher Education Associations Sustainability Consortium (HEASC). DANS' interests in "infusing sustainability into curricula in all academic disciplines,"[5] creating standards (including tenure, promotion, and accreditation criteria)," and "informing policy makers" (Rowe and Johnston, 2013, p. 50) are directly related to assuming this leveraging role at the national level. HEASC – which includes the professional associations of some four thousand US university presidents, facility directors, and planners – already supports efforts of the American College and University Presidents' Climate Commitment (Rowe and Johnston, 2013, p. 50).

Ministries (departments) of education are key players in the external environment of universities. Ministries are especially influential in the South, where sustainable development often is expected to constitute the focal mission of institutions of higher education. The call for systematic and comprehensive evaluation of university sustainable-development initiatives is likely to be taken forward by concerned ministries.[6]

International and domestic NGOs with sustainable-development and watchdog missions[7] also are likely to demonstrate considerable interest in the framework for evaluating university sustainable-development undertakings we have articulated in comprehensive and practical forms. Bilateral and multilateral donors that fund transnational partnerships and individual university sustainable-development activity have an abiding interest in principled outcome- and impact-oriented evaluations. Leading foundations, capital campaigns, entrepreneurial endeavors, government grant programs, professional associations, and prosperous alums are additional prospective external drivers given the common interest of these organizations, individuals, and initiatives in ensuring that tomorrow's graduates are prepared for emerging sustainable-development challenges.

This treatment of external drivers would be incomplete without inclusion of the broader evaluation community. Associations of professional evaluators would be keen to learn from the experiences of Northern and Southern universities that apply the framework for evaluating university sustainable-development activity articulated here.

Conclusion: universities, evaluation, and the 2030 Agenda

In many ways, higher education provides the foundation for sustainable development. Academia is searching for insights into how its contributions to sustainable development can be identified, modified, and advanced. In the interest of preparing effective sustainable-development professionals and enabling engaged Northern and Southern universities to learn about and adapt best practices, we need to know what works and what does not work, in what context, and why, in collaborative academic research, outreach, and learning (Frenk, et al., 2010, p. 1954). In today's linked academic and environmental contexts, this interest requires evaluation of the outcomes and impacts of curricular, research, outreach, and partnering initiatives. Applying a symmetry-sensitive evaluation framework along the lines presented in this book lays the groundwork for catalytic-impact assessments.

Drawing on lessons gained from international-development experience, the framework for comprehensive higher-education evaluation developed in *Universities and the Sustainable Development Future* emphasizes attention to sustainable-development outcomes and impacts.[8] Evaluation is only a tool, not a panacea; it cannot bring about sustainable development on its own (Gibson, 2005, pp. 159, 187). However, rigorous evaluation can and should be the lead contributor to an integrated system of transboundary university sustainable-development initiatives that will make a big-picture difference (Uitto, 2016a, p. 6).[9]

Although methods of sustainable-development and academic-program evaluation are imperfect and consensus on a particular approach will remain elusive, calls for evaluation will continue to escalate. The higher-education sector is specially positioned to influence the ways in which sustainable-development undertakings are evaluated (Derrick, 2013, p. 47) as well as to occupy the forefront of the sustainability transition (Cayuela, et al., 2013, p. 235). Toward this end, the university community writ large can play a leading role in determining and championing what is realistic and meaningful to measure in sustainable-development evaluations.

We submit that internal and external participants in higher-education sustainable-development evaluation would be well-served by drawing upon a comprehensive and principled evaluation framework founded on best-practice experience in the field, theory-based approaches, and principles of symmetry in design, management, capacity-building, and institutional outreach. We look forward to the blossoming of contextually inspired, uniquely carved, and extraordinarily fulfilling university undertakings that are infused with faculty passion, rewarding in terms of student aspirations, informed by progressive outcome and impact evaluations, and responsive to the transboundary, continent-spanning, and marvelously interconnected sustainable-development challenges of the 2030 Agenda.

Notes

1 The framework also calls attention to the need to evaluate the integration of academic undertakings with campus operations (see Cayuela, et al., 2013, pp. 223, 234–235).

2 In short, "the precautionary principle applies *to* sustainability assessment as well as *in* it" (Gibson, 2005, p. 187, emphasis in original).

3 At the deanship level, the issue of resources often becomes less one of total amounts than "the strategy used to dispense them" (Biddle, 2002, p. 39).

4 Incentives for evaluating research and outreach are particularly needed at many Southern universities (see Collins, 2011, p. 196).

5 Alex Ryan and Debby Cotton (2013, p. 164) further maintain that education for sustainability "needs to be more effectively positioned in relation to the broader pedagogic development literature and strategic approaches to curriculum change."

6 GEF experience suggests that timely evaluation reports have more traction among ministries and other stakeholders (Uitto, 2016b, p. 113).

7 Including the emerging education-for-sustainable-development (see Barth, et al., 2016, p. 1) and organizational-learning (e.g., Sylvestre and Wright, 2016, p. 302) communities.
8 Approaches to evaluation where the theory of change is used contextually to identify intermediate states, impact drivers (Todd and Craig, 2014, pp. 63–66, 83), and progress markers (Breton and Engle, 2014); to analyze catalytic outcome-impact pathways; and to explain the contributions of project activities; possess particular promise in both development and academic contexts. Participatory and flexible learning-oriented tools that focus on plausible contributions rather than attribution, such as the most-significant change approach and outcome and impact mapping, are especially valuable in this connection (Hailemichael, 2013, p. 43; Uitto, 2016a, pp. 3–4).
9 In an ideal sense, the progress-directed contribution of a university sustainable-development evaluation would be to "plot alternative possible routes to desired futures, evaluate their feasibility, propose suitable strategies for change . . . at every scale from the local to the global, all somehow linked and mutually responsive, flexible and adaptive, dynamic and open-ended" (Gibson, 2005, p. 159).

Works Cited

Barth, Matthias; Michelsen, Gerd; Rieckmann, Marco; and Thomas, Ian. 2016. "Introduction." In *Routledge Handbook of Higher Education for Sustainable Development*, edited by Matthias Barth, Gerd Michelsen, Marco Rieckmann, and Ian Thomas. London: Routledge. Pp. 1–7.

Biddle, Sheila. 2002. *Internationalization: Rhetoric or Reality?* New York: American Council of Learned Societies.

Breton, Maria E.; and Engle, Nathan L. 2014. "Evaluating Institutional Change and Long-Term Climate Change Adaptation and Resilience Measures: Towards a National Drought Preparedness Policy in Brazil." Paper presented at the 2nd International Conference on Evaluating Climate Change and Development, Washington, DC, 5 November.

Case, Roland; and Werner, Walter. 1997. "Building Faculty Commitment for Global Education." In *Preparing Teachers to Teach Global Perspectives: A Handbook for Teacher Educators*, edited by Merry M. Merryfield, Elaine Jarchow, and Sarah Picket. Thousand Oaks: Corwin Press. Pp. 200–220.

Cashmore, Matthew. 2007. "The Contribution of Environmental Assessment to Sustainable Development: Toward a Richer Conceptual Understanding." In *Impact Assessment and Sustainable Development: European Practice and Experience*, edited by Clive George and Colin Kirkpatrick. Cheltenham, UK: Edward Elgar. Pp. 106–126.

Cayuela, Alberto; Robinson, John B.; Campbell, Ann; Coops, Nicholas; and Munro, Alison. 2013. "Integration of Operational and Academic Efforts in Sustainability at the University of British Columbia." In *Sustainability Assessment Tools in Higher Education Institutions: Mapping Trends and Good Practices around the World*, edited by Sandra Caeiro, Walter L. Filho, Charbel Jabbour, and Ulisses M. Azeiteiro. Cham, Switzerland: Springer International Publishing. Pp. 223–236.

Collins, Christopher S. 2011. *Higher Education and Global Poverty: University Partnerships and the World Bank in Developing Countries*. Amherst, NY: Cambria Press.

Derrick, Stephen. 2013. "Time and Sustainability Metrics in Higher Education." In *Sustainability Assessment Tools in Higher Education Institutions: Mapping Trends and Good Practices around the World*, edited by Sandra Caeiro, Walter L. Filho, Charbel Jabbour, and Ulisses M. Azeiteiro. Cham, Switzerland: Springer International Publishing. Pp. 47–63.

Frenk, Julio; Chen, Lincoln; Bhutta, Zulfiqar A.; Cohen, Jordan; Crisp, Nigel; Evans, Timothy; Fineberg, Harvey; Garcia, Patricia; Ke, Yang; Kelley, Patrick; Kistnasamy,

Barry; Meleis, Afaf; Naylor, David; Pablos-Mendez, Ariel; Reddy, Srinath; Scrimshaw, Susan; Sepulveda, Jaime; Serwadda, David; and Zurayk, Huda. 2010. "Health Professionals for a New Century: Transforming Education to Strengthen Health Systems in an Interdependent World." *Lancet* 376, 9756 (4 December):1923–1958.

Gibson, Robert B. 2005. *Sustainability Assessment: Criteria and Processes.* London: Earthscan.

Hailemichael Taye. 2013. "Evaluating the Impact of Agricultural Extension Programmes in Sub-Saharan Africa: Challenges and Prospects." *African Evaluation Journal* 1 (1):38–45.

Rowe, Debra; and Johnston, Lucas F. 2013. "Learning Outcomes: An International Comparison of Countries and Declarations." In *Higher Education for Sustainability: Cases, Challenges, and Opportunities from across the Curriculum*, edited by Lucas F. Johnston. New York: Routledge. Pp. 45–59.

Rowland, Paul. 2012. "Foreword." In *The Sustainable University: Green Goals and New Challenges for Higher Education Leaders*, edited by James Martin and James E. Samels. Baltimore: The Johns Hopkins University Press. Pp. ix–xi.

Ryan, Alex; and Cotton, Debby. 2013. "Times of Change: Shifting Pedagogy and Curricula for Future Sustainability." In *The Sustainable University: Progress and Prospects*, edited by Stephen Sterling, Larch Maxey, and Heather Luna. London: Routledge. Pp. 151–161.

Sipos, Yona; Battisti, Bryce; and Grimm, Kurt. 2008. "Achieving Transformative Sustainability Learning: Engaging Head, Hands, and Heart." *International Journal of Sustainability in Higher Education* 9 (1):68–86.

Sterling, Stephen. 2013. "The Sustainable University: Challenge and Response." In *The Sustainable University: Progress and Prospects*, edited by Stephen Sterling, Larch Maxey, and Heather Luna. London: Routledge. Pp. 17–50.

Sylvestre, Paul; and Wright, Tara. 2016. "Organisational Change and Organisational Learning for Promoting Higher Education for Sustainable Development." In *Routledge Handbook of Higher Education for Sustainable Development*, edited by Matthias Barth, Gerd Michelsen, Marco Rieckmann, and Ian Thomas. London: Routledge. Pp. 310–314.

Todd, David; and Craig, Rob. 2014. "Assessing Progress towards Impacts in Environmental Programmes Using the Field Review of Outcomes to Impacts Methodology." In *Evaluating Environment in International Development*, edited by Juha I. Uitto. London: Routledge. Pp. 62–86.

Uitto, Juha I. 2016a. "The Environment-Poverty Nexus in Evaluation: Implications for the Sustainable Development Goals." *Global Policy* 7 (3):441–447.

Uitto, Juha I. 2016b. "Evaluating the Environment as a Global Public Good." *Evaluation* 22 (1):108–115.

Wiek, Arnim; Xiong, Angela; Brundiers, Katja; and van der Leeuw, Sander. 2014. "Integrating Problem- and Project-Based Learning into Sustainability Programs: A Case Study on the School of Sustainability at Arizona State University." *International Journal of Sustainability in Higher Education* 15 (4):431–449.

Wright, Tarah S. A. 2002. "Definitions and Frameworks for Environmental Sustainability in Higher Education." *Higher Education Policy* 12 (2):105–120.

INDEX